ROAD TO SUEZ

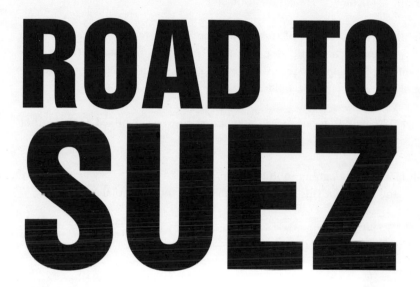

ROAD TO SUEZ

THE BATTLE OF THE CANAL ZONE

MICHAEL T. THORNHILL

SUTTON PUBLISHING

First published in the United Kingdom in 2006 by
Sutton Publishing Limited · Phoenix Mill
Thrupp · Stroud · Gloucestershire · GL5 2BU

British Library Cataloguing in Publication Data
A catalogue record for this book is available from the British Library.

ISBN 0-7509-4447-1

Typeset in 10.5/15pt Photina MT.
Typesetting and origination by
Sutton Publishing Limited.
Printed and bound in England by
J.H. Haynes & Co. Ltd, Sparkford.

Contents

List of Illustrations

Maps

Acknowledgements

A number of people and institutions have been an enormous help in the writing of this book, so it gives me pleasure to be able to thank them. Financially, the British Academy and the Beit Imperial History Fund at the University of Oxford were instrumental in helping macadamise the road to Suez for me. Research in the National Archives of Britain and the United States (the Egyptian official records remain closed) was thus made possible, and I am consequently indebted to the staff at these institutions. The archivists at Churchill College, Cambridge, the Bodleian Library, Oxford, and the University of Birmingham Library were also most helpful. Special thanks go to Diane King and her successor Mastan Ebtehaj at the Middle East Centre Archive at St Antony's College, Oxford. As a graduate student here, I benefited greatly from the scholarly and convivial atmosphere, not least among the seasoned 'PROers' – Dr Lawrence Tal, Dan Somogyi and Dr Martin Bunton.

My subsequent employment as Research Coordinator of the *Oxford Dictionary of National Biography* entailed spending five years in a Georgian building on St Giles with fifty or so in-house editors. I left with an abiding respect for crisp, clear prose. The *DNB*, it should be added, was always a stickler for word limits. Fortunately, my editors at Sutton – Hilary Walford, Jonathan Falconer and Julia Fenn – have proved a little more tolerant in this latter respect, as well as extremely efficient in pushing my manuscript through to publication. I am also grateful to Elizabeth Stone, Ros Robertson and Ann Parry for, respectively, copy-editing, proof-reading and indexing. Ingram Murray, Dr Derek Hopwood, Bruce Schoenfeld, Hoda Gamal Abdel Nasser, Philip Waller, Peter Molloy, Ambassador Frank Brenchley and Adam Watson have also given valuable advice along the way.

The early chapters of this book were sent to several confidential 'readers', one of whom broke cover and wrote to me in generous and encouraging terms. Coming from a scholar of the standing of Professor Wm Roger Louis, it is easy to see why this support meant so much to me, especially when deadlines were pressing. Professor Avi Shlaim was similarly supportive throughout, as well as a vital barometer of progress. Dr Jason Tomes went through the entire manuscript with a fine-tooth comb (striking all such clichés as he went). His help was immense. Dr Tony Shaw cast a sharp eye over what remained and gave assurance at a critical juncture.

Some debts can often go unspoken because they are assumed. This should not happen. My in-laws, Kate and David Wilson, probably do not appreciate the extent of their influence on the completion of this book. After several years of my repeatedly saying that the work was going well, visible results were naturally expected. My own parents, Edward and Susan Thornhill, waited even longer, supporting me in an education which must have seemed abnormally long. I hope they understand my gratitude. Meanwhile, my interest in Bob Dylan – which is sufficiently strong to embrace *Knocked Out Loaded* – helped make sure that the Suez Canal was not always flowing through my home. Finally, this book would not be here but for my wife, Judith Wilson. She has also doubled up as my agent and editor – in more ways than one. As my friends repeatedly tell me, I am very lucky. It is to her that *Road to Suez* is dedicated.

A Note on Spelling

The spelling of names and places in this text follows the usage of British official records at the time, albeit with a few exceptions. Any quotes from American or Egyptian sources retain their given form. With respect to published biographical materials, when the individual concerned has represented their own name in a particular way, this is followed. Khaled Mohi El Din is thus preferred to Khaled Mohieddin. If any of these rules goes against common understanding, they are abandoned.

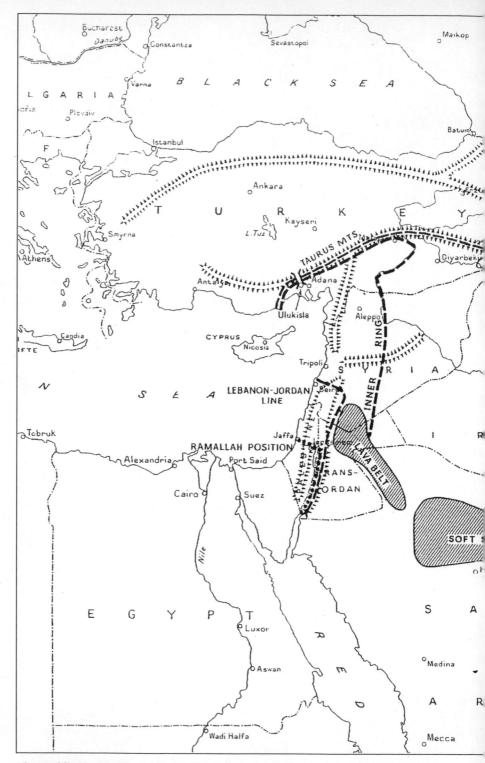

The Middle East, with details of Britain's strategic planning concepts in the early 1950s. *(TNA: PRO DEFE5/35, COS (51) 755, Annex, 18 December 1951)*

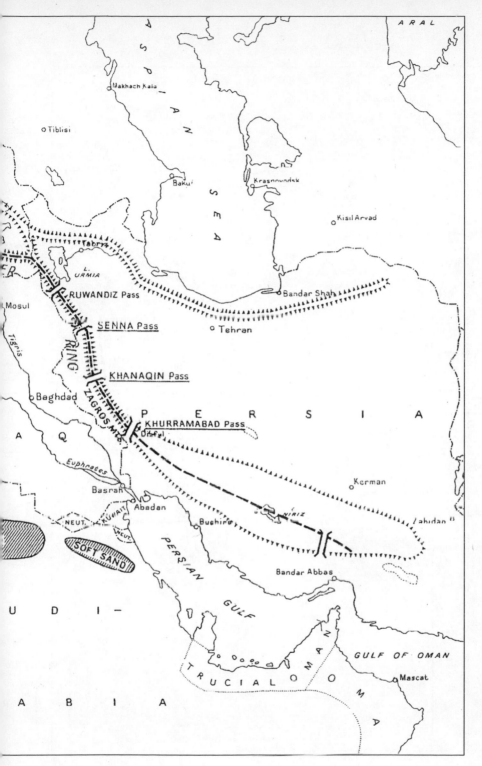

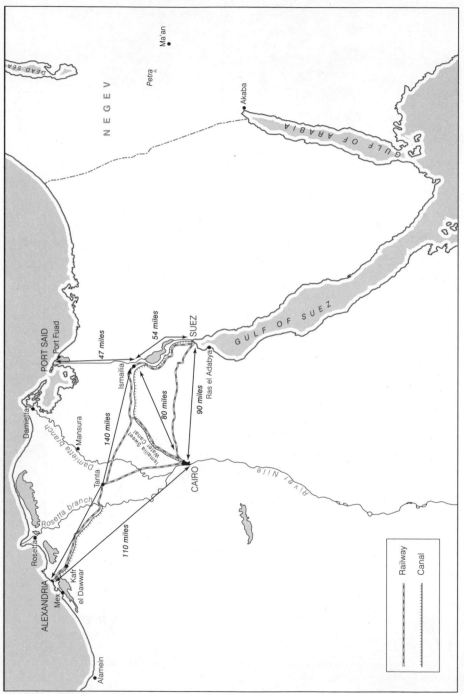

The Isthmus of Suez.

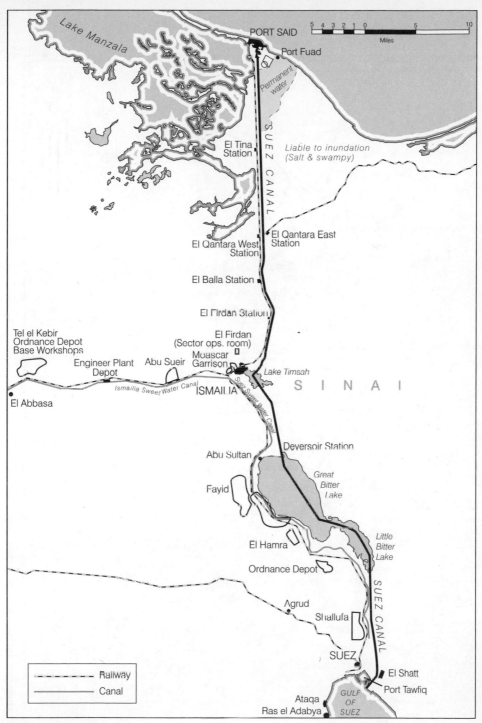

The Canal Zone.

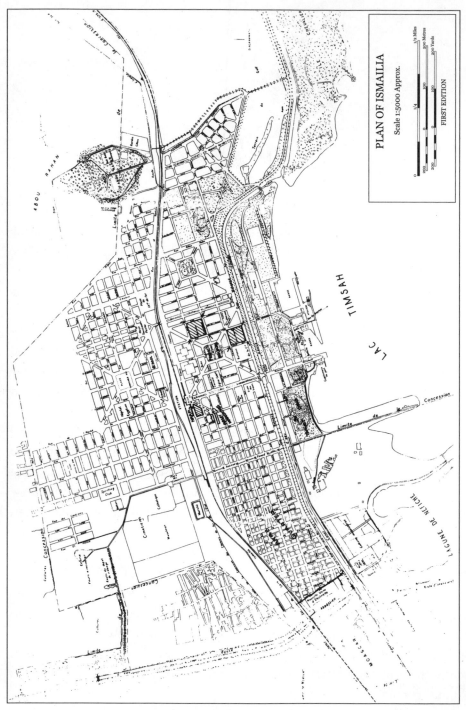

British army plan of Ismailia, 1951. (IWM HW 71074)

Introduction

In a celebrated essay about the English written at the height of the Blitz, George Orwell observed that the only battle poems that had 'won for themselves a kind of popularity are always a tale of disasters and retreats'. 'There is no popular poem', he noted, 'about Trafalgar or Waterloo.' His point was to emphasise how much his fellow countrymen hated war and militarism, and was made in conjunction with another acute observation concerning Englishness, namely its 'respect for constitutionalism and legality'.[1] These remarks, while perhaps a little rose-tinted (Hitler was, after all, pounding at the door), help explain why *Suez* still remains such an emotive word in British politics.

The conflict of 1956 occurred after Sir Anthony Eden's Conservative government had wilfully disregarded legal advice concerning an alleged transgression by President Gamal Abdel Nasser of Egypt (there was nothing unlawful about the nationalisation of the Suez Canal Company, because shareholders were to be compensated). Against all good sense, Eden hatched a secret and highly duplicitous war plot with France and Israel, while keeping Britain's friendly superpower, the United States, completely in the dark; and topping it all, the prime minister abandoned the euphemistically termed 'armed intervention' in the midst of its final phase. Inevitably, Eden, who resigned shortly afterwards, became the main villain of the piece and has since come to be widely regarded as one of the worst British prime ministers of the twentieth century. Not surprisingly, dozens of books have been written about the debacle, although we still await a popular poem.

This book, on the other hand, is about Britain's 'forgotten' Suez campaign, one that occurred in the first half of the 1950s and entailed a political, diplomatic, and military struggle with and within Egypt for possession of the Suez Canal Zone, which at the time was the largest military base in the world. This more drawn-out crisis was pivotal in the making of the modern Middle East, from providing the circumstances for the rise of an Egyptian leader who became the Arab world's most charismatic statesman, to engineering the succession of the United States over Britain as the dominant 'outside' power in the region. Eden, the 'villain' of 1956, once again figures prominently, only this time as a pragmatic, realistic and, for the main part, strong-willed foreign secretary who was anxious to adapt Britain's global responsibilities to the changed and changing circumstances of the post-1945 era. To appreciate fully the irony of his anachronistic imperialist adventure of 1956, it is necessary to understand his role in resolving, against enormous domestic and international pressures, the Suez base dispute of 1951–4.

Winston Churchill emerges from this earlier crisis as a towering and often mischievous presence, cutting a figure that was mulishly reminiscent of a bygone age. A past master in such matters, he also gave the struggle its name, the 'Battle of the Canal Zone'. As prime minister, he did all he could to undermine Eden's efforts at trying to reach an accommodation with the legitimate demands of Egyptian nationalism. Having watched the Labour administrations of 1945–51 lose Palestine, India, and the massive oil complex at Abadan in Iran, Churchill was adamant that the Suez bastion be retained, come what may. Earlier struggles coloured the heated debates. Concessions were equated with appeasement; Munich was said to be on the Nile. There was an added piquancy to the Eden–Churchill tension in that Eden had been given to believe that the keys to No. 10 would be his within a year or so of the Conservatives taking office. But Churchill reneged on this understanding and clung on to power, in large part because he felt that 'Anthony was not ready', as shown by his handling of the Egyptian question. Again, Eden, the weak and ineffective prime minister of 'Suez' repute, stands out as a principled statesman, despite his notoriously quick temper and mood swings. Nevertheless, Churchill's long shadow can be seen to have had an immense influence on Eden's behaviour in 1956.

So what made the Battle of the Canal Zone such a crucial struggle for both disputants? On the British side, the military base astride the Suez artery, which was commonly referred to as 'the jugular vein of empire', bestowed enormous international prestige.[2] At the nexus of Africa, Asia and Europe, Egypt had been a geo-strategic prize for ascendant empires since the pharaohs. Indeed, Britain's encounter with Egypt had begun, paradoxically, when Napoleon Bonaparte seized the Ottoman territory in 1798 in order to undermine British trade with India. An Anglo-Turkish army soon expelled the French, thereby initiating Britain's nineteenth-century policy of propping up the Ottoman Empire, the 'sick man of Europe'. To prevent dependence on one power, Constantinople attempted to balance its relationship with London by allowing France to build the Suez Canal, but this plan backfired when Egypt's reigning khedive (a kind of hereditary Ottoman viceroy) got heavily into debt and was obliged to sell his shares in the venture to the British. Less than a decade later, in 1882, William Gladstone sanctioned an invasion of Egypt and initiated a 'temporary occupation'.

Despite its tentative beginnings, Britain's imperial engagement in Egypt soon developed a logic of inertia that argued for its continuance – hence Churchill's diehard stance seventy years later. The nature of this logic was such that it could run backwards as well as forwards without always being troubled by consistency. Thus, while control of India had drawn Britain ever more deeply into Egypt during the nineteenth century, the granting of Indian independence in 1947 did not have a corresponding effect. Instead, Egypt became the centrepiece of a new imperial system which had Africa as its hub; the Middle East became vital both as a gateway and in its own right because of oil.

The logical gymnastics were not, however, always so specious. The reason why Egypt assumed such a critical role in the story of Britain's disengagement from empire, and why Suez is ultimately remembered as a turning point, was because of a reverse logic associated with 1882.[3] By invading and occupying Egypt, Britain helped spark the 'scramble for Africa' by the European powers. In an inversion of this earlier process, the crisis which affected Anglo-Egyptian relations in the first half of the 1950s – and which flowed into the Suez War of 1956 – was directly linked to Britain's survival as a world power. 'What happens here', remarked Churchill in 1953, 'will set the pace for us all over Africa and the Middle East.'[4]

For Egypt, the Battle of the Canal Zone was known as the Liberation Struggle. After many false starts, the indigenous nationalist movement was prepared by the early 1950s to conduct a campaign of sustained guerrilla warfare against the British military presence. The volunteers called

themselves fedayeen (Arabic for self-sacrifice) and formed liberation
battalions. By means of murder and sabotage, they sought to raise the cost
of the Suez base to a price London was no longer willing to pay. Mass
participation in the struggle was largely confined to its early stages and took
the form of anti-British riots. Egypt's political classes had long manipulated
street demonstrations as a method of displaying their nationalist credentials.
The purpose of manipulation is, of course, control. However, in the winter
of 1951/2, it became increasingly clear that civil disorder had taken on a
life of its own. Genuine outpourings swamped staged spectacles. As the
nationalist ante was upped, leading politicians resorted to courting the
fedayeen, financing them in the hope of being able to regulate their
behaviour.

Their limited success revealed a second fundamental aspect to the
Liberation Struggle – a concurrent struggle for ascendancy in Egyptian
politics. This internal battle pitted the elite, characterised by a fractious and
self-serving party system and a corrupt and sycophantic court, against a
variety of competing nationalist and Islamic pressure groups, operating
outside the parliamentary system. The upshot was that nationalist
opposition to the British presence became intimately connected with an
internal challenge to Egypt's existing political and constitutional
arrangements. The old nationalist demand of 'Egypt for the Egyptians' thus
also came with an implied question – which Egyptians?

It is an oddity of British imperial history that the most notorious crisis of
decolonisation occurred in a country that was, strictly speaking, not part of
the empire. In the early 1950s, Britain maintained military installations in
Egypt by virtue of a bilateral defence treaty, signed in 1936. Similar
relationships existed with Iraq and Jordan, and prompted historian M.A.
Fitzsimons to brand British influence in the Middle East as 'empire by
treaty'.[5] The underlying nature of these interactions was that they were
unequal: Britain was much stronger than its Arab allies and therefore
shaped the terms according to its own interests. After the Second World War,
Labour foreign secretary Ernest Bevin attempted to transform this veiled
system of domination into relationships that better resembled equal
partnership, an approach that sputtered and stalled but was never
completely abandoned, and indeed was effectively picked up by Eden when
the Conservatives came into office in October 1951.[6] The reason for its
resilience, despite frequent and severe setbacks, was brutal necessity.

British policymakers recognised that the world had radically changed during the 1939–45 conflict. Before the war, Europe had dominated international affairs and had shaped a global environment that permitted intervention in, and authority over, 'backward' societies. But with the collapse of this international system, a new infrastructure had begun to emerge based around the competing interests of two superpowers, the United States and the Soviet Union, both of which instinctively, and inconsistently, opposed colonialism. Seen in this light, Britain's partnership approach was effectively a neo-imperialist restructuring effort aimed at maintaining a world role in a changed international order.

In this respect, Egypt resided on the most vulnerable plane of the post-1945 efforts at redefining the empire. Partnership could be reasonably attractive to indigenous peoples when it related to directly administered territories gaining independence and having some sort of treaty connection tagged on as part of the bargain – what imperial historians call a move from 'formal' to 'informal' imperialism. However, when a country was already supposedly a sovereign state (as Egypt was), and yet was bound – and most probably scarred – by an unequal treaty, the attempts to redefine that relationship were likely to be treated with great suspicion. Moreover, given the context of Britain's relative decline (which was evident economically as well as via the rise of the superpowers), the pursuit of new treaty relationships was apt to be interpreted locally as a ruse for resuscitating ties where British influence was already visibly on the wane. 'Informal imperialism', observes John Darwin, 'was not an easy option for a declining power: that was the real lesson of Suez.'[7]

All of which is to say that the Battle of the Canal Zone had as its political core a dispute over how the Anglo-Egyptian defence treaty of 1936 should be revised. Egypt wanted an immediate and complete evacuation of British forces, whereas Britain sought a new settlement which would permit a certain number of soldiers to remain in the Canal Zone. Because the 1936 treaty was an internationally recognised legal arrangement, Britain regarded fedayeen attacks as 'terrorism'. Yet this case was muddied by the size of the troop presence. The maximum permitted in peacetime was 10,000, but the actual number had always far exceeded this. For much of the 1951–4 crisis, 80,000 were deployed. Britain was thus guilty of clinging to one legal point while ignoring another.

It was the 1936 treaty, moreover, that created the Canal Zone in the first place. The name was somewhat misleading in that it suggested a single entity, with a distinct, defensible perimeter. In fact, the various accommodation sites, ammunition depots, airfields, water filtration plants, power stations, stores, hospitals, and workshops were situated in numerous locations within an area still fairly heavily populated by Egyptians. The potential for harassment and sabotage, especially on the linking roads, was therefore enormous. Geographically (see map on p. xv), the northern boundary of the Canal Zone moved across the Mediterranean coast at Port Said. It then dropped southwards to El Tina, forming a narrow corridor, approximately 1 mile wide at most points, along the western Canal bank, and incorporated the Treaty and Canal roads and all camps along these routes. From El Tina, the boundary skirted westwards to Tel el Kebir and El Abbasa, before running south-east to Shallufa. The southern boundary followed the coastline through Ras el Adabya and Suez to Port Tawfiq. The eastern boundary proceeded from Port Tawfiq up the eastern bank of the Suez Canal to the urban boundary of Port Fuad on the Mediterranean coast, again incorporating installations en route.[8] It was, in total, about 750 square miles in size.[9]

Conflicting issues of power and sovereignty lay at the heart of the Anglo-Egyptian dispute. The British presence in Egypt had always been imposed by acts of force. Furthermore, there had never been any formal responsibility for moulding the Egyptian nation. Consequently, a withdrawal of the garrison could not be presented as the fulfilment of the imperial mission. It could only look like a loss or a defeat. British policymakers often tried to deny the realities of this position of power – the power to intervene in Egypt's internal affairs, the power to make and break Egyptian governments. But in moments of crisis, such qualms were quickly overridden. As the distinguished Arab historian Albert Hourani has pointed out, when there is a power in your country which is stronger than the actual government, that power is sovereign despite any pretence to the contrary.[10] One of the key themes of this book concerns Britain's deliberations to reoccupy the Nile Delta, the area between Alexandria, Cairo and Port Said. These debates were to have a crucial influence on the outcome of the Battle of the Canal Zone, as well as on the planning for the re-invasion of Egypt in 1956.

Any student of politics will tell you that power is a relative concept. Egyptian nationalists were well aware that British power was in decline.

It was also apparent to everyone concerned that there was a vigorous new actor on the scene, the United States. Another of this book's main themes, therefore, is to detail how America became embroiled in the Arab Middle East (Washington's connection with Israel already being well known). The irony in this aspect of the story is that British policymakers tried desperately hard to draw their transatlantic ally into the Egyptian dispute, only to rue the day afterwards. Instead of assisting British interests, different agencies of the US government worked assiduously – and often independently of each other – at increasing their influence at the expense of their NATO partner. The struggle for Egypt was thus very much a triangular affair. The nadir in Anglo-American relations during the Suez War of 1956 grew from well-planted roots in the Battle of the Canal Zone.

British commanders in Egypt used to have a bullish saying concerning their plans to occupy the Nile Delta. Seizing control of Cairo, they said, would take one day if unopposed and half a day if opposed. Beneath this flippancy lay an awareness of the real problem in removing disagreeable foreign governments: maintaining civil order after 'regime change' tends to be far more difficult than the initial military operation. In a post-9/11 world, where the United States confronts its enemies with military force rather than contains them through international organisations, this lesson is being relearnt the painful way. As a historian of British imperialism in the Middle East, it has been fascinating, if often alarming, to see the re-emergence of so many familiar themes: Western powers toppling Arab governments; the difficulties of arranging successor administrations; guerrilla warfare conducted by fedayeen; occupation troops becoming bogged down in guard duties; the effect of rising death tolls on morale and opinion back home; internal Arab struggles between secular and Islamic groupings . . . the list could go on. Conditions in Egypt in the early 1950s clearly have a relevance and topicality for events in the Middle East today.

In 2003 the Blair government announced that British veterans of the 1951–4 Suez crisis were finally to be awarded a medal. Years of pressure had at last paid off for soldiers of the 'forgotten campaign'. While not unprecedented, the issuing of a decoration for services some fifty years after the events is highly unusual. Having just committed troops to his own Middle Eastern war, Blair perhaps wanted to right an earlier wrong and give due recognition to the 200,000 servicemen who had served in the Suez base during the Canal Zone crisis. The first request for an appropriate medal was made in January 1952 by Britain's most senior officer in the Middle East. However, it was not properly considered at the time, or indeed for decades afterwards, owing to the political delicacy of Britain's position in Egypt in the early 1950s and the subsequent embarrassment of the Suez debacle in 1956. On the fiftieth anniversary of those latter events, it is high time we more fully understand their antecedents.

ONE

●●●●●●●●

The Politics of Occupation

Ismailia is a city situated at the halfway point of the Suez Canal. Most Egyptians identify the city with the Canal – and all that this implies. What may be regarded as a positive connection today was not always so. Indeed, for a long time Egypt's miseries were blamed on the 100-mile-long waterway that pierced the Suez Isthmus and created an artery from Europe to the Orient. When the French engineer Ferdinand de Lesseps was constructing the Canal in the 1860s, Ismailia (which was briefly called Lessepsville before it was decided to honour Egypt's new ruler, Ismail, in 1863) was envisaged as the Venice of the desert, a great entrepôt for East–West trade. Instead, it became the Washington of the Suez Canal Company, an administrative centre for the foreign-dominated body that piloted the shipping through the Canal and kept the lion's share of the profits. The city naturally developed a French character, with elegant squares and avenues of stone town houses and fine hotels – 'a bit of Paris suddenly transported to the Desert', wrote the London *Times* in 1870.[1] A far less salubrious Arab quarter settled to the east while other (non-French) nationalities settled in the west. Thus, from its very foundation Ismailia was above all else a testament to foreign imperialism. In July 1956 President Nasser of Egypt made himself an Arab hero when he nationalised the Suez Canal Company and finally placed it under Egyptian control. Before this defining moment in Egypt's modern history, Ismailia occupied a special place in the struggle between imperialism and nationalism, astride a fault line at its weakest point.

When members of Europe's royal families gathered in Ismailia for the opening of the Suez Canal on 17 November 1869, the achievement being celebrated was that of imperial France and, more implicitly, the continuing march of European civilisation. Paying for the festivities was Khedive Ismail, grandson of Muhammad Ali, the Albanian volunteer in the Ottoman army who founded Egypt's ruling dynasty in 1805. Ismail saw himself as a great moderniser and was keen to count himself and his country as part of Europe's progress. In the preceding decade Egypt's cities had been radically restructured to fit this grand ambition. The costs were enormous and the public debt was already reaching crippling proportions by the time the Canal was opened. By 1875 Ismail's credit-worthiness among European banks had all but evaporated, leaving him one last source of revenue, 176,602 shares in the Suez Canal Company (44 per cent of the total). Anxious to stop the French acquiring complete control of the Canal, Britain's prime minister Benjamin Disraeli snapped up the shares for £4 million. It was ironic that almost overnight the British government became a partner in an enterprise it had previously done its utmost to block (to stem further spread of French power). Another powerful foreign presence had duly arrived in Ismailia.

VEILED PROTECTORATE AND EMPIRE BY TREATY

In 1879 Egypt's continuing financial problems prompted the British and French governments to compel the Ottoman sultan – the overlord of Egypt's khedives – to depose the profligate Ismail in favour of his son and heir, Tawfiq. This intervention was accompanied by the establishment of Anglo-French 'dual control' aimed at restoring financial stability to Egypt. The partnership broke down in 1882 when Britain, without French help (owing to a ministerial crisis), invaded Egypt and quelled a revolt led by the Egyptian nationalist leader, Colonel Arabi. Tellingly, the British forces, after securing Alexandria, headed straight to the Suez Canal and occupied Ismailia, before decisively defeating Arabi at the battle of Tel el Kebir, which was about halfway between Ismailia and the capital, Cairo. Egypt thereafter became a 'veiled protectorate' with the British residency, especially under Lord Cromer's firm rule between 1883 and 1907, behaving like 'Government House' in a Crown Colony.[2] Nevertheless, it was not until the First World War that London formally ended the nominal sovereignty of Turkey, which sided with Germany and Austria-Hungary, and declared Egypt a British protectorate. This process entailed deposing the reigning khedive, Abbas Hilmi II, because of alleged pro-Turkish sympathies. A successor was appointed – his uncle, Hussein Kamal – with the title of sultan, so indicating the break with the Ottoman sultanate. Kamal's eldest son, Fuad, succeeded him in 1917.

Meanwhile, the war years saw Egypt placed within the imperial grip as never before, and the effect was to stiffen its people's desire for independence.

After the armistice of November 1918, Egyptian nationalists, encouraged by the principle of self-determination espoused by American president, Woodrow Wilson, formed a party called the Wafd (Arabic for delegation) and demanded that they be allowed to attend the Paris Peace Conference. But Britain, having expanded its interests in the Middle East following the collapse of Ottoman rule, was not about to let Egyptian troublemakers threaten them. Thus, it was British officials who represented Egypt at Paris in 1919; the Wafd watched from the sidelines. This marginalisation of Egypt's would-be leaders prompted widespread rioting in Cairo and across the Nile Delta, with Ismailia a prominent trouble spot. In Egyptian nationalist history, these disturbances are known as the 1919 Revolution, but in reality it was a revolution that failed to turn: Egypt remained firmly under British power. Nevertheless, the ferocity of the riots did persuade London to reassess its methods of rule and a form of colonial collaboration was sought to preserve British interests more informally and with less expense. The first step, in February 1922, was the issuing by Britain of a declaration of Egyptian independence, which ended the hated protectorate. At the same time, however, four 'matters' were reserved for the discretion of the British government. These were: imperial communications; the defence of Egypt; the protection of foreign interests; and the administration of the Sudan. Egypt's 'independence' was followed a year later with the promulgation of a liberal constitution. Fuad abandoned the title of sultan and became Egypt's first king; a parliament was established with upper and lower chambers, and regular elections were sanctioned. The electorate for the lower house, the chamber of deputies, was Egypt's adult male population. The upper chamber, the senate, was to be partly appointed and partly elected on a narrow franchise.

Egypt's veneer of democracy masked the realities of the new system. At Britain's instigation, the framers of the constitution ensured that the strength of the nationalist Wafd party would be checked by a powerful and conservative monarchy. The king was granted powers to make and break cabinets, appoint prime ministers, and dissolve or prorogue parliament. As anitcipated in London, a domestic struggle for ascendancy ensued, so diverting attention from Britain's own backstairs domination. Conflicts between the government and the king usually accounted for changes of administration rather than overt British intervention. Somewhat less frequently, the will of Egyptian voters was allowed to make changes at the top. This pattern of rule was established with Egypt's first democratic government, a Wafdist one (as was to be the case after all free elections). It lasted a mere eleven months, after which King Fuad appointed a new prime minister who then proceeded to dissolve parliament. Subsequent palace-appointed governments were profligate in suspending the constitution, falsifying elections, and ruling dictatorially. This systemic abuse of the constitution gradually undermined parliamentary politics in Egypt. Britain's main priority during the interwar years was stability, not political fair play.

Moreover, the fiction of Egypt's independence was always going to be exposed by the continued presence of British military forces: a longer-term solution to the resented issue of 'reserved points' was therefore sought. Britain's goal was to replace the veiled imperial relationship with a treaty recognised in international law. Negotiations repeatedly faltered, however, because of political rivalries in Egypt. Only after Mussolini's Italy invaded Abyssinia (Ethiopia) in late 1935 was urgency added to the process. Within a few months, a 'united front' delegation headed by the Wafdist leader Mustafa al-Nahas Pasha concluded a defence treaty with Britain replacing the military occupation with a treaty of alliance. For British policymakers, this was an instance when it was essential to have the Wafd, and its mass support, on board. Article 1 of the text resoundingly declared, 'the military occupation of Egypt by the forces of His Majesty the King and Emperor is terminated'.[3] The terms of the treaty meant that Britain's mission in Cairo became an embassy, with the high commissioner redesignated an ambassador. London was also committed to reducing the number of its troops in Egypt to 10,000, except in the event of an 'apprehended international emergency'. In the latter eventuality, which was open to broad definition, there was to be no limit placed on reinforcements. (The British signatory, a youthful foreign secretary named Anthony Eden, was honoured with an Egyptian stamp bearing his likeness.) The following year Egypt's capitulations system, in which Britain was entrusted with the judicial protection of foreign interests, was abolished at the Montreux conference, and Egypt was finally admitted to the League of Nations, the litmus test of independent statehood.

But all was not as it seemed with the defence treaty. Most significantly, the twenty-year duration clause came with a hidden catch. Britain's eventual withdrawal from Suez was made conditional on Egypt being able to ensure security of navigation in the Canal. To this end, Britain agreed to assist Egypt in its efforts to modernise and strengthen its armed forces while remaining its sole arms supplier. However, an excuse for reneging on this commitment was planned in advance, namely Egypt's anticipated inability to support the financial burden of a modern army. This duplicitous approach was necessary to overcome the objections of Britain's chiefs of staff to the proposed agreement.[4] Clearly, the military planners in London envisaged a British military presence in Egypt long after 1956. Even without knowing about this imperial skullduggery, many Egyptians felt let down by their politicians for signing up to the treaty. The prevailing attitude was, why worry about the Italian threat when Britain was already in occupation? As a consequence, Egyptian nationalists increasingly turned to pressure groups outside the parliamentary system to vent their demands for complete independence, a trend that further weakened the constitutional order.

The main beneficiary of this disillusionment was the Muslim Brotherhood, an organisation formed in Ismailia in 1928. Its founder and 'supreme guide' Hasan al-Banna had arrived in the Canal city the previous year, having recently graduated from a teacher-training college in Cairo. In Ismailia the realities of occupation were plain to see. The luxurious properties of foreigners stood in stark contrast to the homes of Egyptian workers. Even street signs were written in English. Military barracks dotted the suburbs, while the city's nightlife amply catered to the needs of off-duty soldiers. Nor did the surrounding rural areas offer sanctuary from the occupation forces. Rather, one of Ismailia's draws for Britain was its adjacent scrubland and desert which were deemed perfect for military training and manoeuvres. Like many in his generation, al-Banna had already expressed anti-British sentiments in the 1919 demonstrations. Less common was his fervent religious belief, which stemmed from his upbringing as the son of an imam. The social and political ferment that shook Cairo after the introduction of the franchise in 1923 had spurred al-Banna into action. Instead of seeing the fruits of pluralism in the welter of political activity, he saw only national disunity. What he found most threatening, however, was the increasing secularism of newspapers and books, and the flagrantly European ideas of the elite literary and social salons. The Muslim Brotherhood aimed at rectifying this situation. By 1939 its influence had spread far beyond Ismailia, until it became one of Egypt's largest mass organisations. Its goal was the establishment of an Islamic state free of all foreign interference.

THE SECOND WORLD WAR AND ITS AFTERMATH

The onset of the Second World War highlighted the true nature of British influence in Egypt. The 1936 treaty obligated Egypt to place its facilities, resources and communications at Britain's disposal – not that Britain had reduced its troop levels to the agreed 10,000 in the preceding years. While this was promptly done Egypt did not declare war on Germany – or Italy when it eventually entered the fray – because this was not formally required. Nevertheless, an awkward situation ensued in which many Egyptian nationalists came to see a Nazi victory, which looked likely after the rapid fall of France in June 1940, as beneficial to their cause. Meanwhile, Cairo was turned into the military hub of the British empire (and went on to serve as the headquarters for campaigns in North Africa, East Africa, the Middle East, and south-eastern Europe). However, the British continued to suspect some members of the palace entourage of pro-Axis sympathies. Sir Miles Lampson, Britain's ambassador in Cairo, was more categorical and precise in his assessment: the main problem, he asserted, was Farouk, the young monarch. King Farouk had inherited the throne from his father, Fuad, less than five years earlier, aged 17. Lampson had initially regarded the handsome teenager as a welcome new beginning for Egypt, but this attitude had long since been replaced with ill feeling over his supposed laziness and unreliability. The latter was deemed especially problematic in wartime. On the other side, Farouk disliked Lampson's patronising and dictatorial manner from the start. Beneath this personal antipathy lay the central tension at the heart of Egyptian politics – the continuing British military presence.

The Lampson–Farouk antagonism reached crisis point in early 1942. With an eye to a German victory, Farouk had been resisting British pressures for the recall of the Wafd to government, which was anti-fascist and pro-Allied in the war. Lampson's patience finally ran out on 4 February. The day began with the British embassy delivering an ultimatum to Farouk, instructing him to form a Wafd administration or abdicate. When the 6 p.m. deadline passed Lampson went to confront 'the boy', accompanied by troops and tanks. On being received by Farouk at the Abdin Palace, the ambassador waved a letter of abdication in his face. Visibly shaken by the threat, Farouk did as he was told and brought back the Wafd to power. Lampson then returned to the embassy where a party was in full swing.[5] His entrance later that evening was arm-in-arm with the incoming prime minister, al-Nahas, who was grinning widely. The Abdin Palace incident drove a coach and horses through Egypt's supposed independence. Farouk was disgraced by his capitulation, and the Wafd, which had developed out of opposition to the British occupation, effectively relinquished its position as the standard-bearer of Egyptian nationalism. The al-Nahas administration subsequently survived in office only because of British bayonets. When wartime controls were loosened in October 1944 – signalled by Lampson taking a holiday outside Egypt – Farouk smartly dismissed the Wafd from power.

A common theme among Farouk's biographers is that the king, who was still only 21 at the time of the ultimatum, never recovered from the capitulation, thus offering an explanation for his notoriously reckless behaviour thereafter. Whatever the underlying causes, his misdemeanours were covered up for a while by wartime censorship. For instance, on one occasion he visited Cairo Zoo in the middle of the night and shot dead the caged lions. His sleep apparently had been disturbed by nightmares involving lions, which he equated with the symbolic British variant. After the war his playboy lifestyle became the open gossip of Egypt's coffee shops and salons, and even the European popular press began to take an interest. 'Soon there will only be five kings left,' Farouk famously told a visiting British dignitary, 'the King of England, the King of Spades, the King of Clubs, the King of Hearts and the King of Diamonds.' Behind the devil-may-care attitude lay a lingering hatred for his old tormentor. Referring to the deposition threat of 1942, he told one of Lampson's successors that 'Sir Miles had never been nearer death than on that day!', and maintained that there had been a loaded pistol in his desk drawer. Bursts of 'cackling laughter' punctuated the account.[6] Nevertheless, despite his instability, Farouk still played a pivotal role in Egyptian politics. Britain well understood this and tried to placate him in early 1946 by moving Lampson, by then ennobled as Lord Killearn, to a post in South-East Asia.

This action was part of a wider scheme to redefine Britain's imperial relations in the Middle East after the war. Ernest Bevin, foreign secretary in Clement Attlee's Labour government from July 1945, had set his sights on achieving a new era of partnership in the region. This included encouraging social and economic reform so that the advantages of the British connection could trickle down to the ordinary people. There was even talk of bringing more sections of Arab society into the policymaking process. 'Peasants not pashas,' summed up Bevin – pashas being his catch-all term for the

landowning notables who dominated political systems across the region
(pasha was an Ottoman title equivalent to lord and most accurately applied to
Egypt). The key feature of the partnership approach, however, was the
replacement of the interwar defence treaties with new agreements based on
equality between the signatory nations. To further this process, Bevin
instructed his officials to abandon the practice of intervening in the internal
affairs of independent Arab countries. While this dovetailed nicely with
international opinion in the era of the Atlantic Charter and the United
Nations, another motivation came from the realisation that Britain had
become too embroiled in Egypt's internal rivalries between the palace and the
Wafd. Disentanglement from the machinations of this struggle was
consequently seen as the first step towards the settlement of bilateral issues
between London and Cairo.

In his landmark study *The British Empire in the Middle East 1945–1951*
(1984), Wm Roger Louis meticulously charts the frustrations and eventual
failure of Bevin's 'grand strategy' of bringing about 'partnership' with the
'moderate' nationalists of the region. In the first place, austerity-stricken
Britain was in no shape to provide the resources to make economic aid
programmes to the Middle East work. Indeed, the establishment of an effective
infrastructure for state-driven economic development was never really on the
agenda. While Attlee's administration toiled with the nationalisation of one-
fifth of Britain's domestic economy, in colonial circles old theories of public
finance continued to prevail and these taught that states should live within
their incomes; and as regards seeking new allies among the downtrodden
masses, this had to take a backseat to the realities of trying to secure interests
in the present and near future. This meant conducting negotiations with
existing elites. Even in areas where Britain could have been of help, such as
scientific farming techniques, British policy was met with suspicion.
'Independence not locust control' was the demand of the locals, observed
Economist journalist Elizabeth Monroe (who later wrote *Britain's Moment in
the Middle East 1914–1956* (1963)) following a visit to the region after the
war.[7] In fact, it was this desire for complete independence that ultimately
dashed Bevin's efforts to place Britain's interests in the Middle East on a more
equal footing.

The test case for Bevin's new approach was Egypt, albeit after rioting across
the Nile Delta in early 1946 had pushed Britain to the negotiating table
earlier than it desired. The upshot was an offer to Egypt that became a

millstone for both sides in all subsequent negotiations. In May Attlee stated that Britain would evacuate the Suez base by September 1949 on condition that a joint defence board be established to maintain the base in peacetime. An apparent agreement on these terms was reached between Bevin and Ismail Sidqi, Egypt's prime minister, in October, but the 'Bevin–Sidqi Protocol' soon collapsed amid charges of duplicity. The Sudan issue (see Chapter 6) was the stumbling block as far as Egyptian ratification was concerned. 'Unity of the Nile Valley' had long been one of the rallying cries in Egypt's political life, based on the claims of the Muhammad Ali dynasty to reign over the Sudan. However, the protocol only promised symbolic recognition of these claims, leaving the British administration in the Sudan and the eventual rights of the Sudanese to self-determination unaffected. Protests in Egypt ensued, fuelled by politicians close to Farouk. Anthony Nutting, a British minister intimately connected with Middle Eastern affairs in the 1950s, later contended that Farouk's espousal of 'Unity of the Nile Valley' was a deliberate ploy to protect his throne. By blocking a defence agreement, the Sudan dispute ensured that Britain remained in the Canal Zone. Farouk's logic was that British troops would stave off revolution.[8] Be that as it may, with the onset of the Cold War proper in 1947–8, London felt unable to repeat the 1946 terms. Yet this offer of withdrawal trapped all subsequent Egyptian politicians into having to demand nothing less than the complete evacuation of British forces.

Meanwhile, Ismailia's position at the weakest point in the fault line between imperialism and nationalism had become even more pronounced. During the early stages of the 1946 negotiations, Bevin had tried to demonstrate his sincerity by handing over the British military headquarters in Cairo, which were situated at the Citadel. (The date of the move was intended to send a positive signal – the 4 July Independence Day in the United States.) As a consequence, Ismailia, or more specifically, the suburb of Moascar, became the new command centre for British troops in Egypt. Thus, the old symbol of foreign economic domination, the headquarters of the Suez Canal Company, was hereafter complemented with the overt instrument of military control.

The following year, 1947, was one of stalemate in Anglo-Egyptian relations, despite London's efforts to ease tensions. Most significantly, British forces withdrew from Alexandria and Cairo, in February and March respectively. (As a consequence, the garrison strength in Egypt gradually decreased from 90,000 in early 1947 to 47,000 by October 1948, but still far in excess of the 10,000 allowed by the 1936 treaty.[9]) However, rather than reducing friction between the local population and British forces, the move instead gave succour to Egyptian nationalists. Events elsewhere certainly enhanced the impression that *Pax Britannica* was crumbling and Egypt's turn was imminent. Burmese independence had been promised in December 1946; the problem of Palestine was passed to the UN in February 1947; that same month commitments in Greece and Turkey were effectively handed to the United States; and, above all, in June it was announced that Britain would partition and pull out of India by August. Egypt, meanwhile, had begun the year with a new prime minister, Mahmud Fahmi al-Nuqrashi, along with a new policy – the breaking off of the Canal Zone negotiations and an appeal to the UN for a resolution calling for a British withdrawal. When the UN Security Council responded with a display of disunity in early September, the continuing impasse between Cairo and London played into Bevin's revised approach of standing firm on existing treaty rights. With Egypt relatively secure, Britain decided to cut its losses in its other Middle Eastern trouble spot and a final timetable for disengagement from Palestine was announced on 26 September. The lowering of the Union Jack at the High Commission in Jerusalem was to take place at midnight on 14 May 1948, with major implications for Egypt.

This fateful decision effectively capped Britain's postwar 'crisis of readjustment'. India, the hub around which the rest of the empire had been assembled, was gone, but Britain nevertheless remained committed to its world role. Crucially, the new focus of empire shifted westwards to Africa and the Middle East. True, Bevin's overarching policy of transforming the old imperial system of domination (which largely operated in the Middle East via unequal treaty alliances) into relationships of equal partners had, thus far, been a failure, but perhaps more importantly, at least in the short term, the metropolitan will to remain a world power had been fortified. In this respect, it should be noted that the greatest challenge had come not from Egyptian nationalists or even the Soviet Union, but from Bevin's colleague and boss, the British prime minister.

Since 1945 Attlee had been anxious to bring Britain's commitments into line with the changed circumstances of the postwar world, the imminent loss of India being foremost in his reckoning. He also believed that developments in air power and the advent of atomic weapons needed to be taken into account, especially in light of the deteriorating relations with Moscow. The proximity of Britain's Middle Eastern bases to Soviet oil fields in the Caucasus, he felt, made them a potential source of friction. A major readjustment was further justified by the increasing virulence of anti-colonial sentiment among Arab nationalists. In short, Attlee wanted to withdraw from the Middle East and create a neutral buffer zone between British and Russian interests. In this respect, Bevin's pursuit of partnership, with its talk of social and economic reform in the region, did at least give a socialist gloss (sincere as it was) to his ultimate foreign policy goal of preserving Britain's power.

Meanwhile, the chiefs of staff added their weight to the arguments for staying put. The Middle East, they stated, was vital to British interests precisely because of its geographical position. In a direct inversion of the prime minister's concerns, the region was identified as an ideal location from which to attack the industrial and oil-producing areas of southern Russia and the Caucasus. The service chiefs went on to establish a linkage whereby air attacks launched from bases in the Middle East – including an atomic offensive, courtesy of American input (which had yet to be secured) – would help counter an attack on Western Europe where Soviet forces were far superior numerically.[10] The Foreign Office added its weight to the opinions of the military planners by stressing the importance of Persian Gulf oil and imperial interests in 'Black Africa'. Bevin held that the road to domestic economic recovery began in the African continent. The Middle East was, of course, the gateway to Africa and much else besides. 'My whole aim', wrote Bevin to Attlee in 1947, 'has been to develop the Middle East as a producing area to help our own economy and take the place of India.'[11] Welfare at home was to be paid for by empire overseas. By 1948 the combined might of the chiefs of staff and Bevin's Foreign Office had succeeded in overcoming Attlee's pressure for retreat. In the process, Britain's 'informal' empire of unpopular treaty relationships in the Middle East had become the centrepiece of the post-India imperial system. At the epicentre was Egypt, now regarded as critical to the working of the system as a whole. The need to work with and conciliate 'moderate' nationalists was thus more important than ever. Events in the region, however, were further militating against this very outcome.

THE IMPACT OF PALESTINE

Given the context of events in the Middle East in 1948, there was something rather surreal about Britain's political and military emphasis on the region. On 29 November 1947 the UN General Assembly had voted to partition

Palestine when the British withdrew, a move that was rejected by the Arab states in the Arab League. A civil war then ensued between the Jewish forces in Palestine and the indigenous Arabs, the latter aided by irregulars from other Arab countries. In order to contain and channel popular enthusiasm for the Palestinian cause, the Egyptian government gave assistance to volunteer guerrilla fighters, mainly via the Muslim Brotherhood. On 15 May, when the Israeli state was born, members of the Arab League transformed the conflict into an interstate war by intervening, ostensibly on behalf of the Palestinian Arabs. In truth, the Arab League was riven by rivalries and suspicions of ulterior motives. One of the rumours at the time (and since confirmed by British and Israeli official documents) was that King Abdullah of Jordan had come to an agreement with the Zionist leadership based on his British-led and subsidised Arab Legion seizing the Arab part of Palestine and not attacking the Jewish areas (as defined by the UN).[12] Moreover, Bevin was privy to the collusion and encouraged it because an enlarged Jordan – Abdullah was Britain's most loyal ally in the region – would be better able to defend the northern approaches to Egypt. The unwanted alternative was an Arab Palestine headed by the grand mufti of Jerusalem, Hajj Amin al-Husayni, who had led the Palestine Revolt between 1936 and 1939 and backed Hitler during the Second World War. In this sense, Britain had clearly not given up on the territory of Palestine as an imperial interest.

Meanwhile, it was Farouk's distrust of Abdullah's regional ambitions that largely prompted Egypt's involvement in the war. Dynastic rivalry and a desire to maintain Egypt's position as the dominant power in the Arab League accounted for this attitude rather than any deep sympathy for the Palestinian Arabs.[13] In pressing for war, Farouk undermined the more cautious instincts of the al-Nuqrashi government which knew that Egypt's army was woefully unprepared. When parliament met to decide the issue on 12 May (with a seething pro-war crowd surrounding the building), only Sidqi had the nerve to rise above the clamour and ask whether the army was actually ready. He was thereafter nicknamed 'El Yahud' (the Jew). Farouk, on the other hand, embraced the martial mood by wearing his field marshal's uniform when on excursions to Cairo's casinos.

The First Arab–Israeli War was a disaster for Egypt's king–pasha elite. The advantage Farouk gained by tapping into the popular mood for war backfired on him and his government when events on the battlefield went badly. With no clear strategic objective, the Egyptian army overextended itself across large areas of territory and then settled into stationary positions, all the time avoiding direct attacks on well-defended Jewish settlements. Egyptian leaders wanted quick, symbolic military victories for political purposes at home. As the army advanced further into Palestine it was wrongly assumed that Jewish resistance would become weaker. The upshot was vulnerable supply lines, which allowed the highly mobile Israeli forces to select at will the moments for attack.[14] Meanwhile, in the summer of 1948 the Muslim Brotherhood had opened up a second front by conducting a bombing campaign against Jewish interests in Cairo. Egypt's government, despite considerable powers under martial law, effectively turned a blind eye to these attacks. By the winter, however, with defeat looking imminent, al-Nuqrashi began to prepare the ground for the domestic political consequences of failure in Palestine. The biggest threat was deemed to come from the Muslim Brotherhood, and in early December he ordered its dissolution, having first seized its assets and neutralised Brotherhood battalions in Palestine. Hundreds of arrests followed. On 28 December a member of the organisation responded by assassinating the prime minister. The state authorities retaliated by gunning down al-Banna in a Cairo street on 12 February 1949. The previous month Egypt had signed a ceasefire with Israel, so ending the war. Meanwhile, in November 1948, Farouk had decided to divorce the popular Queen Farida (the birth of three daughters but no son and heir was the apparent motive), thus squandering the last remaining sympathy he enjoyed with the Egyptian public.

Bevin's Palestine policy in 1948 was also to prove disastrous in the longer run. By encouraging a 'Greater Jordan' at the expense of a mufti-led Palestinian state, a new layer of blame was placed on Britain by Arab nationalists. This was in addition to the fact that Israel's very existence could be traced back to the Balfour Declaration of 1917 and its promise of a Jewish homeland in Palestine. Moreover, Britain's aim of preserving influence in the area after the mandate ended, via the rule of Abdullah, failed to anticipate the effects of the ongoing Arab–Israeli dispute, which seriously undermined British interests throughout the Middle East.

On returning from Palestine many Egyptian soldiers blamed defeat on a corrupt high command and the incompetent political elite. With the bonds of combat comradeship still strong, some of the younger officers came together and formed a secret organisation within the armed forces, the Free Officers' society. Led by Colonel Gamal Abdel Nasser, the 'Blessed Movement' shared a

common assumption: there was no point fighting foreign wars until Egypt's
internal problems had been resolved. Looking back a few years later, Nasser
identified these problems as 'a struggle between the nation and its rulers' and
'a struggle between the nation and foreign intervention'.[15] In short, the Free
Officers aimed at the overthrow of the existing political system. Most of the
conspirators shared similar backgrounds. Nasser was born in Alexandria in
1918, the son of a post office manager (a lower middle-class occupation) who
originally came from Beni-Morr in Upper Egypt. During his youth he had
made frequent visits to his father's relations in Beni-Morr and had seen first-
hand the poverty in rural Egypt. Though proud of his *fellahin* (peasant) roots,
Nasser came to resent the power and wealth of the pasha class whose origins
reflected centuries of Turkish domination. Ironically, he was an early
beneficiary of the hated defence treaty of 1936. To bolster its nationalist
image in the wake of the treaty, the Wafd government had permitted for the
first time men from outside the landowning elite to enter Cairo's prestigious
military academy. Nasser became a cadet in 1937; many of the other leading
Free Officers were either in his class or one or two after it. In 1949 these men
had just turned 30 or thereabouts – too young for top posts, but perfectly
placed for commanding the loyalty of the lower ranks. Colonels were typically
the most senior men with direct control over troops in barracks. During the
early days of the conspiracy, it was anticipated that five or six years of
preparations would be needed before a coup could be staged.[16]

In the summer of 1949, with the Muslim Brotherhood banned and
neutralised, the Wafd scented an opportunity to regain power. Since Farouk's
dismissal of the previous Wafd government in October 1944 (the one installed
by British bayonets in 1942), eight coalition administrations had struggled to
govern Egypt. In the meantime, rampant inflation, diplomatic failure on the
'British question', and now military defeat in Palestine had all contributed to
a further weakening of constitutional politics in Egypt. For its part, the Wafd
had used the intervening years to try to rebuild its tarnished nationalist
credentials. It did so by boycotting elections, refusing to join coalitions, and
agitating against the treaty negotiations. Its main achievement, courtesy of
being out of power, was to avoid the full reprobation of the Palestine debacle.
It was highly significant that Britain was also eager for the Wafd's return,
seeing the party as the best hope for political and economic stability after the
turbulence brought on by the Palestine conflict. In the prescient words of
Michael Wright, the Foreign Office official in charge of Middle East policy,

such an eventuality would be 'a critical turning point both in Egypt itself and in relations between Egypt and the United Kingdom'.[17]

First, however, Farouk had to be mollified, the bitter memory of 4 February 1942 still being strong. In pursuit of this end, the British embassy in Cairo acted as an intermediary between senior Wafdists and the palace, assuring the latter that the Wafd fully supported the monarchy. (Bevin's earlier injunction of non-intervention had clearly been abandoned.) At the same time, Egypt's wealthiest industrialist, Muhammad Ahmad Abboud, utilising long-established links with Farouk, sweetened the Wafd–palace rapprochement with large helpings of financial support to both sides.[18] The path was thus cleared for a general election on 3 January 1950. As with all Egypt's free elections, the Wafd swept to victory, taking 228 seats of 319 in the chamber of deputies and polling 54.5 per cent of the vote.

Previous instances of Britain relying on the Wafd – in 1936 (with the threat of Mussolini) and 1942 (Hitler) – had stemmed more from desperation than anything else: the Wafd's mass appeal had been urgently needed. January 1950 was yet another example of this. Egypt's liberal-constitutional system, the political framework designed by Britain to perpetuate its imperial interests in an unobtrusive and inexpensive manner, was in danger of collapsing as a result of the Palestine defeat. With the Wafd and the palace, the system's two centres of authority, no longer able to represent opinion from across the political spectrum, the key question in 1950 was, could the Wafd re-engage with its natural constituency, the nationalists? And if this was possible, what would be the price?

TWO
• • • • • • •

Countdown to Crisis

The start of the Korean War, a second election victory for Attlee's Labour Party in Britain, the beginning of McCarthyism in the United States – there were many blips coming up on the political radar in 1950, but one that largely escaped international detection was the drift towards a full-blown crisis in Anglo-Egyptian relations, the implications of which were to prove as significant in their own way as those of 1882 and the 'scramble for Africa'.

A NEW URGENCY

The Wafd's return to power produced a great surge of optimism across Egypt and there were even hopes that the parliamentary order might redeem itself through wide-reaching social reforms.[1] Yet the Wafd's desire to mend fences with the palace was hardly in line with this and instead resulted in a general sycophancy towards Farouk just as his personal behaviour, following the divorce from Queen Farida, was becoming markedly more irresponsible. Thus, according to one Egyptian press article at the time, a refit of the royal yacht was paid for from the public purse, using up that year's entire budget for the Egyptian navy.[2] Fundamental changes were also occurring within the Wafd party machinery, which affected its ability to govern effectively. After the Second World War a faction representing the interests of large landowners had replaced the previously dominant urban wing of lawyers and government officials. Exemplifying this shift was the promotion of Fuad Sirag al-Din Pasha to party general secretary in 1948 when he was still in his thirties: he became interior minister in the new government at the age of 39.

Sirag al-Din was undoubtedly the most powerful politician in the twilight years of Egypt's parliamentary order, a reputation that earned him the epitaph 'the last pasha' (in part because he defiantly used the title long after Nasser had abolished all such terms of aristocratic privilege). When he died in 2000, aged 90, his demise was seen as a postscript to a momentous chapter in Egypt's history.[3] His prominence in the late 1940s and early 1950s resulted in his becoming a key figure in the subsequent debates concerning the collapse of the old order and the rise of the military junta. To some Egyptians, he was stigmatised as the man who most symbolised the failings of the Wafd and parliamentary politics generally, while to others he was, and always remained, a fervent champion of liberal constitutionalism. His standing in British accounts has tended to be low owing to the animosity that accompanied the Wafd's final fall from power, and yet for a long time before this acrimonious juncture he was seen by British policymakers as a reliable and moderate partner. There is at least one thing upon which the various perspectives implicitly agree. In appearance he resembled what a Hollywood casting director might have assumed a Farouk-era pasha to have looked like. Even in his thirties, Sirag al-Din was corpulent and was rarely seen in public without a large cigar in his mouth or hand. A thick moustache and fez completed the image.

During the late 1940s, Sirag al-Din became the Wafd's main powerbroker by virtue of two crucial alliances. The first was with al-Nahas, the Wafd's leader since the death of its founder, Saad Zaghlul, in 1927. Al-Nahas had moved from humble beginnings to become the main representative of the wealthy landowners, but he still remained popular with the Egyptian masses. Egypt's Nobel prize-winning novelist Naguib Mahfouz has suggested that this was because he had, or at least affected, the 'simple religiosity which appealed to those of rural origin'.[4] Yet this contrasts with most Western accounts of al-Nahas's final years in office, which instead emphasise a heavily perfumed, possibly senile personality who no longer had the will or inclination to be in full control of his party or government.[5] Contemporary explanations for this decline often centre on the influence of his wife, Zainab al-Wakil (al-Nahas had not married until his mid-50s). Although Zainab was the daughter of a pasha, she had never been wealthy, so her new repute for high living may have come as a shock to him, and she was certainly an easy target for criticism from the Wafd's opponents.[6]

The second key relationship making Sirag al-Din the most powerful politician in Egypt by the start of the 1950s was with the aforementioned industrialist, Abboud. To understand Abboud's prominence, it is necessary to grasp the character of Egypt's industrial position and how it resembled the agricultural structure. In both sectors there was hardly any middle class to speak of. Industry was organised along either a multitude of small concerns like craftsmen's workshops, or huge conglomerates managed on 'vertical' lines; landownership was similarly divided between enormous estates and smallholdings.[7] Abboud's rise flowed from a technical education rather than the normal 'legal' route. He was born in Cairo in 1889 and trained as a civil engineer at Glasgow University in Scotland. Work on irrigation schemes in Iraq and Palestine in the 1920s helped cement this British connection, after which he developed his own business interests. By 1950 he had a near monopoly on sugar refining in Egypt and also owned distilleries, an oil refinery, fertilizer factories and a shipping company. Once again, certain stock impressions of this leading Egyptian personality permeate the British and US official records. To the Americans, he was increasingly a powerful associate and adviser, not least as Sirag al-Din's main conduit to US ambassador, Jefferson Caffery.[8] By the same reckoning, as Sirag al-Din's star waned in British eyes, so Abboud's standing also deteriorated. A crucial point to underline about the significance of the Sirag al-Din–Abboud axis is that one of Egypt's largest landowners had teamed up with Egypt's leading businessman.

Meanwhile, opposition within the Wafd to this right-wing, conservative alliance came from reform-minded sections of the party. The leftists tended to be middle-ranking party workers in their forties who saw the rapid rise of Sirag al-Din as a direct threat to their own chances of leading the party once the so-called '1919 cronies', who were all in their sixties and seventies, finally retired. The leading light of the second tier Wafdists was Dr Muhammad Salah al-Din, the foreign minister in the new Wafd administration.[9] The upshot of these rivalries was an internecine and generational struggle for control of the Wafd. As befitted a party whose origins stemmed from opposition to the British, the key battleground concerned the future direction of Anglo-Egyptian relations. Over the next two years Salah al-Din staked his leadership claims on the back of a populist anti-British policy (core vales for the Wafd), aimed at ending the 'occupation' and absorbing the Sudan. Reluctantly at first, but then with great gusto, Sirag al-Din followed suit – with calamitous consequences.

In late May 1950 Britain's most senior soldier, Field Marshal Sir William Slim, visited Cairo in an attempt to persuade the Wafd of the military necessity for Anglo-Egyptian defence cooperation. The trip was timed to follow the Tripartite declaration on 25 May by which Britain, France and the United States had guaranteed the armistice boundaries between Israel and its Arab neighbours, while also promising to control the sale of arms to the region. One of the purposes of the declaration, paradoxically, was actually to facilitate Western arms sales to the Middle East, and specifically Egypt, by reassuring Israel with a territorial guarantee. The background to the declaration was an Anglo-Egyptian agreement signed in February under which Egypt was to be supplied with 158 war jets, 64 tanks, 264 artillery pieces and 3,600 vehicles over a four-year period. This extensive shopping list developed from secret technical talks between British and Egyptian military personnel after the Palestine War. London was hoping that arms shipments might entice Egypt into a joint defence pact aimed at settling the Canal Zone dispute, which had dogged bilateral relations since 1945. Similarly, the Americans saw the sales initiative as a means of easing Anglo-Egyptian tensions and strengthening Egypt's ties to the West. Despite these efforts and the promise of military hardware, Salah al-Din contemptuously dismissed Slim's defence concerns as an ideological extension of the nineteenth-century 'Great Game'. Instead, he argued that the Suez base was more likely to provoke war with Moscow than prevent it, and that Israel was Egypt's real enemy, not the Soviet Union.[10] The outbreak of the Korean War on 25 June served to reaffirm the respective cases of both sides.

Meanwhile, the internal situation in Egypt militated against any signs of concessions towards Britain. The lifting of martial law in May (in place since the start of the Palestine conflict in 1948) had resulted in a more open political atmosphere than had existed for many years, which the Muslim Brotherhood seized upon to edge its way back to legitimacy. It did so by focusing its radicalism on the British occupation rather than on the failings of the king–pasha clite (despite ongoing arms scandals relating to the recent war). As the Brotherhood's views became ever more extreme, so the Wafd, which had been damaged by its sycophancy towards the palace, was obliged to try and regain the nationalist initiative. Finally, on 16 November 1950, Prime Minister al-Nahas, advised by Salah al-Din, announced that Egypt would abrogate the defence treaty of 1936 and the Sudan condominium agreement of 1899 if solutions to the disputes were not found within a year. By this action, al-Nahas set Egyptian political life on a collision course with the British occupying forces.

During the next four months Bevin struggled against increasing personal and political odds to make one last attempt at breaking the deadlock. Ill health eventually forced him to resign as foreign secretary on 9 March 1951, his seventieth birthday. He died on 14 April. New defence terms had been presented to Egypt three days earlier. Although the impetus for these proposals was Bevin's, their final substance was shaped by the military planners. Indeed, the terms starkly revealed how inflexible Britain's strategic requirements in the Canal Zone had become. The process began in December 1950 when Bevin invited Salah al-Din to London for emergency talks. They had already met briefly (and acrimoniously) in New York in September. They now met again on four occasions during an eleven-day period. No progress was made until Bevin made a personal undertaking to examine a whole new approach to the base issue. His 'preliminary thinking' envisaged an early withdrawal of the front-line (fighting) troops of the British garrison, as well as the military headquarters in Ismailia. The subsequent maintenance of the base, he suggested, could be carried out by technicians in civilian clothes until the expiration of the 1936 defence treaty in 1956. In return, he expected the right of immediate re-entry for British forces in the event of war. The cabinet's 'considered view' of these thoughts was promised by the middle of January 1951, or as soon afterwards as possible.[11]

Consideration of Bevin's ideas quickly turned into an exercise by which Britain's military planners reasserted the importance of retaining a fully working base in Egypt during peacetime. Officials in the Foreign Office looked on with mounting concern. There was already an undercurrent of opinion in the African department (under which Egypt was subsumed) which held that Britain was not doing enough to settle its differences with Egypt. Shaping these thoughts was the departmental head, Roger Allen.

Allen had taken up this post in February 1950 at the relatively late age of 40, having pursued a career as a barrister before the Second World War. His approach to the Egyptian dispute was fundamentally progressive and enlightened, although he was always careful to shade his crisp recommendations with an air of worldly pragmatism. His thinking in early 1951 was certainly ahead of its time, at least in London's policymaking circles. In an introductory brief for Herbert Morrison, Bevin's successor as foreign secretary, Allen observed that the only alternative to a settlement with Egypt was for Britain 'to maintain the present position in the teeth of the Egyptian Government'; not only was this legally and morally difficult to justify (Britain far exceeded the 10,000-troop cap in the Suez base), it was also, he stated, a course with 'incalculable' political repercussions. Allen consequently busied himself with trying to make the stance of the military planners more palatable to the Egyptians. For example, the withdrawal timetable ought to be brought down from five years to three (in accord with the 1946 offer), and the Anglo-Egyptian joint defence board should at least look as though it had some Egyptian input.[12]

Three weeks before he resigned, Bevin had warned Attlee that the chiefs of staff's approach was far less likely to be acceptable to the Egyptians than the measures he had outlined. Britain's ambassador to Egypt, Sir Ralph Stevenson, who visited London in March to present the Cairo embassy's views, put it more bluntly: he 'did not think for one moment that the COS proposals, as they stood, would be acceptable to the Egyptian Government'.[13]

Stevenson had taken up his appointment in June 1950, aged 55, knowing that the task at hand was about as sensitive and important as any in the diplomatic service. His underlying conviction, like Allen's, was that more had to be done to satisfy the demands of Egyptian nationalism, otherwise the Canal Zone bastion would become a costly liability. In this he echoed the views of his senior advisers, as evidenced in the internal files of the Cairo embassy. Like a government department, the Cairo embassy benefited from having officials (some not all) spend large parts of their careers in one posting. Expertise could be linked to continuity, especially with the resident Arabists, the oriental counsellor and political counsellor. There were also occasions when the head of mission stayed in position for far longer than was customary with diplomatic appointments – Cromer and Lampson being the most notable examples. In a crucial way, Stevenson and his advisers were steeped in the legacy of these towering figures, only now there was a pressing desire to distance themselves from past practices. If Stevenson's modus operandi could be summed up in a few words, it would be that he was *not* another Lampson.

Yet to the Egyptians, certain symbols remained the same. The British embassy was an even more palatial establishment than it had been during Cromer's heyday. Having been constructed in the 1890s to specifications that befitted the imperial ambitions of the time, it had since been extended on several occasions, while additional land purchases had permitted the southwards expansion of the gardens all the way down to the banks of the Nile. Its nickname among locals was Bayt Al Lurd (the Lord's House).

Although Stevenson did not drive through the streets of Cairo with two motorcycle outriders blowing whistles before him, as Lampson had imperiously done, the impression of foreign occupation nevertheless remained.

Meanwhile, the mood in Britain's Parliament was consistently hostile to conceding anything to the Egyptians. Like the military planners, the Conservative opposition held that the imperial position at the Suez jugular was vital to Britain's survival as a world power. Prestige was central to this assessment. 'The life and honour of Great Britain depends upon the successful defence of Egypt,' stated Churchill in 1941.[14] This conviction had, if anything, since been strengthened. For its part, Labour, with its tiny majority of five, was wary of being labelled as appeasers. When the Foreign Office's African department suggested in March that nineteen obsolescent Spitfires be sold to Egypt in line with Britain's arms sales obligations of February 1950, Morrison vetoed the suggestion: 'Anything for Egypt just now is Parliamentary dynamite,' he commented.[15] (Britain's own needs in Korea had already put paid to the earlier commitment of supplying Egypt with jet fighters.)

Morrison's extreme caution in this respect stemmed from a House of Commons debate on 20 March concerning the recent conclusion of the Anglo-Egyptian sterling releases agreement. As foreign secretary for less than two weeks, he had little to do with this Treasury-negotiated treaty. Nevertheless, its stormy Commons reception was his political baptism on Egyptian issues, and indeed it was a cautionary tale for the Attlee administration as a whole.

The sterling negotiations had begun the previous November and had provided British officials with their first real insight into the Wafd's internecine feuding. The purpose of the talks was to agree on a long-term repayment schedule for the debt owed by Britain's banks and financial institutions to Egypt. The debt topped £400 million at the close of the Second World War, but had been reduced to £242 million by 1951 (albeit with restrictions on the liquidity of the accounts). Being a consummate politician, al-Nahas had balanced the abrogation threat in November 1950 – which strengthened Salah al-Din's hand – with the appointment of Sirag al-Din as finance minister, who was already the interior minister and Wafd party general secretary. This addition to Sirag al-Din's roll call of responsibilities was resented by the foreign minister, who was therefore keen to see the sterling negotiations fail. Thus, when an agreement was reached in March 1951, Salah al-Din did not conceal his irritation. Meanwhile, British Treasury officials had come to regard Sirag al-Din as 'most affable', and even a friendly figure of fun. Their nickname for him, the 'big boyfriend', referred to his wide girth and tactile behaviour (the latter was common in the Arab world, though perhaps unfamiliar to Treasury civil servants usually based in London). At the culmination of the negotiations, Leonard Waight jokingly reported back to London that he had to 'endure another parade down [Sirag al-Din's] drive to the car with his hand around my waist, and more hand-stroking, but in more concentrated form'. 'This affront to my manhood', Waight commented, 'cost the Egyptian Finance Minister £1 million worth of dollars.'[16]

The mood in the Commons debate on the 20th, however, was anything but friendly. The Conservative opposition argued that too many concessions had been made on the financial side without considering the wider defence picture. Anthony Eden, the shadow spokesman for foreign affairs, went so far as to barrack the chancellor of the exchequer, Hugh Gaitskell, for lacking full control over his officials.[17] This scene made a profound impression on Morrison, as did the chorus of voices on both sides of the House for a tougher Middle East policy. Labour scraped a majority of three in the subsequent vote.

It was a chastened cabinet that met on 5 April to discuss the defence proposals. Consequently, even in their rigid imperial form, it was no easy matter getting the terms accepted. Attlee clearly wanted to avoid further controversy on Egypt. A memorandum circulated to ministers by Morrison, dated 30 March, had stated that one of the most important aims of the proposals was 'to spin out the negotiations for some time'.[18] After much deliberation, the Labour administration decided to proceed with the new terms, which were presented to Egypt on 11 April.

Assessing the situation from the Cairo embassy, Stevenson believed that the greater danger was not Egypt rejecting the terms, but it suddenly becoming tractable and agreeing to them. He confided to his American counterpart that even if Egypt accepted the British offer, there remained the 'distinct possibility that the Labour Government would wish to stall still further because of its fear that no agreement with Egypt could muster sufficient votes to get through Parliament'.[19] He need not have worried. Less than two weeks later (and with a speed that shocked seasoned diplomats), the Wafd government responded by forwarding its own counter-proposals. These amounted to a point-by-point rebuttal of the British offer, followed by a reiteration of the twin rallying cries of Egyptian political life – 'Unity of the Nile Valley' and 'immediate evacuation'.[20] The defence negotiations were no longer useful even as a stalling device.

In retrospect (see Chapter 9), Bevin's informal suggestions of December 1950 – the immediate withdrawal of front-line troops and the maintenance of the base by technicians in civilian attire until 1956 – can be seen as an inspired assessment of the minimum requirements of Egyptian nationalism in the 1950s. As an estimate of Britain's own strategic planning requirements, however, they were a considerable diplomatic blunder. By unrealistically raising Egyptian expectations and then dashing them with the subsequent offer, the British government inadvertently succeeded in strengthening the hands of the Wafd's abrogationists led by Salah al-Din.

SECURING US BACKING

From late May 1951, British policy became dominated by plans to create a Middle Eastern defence organisation, with American participation, as a means of solving the Canal Zone dispute. This multilateral approach was prompted by the Truman administration's announcement to Congress on 24 May of a Mutual Security Programme worth $100–125 million in military and economic aid to the Arab states and Israel. London was assured that the plan was to help rather than replace British prestige in the area, with the objective of 'stability in depth'.[21] It was clear that American anxiety about the state of Anglo-Egyptian relations was a major motive behind the new policy. Washington had previously held the view that defence planning in the Middle East was a British and Commonwealth responsibility. Extensive military responsibilities in the Far East and Europe, together with the recent outbreak of war in Korea, had shaped these priorities.

During the last twelve months, however, State Department pressure for a more interventionist role in the Middle East had gradually weakened Defense Department resistance to additional military commitments. Assistant Secretary of State George McGhee, an Anglophile since his days as a Rhodes Scholar at Oxford, was the main advocate of intervention, arguing that Britain's ability to maintain Western interests in the region depended on a greater measure of American support. He was backed by the reporting of the US ambassador in Egypt, Jefferson Caffery, albeit for different reasons. Before being posted to Cairo in 1949, Caffery had been the first career diplomat to serve as American ambassador to Paris (normally a political appointee would take this plum appointment). Playing second fiddle to British interests in Egypt was hardly in keeping with this record of achievement. With his Irish–American roots, the Foreign Office suspected Caffery of having an inbuilt anti-British bias. His gloomy assessments of Britain's methods in Egypt – 'it is at least a minor miracle that serious disturbances have not already occurred', he noted in February 1950 – were crucial in enabling the State Department to convince the National Security Council that American help was urgently needed to bolster Britain's precarious position in Egypt.[22] The Mutual Security Programme was thus the first elaboration of the US's new direction.

British officials were quick to see the potential for linking aid packages with a regional pact. On 29 May a Foreign Office working party met for the first time to examine these possibilities. Two potential differences were immediately identified between British and American conceptions of regional defence. The first was that the British fully expected the Middle Eastern states to be unwilling to join an organisation that included former imperial powers like Turkey and present ones like itself. The working party consequently concluded that a Middle East Defence Board should be formed irrespective of whether the states of the region joined or not. The second potential difference related to Britain's primary motivation for pursuing the regional defence idea. This was unequivocally stated as being to provide a cloak for a continued military presence in Egypt and elsewhere in the Middle East at a time when bilateral arrangements were coming under increasing pressure.[23] This meant overturning Washington's conviction that control of the Canal Zone, though desirable, was not essential to Western interests. (The upshot of this American thinking was that the base should be evacuated for the greater goal of an Anglo-Egyptian political understanding.) Britain's aim, therefore, was to 'marry up' the so-called Middle East Command proposals with the need for a working base in peacetime. The co-sponsorship of Washington was considered vital to the whole plan.[24]

To buy time while the new multilateral approach was being formulated, Morrison persuaded the cabinet to approve the opening of talks with Egypt on the Sudan. An aide-mémoire was consequently presented to the Egyptian government on 8 June; the expected rejection was received on 6 July. However, it took until the end of July to work out the basics of the proposed organisation, the main difficulty – according to British officials – being the

State Department's 'almost exaggerated attention . . . to Middle Eastern susceptibilities'. Whereas the Americans wanted the Arab countries involved from the start on an 'equal to equal basis', liaison status was the most Britain was willing to concede. In the end, a defence board was agreed upon with a British supreme allied commander, alongside American, French and Turkish members. As a special 'honour', Egyptian officers would be invited to join the organisation at its inception; the other Arab countries would have to wait until they were able and willing to contribute substantially to the defence of the region.[25]

While the British and Americans were working out these details, the political situation in the region took a turn for the worse. July began with Egypt seizing a British ship in the Gulf of Aqaba in line with its policy of blockading all Israel-bound vessels using the Suez Canal. This had the effect of re-igniting restlessness in the House of Commons on Egyptian matters and pressured Morrison into taking a tough stance on the restrictions issue, even though it risked upsetting the multilateral defence approach.[26] In addition, on 20 July news of the assassination of King Abdullah of Jordan, by a Palestinian, reverberated across the Middle East. The murder demonstrated the dangers of compromising with colonial powers. Meanwhile, the principled social reformers within the Wafd administration, upon whom such high hopes for wide-reaching reform had been pinned, left office. Ahmad Husayn, an internationally renowned expert on Egyptian agriculture, resigned as minister for social affairs in June, frustrated by the conservatism of the Sirag al-Din–Abboud axis. The other key reformer, Egypt's leading intellectual, Taha Husayn, lasted as minister of education until September. But by then the Wafd were staggering on amid allegations that ministers had rigged cotton prices for personal gain. Despairing of these scandals, Salah al-Din admitted to the British ambassador in July that the Egyptian government was deliberately seeking foreign complications as a distraction from its internal shortcomings.[27]

In August the expectation of rioting across the Nile Delta was strong. On the 6th, al-Nahas informed the Egyptian parliament that Britain's foreign secretary had closed the door on the defence talks because of a hostile speech he made in the Commons on the Suez Canal restrictions issue.[28] In anticipation of the fifteenth anniversary of the signature of the 1936 defence treaty, due on 26 August, British forces in the Canal Zone prepared for major disturbances. These preparations brought home to British officials the full scale of their Middle East predicament in 1951. In May, Iran's parliament had nationalised the Abadan oil refineries, Britain's largest overseas possession, and for a while it looked as though the Attlee government might intervene militarily. However, US backing was not forthcoming and the plans (code-named Operation Buccaneer) were put on hold. Nevertheless, Buccaneer's implementation was not ruled out if British lives were threatened in the Iranian oil fields. The problem in August was that Canal Zone troops earmarked for Buccaneer might also be needed in Egypt. In the event, the treaty anniversary passed with only minor disturbances.

The race to finalise the multilateral defence proposals went on unhindered by the British expectation that Egypt would reject the new approach. Almost from the start, the Cairo embassy warned London that the Wafd government would not accept an allied military presence in place of British forces. By September the Foreign Office was in full agreement and recognised that no amount of 'spectacular "window dressing"' would work until there was a well-disposed Egyptian government willing 'to sell the new Anglo-Egyptian defence agreement to the Egyptian public'.[29] William Strang, the most senior official in the Foreign Office, had already begun to wonder whether the time had arrived to throw Salah al-Din 'to the wolves' – there is no elaboration on the presumably covert methods.[30] On 4 September Britain's cabinet concluded that a settlement was 'unlikely to be reached with the present Egyptian government or with any party government in Egypt. Only an all-party administration in Egypt [as in 1936] and the influence of the King could lead to a helpful compromise.'[31] Despite this attitude, the British government resolutely pressed ahead with the Middle East Command in the autumn of 1951.

The final countdown to the impending rupture began on 27 September when Salah al-Din informed the Americans that the abrogation legislation would be ready to present to Egypt's parliament in ten days' time, a month ahead of the schedule London had been expecting. Britain's embassy in Cairo reacted by arguing that the presentation of the Middle East Command proposals should be postponed until the Wafd had fallen from power or at least until Salah al-Din had been removed from office. Instead, the embassy believed that Britain should ride out the impending storm, while pursuing a covert policy of destabilising the Wafd administration. The attitude was, why waste the complicated multilateral approach on a government bound to reject it?[32]

This thinking was squarely rebuffed, however, in favour of tactics that made no bones about Britain's willingness for a military showdown. By presenting the proposals and having them rejected, Britain sought to cast Egypt as the quarrelsome party. This would then help harness US diplomatic support in anticipation of the post-abrogation disturbances when the use of force was expected. Two other considerations had a major influence on this course. A few weeks earlier Attlee had decided that his government's small majority was no longer workable and had taken the decision to dissolve Parliament in the first week of October, ready for a general election on 25 October. The second key factor was the spectacle of the last British technicians leaving the Abadan oil refineries on 3 October. A day late, when the evacuation was reported critically in the press, the cabinet convened a special committee to consider the Egyptian situation. The meeting endorsed the Foreign Office's case for the immediate presentation of the Middle East Command proposals. Meanwhile, the Iranian connection was also watched closely in Egypt. 'This is the example we must follow in our struggle with the British,' wrote the *Bourse Egyptienne* on 4 October: 'It is only the weak who they oppress. Their prestige in the Middle East is finished.'[33]

The crux of the British Middle East Command approach was thus to make a new and reasonable offer to the Wafd government before the abrogation bills (which were presented to the Egyptian parliament on 8 October) became law. These tactics privileged the short-term advantage of strengthening Britain's position in the eyes of domestic and international opinion over the long-term aim of securing a lasting settlement to the Canal Zone dispute.[34] As Morrison wrote to Attlee on 12 October:

It is essential that we carry, in the first instance, the old Commonwealth governments and the United States with us in these two policies (not being kicked out of Egypt and pressing on with the MEC) and that we should then rally other governments and public opinion generally to our view. In presenting the issues at stake to the United States, we should do well to emphasise the second policy which will appear to them more constructive and less egotistical.[35]

These tactics, however, also drew Britain into a confrontation with Egyptian nationalism, the virility of which had not been tested in the post-Palestine War era. On 9 October Morrison managed to convince a reluctant

Dean Acheson, the US secretary of state, to proceed with the Middle East Command proposals, and public statements to this effect were made on 9 and 10 October (British and American respectively).[36] Seeing that the Cairo embassy was still not sure of the Attlee government's real motives, the Foreign Office wired an urgent telegram to the ambassador on 11 October: 'This operation is no longer regarded as a negotiation but rather a confrontation with the Egyptians.'[37] With misgivings, Stevenson presented the new approach to Salah al-Din two days later.[38] On 15 October, in a show of national unity with the Wafd, Egypt's parliament convincingly ratified the bills terminating the 1936 defence treaty and the 1899 Sudan agreement. As in the past, the first flashpoint was Ismailia.

THREE

•••••••••••••

Canal Zone Siege

'For Egypt I signed the defence treaty and for Egypt I abrogate it,' declared Prime Minister al-Nahas when he presented the abrogation bills to the Egyptian parliament.[1] Yet despite the lordly rhetoric it was by no means clear how the new legislation was going to be implemented. A consensus has since emerged, from Egyptian historians no less than British and American, that the Wafd government stumbled into the 'abrogation' crisis as a means of diverting attention from its domestic problems, and that it had no overall strategy. Of course, there would be street demonstrations, but these were a staple of the national struggle – hardly a bold new response to a dramatic heightening of tension. Furthermore, the theatre of public disorder – the manipulation of the mob through the bribing of rabble-rousers with the covert involvement of the security forces – was in truth a symptom of weakness. Such demonstrations symbolised nationalist resistance, albeit often bloodily, at a time when the battle against foreign occupation was too unequal for other kinds of confrontation. But in the wake of the Palestine War (during which Egypt's state authorities had encouraged the deployment of guerrilla units), it remained to be seen whether staged demonstrations would be enough to contain the heightened nationalist opposition to the British presence.

BATTLE LINES

On Tuesday 16 October, a day after the abrogation measures became law, students from Cairo converged on Ismailia and gathered in the square by the railway station. Shortly after 8 a.m. ringleaders began setting fire to British cars and trucks, and the crowd was soon transformed into a rampaging mob.

The next target, barely an hour later, was the NAAFI grocery store, adjacent to the square; staff and service families were forced to run and hide in the back with only four military policemen for protection. After pelting the premises with rocks, the mob pulled down the perimeter fence and set it alight. A frenzy of looting ensued, abetted by uniformed Egyptian police officers. Some of the crowd moved off towards a nearby residential block for married British servicemen and attempts were made to enter it by a cellar door.

By this point, British forces from the barracks in Moascar, 2 miles away, were ready to intervene. Their immediate priority was the trapped staff and families at the NAAFI. Bren guns were deployed, covering the main roads on to the square. A couple of empty lorries then proceeded to the NAAFI building, accompanied by a platoon of troops. The rioters briefly dispersed, but they soon closed in again to throw stones and bottles at the rescuers. Two rounds were fired in response, driving the crowd back and allowing the mission to be completed. The British commanding officer then decided to remove the mob from the European area and barricade it in Arasha, the district of Ismailia that the British nicknamed Arab Town. This entailed clearing the square with a few more shots over the heads of the crowd. When the demonstrators regrouped in the side streets, British soldiers fixed bayonets and attempted to edge them away, but failed to move all but the first rows. A few bursts of Sten-gun fire aimed into the ground – the noise echoing around the built-up streets – proved far more effective in that it panicked those at the back as much as those at the front. The mob rapidly melted away.

By 1 p.m. order had been restored and a cordon was established around Arasha. Later in the afternoon this new perimeter, with empty oil drums with rocks for ballast and barbed wire in between, served as a focus for the regrouping crowd. A British army account of the day noted the changed character of the demonstration: 'They were not a vast mob out of control under the influence of mob hysteria as the morning rioters had been. They contained an equal number of extremists and talkative individuals who were urging moderation on the former and curious onlookers.'[2] Although a couple more rounds were fired to preserve the hastily constructed barrier, the worst of the day's troubles was over and the night passed peacefully, aided by a British-imposed curfew from 7 p.m. These events in Ismailia began a new chapter in the nationalist struggle against the British presence in Egypt.

In the Post-1945 Conflicts section of the Imperial War Museum in London, there is a special exhibit on what it calls the Canal Zone Emergency of

1951–4. Yet the term 'emergency' was never used at the time. Rather, it was adopted decades later when the distinctions between nationalist insurgencies in informal parts of the empire like Egypt and formal British possessions like Cyprus and Malaya (both of which had officially declared emergencies in the 1950s) were less contentious, in any case outside academia. During the early 1950s, however, Britain's politicians adamantly refused to acknowledge – at least publicly – anything like a concerted anti-British campaign in Egypt; and even in top-secret cabinet papers fairly nondescript headings were used such as 'Measures to maintain our position in the Canal Zone'. In the meantime, rarely a week went by without Egypt being on the cabinet's agenda – proof one would think of a concerted struggle. Nevertheless, the political circumstances of the time dictated a stance that emphasised Britain's legal right in international law to maintain a garrison in the Canal Zone. Emergencies were connected with formal empire and declarations from Government House, not with the backstairs manipulation that Britain had exercised in Egypt since 1922. An official acknowledgement of a state of emergency would thus have had overt colonial implications inappropriate to Egypt's informal imperial context. This, in turn, would have hindered the ongoing attempts to negotiate a new basis for Britain's defence interests in Egypt. Little wonder, then, that British ex-soldiers have since described the Canal Zone experience of 1951–4 as the 'forgotten campaign'.

In October 1951 Britain responded to the renewed nationalist challenge in Egypt by pursuing a policy aimed at toppling the Wafd government. Reshuffling the Egyptian political deck of cards had been the mainstay of interwar imperial policy, but it was far from certain whether Egypt's decaying constitutional system could now withstand the additional weight of overt British intervention. Farouk was widely despised, the Wafd was beset by feuding and scandals, and in the growing vacuum the Muslim Brotherhood had become Egypt's second largest mass organisation; it regarded parliamentary rule as a Western corruption of Egypt's Islamic path.

The extent to which the Labour government shaped British policy, despite losing a general election ten days after the crisis erupted, should not be underestimated. Having chafed under cabinet constraints throughout the recent Iranian dispute (American pressure had persuaded Attlee not to pursue a military solution to the problem of Mossedeq's nationalisation of Britain's oil refineries at Abadan), Foreign Secretary Herbert Morrison clearly relished the opportunity to assume an 'attitude of resistance' on Egyptian matters.[3] In a letter to US Secretary of State Dean Acheson on 12 October, Morrison underlined Britain's determination to stand by its treaty rights and hold on to the Suez base in the interests of the free world; to this end, American backing was formally requested. The response five days later promised political and diplomatic support, though only for measures deemed necessary for 'protecting the Suez base and keeping the canal open'. The Foreign Office recognised the tone. The Americans were wary of giving Britain too much encouragement; care therefore had to be taken 'not to scare them off'.[4]

On 25 October the Conservatives, led by Winston Churchill (who turned 77 in November), secured a majority of seventeen in the general election. Anthony Eden, the incoming foreign secretary (and architect of the 1936 defence treaty) was informed by his officials that the outgoing government's policy was 'to work for the establishment of an Egyptian government which will be prepared to reach a reasonable settlement [on the Canal Zone question]'. He reaffirmed this policy for the benefit of the Cairo embassy on 2 November.[5]

Collusion with Farouk was seen as the best means of achieving this result. The signals from his palace entourage were encouraging. Egypt's Oxford-educated ambassador to London, Abdel Fattah Amr, reported that Farouk was so 'deeply disturbed' by the behaviour of the Wafd government that he intended to dismiss it or at least make changes to it as soon as he could. Amr had fallen out with Salah al-Din over the policy of confrontation with Britain and had been reporting directly to the king since the summer.[6] (Interestingly, when Amr had first been appointed to London in 1945, Lampson had felt rather frustrated: this most pro-British of Egyptian officials, he argued, was more needed in Cairo. The disappointment was subsequently lessened, however, when Amr undertook to send direct reports to Farouk by way of Foreign Office diplomatic bags.[7]) The main problem for Eden that winter was how to galvanise Farouk without making it appear that the British had pushed him.

THE DEBATE OVER OIL SANCTIONS

While Britain's policy of ousting the Wafd relied in the first instance on political intervention, the application of 'rigorous sanctions' was not ruled out.[8] However, Eden (like Morrison before him) first wanted to exhaust the backstairs means of pressure. An indication of what more vigorous methods might entail was nevertheless glimpsed in the first week of the crisis when Britain's military authorities in Egypt briefly stopped oil supplies getting through to the main cities. Two-thirds of Egypt's oil was produced locally and transported either by train or pipeline through the Canal Zone to the main population centres, so making the Egyptian economy highly susceptible to oil sanctions. (The Attlee government's defence committee had earlier identified the blockading of the Agrud–Cairo pipeline as 'the most immediately effective counter-measure not involving force that is available to us in Egypt'.[9]) Although only black oil supplies were affected by the initial blockade, kerosene and other white oils used for domestic purposes also became subject to shortages because of panic buying. Britain's military commanders naturally concluded that this was the way to maintain the initiative during the crisis. They were therefore most unhappy when the order came from London on 23 October instructing them that the oil blockade should only be used for short periods in retaliation to Egyptian actions.[10]

In an attempt to change this policy, General Sir Brian Robertson, the commander-in-chief of British Middle East Land Forces, wrote to the chiefs of staff on 27 October urging them to allow the use of oil sanctions as an offensive weapon. The objective, he stated, should be to 'apply a stranglehold on the Egyptian economy and deprive the population of Cairo and the Delta of power on which sewerage disposal amongst other things depends, on kerosene for cooking, and of petrol'. He concluded that passive defence was as fatal in the present circumstances as it was in war: Britain must therefore work for the complete collapse of the Wafd government, using troops if necessary. At a chiefs of staff meeting two days later, the chief of imperial general staff, Field Marshal Sir William Slim, gave his backing to this tough approach.[11]

Although Robertson's language may, in this instance, have sounded blimpish, his record of service was that of an outstanding soldier-administrator. The son of Field Marshal William Robertson, Sir Brian had broken up his army service, which began in 1914, with a spell as managing director of Dunlop South Africa from 1935 to 1940. The logistical and management skills developed as an industrialist were once again called upon by the army during the Second World War. After 1945, his crossover skills were put to use as military governor in the British zone in Germany and then, in a seconded appointment, as UK commissioner in Germany's Allied High

Commission. Konrad Adenauer spoke of him as 'a great soldier statesman'.[12] But in the autumn of 1951, Britain's ambassador to Egypt perceived little of the cool judgement and acumen for which Robertson was renowned. In fact, Stevenson felt that Robertson's fiery recommendations might easily lead to the onset of formal British rule in Egypt. The embassy's preferred approach was, instead, to allow Farouk more time to dismiss the Wafd, the thinking being that his task would be made easier once the euphoria of abrogation had worn off.[13]

On 28 October Churchill, in his first intervention on the Egyptian issue as peacetime prime minister, advised Eden not to do anything that was either 'sharp or sudden'.[14] (Churchill's early caution on Egypt was to prove highly uncharacteristic and was probably a fleeting legacy of the election campaign, on the last day of which the *Daily Mirror* had devoted its entire front page to the question, 'Whose finger do you want on the trigger?') On 2 November Britain's policy was reaffirmed as the use of oil sanctions on an intermittent basis only, the aim being 'to make the show pinch without actually setting up gangrene'. As a thinly veiled rebuke to Robertson, Britain's military authorities in Egypt were told to cooperate closely with the Cairo embassy when deciding to cut supplies.[15] The American ambassador in Egypt, Jefferson Caffery, also closely monitored the oil dispute and reported to Washington that his British counterpart was in a 'state of despair' over the disagreements with Robertson. Like Stevenson, Caffery strongly believed that the excessive use of oil sanctions would end in political disaster: 'What would mobs do in dark streets?' he asked on 25 October. It was on his advice that the State Department made representations to London on the need to keep the Canal Zone military in check. Britain's policy statement on 2 November was therefore welcomed by US officials. London was indeed being careful about keeping the Americans on side.[16]

The failure of the military authorities in Egypt to persuade the new Conservative government to adopt a more rigorous use of oil sanctions prompted Robertson to conduct his own post-mortem of the episode. While acknowledging that his telegram to the chiefs of staff on 27 October, with its bellicose language, had probably done 'more harm than good', he nevertheless concluded that the underlying fault lay in the organisational apparatus of Britain's forces in Egypt: 'too many cooks [were] stirring the broth', he observed, and it was 'very difficult to keep the pot steady as a consequence'.[17]

Britain's military decision-making in Egypt was certainly a complex business. Robertson, based in Fayid (on the banks of the Great Bitter Lake), was top of the hierarchy and wore two hats: one as chairman of the Middle East Defence Co-ordinating Committee, whose geographical remit covered the northern Mediterranean coast, the Balkans, Africa, Central Asia and the Indian subcontinent, and the other as commander-in-chief, Middle East Land Forces. As such his main responsibility was to prepare for an all-out war with the Soviet Union. Another responsibility was to liaise with the commanding officer of British troops in Egypt, Lieutenant-General George Erskine (formerly his deputy in Germany), who was based in Ismailia. Erskine's remit was the security and action of troops in the Canal Zone. Military measures taken by him to deal with local difficulties frequently overlapped into Robertson's area of general policy. Further complicating matters was the need for consultation with two civilian bodies, the Cairo embassy and the British Middle East Office (BMEO), the latter headed by Thomas Rapp who held ambassadorial status.[18] The Political Division of the British Middle East Office had hastily moved to Fayid at the start of the crisis while the Development Division moved to Beirut so that it could function undisturbed by Egyptian politics. Decision-making on a day-to-day basis entailed Rapp liaising with Robertson and Erskine, while the embassy was represented by John Hamilton, a long-standing political officer who had relocated from Cairo to Ismailia at the start of the troubles. Crisis decisions were thus the product of an intricate network of interaction between civil and military authorities.[19] Robertson did indeed have a point: chafing and confusion were hard to avoid in such a set-up.

Not that Britain's most senior soldier in the Middle East was going to strive for greater emollience when dealing with his diplomat colleagues. Rather, his response to Eden's policy directive on 2 November had the contrary effect of spreading the civil–military divide to the corridors of Whitehall. Unable to contain his frustration, Robertson fired off a personal telegram to the vice chief of imperial general staff: 'If these sanctions are necessary to achieve our end,' he puffed, 'then we should not be detained by the bleats of any Ambassadors.'[20] The chiefs of staff agreed and decided to write to William Strang, the permanent under-secretary at the Foreign Office. Their letter, dated 8 November, pressed for the 'reintroduction' of a 'positive policy' in Egypt. 'At present,' the service chiefs stated, 'the situation appears to us to consist of a contest between British forces in the Canal Zone and the Egyptian government, with the Ambassador acting as a somewhat nervous referee.

This situation, if it continues, is likely to frustrate all activities which the C-in-C ME attempts to undertake to maintain our position in the Canal Zone.'[21]

The Foreign Office was incredulous. Eden commented that he could not recall seeing such a 'strange document' in all his previous experience.[22] Strang's measured reply reminded the military that 'political operations of this kind' required 'time and patience, above all patience, combined with firmness':

They are not usually to be successfully performed by the method of ultimatum or threat of violent sanction, though at the proper time these may be called for. If we want to make an agreement with an Egyptian Government, there must be a Government of a kind we can make an agreement with. Such a Government would be unlikely to emerge from the welter of riot, disease, murder and armed intervention that would almost certainly follow any long-continued interruption on the movement of oil from Suez to the Delta.

Britain was therefore committed, for the moment at least, to maintaining 'various means of pressure' on Farouk. Official policy, observed Strang, was designed to avoid the 'extremes which would upset the applecart altogether'.[23]

STALEMATE

By the second week of November, the latest intelligence from palace insiders was that Farouk was not willing to budge until he had secured a private undertaking that Britain would make a substantial concession to Egypt's national aspirations. But London was loathe to contemplate such a move in advance of negotiations, let alone for the benefit of an Egyptian government yet to be formed. While Farouk understandably wanted to see the colour of British money before he embarked on the risky course of removing the Wafd, Britain was equally anxious to avoid the impression of being pushed into compromises by nationalist disturbances.[24] The upshot was a damaging stalemate.

Britain's loosening grip on Egypt's internal political situation was further evidenced by its ineffective attempts to collude with the Wafd's domestic opponents in the search for an alternative government. Opposition leaders were worried that heavy-handed British action would force the Wafd from power in a blaze of glory. Secret talks on the possible composition of an anti-Wafd coalition struggled to get off the ground. As a former Egyptian prime minister, Ali Maher, explained, no politician in Egypt could hope to survive merely by going back to the pre-abrogation situation.[25]

While these political manoeuvres played themselves out, the situation in the Canal Zone gradually worsened. A siege mentality had developed during the early days of the crisis as a result of the walkout of the 40,000-strong Egyptian labour force which was directly employed by the British. Another 40,000 employed on a contract basis also joined the boycott, or were intimidated to do so by nationalist agitators. The Muslim Brotherhood imposed road blocks and confiscated passes to military camps. Civvie jobs such as manning the power stations, the sewage works and the water filtration plants had to be assumed by hard-pressed British soldiers. The image of Britain's mighty garrison, which had been reinforced to 64,000 (from 35,000)[26] since October, being committed to menial labour and guard duties was a telling indication of a power in decline. To the Wafd's opponents, such a power did not make an attractive ally.

Although Egyptian sovereignty over the Canal Zone was never formally terminated, in practice the infringements were legion. Security checks and restricted access for locals were only part of the story. On 18 October, following a skirmish between British and Egyptian soldiers at the El-Firdan swing bridge, General Erskine requested that the senior Egyptian officer withdraw his forces behind a line running between 18 and 32 miles away from the Canal. The subsequent retreat of the Egyptian army to the so-called Erskine Line registered a further blow to its military honour, having already been damaged by poor leadership during the recent Palestine campaign.

Another new manifestation of the nationalist challenge – the one that upped the ante more than anything else – was the formation of guerrilla units known as liberation battalions, inspired by the fedayeen in the Palestine War. The Muslim Brotherhood was again instrumental in this development, but squads were also formed by the Socialist Party, led by Ahmad Husayn, a long-standing rabble-rouser.[27] He had first come to Britain's attention in the late 1930s when he founded the Young Egypt Party, influenced by Hitler's Brown Shirts. By November, 'commandos' from the liberation battalions were taking the battle directly to British personnel and installations, sniping at guards, cutting cables and attacking convoys on roads between sites, usually under the cover of darkness. The volunteers, men, women and teenagers, came from all walks of life and from all over Egypt: doctors, mechanics, students, lawyers, engineers – anyone with a grievance against the British presence. But it was the residents of Ismailia, the ones who had done the menial jobs in the Canal Zone, who most willingly volunteered in the months and years to come, the very people whose houses were now being routinely ransacked by British soldiers as they searched for 'terrorists'.[28]

The Wafd regarded this escalation of the struggle with concern: the fedayeen might one day embarrass or turn on the government. But rather than suppress an apparently popular manifestation of nationalist anger, the Wafd instead tried to co-opt it. A month into the crisis the interior minister, Sirag al-Din, announced that the government would henceforth take responsibility for organising the liberation battalions; and yet despite the financial ties, the guerrilla units still operated largely outside governmental control.[29]

Ismailia continued to be the focus of the struggle, not least because of the 1,000 auxiliary police (*Bulak Nizam*) who were dispatched to the town after the riots of 16 October. This irony was not missed by the British. In normal times the auxiliary police were the Egyptian state's means for controlling disturbances, but from October 1951 many of the auxiliaries moonlighted – literally, given the night-time raids – as fedayeen in the liberation battalions.[30] But even the daytime pretence of being riot police was not always adhered to. One particularly brutal incident was to have an impact on all the British service families in Egypt.

On 17 November two army officers took advantage of a period of relative calm in the Canal Zone by escorting their wives and children on a shopping excursion into Ismailia, albeit with Sten guns at the ready. As their vehicle went past the police station, they were fired upon. The officers quickly shepherded the women and children into a side street and sheltered them behind a wall, all the time bullets ricocheting across the brickwork. Needing a safer refuge, the two women and three boys dashed to a nearby house owned by a French family, their progress shielded by covering fire. The two officers then continued as best they could with the unequal fire-fight. When it all went quiet in the street one of the wives went to the window and called out for her husband. There was no response. After a night huddled at the back of the house, the women and children were rescued by a heavily armed British patrol. Later that day news was received that the two officers had been found. Their bodies, which had been dragged through the streets as trophies in the national struggle, were riddled with bullets and badly beaten. Erskine concluded that Ismailia was no longer safe for service families (some 1,100 resided there), and they were evacuated between 20 and 23 November.[31]

Not surprisingly, policymakers in London became increasingly nervous about the well-being of all 27,000 British civilians resident in Egypt. This, in turn, led to further discord between the Cairo embassy and Britain's military authorities in Fayid and Ismailia. The latest area of dispute focused on the feasibility of the secret military plans to protect foreign nationals in Cairo and Alexandria, should widespread disturbances erupt. The operation for Cairo, code-named Rodeo Bernard, was simple enough. A mobile armoured column would move from the Canal Zone to the Almaza airfield on the outskirts of Cairo, about 70 miles away. If order was not restored by this action, the forces were to proceed to key strategic areas throughout the city. In contrast, the plan for Alexandria, where most foreign nationals resided, involved the deployment of troops from bases in Libya and Cyprus, using cruisers, naval air support and RAF transports. The distances involved and the complexity of the operation meant that seventy-two hours' notice would be needed to enter Alexandria. Embassy officials were acutely aware that many lives could be lost in the interim and therefore suggested the deployment of a smaller and faster force. However, Robertson and Erskine resolutely opposed any plans that used fewer troops than the existing operations.[32] If the military could not influence political decisions (as in the use of oil sanctions), the diplomats were certainly not going to be allowed to shape military operations.

The service chiefs did at least show some unanimity of purpose with the diplomats when it came to the issue of whether the Canal Zone should be legally severed from Egypt. A proclamation of military government over the area would have entailed having to feed 300,000 Egyptian residents. Food for this population came almost entirely from the Nile Delta, a line of supply that the Wafd government could be expected to cut. British War Office figures estimated that 3,000 tons of foodstuffs a week would have to be imported; regular supplies would take six weeks to arrange. The enormous expense and inconvenience of such an exercise was sufficient to check all but the most enthusiastic firebrands in military circles. The Foreign Office, for its part, also stressed the incalculable international repercussions and the creation of another long-term irredentist grievance in Egypt.[33] These strands of opinion together wove a thread that was strong enough to withstand frequent surges of pressure – usually after the brutal murder of soldiers – to formalise Britain's military authority in the Canal Zone.

There was also caution as to how captured Egyptian 'terrorists' should be treated. In early December Robertson requested permission to hold trials and punish offenders, but the cabinet refused. The prospect of death sentences being meted out would not only stir up Egyptian opposition, it would also blacken Britain's name internationally. Instead, Eden helped forge a compromise which permitted the detention of offenders without trial for as long as the military authorities saw fit.[34] At the time of writing, this might be called the 'Guantanomo' solution.

As weeks passed (and with little sign of the Wafd's dismissal), friction became more evident in relations between London and Washington. The State Department wanted Britain to stop looking 'hopefully to the King' to provide a new administration and felt instead that attempts should be made to work with moderates within the Wafd. This thinking reflected the continuing influence of Sirag al-Din in American circles. As both interior and finance minister, his credibility was linked to his close association with Abboud, whose extensive business contacts with US companies were an important part of the equation. American confidence in Sirag al-Din was premised on the assumption that he could control the liberation battalions.[35] British officials, on the other hand, felt strongly (and correctly) that this was not the case. As a late convert to the anti-British campaign, the interior minister was now doing his utmost – or so it seemed to London – to prove his nationalist credentials. Moreover, the fact that it was he and not Salah al-Din who announced Egypt's rejection of the Middle East Command approach a day after the abrogation laws were passed was taken in London as a signal that the Wafd's fractious leadership had pulled together for the crisis. For as long as the party remained united, Britain wanted nothing to do with it.

Britain's inability to reach an agreement with either Farouk or opposition elements, despite their shared wish to see the Wafd ousted from power, signified two decisive developments in the Egyptian question by the end of 1951. The first related to the decline of British power and prestige, and Egypt's realisation of this. For six years Ernest Bevin had effectively disguised the perilous foundations of Britain's postwar position in the Canal Zone by insisting on a policy of non-intervention in Egypt's internal affairs, which by and large had been adhered to. However, the reintroduction of overt interventionism in October 1951 served to expose the true state of affairs: Britain's backstairs manipulation of Egyptian political life had all but ceased to be effective. Neither the palace nor the minority parties believed it to be in their interests to side with the British. As a consequence, the second major development in the autumn and winter of 1951 was that military might, hitherto the final arbiter of Britain's influence (as in 1942), was becoming, to all intents and purposes, the only arbiter. Between 16 October and 3 December 1951, 117 Egyptian civilians were killed in clashes with British forces, together with another 440 injured.[36]

THE DRIFT TO MILITARY INTERVENTION

By the start of December, policymakers in London were finally thinking of setting a time limit for the political approaches to run their course. The Foreign Office wanted to allow Farouk another two or three weeks to dismiss the Wafd before resorting to tougher methods. Slim and the other military leaders accepted this timetable with the proviso that it be shortened if the situation deteriorated.[37] However, just as civil–military policy formulation was proceeding in this uncommonly harmonious fashion, a succession of local security measures in the Canal Zone inadvertently escalated Britain's military response to the abrogation crisis.

On 5 December Erskine issued an order permitting British troops to secure the routes to a water filtration plant in the village of Kafr Abdu, near Suez. 'Buildings may be levelled', it stated, 'if there is evidence that they are being used for firing into our camps or along our necessary routes.'[38] This action, which was aptly called Operation Flatten, came as a response to the guerrilla tactic of targeting essential utilities. The Kafr plant supplied water for the British military installation at Suez, as well as for ships at Ras el Adabya. It had already been damaged by one bombing. The last straw for Erskine came on 4 December when relief guards en route to the water plant were ambushed, resulting in a fierce fire-fight. To avert a repetition and to avoid all contact with the local population, a decision was taken to build a new approach road 460 yards long and to demolish such buildings as lay within 100 yards on each side.

Officials in London were informed of the proposed operation in terms that made no reference to its true scale. The Foreign Office, for instance, was supplied with a copy of a note that Stevenson had passed to Sirag al-Din (in his capacity as minister of interior) which stated that the construction of the road would involve 'the disappearance of only a few mud huts'.[39] It was not that the British embassy intended to deceive the Conservative government or for that matter Sirag al-Din; rather, Erskine's staff had failed to inform Stevenson of the operation's real size. Indeed, even Erskine probably had little idea as to the number of buildings due to be destroyed. (According to John Hamilton, who was acting as the embassy liaison at the Ismailia HQ, Erskine subsequently disciplined one of his officers for not giving an accurate account of the scale of the operation.[40])

The Foreign Office became aware that uproar was likely during the night of 7/8 December after the Cairo embassy sent two telegrams warning that the Wafd government was calling for violent resistance at Kafr. Despite the late hour, Eden was immediately brought into the picture. As the head of the African department recounted a few days later: 'By that time the military authorities had apparently made it plain that they were determined to carry the operation through, and the Secretary of State, whom we got out of bed at 1am, felt he must back them. We had indeed no material on which to assess the need or justification for the operation.'[41]

Operation Flatten entailed British paratroopers guarding the outer limits of Kafr while bulldozers set about levelling over 100 buildings, a third of which were roofed dwellings. Between 250 and 300 inhabitants were displaced.[42] What amounted to a small village was destroyed. Churchill sent a personal telegram congratulating Erskine on the action.[43]

Faced with overwhelming force, it was hardly surprising that Egyptian popular resistance failed to materialise. This left Sirag al-Din looking weak and vulnerable. In the days that followed, the Egyptian press, after violently denouncing the British, unanimously turned on him and the Wafd for not preparing effective counteraction. As a consequence, British officials became increasingly concerned about the measures al-Nahas might take to salvage his government's credibility. It was fortunate for all concerned that the US embassy in Cairo worked hard behind the scenes to limit the Egyptian response to the recall of Amr, the pro-British ambassador in London (announced on 13 December). To appease the hardcore nationalist elements, Sirag al-Din also made a show of giving an additional £E100,000 to the liberation battalions.[44] While Britain was fortunate to escape the Kafr mess with these modest reprisals, the Wafd government recognised that it could not afford another comparable failure. The ramifications of Operation Flatten were not yet over.

Meanwhile, the pressures on Britain's ambassador in Egypt were immense and worsening. On the one hand, there was the deep conviction of most of his embassy staff that punitive action by the British garrison would assist the extremists to the lasting detriment not only of the Canal Zone base but also Egypt's faltering constitutional system. On the other, there was the almost daily occurrence of servicemen being sniped at, ambushed and occasionally murdered. Reports of mutilated bodies of young soldiers being dragged from the Sweet Water Canal were particularly upsetting. These conflicting stresses affected Stevenson's reporting: mostly he advised caution, but occasionally he called for a tough line. (According to Caffery, the British ambassador was being 'pushed hither and yon by the Generals and one of his advisers'; Roger Allen in the Foreign Office similarly felt that he too was 'fighting not only the whole of the Egyptian Government but also all the British soldiers'.[45]) The upshot of Stevenson's inconsistency was that Eden began to lose confidence in the Cairo embassy's reporting. 'I find it increasingly difficult to know what Stevenson really wants', the foreign secretary minuted on a telegram dated 22 December; on another a couple of days later he testily scribbled, 'quite incomprehensible'.[46] Rumours began to circulate that Stevenson might be replaced. Robertson for one was keen to see a kindred spirit installed at the Cairo embassy. Earlier in the month he had intimated to the War Office that Rapp of the British Middle East Office would be a welcome successor.[47]

Underlying the differences between the Foreign Office and Britain's Cairo embassy was a fundamental divergence of opinion as to the permanence of anti-British feeling in Egypt. Significantly, Stevenson's attitude was more in line with American officials than with his colleagues in London, as shown by a joint US–UK embassy estimate in December. The State Department held that Egyptian nationalism was a 'deeply-rooted movement' which would 'neither subside nor alter its course by mere passage of time'. The current high pitch of national fervour was thus taken as a substantially accurate expression of popular feeling. As a consequence, the danger in the existing situation was that the Wafd government would be replaced not by 'more reasonable politicians' but by 'extremist elements which may lead Egypt down [the] road to chaos and anarchy'. (These views were conveyed to the Foreign Office a week after the Kafr incident – a warning perhaps against the continuing efforts to oust the Wafd.)[48]

In contrast, the view from London was wilfully more optimistic. James Bowker, the Foreign Office official in charge of the Middle East, explained the Whitehall rationale in a letter to the embattled Stevenson. It is a highly illuminating document for understanding Britain's response to the Egyptian nationalist challenge to the Suez bastion:

> Suppose there were an Egyptian government pledged to reach a reasonable settlement with us . . . and to join with the western powers in a military association. Suppose further that this government were determined to implement its policy by every possible means, for example the ruthless suppression of terrorism and gangsterism, and the publication of truth in the Egyptian press. What would be the chances of survival for such a government? And if it did survive, with the backing of the King and army, for say a couple of months, how far would hatred of the British in fact decline?

Bowker's response to his own questions tacitly conceded the need for a deliberate suspension of realism:

> Unless the answers to them are purely negative, we think we must proceed on the assumption that there is a chance of our securing such a government and reaching agreement with it. The chance may not be a very big one but the alternatives are too uncomfortable for us to accept without a struggle.[49]

Despite being a public relations disaster (even the imperialist-minded *Spectator* objected), the Kafr incident did not stop London from keeping to its timetable for deciding when stronger tactics could be used to force the Wafd's dismissal.[50] The political methods were in any case critically undermined by Eden agreeing to see Salah al-Din at a UN General Assembly session in Paris in mid-December. Nothing of substance transpired during the private meeting, but its very occurrence was taken as a victory for Egypt's foreign minister, so making Farouk's task of replacing the Wafd administration still more difficult. Al-Nahas even seemed to think that Britain was about to give way.[51] Eden returned to London convinced that the time had finally arrived for Stevenson to see Farouk and request that the Wafd be removed from office: if this was not done, Britain would be 'compelled to resort to further measures which may damage the situation beyond repair'.[52] Stevenson regarded these instructions with distaste, telling Caffery that they amounted to 'lecturing the king in the "Miles Lampson way"'.[53] Given his attitude, it was possible that the British embassy in Cairo, or for that matter the American mission, warned the Egyptian palace of the impending threat. In any case, on 24 December, just as the sabre-rattling was about to take place, Farouk announced two highly significant appointments. Dr Hafiz Afifi, a renowned Anglophile who had written a book entitled *The British in Their Country*, was made chief of the royal cabinet. As president of the Misr Bank since 1939, he was the main rival to Abboud's business empire. The impression was thus created that Farouk was readying himself to challenge the axis formed between Sirag al-Din and Abboud. The second, equally telling appointment saw Amr, barely a week after his recall from London, installed as royal counsellor on foreign affairs. (Perhaps there was still something left of Britain's informal influence after all.) Egyptian nationalists regarded Farouk's moves as a dastardly stab in the back. Nevertheless, the king had bought himself some more time with London.

By the start of 1952, British soldiers in the Canal Zone were beginning to develop more proactive responses to the daily sniping and sabotage attacks. A particular trouble spot was the Moascar to Tel el Kebir road, which was used extensively by military vehicles (Moascar being the HQ for the Canal Zone garrison). Beside the road ran the Sweet Water Canal, which had high banks and thus provided excellent cover for snipers who could easily retreat into nearby hamlets. Motorised patrols had tried to hit back at the snipers, but with little success. Consequently, a new approach was initiated whereby foot patrols were deployed behind the Sweet Water Canal, in what was regarded as enemy territory. Clothing on the nocturnal missions was more akin to civilian attire than military kit: sweaters and denim slacks, caps for headgear, and gym shoes for speed and quiet movement. Wet cocoa powder was applied across faces, necks and hands as a final touch. Erskine took a personal interest in the fresh tactics – an Egyptian newspaper was offering a £E1,000 reward for his assassination and £E100 for each British officer killed – and was pleased when, as he put it, 'bags' were achieved. Indeed, on the very first night of the foot patrols a fedayeen unit was intercepted (having just killed an RAF serviceman and wounded two others) and duly dealt with; two of the three guerrillas were also killed.[54]

While events on the ground were escalating the military struggle, Churchill and Eden made a visit to Washington for talks with the Truman administration. Egypt was high on the agenda. British policy, as defined in Eden's brief for the trip, was 'to steer a course between making any concessions to Egypt which would prejudice our military requirements in the Middle East and landing ourselves with a commitment for which we are not prepared'; the possibility of military government in the Canal Zone and even elsewhere in Egypt was not to be ignored, however. The memorandum noted that US officials had shown 'a characteristic reluctance to face the less palatable implications' of Britain's attempts to maintain its position in Egypt.[55] One of Eden's primary tasks, therefore, was to prepare the Americans for the worst.

Somewhat more ambitiously, Churchill set out to enlist US military support for what he had started calling the Battle of the Canal Zone. At preliminary meetings on 5 and 8 January, he suggested that the US send a brigade of marines to Egypt to assist in the defence of the Suez Canal. American officials were far from impressed with the idea, but rather than cause embarrassment by officially rejecting it, the State Department asked Norman Brook, the cabinet secretary, to advise Churchill not to repeat the proposal in any of the plenary sessions.[56] Frustrated by this rebuff, Churchill saved a parting shot for the speech he made to Congress on 17 January. As ever, a sense of history and emotion imbued the prime minister's address. He began by explaining that it was no longer possible for Britain 'to bear alone the whole burden of maintaining the freedom of the famous waterway of the Suez Canal. That has become an international rather than a national responsibility.' He concluded: 'It would enormously aid us in our task if even token forces of other partners in the Four Power [Middle East Command] proposals were stationed in the Canal Zone as a symbol of the unity of purpose which inspires us.'[57] But before the British and Americans had a chance to disagree with each other publicly on Egyptian policy, events in the Canal Zone once again intervened.

THE BATTLE OF ISMAILIA

By mid-January, thirty British servicemen had been killed and sixty-nine wounded since the start of the crisis. London's patience with the Egyptian insurgents finally ran out on 19 January when a bomb hidden in a barrow of oranges exploded in Ismailia, killing two more British soldiers and injuring six others. The explosion was followed by fedayeen, many of whom were doubling-up as Ismailia's auxiliary police, firing off their weapons in celebration. Later that day a battle erupted on the western edge of the town, close to a bridge on the Sweet Water Canal. In an effort to strike at the guarded bridge, Egyptian irregulars took up positions in a nearby convent. During the ensuing fight an American nun, Sister Anthony, was shot and killed. According to a British account in the garrison's own newspaper, the *Canal Zone News* (established early in the crisis to counter Wafd propaganda), Sister Anthony had been murdered after she had remonstrated with an Egyptian about to throw a grenade on to the bridge. Back in December 1951, Stevenson had alerted the Conservative government to the possible need to disarm Ismailia's auxiliary police. A warning had also been made: 'Such measures can hardly fail to bring the situation to a head.'[58] That moment was now close at hand.

The day after the killing of Sister Anthony, Britain's Third Infantry Brigade Command (based in Ismailia) was instructed by Erskine to begin preparations for the disarming of the auxiliaries. The political authorisation to carry out this action, which was code-named Operation Eagle, was received from London on 24 January, ready for implementation the next day. During the evening of the 24th, Eden chaired a special meeting of the chiefs of staff to discuss the circumstances in which the Rodeo operations would be launched, should events in Ismailia prompt a widespread breakdown of order across Egypt. The meeting concluded that the final say must come from ministers. (The troop movements involved in the Rodeo plans would look to the outside world as though Britain was trying to retake control of Egypt.) In the meantime, both operations were placed on forty-eight hours' notice. The US government was warned of the impending action at Ismailia and responded by placing ships and aircraft in the vicinity on standby, ready to help evacuate foreign nationals if need be. No one was under any illusions that a major confrontation was about to take place. Meanwhile, Churchill, who was sailing back from North America on the *Queen Mary*, was kept fully informed of events and wholly agreed with the proposed measures.[59] His earlier caution – witnessed on the issue of oil sanctions soon after assuming office – had long since evaporated.

A wider explanation as to why Britain was willing to instigate a major international incident over events in Ismailia may be gleaned from a memo written by a senior Foreign Office official on 23 January. 'Thinking over our difficulties in Egypt,' observed Pierson Dixon, 'it seems to me that the essential difficulty arises from the very obvious fact that we lack power. The Egyptians know this, and that accounts for their intransigence.'

On a strictly realistic view we ought to recognise that our lack of power must limit what we do, and should lead us to a policy of surrender or near surrender imposed by necessity.

But the basic and fundamental aim of British policy is to build up our lost power. Once we despair of doing so, we shall never attain this aim. Power, of course, is not to be measured in terms alone of money and troops: a third ingredient is prestige, or in other words what the rest of the world thinks of us.

Here the dilemma arises. We are not physically strong enough to carry out policies needed if we retain our position in the world; if we show weakness our position in the world diminishes with repercussions on our world wide position.

The broad conclusion I am driven to is therefore that we ought to make every conceivable effort to avoid a policy of surrender or near surrender. Ideally we should persuade the Americans of the disaster which such a policy would entail for us and for them, and seek their backing, moral, financial and, if possible, military, in carrying out a strong policy in Egypt.[60]

This belief that events in Egypt would help determine the fate of Britain's world power status continued to be a crucial influence on British policy throughout the Egyptian troubles.

At 5 a.m. on 25 January 1952 Operation Eagle was set in motion. It was a Friday, the holy day for Muslims, but too early still for the muezzin to have summoned believers for dawn prayers. The British officer in charge was Brigadier R.K. Exham of the Third Infantry Brigade. His first task was to establish a close cordon around the Bureau Sanitaire, the temporary lodgings of the auxiliary police (formerly hospital buildings). Two troops of the 4th Royal Tank Regiment and four troops of the Royals were detailed, along with eight Bren-gun carriers and accompanying infantry sections. A state-of-the-art Centurion tank was also assigned, along with several armoured cars. Exham's next task was to seal off Arasha where most of the locals lived. Again, little was left to chance. The forces allotted were the 2nd Parachute Battalion, the 1st Battalion of the East Lancashire Regiment, and the Royal Lincolnshire Regiment. Both cordons were in place by first light.

At 6.20 a.m. a British loudhailer van, shielded by the Centurion tank, issued a message calling on the Egyptian police to surrender. A veterinary surgeon and his family were the sole people to leave the compound. The other occupants, numbering close to a thousand, seized the opportunity to man already sandbagged and fortified positions on the roofs of the buildings and in the yard below. Meanwhile, the Egyptian officer in charge took advantage of the fact that his telephone line had not been cut and rang Cairo asking for instructions. The order came through from the very top – from Sirag al-Din, the minister of interior – for the men to resist. After the Kafr incident the Wafd could not afford another humiliation. Two more calls for surrender were made by the British in the half hour after 6.20 a.m., punctuated, as a notice of intent, by the Centurion crashing through the main gate of the compound and demolishing part of the front wall. At 7 a.m. the tank fired a blank round as a further warning, but the Egyptians took this as the signal that the battle had commenced. An intense exchange of small-arms fire followed, backed up on the British side with the dispatch of six 20lb rounds from the Centurion. Two more surrender broadcasts were made – and ignored – at 7.45 a.m. and 8.20 a.m., after which Exham gave permission for all necessary force to be used to complete the action. Almost four hours were needed.[61]

The ferocity of the fighting was such that midway through it General Robertson wired an urgent message to the chief of imperial general staff in London requesting further reinforcements for the Suez base. This telegram can be seen as the first expression of a momentous shift in British thinking towards Egypt. Robertson's message was that Egypt's politicians had succeeded in 'whipping up the fanaticism of the nation' to such an extent that the situation had fundamentally changed: 'Whereas we once thought that all Egyptians are cowards and would pack up when confronted by force, that is certainly not the position today. Events taking place in Ismailia this morning are an example of this new attitude.' As a consequence, Robertson now believed the Rodeo operations to be fatally flawed:

If I thought that the arrival of our troops in Cairo and Alexandria would bring about the immediate collapse of resistance both there and in the Canal Zone I should have no further representations to make. In view of the present Egyptian attitude I consider that such an impression is quite unjustifiable and that on the contrary we must expect to be confronted with a fierce guerrilla struggle against our troops and communications. As you know so well such a situation inevitably absorbs a very large number of troops.[62]

The impact of Robertson's telegram can be gauged by the marked reluctance of British policymakers to enact the Rodeo operations during the turbulent days that followed, and indeed throughout the final years of the British presence at Suez.

Operation Eagle resulted in the death of fifty Egyptian auxiliary policemen with many more injured; about 800 were taken into British custody. On the other side, four British soldiers were killed and ten wounded. One of the first visitors to the battle scene was Thomas Rapp, the head of the British Middle East Office. 'The corpses had been removed', he later wrote, 'but the blood and brains that were still scattered about the ruins were a sufficiently gruesome sight vividly illustrating the sharp nature of the encounter.' His subsequent assessment is worth quoting in full:

> Yet what sickened me most was the conviction that something had gone wrong and that the bloodshed was unnecessary. The Egyptians had finally provoked our troops into a ham-handed operation, which could easily nullify all the political advantage of our previous exemplary forbearance and humanity. Psychologically, it had certainly been a blunder. The Egyptian common soldier is a brave man in defence and when cornered, as he had been, without an escape route, he will fight to the death. It had been foolish, moreover, to attack so early in the morning when all the senior officers – no tough characters like their men – were comfortably in bed elsewhere. It had been unnecessary too to give so peremptory an ultimatum: time for reflection and parleying would have resulted in peaceful submission. And then there was the question of the uncut telephone line: why had it been overlooked?[63]

The brave resistance of Ismailia's auxiliary police on that fateful Friday morning was to have a far-reaching impact on the subsequent course of Anglo-Egyptian relations.

FOUR

· · · · · · · · ·

The Burning of Cairo

On Saturday 26 January 1952 the centre of Cairo was set ablaze amid ferocious anti-British riots. The 'Burning of Cairo' or 'Black Saturday' has since been seen as a defining moment in the history of modern Egypt. Psychologically, a corner had seemingly been turned and the events of the next six months, until the coup of 23 July, soon became part of a revised narrative which saw the period as one of prologue to revolution. Whereas the old nationalist perspective equated the struggle for Egyptian independence with the rise of the Wafd party, the new version emphasised the decline of the Wafd and the intrinsic failings of Egypt's parliamentary framework. As Anwar Sadat, one of the coup leaders and a future president of Egypt, stated in his influential account, *Revolt on the Nile* (1957), the politics of Egypt in the thirty years prior to July 1952 resembled a pendulum that oscillated between the palace and the Wafd. The oscillation, he observed, was regulated by Britain.[1]

Sadat's point would not have been lost on a generation or two of British policymakers; Egypt's political framework after the First World War had indeed been designed to perpetuate Britain's imperial position by indirect, or informal, means of backstairs influence. And while there was an attempt by the British after the Second World War to stop interfering in internal affairs, this was categorically abandoned during the abrogation crisis and the siege of the Canal Zone. During the winter of 1951/2, the Wafd's removal from power was the first aim of British policy in Egypt. Ironically, these renewed attempts at intervention revealed how little influence Britain still exerted. The movement of the pendulum had all but ceased.

BLACK SATURDAY

Egypt's interior minister, Sirag al-Din, was allegedly having a bath when he received the call from Ismailia's auxiliary police commander asking for instructions on how to respond to the British ultimatum on 25 January. In the rumours that subsequently circulated, the minister was also smoking one of his signature Havana cigars. The connection being made was never too subtle: the overweight pasha, smoking his expensive cigars, giving the callous order for the police to fight to the last man. Whether true or false, such accounts nevertheless became an important part of the mythology surrounding the events that followed.[2] What is certain, however, is that Egypt's auxiliary police felt utterly betrayed by the Wafd government.

The next morning, Saturday 26 January, Cairo's auxiliaries took to the streets in protest.[3] They marched from their barracks at Abbassia on the outskirts of the city to the traditional meeting point for demonstrations, the Abdin palace. A familiar marching detour was taken past the Fuad I University so that supporters could be gathered en route. It soon became clear that the anger of the demonstrators was as much against Egypt's political elite as at the massacre in Ismailia. Farouk happened to be at the Abdin palace owing to a celebratory banquet due to take place that afternoon. Ten days earlier his second wife, Queen Narriman, whom he had married in May 1951, had given birth to a first son, Ahmed Fuad. Six hundred senior military and regular police officers were to attend the feast. Upon reaching the palace gates, the demonstrators turned their anger on Egypt's royal family. One chant articulated the widespread belief that Farouk had only remarried once his bride-to-be had produced a male heir: 'Narriman, Narriman, why does your baby have teeth?' A second marriage and the royal birth had obviously failed to rekindle the goodwill that the monarch had earlier enjoyed from the Egyptian people.

For the Wafd government, the most worrying aspect of the demonstration was that members of the auxiliary police – the state's usual means for controlling serious disturbances – were leading the fray. In an apparent effort to pacify the marchers, Abdel Fattah Hassan, the minister of social affairs and a close ally of Sirag al-Din, met some of the ringleaders, but to little avail. There are other particulars that day which, like the bath story, may be apocryphal, but nevertheless gained wide currency and are therefore significant. The prime minister, Mustafa al-Nahas, supposedly spent his morning having a pedicure; Sirag al-Din was said to be busy conducting a private land deal.

Around midday, just as the demonstration was winding down, word spread that fires were being deliberately started in the Europeanised heart of the city, less than a mile from the Abdin grounds. The effect was magnetic. As the crowd relocated to the quarter that Khedive Ismail had hastily constructed in the 1860s to impress visiting dignitaries at the opening of the Suez Canal, well-organised gangs arrived at prearranged sites, primarily British-owned properties but also foreign establishments in general, and systematically set them alight. Fuel trucks were on hand to supply the necessary flammable materials. Bars, cinemas, department stores, nightclubs, banks – all were torched. The absence of police control of any sort allowed the watching crowd, which included many of the auxiliary police, to develop quickly into a looting, rampaging, murderous mob. In a particularly gruesome incident nine members of the Turf Club, which was frequented by the upper echelons of the ex-patriot community, tried to escape the burning building. They were beaten to death and stripped before being tossed back into the flames. Their retrieved bodies revealed broken bones and wounds to the genitalia.[4] An Egyptian eyewitness described the frenzied destruction:

> I saw the body of a dead Briton on the sidewalk being kicked time and again by half a dozen fuming rioters. A short distance away, I saw Groppi's, a renowned Swiss-owned confectionary, set aflame after being smashed up with iron bars and sticks. French pastry, broken bottles of syrup and juice, all kinds of cookies, pieces of cheese and cold meat littered the street outside and the rioters kept trampling on them.[5]

The Shepheard's Hotel, an establishment emblematic of the British empire ('Patronized by Imperial and Royal Families' went its advertisement), was reduced to a burnt-out hulk. The symbolism must have been difficult to resist.[6]

With wholesale destruction of Western-owned properties occurring in central Cairo, it is necessary to ask why Rodeo Bernard, the British military operation to save the lives of Britons and other foreign nationals in the Egyptian capital, was not implemented. Forces in the Canal Zone had, after all, been placed on short notice for such an eventuality since 24 January. There are two related reasons for this decision. The first concerned the presence of a couple of Egyptian brigade groups with tank support dug in on hillside positions on the western edge of the Canal Zone. To get past these forces would almost certainly have entailed a major clash between the Egyptian and British armies – a swift one, in the expectation of Lieutenant-General Erskine, but a battle nevertheless. Such an eventuality could easily have been construed as an act of war.[7]

The second reason for Rodeo Bernard not being implemented concerned the attitude of Britain's Cairo embassy. Throughout the abrogation crisis, Ralph Stevenson had been deeply apprehensive about the possible reintroduction of military government in Egypt. Although the final decision for launching the Rodeo operations was a ministerial one (as clarified by Eden during the previous twenty-four hours), ministers back in London nevertheless relied upon advice from the Cairo embassy, and here the ambassador's apprehensions held sway.[8] Provided the disturbances remained confined to the business heart of Cairo, Stevenson felt that there was no need for Canal Zone forces to intervene. The main point of the military operations was always to protect lives, not property. If the mob had moved on to nearby European residential areas, however, then Rodeo Bernard would have been near impossible to avoid. Another danger, for reasons of prestige, concerned the British embassy itself being attacked. An unruly crowd had approached the compound midway through the afternoon, but had been seen off by three rifle shots aimed to hit.[9] Thus, despite the intense pressures of the day, Stevenson held his nerve and a potential act of war, with consequences which could easily have resulted in a re-imposition of British rule à la 1882, was narrowly avoided.

Also holding his nerve was King Farouk. He continued with his banquet as the mob ran amok, the smoke of downtown Cairo visible from his palace ballroom. Conclusively fathoming his motives is impossible, but it was probable that he saw the disturbances as a pretext for dismissing the Wafd administration. According to Sirag al-Din's own account given to the Wafdist newspaper El Misr a few weeks later (in an effort to refute assertions that he had not done enough to quell the rioting), the interior minister claimed that from around 1.30 p.m. he had repeatedly tried to telephone the commander-in-chief of the Egyptian army, General Haydar, who was at the Abdin palace event. The telephone calls, however, were not put through. (Haydar and Farouk were nevertheless seen in frequent huddled conversations as the banquet progressed.) Sirag al-Din stated that he eventually drove to the palace and insisted that the commander-in-chief see him, which he did at 2.45 p.m.

Haydar duly assured him that the army would be in the city by 3.30 p.m.[10] In fact, the first army units did not arrive until 5 p.m.[11]

Several hours of anarchy thus elapsed before Egyptian forces arrived to restore order. They only did so then, in Stevenson's opinion, out of fear that the British would otherwise intervene.[12] In the meantime, over 700 buildings were destroyed, while nine Britons and twenty-six Westerners in total were killed. The political impact was to prove seismic. Unlike Ismailia, which was a relatively recent invention of European imperialism, Cairo was a metropolis of enormous historic and contemporary importance. It was, as one British official aptly put it, 'the Hollywood, the Oxford, the Paris and the Moscow of the so-called Arab world'.[13] To observers and participants alike, Egypt's political system seemed to be visibly collapsing.

In the weeks after Black Saturday, British and Egyptian investigations were conducted as to who was responsible for the rioting and why it had not been suppressed. While much of the evidence pointed to Ahmad Husayn's Socialist Party, the influence of the Wafd's interior minister never seemed far removed. A British embassy report in February, based on contacts with the Muslim Brotherhood, stated that Husayn 'had so much help from Sirag al-Din in the form of money, arms, incendiary equipment and police protection that organising the events on Black Saturday had not been difficult'. Husayn was detained soon after the riots. The British report also acknowledged that the interior minister had received far more than he bargained for: 'Right up to the end', it concluded, 'Sirag al-Din had been stupid enough to believe that these facilities would be used in the Canal Zone. He had expected and wanted a riot in Cairo on 26 January, but only a "normal riot".'[14] Other evidence, which was not necessarily contradictory, suggested that Farouk may also have given encouragement to Husayn to start a riot which could then be blamed on the Wafd. The idea that Husayn double-crossed both of them would certainly accord with his party's vitriol against the Egyptian elite and its capitalist cooperation with the British.[15] In any case, the crucial difference between a 'normal riot' – whether encouraged by Sirag al-Din, Farouk or both – and the events of Black Saturday was, of course, the role played therein by the auxiliary police.

EYE OF THE STORM

On Sunday 27 January, King Farouk seized his moment and dismissed al-Nahas's Wafd administration for failing to maintain order. Britain thus achieved the goal it had established at the outset of the abrogation crisis in October 1951, the toppling of the Wafd. It was a victory no one cared to celebrate. The incoming palace-appointed prime minister was Ali Maher. His political career spanned Egypt's constitutional era. Born into a landowning family famous for its opposition to the British, Maher had spent his professional life bolstering that reputation. After flirting with the Wafd in 1919 he soon drifted to the other centre of Egyptian politics, the court. As a leading lawyer, he chaired the body that drafted the constitution of 1923, before being elected to parliament as an independent in 1924. Cabinet posts followed, albeit only when the Wafd was out of power. He served as prime minister in 1936 (briefly) and again in 1939–40, until his pro-Axis sympathies prompted Lampson to insist on his dismissal. As Farouk's closest adviser, he nevertheless continued to be a nuisance to Britain's wartime interests. British officials considered having him abducted and smuggled out of Egypt, but in the end he was placed under house arrest, courtesy of the Wafd government installed by Lampson in February 1942. The French historian Jacques Berque has memorably described Maher as having 'the face of a crafty musketeer' – 'stubborn wrinkles', 'a suggestion of a beard', and an 'impassive gaze'. 'To his friends and supporters, he seemed an authentic personality', and yet he was also 'unpopular, even detested, according to some people, for all his shares in the intrigues against the Constitution since 1923'.[16] In late January 1952, Maher was once again entering office at the behest of the palace, with scant regard for Egypt's façade of democracy.

Immediately upon assuming office, Maher told the British that he intended to reach a new defence agreement within three months.[17] The liberation struggle was officially called off (though suspended is a more accurate description with hindsight) and Egyptian workers in the Canal Zone towns and villages were encouraged to return to their former jobs. At the palace's insistence, a tough anti-Wafdist politician, Ahmad Mortada al-Maraghi, was appointed as interior minister and he immediately started weeding out anti-British elements within the auxiliary police. The fate of the Ismailia detainees, who were being held in a makeshift prison encampment in the Canal Zone, was ignored. Meanwhile, Maher's pledge and early actions coincided with Eden's desire to reach a quick settlement with Egypt over the Suez base while its people were supposedly in a chastened mood. On 28 January he informed Stevenson that there was 'no wish to maintain indefinitely British troops in the Canal Zone contrary to the wishes of the Egyptian government', and that the defence of the area might instead be gradually assumed by Egypt's armed forces. When Churchill read a copy of the telegram that same day, he was flabbergasted, scribbling tetchily in the margin in his distinctive red ink, 'complete "clear out"'.[18]

This abrupt dismissal of Eden's instincts on the base issue created a full-blown rift between prime minister and foreign secretary over Egyptian matters which lasted for the rest of the Canal Zone dispute. Indeed, all subsequent British dealings with Egypt in the 1950s bore the messy imprint of this division. After the killings of Black Saturday, Churchill felt that Egypt was no longer a fit country to negotiate with: 'I think we should be very careful lest in our desire to have an easier settlement in Egypt we do not take account of the degree of atrocity committed by the Egyptians in the murders and massacres in Cairo,' he told Eden on 30 January.

> The horrible behaviour of the mob puts them lower than the most degraded savages now known. Unless the Egyptian government can purge themselves by the condign punishment of the offenders and by the most abject and complete regrets and reparations I doubt whether any relationship is possible with them. They cannot be classed as a civilised power until they have purged themselves.[19]

Evidently, the British killing of fifty Egyptians at Ismailia was conveniently forgotten. In the weeks to come, Eden's stance was backed by the usual advocates of an accommodation with Egyptian nationalism (Britain's Cairo embassy, US officials generally and the large foreign commercial community in Egypt), but this did not mean that it was business as usual on Egyptian matters – in fact, far from it.[20] The events of 26 January had psychologically scarred many British residents, whether they were directly affected or not.

A sense of shock permeated the embassy and soon registered with an iconoclastic reappraisal of Britain's position in Egypt. The review was initiated by John Hamilton, the embassy's political counsellor (who was to play a key role in later events). Hamilton had first come to Egypt in 1932 as Sudan agent, a position akin to an ambassador for the Sudan government, the Sudan being directly administered by British officials.[21] After three years, he was seconded to the Egyptian government and served in the European department of the Ministry of Interior, which was the centre of British intelligence operations in Egypt. Following the signing of the Anglo-Egyptian defence treaty in 1936, he moved for good to what henceforth became the Cairo embassy.[22] (One of the great strengths of the Cairo mission was that it could employ officials who were not obliged to move to other postings every two or three years like most diplomatic service appointees.)

On 13 February Hamilton wrote a highly significant internal embassy memorandum suggesting that Britain should relocate its forces from the Canal Zone to a series of northerly bases in Turkey, Lebanon, Greece, Cyprus and, most interestingly, Israel. His argument was underpinned by the conviction, born of twenty years' first-hand experience, that Egypt was 'rapidly and disastrously heading towards financial bankruptcy, administrative chaos and possibly civil war'. The number two at the embassy, Michael Creswell, and the former oriental secretary, Walter Smart – the example par excellence of expertise linked to continuity – both agreed with Hamilton's thesis.[23] Thus, less than three weeks after Black Saturday, the most senior advisers to the ambassador, plus a legendary old hand, were all voicing momentous doubts about the usefulness of Britain continuing to maintain a military presence in Egypt.

In a dispatch to the Foreign Office exactly one month after the Ismailia action, Stevenson adopted the line taken by his staff and advised the government to place Britain's Middle Eastern defence requirements 'on firmer foundations than those of the Egyptian political scene'. His telegram added that if Britain provided evidence that it was 'willing to fall back upon such an alternative plan and were indeed prepared to isolate Egypt as a potential enemy', then it 'would also have the incidental advantage of stimulating the Egyptians themselves into adopting a more realistic policy towards us'. 'They are', he concluded, 'still convinced that they are indispensable to us – a fact which makes them blindly intransigent.'[24]

But London's reaction to this radical new approach was unenthusiastic to say the least. Five day earlier Eden had persuaded a reluctant cabinet to accept new instructions for the Cairo embassy regarding the restart of the defence negotiations. As Roger Allen, the head of the Foreign Office's African department, stated in a minute attached to Stevenson's telegram, officials were already 'straining every nerve to try and find the basis for an agreement with the Egyptians' and they did not want any additional complications. The decision was therefore taken to keep these 'new doubts' away from the negotiating process. Tellingly, Eden was not even consulted, presumably because his views on the matter were well known.[25]

The British military establishment in Egypt also remained deeply troubled by Black Saturday, not least because these events were linked to alarming new assessments of Egyptian resistance capabilities following the showdown at Ismailia. Robertson was gloomily expecting a prolonged period of guerrilla warfare should there be another break in relations. Nor was he overly impressed with the calm produced by the martial law measures introduced by the Wafd as its last action in office. The Egyptian press, for instance, did not even mention the riots until 12 February, and only then to publicise Farouk's decision of the previous day to forgo his usual birthday celebrations and instead donate the money to those suffering as a result of the 'latest accidents'.[26] In mid-February, Robertson wrote to the War Office expressing his concerns that policymakers in London had been too eager to downgrade the possibility that further drastic action might still be required. Had we, he wondered, 'passed through the hurricane' or were we 'only at its centre'?[27] Two weeks later, the vice chief of imperial general staff replied in reassuring terms: if the need for military measures arose, there would be 'no hesitation on the part of the Prime Minister as to what we should do'.[28]

As February drew to a close, a new crisis loomed in Egyptian politics. Eden's early confidence in Maher had dwindled because of the prime minister's marked reluctance to bring charges against the Wafd leadership for criminal negligence during the Cairo riots, despite Egypt's public prosecutor placing some of the blame on Sirag al-Din. The value of negotiating with the Maher administration was therefore considered doubtful, especially after all the wrangling to get the green light from Churchill. Another negative sign late in the month was Maher's insistence that the Ismailia auxiliary police detainees be handed over to the Egyptian authorities. Al-Maraghi, the supposed 'strong man' of the cabinet, was clearly becoming marginalised. According to the released police commander (after he and several officers were taken to Cairo to see the interior minister), al-Maraghi 'did not seem particularly happy to see us alive'.[29] Farouk was another who felt increasingly dissatisfied with Maher's behaviour. The last straw for all concerned came when Maher attempted to establish a working relationship with the discredited Wafd.

In response, and with British and American foreknowledge and possibly collusion, Farouk instigated a cabinet crisis aimed at forcing Maher's resignation. On 1 March the head of the royal cabinet presented Maher with a decree signed by the king (but not dated) stipulating the suspension of parliament, which the Wafd still dominated as per the election results of January 1950. Meanwhile, that morning's press had included palace-inspired reports that the government was intent on suspending parliament, the aim being to drive a wedge between the Maher–Wafd rapprochement. Another layer of intrigue was that Maher had been due to meet Stevenson at 9.30 a.m. for the formal restart of the defence negotiations, but the ambassador had cancelled at the last moment, citing the onset of a severe cold. Without the excuse of being busy with the British, Maher was obliged to call an emergency cabinet meeting to discuss Farouk's decree. Al-Maraghi and the likeminded finance minister, Zaki Abd el-Motaal, used the session to urge the prime minister to take a tougher stance against the Wafd and corruption generally. When he refused they promptly resigned. Maher then tried to arrange an audience with the king, but was palmed off with a courtier. Outmanoeuvred all round, the beleaguered prime minister tendered his resignation.[30]

Although the evidence directly linking Britain to the affair is partial, it is nevertheless persuasive. It centres on a telegram written by Stevenson on 1 March in which he refers to an earlier report dated 28 February (still classified, as are many others concerning this crisis) which accurately predicted the timing of Maher's fall. The reliability of the intelligence source may be gauged by the fact that Rodeo Bernard, the operational scale of which was very large, was immediately placed on twenty-four hours' notice.[31] It would thus seem that Stevenson's flu on the morning of 1 March was indeed a 'diplomatic' illness.

Details about US participation come from the memoirs of Miles Copeland, a former CIA operative, who writes that the March crisis was instigated by the CIA's Middle East specialist, Kermit Roosevelt (a grandson of President Theodore Roosevelt), who had gone to Egypt in February with the brief of working with Farouk, a friend from the war years, to clean up the machinery of government.[32] Copeland's testimony needs to be treated with caution, yet his account is in accord with verifiable US diplomatic records.

The premise of greater American involvement in Egyptian affairs flowed from the conviction that Britain was making a dreadful hash of things. Secretary of State Dean Acheson had been appalled at the 'splutter of musketry' tactics deployed at Ismailia on 25 January.[33] A week later, the American missions in London and Cairo were alerted that changes were afoot: 'We have had a very close shave', Acheson stated, and we should now 'take advantage of the present opportunity which may not last long' to prevent revolution in Egypt.[34] Working with al-Maraghi (after securing the reluctant approval of the British), the US administration had embarked on an initiative aimed at creating a motorised and armoured police battalion modelled on Italy's *carabinieri*, an intermediate organisation between the regular police and the army which could be relied upon for tackling serious disturbances.[35] To be sure, Egypt's auxiliary police were no longer useful in this respect.

LIFE IN THE CANAL ZONE

The unease among the governmental elites was mirrored in the attitudes of the rank-and-file soldiers who had little choice but to experience the discomforts of the Canal Zone base under active service conditions. It might be illuminating at this juncture, therefore, to step back from high-level politics and instead try to recapture some of the sensibilities and ways of life of British soldiers in Egypt in the twilight years of empire.[36] There is also a wider point to this exercise. The increasing reluctance of national servicemen to sign up for regular soldiering positions was to prove a powerful influence on British politicians in the movement towards imperial disengagement from Egypt.

The easing of tensions after Black Saturday did not result in a marked improvement in life for personnel and families in the Canal Zone garrison. If anything, it allowed them greater time to consider their uncomfortable surroundings. Moreover, the rapid increase in the garrison size during the previous winter – to *c.* 80,000 by early 1952 – put enormous strains on the existing facilities. Even the accommodation at the General Headquarters for British Forces in the Middle East at Fayid was basic, a reflection of its origins as a temporary replacement for the Citadel HQ in Cairo when it was evacuated as a gesture of goodwill in 1946. (When the British Middle East Office's political division was obliged to move from Cairo to Fayid at the start of the abrogation crisis, Thomas Rapp and his deputy, Hugh Stephenson, were invited to join No. 1 mess, but this hardly compensated for the abandonment of villas in Gezira on the outskirts of Cairo, close to the pyramids.[37])

The service families evacuated from Moascar in November 1951, where many had lived in tidy bungalows, were relocated to temporary compounds. The wife of a warrant officer later recalled the conditions in Fayid:

These double-skinned EPIPS tents – European personnel, Indian pattern – had sand floors and only basic necessities like beds and bedding, a Tilly lamp, washbasin and stand and a couple of chairs. Home sweet home. It might have been primitive but we felt much safer here than we had for some time.[38]

A flight back to Britain could often not come soon enough. However, for the regulars and national servicemen, many of whom were still teenagers, flying home was not an option. For them, tented accommodation in the desert, usually ordered in featureless rows for security purposes, was a fact of life, not an emergency recourse. Luckier ones might find themselves in Nissen huts, tunnel-shaped corrugated iron structures. As the recent reinforcements to the Canal Zone were already finding out, springtime temperatures were hot enough, let alone the summer highs of 40°C or over. It was something of a mixed blessing, therefore, that night-time temperatures could drop to near freezing. Needless to say, flies were an irritant during daytime, while mosquitoes took over at dusk.

Primitive sanitation was a predicament shared by all. At some depots a hole in the ground crossed with a horizontal telegraph pole and shielded by a Hessian sheet served as a multi-seated toilet. As a substitute for flushing, diesel oil was periodically poured down the hole and set alight. Shacks with buckets were luxurious in comparison. This being the British armed forces, however, there were still issues of hierarchy. Of the ten lavatories at El Qantara railway station, 'three [were] for officers (one each for European, Asiatic and Coloured users), three for other ranks of each race and one for the smaller number of servicewomen'.[39] Yet pecking orders were absent when it came to 'Gyppie tummy' (to use one of its politer names): diarrhoea was a sickness suffered by all at one time or another.

Guard duties remained the primary preoccupation of the British garrison. The most difficult installations to defend were the airfields, because of their lengthy perimeters. (Well-defended army garrisons had been less troubled by guerrilla attacks during the recent crisis.) Installations were typically ringed by 9ft-high security fences strung with barbed wire. In addition, there was usually an inner space of 10–12ft filled with rolls of danert wire. These enclosed areas were patrolled by armed guards, backed by searchlight towers, on the lookout for infiltrators or evidence of entry. Fedayeen would cover themselves in grease and roll in the sand for camouflage. At the Abu Sultan camp the outer perimeter sands were swept every evening by a vehicle pulling a mat so that any fresh footprints would be visible. Outlying areas were sometimes protected with anti-personnel mines. For particularly susceptible targets, such as ammunition and arms stores, trip wires and flares were fitted. The ordnance depot at Tel el Kebir had a 25-mile-long perimeter and required 280 sentries at any one time. Despite all these measures, however, the problem of theft remained. The clothing favoured by locals – a baggy shirt called a *djellabah* – was perfect for concealing weapons or stolen goods. Road patrols remained the most dangerous job. The Ismailia to Tel el Kebir road was nicknamed Terror Alley or Sniper's Alley. Another prime target was the Ismailia to Fayid road, the route most frequently used by the top brass. General Robertson was driven around in a bulletproof Bentley. Land Rovers engaged in escort duties kept their windscreens down so that they had a free field of fire if ambushed.

During the spring of 1952, the expectation of renewed guerrilla struggle remained strong among British soldiers. The Canal Zone's alert settings stayed at 'red-and-amber' or 'amber' and the troops were constantly reminded that they were engaged in active service conditions. Douglas Findlay, then a leading aircraftman, has described how the various states of alert affected the troops:

Red was when things were really rough, with everyone confined to camp unless on essential duty. Vehicles would carry escort guards and travel in convoy, led by redcaps [military policemen] driving a Land Rover with a wire-cutting piece of angle iron mounted in front. Red-and-amber indicated a slightly less dangerous state of affairs. At this level we could travel in convoy but could cut down on the escort guards and dispense with the Land Rover. While we were out of camp we had to keep in groups, each man armed with a rifle and ten rounds of ammunition . . . The next state was amber, when a pickaxe handle was substituted for the rifle. This was more or less the prevailing state if you were allowed out of camp at all, and whole regiments were issued with pickaxe staves. I never saw a green alert in operation [he was present from 1951 to 1953], but old sweats used to wax lyrical about the good times when the only condition was green.[40]

Although military censorship in the Canal Zone meant that rank-and-file personnel had been kept ignorant of the full range of fedayeen activities during the previous winter, word of mouth, if not first-hand experience, ensured that few were uninformed about the circumstances surrounding the deaths of comrades. Grisly details of mutilation resonated with young men, many of whom were not only away from Britain for the first time, but also, apart from basic training postings, away from home. Egypt was an alien country 3,000 miles away where the locals could brutally turn on them at any moment. Harassment of Egyptians, not empathy, was the standard response, thus further exacerbating nationalist grievances, as well as acting as a powerful recruiting agent for future fedayeen.

Social outlets for the garrison were scarce. There were no trips to the pyramids and the Sphinx, as there had been when British troops were stationed in Cairo. A particular problem for personnel when allowed out of the camps was how to gauge the mood of the local population. The safest option by far was to stay on base and have a drink. RAF Ismailia had an impressive outdoor cinema, but film performances had been distracted by hand grenades tossed from over the perimeter fence. In addition, the age-old soldierly distraction of brothels, which were located in the main Canal Zone towns, might easily be traps. Moreover, the nightspots for which Ismailia had once been renowned were now out of bounds. Even buying fruit from the locals had proved fatal in recent events and was treated with great caution. Clearly, the heightened struggle of the Canal Zone siege was not about to be forgotten by any of the participants, no matter how calm the situation might appear in the short term.

CLEANING UP THE HOUSE

On 2 March Farouk turned to Ahmad Naguib al-Hilali, a leading opponent of the Wafd, to form a new government. Significantly, on 27 January he had been the king's first choice as prime minister, but had declined the offer because he felt unable to balance his plans for internal reform with progress on the base issue. He was probably also following his own advice to the British from the previous October, which was to avoid negotiating with the immediate successor to the Wafd and instead save any concessions for when the situation had quietened down – more light, perhaps, on Maher's fall. Al-Hilali's credentials as an anti-Wafdist followed a familiar pattern: he had previously been one of its most important figures (Egypt's party system being largely the product of defections and divisions from the mother organisation).

Moreover, his grievances were still fresh, for he had been expelled in October 1951, ostensibly because of a dispute with Sirag al-Din over illegal wire taps, but really because of al-Hilali's drive against internal corruption.[41] Beneath a mild-mannered exterior, as befitted a 60-year-old former professor of law, was a man determined to clean up Egyptian politics.

Eden warmly welcomed the changes (as well he might), telling his ministerial colleagues that the new administration was 'about as good as we can hope for in Egypt'.[42] But Churchill was not convinced: 'I cannot think it good policy to hasten to make an agreement with this fragile Palace Government,' he told Eden on 9 March.[43] Eden's reply a day later was equally forthright.

> The plain fact is that we are no longer in a position to impose our will upon Egypt, regardless of the cost in men, money and international goodwill both throughout the Middle East and the rest of the world. If I cannot impose my will, I must negotiate. This is the best Government we have yet had to do so.[44]

Al-Hilali's early actions lived up to Eden's estimate. His first move, on 2 March, was to issue a royal decree suspending parliament for a month. When pro-Wafdist demonstrations followed at Cairo's Fuad I University, al-Hilali promptly suspended all lectures. The ground was thus readied for his 'purification' campaign aimed at exposing and punishing governmental corruption. All exceptional promotions in the civil service were to be cancelled; 800 suspected rioters were put on trial; and Sirag al-Din and his protégé Abdel Fattah Hassan, now regarded by British officials as the Wafd's two principal 'gangsters', were banished to the provinces and placed under house arrest.[45]

Having enacted these measures, al-Hilali felt that concessions from London were in order. As an initial gesture he wanted Britain to commit itself publicly to the principle of evacuation before the negotiations formally restarted. As in the past, however, this was firmly resisted even after US pressure was applied. He consequently changed tack. On 23 March he dissolved the Egyptian parliament and announced elections for 18 May. As everyone in Egypt knew, free elections always produced Wafdist victories.[46] The Foreign Office was therefore under no illusions as to the nature of al-Hilali's action: it was a gambit by which the cancellation of elections would be used as a bargaining chip in the defence negotiations, the assumption being that Britain could not afford to let his administration collapse. But what al-Hilali had failed to anticipate was the divide between Eden and Churchill on Egyptian matters. Significant concessions were just not possible.[47] Meanwhile, the expectation of polling produced a great deal of political activity in Egypt, but as was the norm, only the Wafd filed candidates for all constituencies.

After an elapse of nearly three weeks, al-Hilali had little choice but to accept that his bluff had been called. On 12 April he consequently backtracked and announced the suspension of elections. The excuse given was that the Wafd had tampered with the registration details of voters during their previous administration.[48] Even then, however, al-Hilali's hopes for an immediate restart of the defence negotiations were dashed owing to Churchill's stonewalling in Britain. A string of cabinet meetings in early April had confirmed and exacerbated the growing split over Egyptian policy.[49] The recall of Stevenson from Cairo later that month did little to assist Eden in his struggle with Churchill.[50] Meanwhile, a sure sign of al-Hilali's desire to do business with Britain had been his appointment of Amr, Egypt's former ambassador to London (who had been recalled after the Kafr incident in December 1951) to be foreign minister. Yet when Amr visited London in early May to work on a joint formula with which to restart the negotiations, Churchill subjected this most pro-British of Egyptian officials to a long and violent lecture on Egypt's shortcomings.[51] While a joint statement was eventually agreed upon, it was so emasculated as to be worthless for the negotiations.[52] The talks on the future of the Canal Zone were thus stifled before they had a chance to begin.

Egyptian constitutional politics, however, could no longer afford these prevarications. After the Canal Zone siege of the previous winter, all Egyptian governments, whether they liked it or not, were being measured by the results they achieved on the 'British question'. Domestic reforms came a poor second to the overriding issue of ridding the country of all foreign troops. After the glories of the liberation struggle, which had seen the empowerment of the Egyptian masses via the guerrilla tactics of a few, the post-Black Saturday truce in the Canal Zone could only be temporary. The formation, training and deployment of the liberation battalions were not privileges for the politicians to take away – they had become a national right. Moreover, the subdued public mood in the wake of the Cairo riots would not last for ever. It was nevertheless to al-Hilali's advantage that he enjoyed relatively cordial relations with the Muslim Brotherhood (owing to his 'clean' reputation). Having taken the lead in the development of guerrilla tactics, the politicised Islamic organisation was now willing to give al-Hilali some much-needed leeway.

There may also have been other motives for this latitude. According to British intelligence sources, the Muslim Brotherhood's leadership was riven by divisions over how best to respond to the large influx of new members since October 1951. On the one hand, the paramilitary wing was emboldened by the recent guerrilla campaign and saw this as the best way forward; on the other, Hasan al-Hudaybi, al-Banna's successor as supreme guide, wanted to focus more on mainstream politics and rehabilitate the organisation after the spate of assassinations during the late 1940s.[53] In any case, the practical effect of the Muslim Brotherhood's attitude to al-Hilali was that a temporary domestic compromise was shaped whereby the liberation battalions were confined to the university campuses and kept out of the Canal Zone. As a consequence, Fuad I University resembled a guerrilla training camp during these months; meanwhile, students at Alexandria University were kept busy learning the art of using explosives.[54] To put these developments into proper context, it is necessary to remind ourselves that a pivotal definition of political sovereignty is that the state alone wields the coercive instruments of power. It was a telling sign of Egypt's ebbing political system that this was no longer the case in the first half of 1952.

Al-Hilali's lack of progress in the defence talks eventually prompted him to return his focus to tackling internal corruption. To this end, in June he introduced legislation that required all past and present ministers to declare the sources of their wealth. A rumour quickly circulated that the government was going to pursue Abboud, Egypt's wealthiest industrialist (and Sirag al-Din's ally), for unpaid taxes amounting to £E5 million. Taking the stories seriously, Abboud paid a large sum of money to two palace insiders, Elias Andraos and Kerim Thabet, to engineer the prime minister's downfall. Al-Hilali was tipped off and urged Farouk to expel the plotters from his clique. The king refused and al-Hilali resigned in protest on 28 June.

The longest cabinet crisis of Egypt's constitutional era followed, with Farouk struggling to find any reputable politicians to form an administration which many thought was already paid for in advance. It was not until 2 July that Hussein Sirri, an engineer and administrator who had been prime minister twice before (1940–2 and, briefly, 1949–50), accepted the premiership and formed a new government. Despite his being a non-partisan politician, Britain suspected Sirri's administration of being the precursor to the Wafd's return and so preparations were taken to intervene once again in Egypt's internal affairs.[55] The plan was for joint Anglo-American pressure on Farouk to banish Thabet and Andraos from the palace clique. However, the State Department refused to be involved on the grounds that the action would not only be resented, but also most probably ineffective.[56] The proposed intervention was consequently abandoned and instead Britain resorted to letting the new government 'stew in its own juices'. The Canal Zone negotiations were indefinitely put on hold.[57] On 17 July the release of Sirag al-Din from house arrest confirmed the earlier British suspicions about the character of Sirri's government.[58]

British and American officials were divided on the causes of al-Hilali's fall. The latter believed that the rigidity of London on the base dispute had made his domestic position vulnerable. On the other side, Britain blamed endemic sleaze and corruption in Egypt, and had a few choice words concerning Caffery's 'unhelpful' links with Abboud.[59] At the same time, however, there were some Foreign Office officials who shared the view that the Conservative government, and Churchill in particular, had not been doing enough to satisfy the legitimate demands of Egyptian nationalism.

The informal and candid correspondence between Roger Allen and Michael Creswell is particularly illuminating in this respect. Both were ideally positioned in 1952 to comment on the Egyptian situation, Creswell from his vantage as minister (i.e., chief political adviser to the ambassador) at the Cairo embassy, and Allen as head of the Foreign Office's African department. In late February, Allen considered the prospects for negotiations as follows: 'At the moment I can see no hope whatever of our reaching agreement with the Egyptians. We are not at present prepared to make the minimum concessions necessary to secure an agreement, and it seems impossible to make people here realise this fact and to understand the possible results of failure to reach an agreement.'[60] Three months later he had become, if anything, more pessimistic:

For my part I do not think any agreement is in sight. If African department appear to have been optimistic, it is probably because in public we shoot a line that it is Egyptian intransigence over the Sudan which is holding the whole thing up [see Chapter 6] and that therefore it is their fault that we cannot reach a settlement on defence. But in fact we realise, even if we do not feel it with quite the same intensity as you, that we have not even begun to settle the large numbers of tiresome points outstanding if agreement is to be reached on defence.[61]

Creswell shared Allen's gloom. In early March he had predicted that the effect of the next failure in the defence talks would be 'a military dictatorship rather than an immediate outbreak of revolution'.[62]

REVOLUTION IN THE AIR

Meanwhile, the mood of Egypt's king–pasha elite was remarkably complacent about the dangers of radical upheaval. This complacency stemmed from the Cold War and the effect it had generally on smaller powers caught up in the East–West struggle. Egyptian politicians were convinced that London – and Washington – would prop up their political system owing to the fear that if it collapsed, communism would be the result. This type of thinking also encouraged Egyptian intransigence in the defence negotiations, along the lines that Egypt's cooperation was so necessary to the West's defence of the Middle East that it could dictate its own terms. (Egypt's privileged position in the proposed Middle East Command was taken as further evidence of this.) It was felt, not unreasonably, that Washington's preoccupation with the spread of communism would lead the United States to insist that Britain make concessions. For his part, Farouk remained unconcerned about abusing his constitutional position. Britain had, after all, encouraged him to do precisely this on many occasions. He was therefore confident that if widespread disturbances broke out again or there was an uprising, British forces would intervene to save his throne.[63]

British policymakers were acutely appreciative of this Cold War logic on the part of the Egyptian elite, but struggled to dispel it. During al-Hilali's last weeks in office, Britain was busy conducting a covert propaganda campaign aimed at making Farouk in particular, and Egypt's moneyed classes generally, more apprehensive about the political stability of their country. A corollary of this was to make the Egyptian elite anxious over the deadlock in the talks on the future of the Canal Zone. The campaign's code name was Operation Jolt. Its central theme, propagated via inspired newspaper articles based on briefings from the Cairo embassy's information office, was that Britain would not intervene to save the existing order if revolution occurred.[64]

While the overt aim was to revive middle- and upper-class fears of another Black Saturday, it was possible (though this cannot be verified) that Britain's Secret Intelligence Service (MI6) had another end in sight. Was a signal being sent to known elements within Egypt's armed forces? The central approach of the propaganda campaign appears very telling in retrospect:

> If we have to send forces into the Delta, it will be in order to safeguard the position of our own forces in the Canal Zone and to save lives of the British community and certainly not to preserve Pashadom or the Egyptian monarchy. In the event of an internal collapse we would be willing to enter into relations with an Egyptian Gandhi or Ataturk as we should a pseudo-constitutional Prime Minister or a sociable monarch.[65]

Propagandists always assert that truth is the most powerful tool in their arsenal.

The possibility that a young Ataturk-type figure was being actively encouraged to take the stage is not so far-fetched when one considers Britain's dim view of democracy, as practised across the Middle East. The accepted wisdom among Britain's so-called Camel Corps experts by the early 1950s was that democratic practices had been prematurely grafted on to the region, the upshot being the rise of nationalism. 'The Spirit of Nationality', concluded a Foreign Office information paper circulated in March 1952, 'is a sour ferment of the new wine of Democracy in the old bottles of Tribalism.'[66] Britain's own role in first establishing these methods of rule and then corrupting them was, needless to say, left unmentioned. Roger Allen, the official directly responsible for the political aspects of the Canal Zone negotiations, minuted quite matter-of-factly in February that Egypt was 'too unstable to provide the basis upon which democracy can work'.[67]

It is thus possible to see in these views the seeds of how Britain first came to deal with the revolutionary states in the Middle East in the 1950s. The prospect of 'a man on horseback' who could push through reforms and modernisation, as well as more 'equal' defence treaties, was not an unattractive prospect, even if the reality in the end proved rather different. But Egypt's king–pasha elite was plainly not paying any attention to whatever veiled messages Britain was sending out in the summer of 1952. Indeed, they signally failed to foresee the emergence of the military as a force in Egyptian politics. In this respect, the army's entry into Cairo on Black Saturday may be seen as both a symptom of decline and a portent of revival.

British observers had long held two views of the Egyptian armed forces. The first focused on their military capabilities, which were generally considered to be poor. Typical of this thinking was Professor Bernard Lewis's contribution to a meeting of the Middle East Discussion Group at the Royal Institute of International Affairs (Chatham House) in March 1952. 'As long as Egypt remains at her present level of literacy, technical education, and broadly retaining the Middle Eastern patterns of social loyalties', he stated, 'I see no prospect at all of Egypt being able to produce any sort of army which would be effective in modern warfare, either to meet the Russians or to look after the base.'[68] (For their part many Egyptians felt that Britain, via its monopoly of arms sales, had deliberately kept the Egyptian army weak so that it would not pose a threat to the occupation forces.[69])

The second way in which British observers saw the Egyptian military focused on its domestic influence, both from the standpoint of internal security and national pride. During the previous winter's insurgency, Britain's military commanders had done their utmost to keep the Egyptian army out of the ring, realising that its prestige could make the difference between stability and revolution.[70] The manner in which the army moved to restore order on Black Saturday (when called to do so) appeared to vindicate this approach.[71] In light of subsequent events, the question as to why Chatham House was deliberating on the role of the Egyptian army in March 1952 is, of course, a fascinating one.

Opinion among British diplomats about the political importance of the Egyptian army was divided. When asked in April if the offer of arms would bring Egyptian politicians to the negotiating table, Stevenson replied that it would be pointless as the armed forces 'had little or no influence'.[72] As we have seen, his deputy, Michael Creswell, regarded the prospects of a military dictatorship as a distinct possibility. It was left to Creswell – Stevenson went on leave from 8 June – to assess the significance of Farouk's role in the fall of al-Hilali's administration: 'Perhaps never before has [Farouk] so clearly shown that where the interests of his own country and his own selfish ends conflict, he has no hesitation whatsoever in choosing the course of self-gratification.'[73] Creswell, it should be noted, was in charge of the British embassy during the momentous days of late July.

On 20 July an intelligence report reached the British mission in Alexandria (the seat of government during the summer months) stating that a number of Egyptian army officers in Cairo had refused to obey orders, and that some troops were on the move to Alexandria. Creswell took the report seriously and advised General Robertson to place the two Rodeo operations 'on very short notice': 'Some form of military rising' was 'quite possible.' Rodeo Bernard and Rodeo Flail were consequently reduced from ten days' notice to forty-eight hours.[74] The eruption in Anglo-Egyptian relations of the previous winter was about to produce its biggest aftershock.

Since forming in the wake of the Palestine defeat in 1949, the Free Officers' movement had largely contented itself with producing anonymous pamphlets which exposed Egyptian political scandals and criticised corrupt senior officers. This began to change after October 1951 with the onset of the abrogation crisis and the ensuing Canal Zone siege. While individuals within the Free Officers' movement had helped train and equip the new liberation battalions, the main effect of the guerrilla campaign was to highlight how marginalised the armed forces were becoming in Egypt's nationalist struggle. This was no doubt a factor as to why the Free Officers' society had finally decided to come out of the shadows in December 1951.

Each year commissioned ranks within the Egyptian military took part in elections for their Officers' Club. These elections were rigged in that the reigning monarch alone, as head of the armed forces, decided upon the nominations for both the board and the presidency. However, on this most recent occasion the Free Officers broke with tradition and put forward their own candidate for the presidency, General Mohammed Neguib. Neguib, one of the few war heroes among senior officers from the Palestine conflict, was not actually a member of the clandestine society. An element of separation was thus maintained for security purposes; Nasser, the leader of the secret movement, remained well hidden. Neguib's subsequent election victory at the start of 1952 was meant to send a message to Farouk to cease meddling in army appointments. 'It was a trial of strength', wrote Sadat in *Revolt on the Nile*, 'which enabled us to demonstrate publicly our opposition to the monarchy.'[75] True to form, however, Farouk ignored the warning. In the months that followed, the Free Officers responded to the advanced institutional decay around them and brought forward their preparations for a *coup d'état*.[76] The planning thus began in earnest.

In mid-July, with the domestic scene seemingly calm, Farouk ordered the commander-in-chief of the Egyptian army, General Mohammed Haydar, to abolish the elected governing board of the Officers' Club and replace it with one comprised of palace-nominated members. When Haydar did as instructed on 16 July, uproar occurred in the army. Excited barrack-room meetings took place across Egypt. In an attempt to calm the situation, Farouk offered Neguib a cabinet post as minister of war, which he declined. Riled by the rejection, Farouk stood firm by his earlier abolition order. Worried by the quarrel (the army had been the only source of authority left during the Cairo riots), Sirri stepped in and urged the palace to compromise. Again, Farouk refused to shift. The prime minister consequently felt that he had no choice other than to offer his resignation, which he did on 19 July. Thirty-six hours later, on Monday 21 July, Farouk reluctantly accepted the resignation, so bringing about a second change of government within three weeks.[77]

By this point, the Free Officers had decided on a timetable for a purge of the upper echelons of the army. On 19 July, Neguib, who was still not a member of the movement's executive committee, tipped off the dissidents that the high command had a list of their names. A day later reports came that a new war minister was going to be appointed with the brief of rooting them out. This threat to themselves forced the Free Officers into immediate action. The need to manoeuvre units into key locations meant that the actual seizure of power could not begin until the early hours of Wednesday 23rd.[78] Meanwhile, al-Hilali was tempted back as prime minister, assuming office at 4 p.m. on 22 July. It was to be the last, and shortest, government in Egypt's thirty-year constitutional experiment.

FIVE

·········

Coup d'état

Shortly before midnight on 22 July 1952, about 300 middle-ranking Egyptian army and air force officers, with about 3,000 men under their direct command, mutinied against their senior commanders. There are conflicting accounts of how the mutiny began. One version states that Colonel Gamal Abdel Nasser, the leader of the uprising, brought forward the plans by an hour so as to capitalise on a tip-off that General Haydar, the new minister of war, was holding an emergency meeting of the military high command in response to reports of unrest in the armed forces. With characteristic flair, Nasser turned the problem into an advantage: 'It will save us time and trouble,' he supposedly stated: 'We can take them all together, instead of one by one at their homes.'[1] A motorised infantry column led by Lieutenant-Colonel Youssef Seddiq was duly dispatched to arrest the senior officers en masse. However, another version of these same events is less self-serving. It contends that Seddiq's actions were in fact premature and came about because of miscommunication.[2] Thus, from the very first actions of the uprising, a blurriness surrounds proceedings.

It is worth emphasising at the start, therefore, that whenever possible this chapter relies on British and American government documents, before comparing these fixed perspectives with the accounts given in the memoirs of insiders and subsequent secondary sources. Whereas the former materials were written hastily during fast-moving events (but by participants in the power struggle nonetheless), the second types were written later, often with an eye on current political debates. The upshot of this approach should be a more reliable – and verifiable – account of one of the key events in the making of the modern Middle East, even if that reliability must at times recognise uncertainty. Coups are, after all, murky affairs.

CROSSING THE RUBICON

With the high command arrested, the mutineers proceeded to secure strategic locations throughout Cairo. A German journalist writing in 1960 evokes the drama, while also giving proceedings a (dubious) sense of inevitability: 'Riding in trucks escorted by tanks and half-tracks, steel-helmeted troops occupied the radio station, the telephone and telegraph offices, police stations and Ministries. There was no resistance. Like over-ripe plums, these key points yielded softly at the first touch.'[3] Nasser, dressed in civilian clothes, supervised the operation by driving around from unit to unit in his small black Austin car (and was temporarily arrested by Seddiq's overzealous troops).[4] At around 3 a.m., the Free Officers shifted their attention to the critical problem of Britain's effective veto power over the uprising: a defining feature of Egypt's national consciousness was the memory of Arabi's crushed uprising in 1882. A plan was already in place and this was to try and use American influence as a trump card. To this end, a Free Officers' emissary, Wing-Commander Ali Sabri, the director of intelligence of the Royal Egyptian Air Force, visited the US embassy and asked that a message be passed on to the British. This message was that any foreign intervention would be forcibly resisted by the Egyptian army; at the same time, however, reassurances were given that foreign lives would not be endangered. The coup leaders no doubt hoped that the Americans would counsel caution when passing on what was tantamount to a threat; to have gone directly to the British might have come across as inflammatory.[5] Another reason for dealing with the US embassy at this early stage was to renew contacts with a friendly official, the assistant air attaché, Lieutenant-Colonel David Evans. For several months, the Free Officers, via Sabri because of his pro-American outlook (bolstered by attendance at an intelligence officers' course at Lowry Air Force Base in Colorado the previous autumn), had reassured the American embassy that they were not a front organisation for the communists.[6] Having kept the Americans in the dark about the uprising, Nasser now wanted to get them on side as quickly as possible.

The precise nature of the connection between the Free Officers and the US government is one of the most controversial aspects of Nasser's rise to power. It is worth pausing briefly, therefore, to evaluate the debate and the nature of the evidence as it affects the Officers' seizure of power. A key text, if rather gung-ho in its tone, is Miles Copeland's *The Game of Nations* (1969), which contends that America was closely involved with the coup leaders from early

1952 and had been encouraging a military takeover in response to Egypt's endemic political instability. However, a more measured memoir by another ex-CIA operative, Wilbur Crane Eveland, published in 1980, seemingly disputed Copeland's account by asserting that the coup had 'caught the CIA completely by surprise'. Eveland added that Copeland's chief protagonist, Kim Roosevelt, had become modest about claims that he had arranged Farouk's dismissal since he had now formed business contacts with the Shah of Iran and the Saudi royal family.

But Eveland's observations themselves require closer scrutiny. Firstly, the notion that the coup came as a surprise to the CIA does not mean that US officials were unaware of the plotting or were not encouraging a takeover. Secondly, Eveland's assessment of Roosevelt's new-found modesty implies worldly pragmatism, rather than a denial of earlier association with the coup. (Roosevelt had told Eveland that 'he'd never have been able to gain the confidence of his customer monarchs if he'd really ousted Farouk'.) Thus, Copeland's assertions of pre-coup contacts, if not direct involvement, remain persuasive.[7]

We might then ask how much light declassified US records shed on this affair. According to diplomatic historian Peter Hahn (in his study, *The United States, Great Britain, and Egypt, 1945–56*), the answer is not much: 'Even if the CIA expected the Egyptian army rebellion, the State Department apparently did not, and all American officials seemed surprised by its suddenness.'[8] While a 'smoking gun' has still to be found in the archives, there is nevertheless plenty of evidence that highlights a greater US role since the tumultuous events of January 1952. The previous chapter has already shown how Secretary of State Dean Acheson was anxious to become more involved in Egyptian matters, as witnessed by the American assistance given to the formation of a motorised gendarmerie. There had also been the appointment of a new assistant secretary of state for Near Eastern affairs, Henry Byroade, in April. Aged 39, Byroade had started his career in the army where he had attained the rank of general at the remarkably young age of 33.[9] In May he visited US missions throughout the Middle East to gain first-hand experience of the local and regional situation. His return journey included a stopover in London to discuss Egypt with Britain's foreign secretary, Anthony Eden.[10]

Byroade's subsequent report suggested that Britain was in danger of extricating itself from the region 'in a rather disgraceful way'.[11] 'It is becoming more and more difficult to give support to the British in the measures they desire since we are less and less convinced of the correctness of this position', he informed Acheson in a letter dated 21 July. The time had therefore come, he concluded, 'to make greater use of our position in Egypt'.[12] Two days later, the Free Officers initiated their seizure of power. They were not the only ones crossing the Rubicon in Egyptian politics – the United States followed closely behind, in what became a thinly disguised bid to replace British influence.

Egyptian perspectives on pre-coup contacts between the Americans and the Free Officers are refreshingly straightforward in comparison. Key participants in the uprising have long acknowledged that in the months before July 1952, special efforts were made to reassure US officials that the Free Officers' movement was not pro-communist. To this end, they dropped all references to 'American imperialism' in their pamphlets.[13] There is, moreover, a certain pride in showing how Nasser handpicked pro-Western colleagues to act as liaisons with the Americans while diligently keeping leftists out of sight. This was Nasser at his pragmatic, calculating best. Another area of little contention relates to American contacts being helpful in the first hours of the uprising when the fear of British intervention was at its strongest.[14] That said, the extent to which the Free Officers *needed* Washington's pressure on Britain is clearly a sensitive topic. The preferred line still emphasises the Egyptian army's own show of military strength along all routes to the Canal Zone.[15]

When considering the role of foreign involvement in the July coup, there also remains the tantalising question of how Britain's propaganda campaign, Operation Jolt, fitted into the events. If a signal was indeed being sent to the Free Officers that Britain would not intervene to rescue the king–pasha elite should an uprising be attempted, what evidence is there in Egyptian accounts for this message actually being received? Moreover, if it was received, how did it influence decision-making during the actual seizure of power? In *Memories of a Revolution* (1992), one of the coup leaders, Khaled Mohi El Din, admits that the British 'entertained thoughts of establishing contact with the Free Officers', but somewhat frustratingly only goes on to explain the context:

The few months following the burning of Cairo – from the end of January to the beginning of July 1952 – witnessed concentrated activity on the part of the Free Officers. A large number of officers joined us in this period, and we became a very strong organisation that attracted the attention of foreign powers who were concerned with maintaining their influence in Egypt and safeguarding their interests.[16]

One might nevertheless ask how Mohi El Din could have known of British 'thoughts' unless contacts were actually made? Intriguingly, he adds that London may also have been honing in on the immediate causes of Egypt's chronic instability, namely Farouk. A leader of the Muslim Brotherhood was apparently approached by British agents during this period and asked if his organisation would assassinate the king.[17]

As for the question of how Britain's covert signals influenced decision-making during the course of the coup, one point above all needs emphasising: even with assurances of American help, the fear of British intervention remained inescapable and palpable. The reason was simple. Newly marginalised or threatened political elements in Egypt could bypass tackling the army rebels themselves by instead arranging the murder of a couple of dozen Western civilians. This could prompt, in turn, a full-scale 'rescue mission' for foreign nationals from the Canal Zone garrison and, in the process, destroy the coup at birth.

WAKING UP TO KHAKI

It was during the early hours of 23 July that the mutineers renewed their contacts with the man who was to become their public leader, General Mohammed Neguib. Since his election as president of the Officers Club in January, the relationship between Neguib and Nasser's secret movement had been cordial, though distant. Neguib had not been invited to join the Free Officers' executive committee, its decision-making body which Nasser chaired, nor was he informed of the plans for the night of 22/23 July, despite his role in tipping off the younger officers that the high command had a list of their names. Trust was not the issue; rather Neguib was a visible figure whom the authorities could monitor. But this prominence was now to be used by the mutineers to excellent effect. A grey-haired pipe-smoker, Neguib was to be cast as the avuncular commander of the uprising to reassure both Egypt and the world. This would allow the real leaders, junior officers in their mid-30s (and so liable to be perceived as hot-headed youngsters), to remain in the shadows. Nasser was only 34. While not a well-known personality, Neguib was at least a recognisable figure in political circles. His past, moreover, would be ideal for creating mass popular appeal. Apart from his war hero status (he was thrice-injured in Palestine, once gravely), he had also achieved prominence inside the Egyptian armed forces by attempting to resign his commission after the 1942 Abdin Palace humiliation (his letter, however, was rejected). To the Free Officers, 1942 and 1948 were crucial milestones on the road to their uprising.

Just before 7 a.m., Michael Creswell, the chargé at the British mission in Alexandria, wired an emergency telegram to the Foreign Office:

> I am reliably informed that the military led by a group of dissident officers took over control in Cairo during the night and that the police are obeying the orders of this group. Its members have passed a message to me through a member of the US embassy to the effect that they will offer organised resistance to any British intervention and that the movement is not concerned with any foreign issue, but solely with the suppression of corruption in the country.[18]

Things only became marginally clearer after the Egyptian Broadcasting Service's first news programme of the day, at 7.30 a.m., an hour later than usual because of a brief struggle at a transmission station. Inside the studio, the presenter was joined by Anwar Sadat and several other Free Officers. It was Sadat who read out the first news item, which was a message from the mutineers to the Egyptian nation. As instructed, the presenter did not introduce him personally and instead the statement was made in the name of General Mohammed Neguib and the 'General Command of the Armed Forces'. It reported that several senior officers had been detained during the night and that the army was 'now in the hands of men in whose ability, integrity and patriotism you can have complete confidence'. The statement also contained a plea (and warning) that 'no acts of violence or destruction be committed'. 'Such acts can only harm Egypt. They will be regarded as acts of treason and will be severely punished. The Army, in cooperation with the police, will be responsible for law and order.'[19] Sadat left the building immediately afterwards (though some officers remained encamped in the studios for the next few weeks) and so did not hear the next news item, that Farouk was due to receive al-Hilali, the newly appointed prime minister from the previous day, to discuss the formation of a cabinet.[20] The juxtaposition of the two news stories only added to the questions on people's minds.

The news of the mutiny – coup, let alone revolution, would be too strong a description at this stage – was warmly received in Cairo's streets, despite the limited information available. Calibrating popular enthusiasm, especially during the earliest stages of the uprising, is impossible in retrospect and so it is necessary to rely on sources that have proved themselves dependable. Jean and Simonne Lacouture's excellent *Egypt in Transition*, first published in Paris in 1956, fits this bill. 'The city', they write, 'had awakened in a mood of surprise and joy. It would be an understatement to say that the army's action was popular from the start: it was welcomed with relief, as though some decaying whitlow had been removed.'[21] A highly respected British journalist in Egypt, Tom Little, was equally positive: 'The mass of people, dumbly despairing of the country's condition, received the news at least with pleasure, in most cases with delight.'[22]

Given that no political aims had thus far been mentioned by Neguib's General Command, it may be surmised that the hopeful mood was very much a reaction to the failures of the parliamentary order, rather than a positive endorsement of some alternative political programme, let alone structure. It should also be pointed out that the sight of tanks and soldiers on the streets, with planes flying low overhead, would also have helped shape an outwardly positive response.[23] As for the possible wider goals of the mutineers, speculation could only have been rife. The Lacoutures suggest this with an affectionate anecdote (much-repeated in other accounts) of the steely pragmatism of Cairenes: 'The fruit juice vendors, shrewdly patriotic but with an eye to business, offered a few free drinks "In the name of the Revolution".'[24]

Later that morning, the Free Officers persuaded Ali Maher (a friend of Sadat's since they had been imprisoned together for pro-German activities during the Second World War) to return as Egypt's prime minister; al-Hilali willingly stepped aside. Maher made his acceptance conditional on Farouk's approval, which was reluctantly given. On assuming office, Maher immediately announced that parliamentary elections would soon be held and promised that martial law, which had in effect been in place since Black Saturday, would be lifted in the near future. The Free Officers then made their first direct communication with the British embassy, stating that their movement was solely concerned with the eradication of corruption.[25] The import of the day's events was thus becoming clearer: the Egyptian military's involvement in politics was to be brief and in the meantime they would act as

guardians of the constitution. In the view of Joel Gordon's meticulous study
of Egyptian internal politics at the time of the coup, this was 'hardly the
mark of a movement with a radical vision for the future'.[26] Yet such an
interpretation may well underrate the deftness with which Nasser and his co-
conspirators were shaping the political battlefield.

The choice of Maher as civilian prime minister served several functions.
The appointment of an establishment grandee reassured the pasha elite that
they were not about to be swept away. The appearance of continuity and the
rule of law, important domestically and internationally, was thus maintained.
Left-wingers around the world might grumble that it was a rightist coup – as
did eminent *Le Monde* journalist Eric Rouleau[27] – but this was the whole
point. The Americans needed to be kept on side; the British needed to be kept
still. Maher had been Egypt's leading 'court' politician under Fuad's reign and
during Farouk's early years, and so the appointment was also almost
certainly intended to reassure royal circles. All in all, this was a masterful
piece of statecraft on the part of the young officers, irrespective of whether it
was decided under the pressure of events or part of a prearranged plan. In
his 'practical handbook' on military coups, political scientist Edward Luttwak
notes that success is largely dependent on the passivity of the existing state
apparatus.[28] Maher's elevation as prime minister on the morning of the 23rd
was instrumental in bringing about such compliance from the British, the
palace, and the main political parties – in other words, from Egypt's quasi-
colonial state-executive.

As the first day of the crisis progressed, the apparent moderation of the
mutineers secured the desired 'wait and see' policy on the part of Britain.
Information was sketchy and officials thought it best to avoid the impression
of taking sides while events were still unfolding. 'We should not wish to queer
our pitch in advance', wrote Roger Allen, the Foreign Office official
responsible for Egypt, in reference to the possible emergence of a military
dictatorship. Moreover, the idea that Farouk might be reduced to a titular
monarch seemed particularly appealing in London.[29] This approach also
accorded with the main themes of the earlier propaganda campaign,
Operation Jolt. However, not all British officials were happy with the adopted
line. Creswell in Alexandria was unimpressed with the army's early signs of
moderation and warned the Foreign Office of a 'Kerensky type regime' that
would 'later be swamped by extremists'. His preferred approach was to place
the two Rodeo operations on twenty-four hours' notice, even though

implementation of these was tantamount to an act of war against the Egyptian army. He also advised that troops be moved forward to the 'Erskine Line' (delineated during the previous winter's struggle), and recommended a fleet demonstration off Alexandria. These actions, he argued, would have a steadying effect on the insurgents and deter them from a revolutionary programme. At the same time, however, he also acknowledged that the appearance of warships *à la* 1882 might actually provoke anti-British riots.[30] The Foreign Office saw his recommendations as counter-productive, because of the increased danger to civilian lives, and rejected them outright. There was also a desire to avoid any policy akin to 'back-seat driving'.[31]

Farouk, in the meantime, could hardly believe that Britain was doing nothing to help him. Operation Jolt had clearly washed past him. His efforts to enlist British intervention started half an hour after the Officers' first news broadcast when he telephoned the US ambassador to tell him that only foreign intervention could save his throne. Farouk's views were passed on to the British embassy.[32] A few hours later, Egypt's ambassador in London urged Britain to take visible preparatory measures in the Canal Zone to convey the impression that its forces were ready to move in defence of Egypt's constitutional order.[33] Maher's appointment that morning had clearly failed to assuage Farouk. When still no action was taken, Farouk telephoned Creswell directly and in a state of agitation equated Britain's inactivity to encouragement for the coup leaders, even alleging that London might be behind the plot. But by this time British officials were far more interested in reports that Egypt's front-line Sinai army had signalled its support for the mutineers.[34] With Cairo secured (as national radio broadcasts duly emphasised), other contingents of the armed forces around the country gradually declared their adhesion to the movement.

'THEY HAVE LOST THEIR KING!'

The next day's newspapers carried the first pictures (taken on the morning of the 23rd) of the self-styled General Command: tired-looking, perspiring and dressed in open-necked khaki tunics, the mutineers gathered earnestly round their 'leader', General Neguib. The notion that they were acting as watchdogs over the constitution was faithfully reflected in the accompanying coverage. *Al-Ahram* reported that the army had conducted a peaceful move aimed at protecting public services and was 'working in the interests of the country

and within the framework of the Constitution'. Commentary was provided by
the editor-in-chief who underlined the 'limited' objectives of the military and
how they were trying to reinforce democratic rule.[35] Meanwhile, news of the
coup and talk of imminent elections prompted Egypt's politicians to cut short
their summer vacations – al-Nahas and Sirag al-Din both happened to be in
Europe. Later that morning the king came under pressure from the new
regime, acting through Maher, to dismiss corrupt elements from his
entourage. Despite being convinced that the coup leaders were getting
'saucier and saucier', Farouk stubbornly refused to comply.[36] With the
possibility of British intervention hanging over them, the Free Officers
refrained from taking more drastic measures. For London, it was a deliberate
policy of keeping the mutineers guessing in order to encourage moderation.

This approach was modified, however, as a result of a historic meeting
between a British official and a representative of the mutineers at the
Abbassia barracks on the outskirts of Cairo at 10 p.m. on the 24th. With
Ambassador Stevenson on leave and Creswell in Alexandria, it fell upon John
Hamilton, one of the embassy's long-serving 'oriental' advisers, to represent
Britain. Neguib represented the Egyptian side, so maintaining the fiction of
his leadership for all official business, secret diplomacy included. It was
during this meeting that Hamilton formally told Neguib that Britain viewed
the unfolding events as an internal matter for Egypt, and that British forces
would only intervene if foreign lives were threatened.[37] 'Y' know Hamilton,'
remarked Neguib (who was born in Khartoum and educated at a British-
founded school) as he committed to paper what was being said, 'this reminds
me of taking down dictation at Gordon College.'[38]

The message amounted to a momentous shift in Britain's approach to
Egyptian affairs. As Hamilton later recounted, 'there was no mention in it of
King Farouk, or indication that we regarded Neguib and his officers as
mutineers against the lawful sovereign'. The implication of what was said did
not go unnoticed.[39] Britain had effectively given the Free Officers a green light
to depose Farouk. In 1882 Britain had occupied Egypt in order to prop up its
lawful ruler, Khedive Tawfiq (Farouk's great uncle), in the face of Colonel
Arabi's military revolt; seventy years later, Britain was all but encouraging
Arabi's successors to topple the king.[40] The Hamilton–Neguib meeting paved
the way for the Free Officers' executive committee to deliberate later that
night on whether Farouk should be tried and executed, or expelled. Nasser led
a two-thirds majority in favour of exile.[41] This subsequent Officers' meeting

features prominently in the secondary literature, which is based on the memoirs of participants, but the manner in which Britain's message at Abbassia influenced the course of events has, until now, been ignored.

British official papers also offer a new perspective on the immediate motive for the exile decision, which seems to have been taken shortly after 4 a.m. According to reports from Creswell (via Caffery), this was when Farouk, who had remained in Alexandria throughout the crisis, discovered that the royal bodyguard had declared its allegiance to the mutineers. Panic set in and he telephoned the American embassy and asked for a warship or aircraft to evacuate his family. Caffery advised him to remain calm and stay in Egypt but the king's anxiety failed to abate, and once again he urged the American ambassador to request British intervention on his behalf.

It was at this point that the Free Officers learnt of Farouk's requests for outside intervention. British diplomats suspected telephone interception as the means, but given subsequent relations between the Americans and the Free Officers, a tip-off seems more likely.[42] Even after the Abbassia meeting, the mutineers could not disregard the danger of the Canal Zone forces. (A few days later British officials were informed by the new regime that Farouk had ordered his political police to arrange the murder of some prominent Britons in order to prompt intervention.[43]) Urgency was thus added to the Free Officers' deliberations, with Nasser stating during the early hours of Friday 25 July, 'the king must be expelled today, or tomorrow at the latest'.[44] To this end, troop reinforcements were transported by train and road to Alexandria throughout the day, ready for a showdown. Meanwhile, the Egyptian population was again reminded that the army's 'clean up' programme had a limited duration: 'All those who find themselves in positions of leadership in this blessed movement', read a new public statement, 'will return to their normal posts as soon as they are satisfied that the country is in good hands.'[45]

Later that same day, the British government – and here the evidence is particularly fragmentary – may well have been sounded out about the Officers' plan to depose Farouk. *Sunday Times* journalist John Slade-Baker, who had a wealth of prominent Egyptian contacts from his years as the paper's Cairo correspondent, was approached in London by Egypt's military attaché, Lieutenant-Colonel Moghabi, and told that the officers involved in the plot were greatly concerned that Farouk would never forgive them for their actions. This nervousness about their future, Moghabi stated, had led them to

consider forcing the king to abdicate. Slade-Baker's note of this conversation –
'Coup d'état by Egyptian army' (which is deposited with his private papers at
St Antony's College, Oxford) – is, to my knowledge, the only surviving
reference to this conversation, at least in the public domain. Moreover, Slade-
Baker would appear to have been no ordinary journalist. His relationship with
the British government was particularly intimate, due perhaps to his military
background. In April 1951, for instance, when the Attlee administration was
presenting new defence proposals to Egypt, the Foreign Office had instructed
Slade-Baker to investigate the reports of a split in the Wafd government. If the
rumours were true, Britain hoped to exploit them to secure the dismissal of
Salah al-Din, the anti-British foreign minister.[46] Interestingly given
subsequent events, Slade-Baker's response to the abdication tip-off was not to
warn against getting rid of Farouk, but rather to suggest a regency council
during the minority of his son, Ahmed Fuad.[47]

At 7 a.m. on the morning of 26 July, the royal palaces of Montazah and
Ras el-Tin along Alexandria's seafront were surrounded by Egyptian troops.
A brief exchange occurred with the palace guard at Ras el-Tin where Farouk
was in residence, but before long Maher, acting on instructions from the Free
Officers, was allowed to enter. Ashen-faced, he presented the king with an
ultimatum.[48] It read:

From General Mohamed Neguib, on behalf of the officers and men of the
Army to His Majesty the King.

Whereas complete anarchy has spread lately throughout the country as
a result of your misrule and violation of the Constitution and your
disregard of the will of the people, so that no individual feels that his life,
liberty and property are safe;

Whereas you have done harm to Egypt's reputation in the eyes of the
peoples of the world by your persistence on this path, so that traitors and
bribe-takers have found protection, security, immense wealth and
shameless luxury in your shadow, at the expense of the poor and hungry
people;

Whereas a clear sign thereof was the Palestine war and the subsequent
defective arms scandals, your open interference with the course of justice,
corrupting the truth and shaking confidence in their crimes, enjoy their
wealth, and indulge further in their unlawful acts, and how could it be
otherwise, since "people follow their kings?"

Therefore the Army, representing the force of the people, has authorised me to demand that Your Majesty abdicate in favour of your son, Prince Ahmed Fuad, before twelve o'clock today, Saturday, July 26, 1952 and leave the country before six o'clock of this very day.

In case this ultimatum is not complied with, you will be responsible for all consequences.[49]

Farouk tried to look calm while reading the document, but tell-tale signs of nerves revealed his inner turmoil. The tensions eased when he realised that his life was being spared. He readily agreed to the terms and an instrument of abdication was drafted that morning by jurists. At the specific behest of the Free Officers, it included a reference to the 'will of the people'. Farouk signed the document at noon.[50]

Shortly before the 6 p.m. deadline Farouk, with Maher and Caffery as witnesses, boarded the royal yacht with his wife and children and left Egypt for the last time, bound for exile in Italy. Neguib and some younger officers belatedly arrived at the landing stage and, according to Caffery, looked disappointed at missing the event. The new rulers of Egypt nevertheless recognised the need to legitimise themselves and so press reports were inspired which spoke of a dignified affair presided over at the quayside by Neguib.[51] In the first book about the events, Dr Rashed el-Barawy's *The Military Coup in Egypt*, published in Cairo later that year, a moving but wholly fictitious occasion was described which detailed flags being lowered, 21-gun royal salutes, the playing of the national anthem and earnest farewells:

Against the advice of his friends, Lieutenant-General Neguib went on board [the royal yacht] to say goodbye to Farouk. The latter said that he hoped the army would be taken care of and Neguib retorted that the army was now in honest hands. Such was the respectful treatment offered to a man who had not during his fifteen years [as king], respected people, honour, integrity or democracy.

El-Barawy was very much an insider with the new regime. His assessment of the longer-term causes of the deposition is thus also worth quoting. Farouk, he observed, was 'paying for the recklessness of Said, the extravagance of Ismail, the appeal to the British to save Tewfik's throne, the autocracy of his father and finally his own faults and crimes'.[52]

Perhaps the most remarkable feature of the coup in retrospect was the ease with which a cabal of young, relatively inexperienced soldiers destroyed the power of the Muhammad Ali dynasty with barely a murmur of protest within Egypt, let alone the international community. 'They have lost their king!', scribbled Britain's prime minister Winston Churchill in the margin of a Foreign Office telegram reporting the news.[53]

One point linking all the versions of Farouk's final moments on Egyptian soil – apart from his wearing an admiral's uniform – is that no British representative was present at the quayside. This was to prove highly indicative of the times to come. Creswell as chargé seemed to register this slippage more acutely than any other British official (it had, after all, happened on his watch). Frustrated with London's rejection of his recommendations on the first day of the crisis, he decided to place on record his conviction that Britain had 'directly contributed' to Farouk's deposition. The policy of inaction, he told the Foreign Office on 28 July, had amounted to 'intervention by default'.[54] It was arguably Britain's last artful involvement in Egypt's internal politics. After the July coup, the United States became the main external player in Egyptian affairs, much to the frustration of British policymakers who were instead increasingly obliged to struggle with the practicalities of disengagement.

'TASTING POWER'

After Farouk's removal from power, the next big decision taken by the military regime was on 31 July when it backtracked on the earlier promises of elections and instead announced a six-month hiatus to allow for a purification of the political process. Parties were called upon to purge themselves of undesirable elements and declare publicly their hierarchies and platforms.[55] This latest action was shrewdly coupled with the formation of a regency council for the minority of Ahmed Fuad II. The inclusion of a nephew of Saad Zaghlul, the founder of the Wafd, in the three-man body was intended to appease Egypt's most powerful political party for the delay in returning to parliamentary procedures.[56] In fact, it was the feverish activity of the Wafd that had prompted this major shift. For their part, many Wafdists viewed Farouk's removal as a great triumph for themselves, and were now condescendingly seeing Neguib and his General Command as potentially docile allies after their own return to power. When a group of Officers met

Sirag al-Din, they came away feeling that the ex-minister was barely taking them seriously. Salah al-Din was more respectful but no less ambitious: his approach entailed trying to form a 'young Wafd' party with a view to acting as the political wing of the army movement.[57]

Having advised Maher, on 24 July, to put off 'premature' elections and concentrate instead on getting Egypt 'back on an even keel', Britain was pleased with these developments. The last thing that London wanted at this moment was the disgraced Wafd returned to office, as always happened when free elections were held. In the weeks after the coup, Britain thus pursued a policy of giving Maher 'every encouragement' to keep the military under control while he sought to bring much-needed stability to Egyptian politics.[58] To this end, British diplomats dealt only with the prime minister and avoided direct contacts with the military high committee. Neguib was viewed as moderate, but little was known about most of the younger officers behind him. Meanwhile, Maher tried to give the impression that he was in charge. Two weeks into office, he was confidently telling the British embassy that within a year he could dispense altogether with army support.[59] However, by mid-August, Britain's ambassador, Ralph Stevenson, having returned to Egypt after the coup, realised that Maher was in fact little more than a 'political instrument' of the junta.[60] In seeking to bolster Maher over the military, London had backed the wrong horse.

While Britain clung to the last vestiges of Egypt's collaborative pasha class, the United States was busy cultivating a wide range of contacts with the new regime. The pronounced formality of the American embassy in Cairo (even by the standards of the diplomatic profession) proved beneficial in this respect. Ambassador Caffery was the US's most experienced diplomat in the early 1950s. The son of a prominent Louisianan lawyer and mayor of Lafayette, he had himself briefly practised law before joining the newly established career diplomatic service in 1911. By the time he reached Cairo in 1949 (after five years as ambassador in Paris) he had headed missions for over twenty years. Caffery's posting to Egypt was thus a mark of the region's growing Cold War importance to America. While his personal reputation was for being starchy and self-important, his professional standing was such that when he reached the normal retirement age of 65 in December 1951, he was asked to stay on in Cairo.[61]

Before the July coup, Caffery had chafed under the constraints of bolstering British interests in Egypt; afterwards he clearly relished the prospect of building up America's position, while always making sure that precise diplomatic etiquette was maintained.[62] It was a matter of great principle for him to deal only with the head of state or representatives with sufficient status. This therefore entailed formal transactions with Neguib and Maher, but not the younger officers, so leaving the ground clear for other embassy officials to cultivate relations with the real leaders of the military regime.

It was William Lakeland, the embassy's political officer (with the grade 'second secretary', a relatively junior appointment), who came to develop the closest relations with the junta, owing to a friendship he formed with the similarly-aged Nasser. While Caffery conducted business with Neguib, Nasser and Lakeland began visiting each other's apartments for lengthy late-night chats about policy and strategy. Despite his highly significant role, Lakeland barely gets a mention in accounts of American foreign policy towards Egypt in the 1950s. Even in a book specifically about American Arabists, Lakeland receives only the blandest of assessments, with a colleague remembering him as 'very much a supporter of Arab nationalism, Nasser, and Sunni majority rule'.[63] In an exception to this rule, Jon Alterman's *Egypt and American Foreign Assistance 1952–1956* offers a glimpse of Lakeland 'spending evenings watching Esther Williams films with Gamal Abdel Nasser in the embassy canteen and enjoying dinner parties at the officers' houses'.[64]

But lest this still rather anodyne impression remain, it might be salutary to move ahead and quote a senior State Department official in early 1954: Parker T. Hart felt that Lakeland had become 'a very thin line' to the 'small gang' around Nasser. There was, he added, 'something nineteenth century or even eighteenth century about this kind of diplomatic contact'; it was 'not the stuff out of which modern international relations are made'.[65] Given this rather sour assessment by a visiting diplomat, it may be that Lakeland was actually a CIA officer working under embassy cover. According to Copeland's *Game of Nations*, the 'autocratic and aloof' Caffery valued only two of his officials – while holding most of the others in contempt – and those two were David Evans and William Lakeland.[66] While Copeland is undoubtedly guilty of inflating the role of the CIA in the 'Egyptian revolution', the connections developed by Evans and Lakeland do at least support the claims that America attained a significant stake in Egypt's new era. One measure of Lakeland's role may be the hostility soon felt towards him by embittered British officials in Egypt, frustrated that their own influence was being replaced.[67]

A critical moment in cementing the US–Free Officers connection was a workers' strike at Kafr el Dawwar, a textile-producing town 19 miles from Alexandria, on 12 August. Although the industrial action was prompted by hopes raised by the July coup, the labour grievances were far from new. At about 7 p.m. on the 12th, workers from the Misr Fine Spinning and Weaving Company assembled in front of the plant (which employed about 10,000) and demanded redress of their grievances 'in the name of Muhammad Neguib and the revolution'. The board refused outright and called upon the police to disperse the crowd. The fracas that ensued left many wounded on both sides and one worker dead. Two office buildings were also set on fire. During the early hours of the next morning, 500 troops arrived and surrounded the factory with the strikers still inside. The ringleaders were rounded up and arrested. On 14 August a military tribunal was hastily convened under the direction of Lieutenant Colonel Abdel Moncim Amin of the military high committee. On the 18th, two strikers were found guilty of 'a grave crime against the state' and hanged in the factory grounds. Fourteen others were given sentences of hard labour.[68] The message to the Egyptian population was unequivocal: nothing could threaten the stability of the new regime. The signal to the Americans was equally clear: the Free Officers would have no truck with communist agitation, whatever the guise.

Amin subsequently acquired a reputation as 'America's man' in the military regime.[69] A secret briefing document produced by the US embassy in Cairo in October 1952 provides a window into the manner in which American officials came to know the new rulers of Egypt, and also illustrates the skilled pragmatism of Nasser's leadership in promoting a positive perception of the regime. Amin, the entry reads, is 'a suave good-looking man in his forties' with 'an erect military bearing' and 'deliberate manner'; he 'speaks excellent English and is quite Westernized and moderate in his views'. It continues:

Within the group of officers who organized the military coup d'etat and who have subsequently surrounded Major General Neguib, Amin is one of the strongest and most responsible members. His office is now located next door to that of Neguib and recently he has, on several occasions, acted as the mouthpiece for the High Committee at important meetings. His voice is listened to by all concerned and he is usually saying what, from the Western point of view, would be considered the right things. He has acquired most of his influence since the coup d'etat as he was not even a member of the High Committee before July 23. As one of the most influential men in Egypt today, he may be counted on to use that influence constructively.

In the same document, Amin's wife was also accorded attention for being 'a cosmopolitan, intelligent, attractive and wealthy woman':

As a couple, the Amins are friendly and socially active. They are the only members of the inner circle of the new regime who are also at home with the luxuries of life, club memberships, and European holidays normally associated with their predecessors as Egypt's rulers. They have a delightful apartment overlooking the Nile in which they have dinners and receptions at which they introduce the rulers of new Egypt to leading personalities whom they have not met. These were, in fact, the circumstances under which Major General Neguib and the American Ambassador had their first long talk after the coup d'etat.[70]

It should be noted that by 1953 Amin had served his purpose of reassuring the Americans and so was dispensed with from the junta; he subsequently served as ambassador to Bonn between 1954 and 1956, before leaving public life altogether for a business career.

The US assessment of Nasser in the same biographical briefing paper was more circumspect: 'Abd Al-Nasir is a rather quiet, slow spoken, and reserved individual whose appearance and manner somewhat belie the qualities of personal dynamism and shrewdness which he possesses. His natural reserve together with a somewhat limited command of English, make him less "approachable" than some of the other members of the High Committee.' Lakeland's influence nevertheless comes through in the sketch, even if Neguib was still being perceived as the real leader of the junta a full two months after the coup:[71]

Lt. Col. Abd Al-Nasir has revealed a sense of deep personal attachment not only to his military comrades, but to the men of the Egyptian Armed Forces. He is imbued with the desire to give to the 'little people of Egypt' a stake in the country's future and instill [sic] in them a real sense of national consciousness. He was an instructor at the General Staff College

[and] has many of his former students among the younger officers of the Army. He is believed to be widely loved and respected throughout the military service and next to General Neguib himself, may well be the strongest man in Egypt at present.[72]

It almost goes without saying that there were no British guests at the Amin dinners, and the knowledge that US officials were gradually acquiring on the inner workings of the military regime was certainly not passed on to their main NATO ally: the Anglo-American 'special relationship' was decidedly lacking in regard to Egyptian matters. Nasser was as much an enigma to the British at this point as he was to the Egyptian public. If he was known at all to the latter, it was for going 'about furtively with bent head, shut lips and lowered eyes in the wake of the popular general'.[73]

Apart from bolstering the American connection (because of its anti-leftist character), the suppression of the Kafr el Dawwar strike was also significant for providing an early indication of how Nasser would respond to the pressures and demands from within the Free Officers' movement. Since its inception, the movement had been akin to an umbrella organisation inside the armed forces: all opposition elements could join it, provided that any other ties came second to those of the secret society. 'I don't accept communists,' Nasser reportedly said, 'I accept officers. If they want to join us as officers, alright.'[74] Within the military high committee there thus existed both communists and members of the Muslim Brotherhood. The ability of the movement to accommodate both the hard left and the conservative right had been in large part due to the deliberate policy of keeping its political goals vague before the coup.

In June 1953 Nasser told the *Al-Ahram* newspaper that he and the other leading officers had been anxious to avoid a split in the army movement: 'The political ideas of the Free Officers differed according to their temperaments and the family or social milieu from which they came . . . What we all wanted was to purge the army, rid the country of foreign occupation and establish a clean, fair government which would work sincerely for the good of the people.' The downside of this approach was that on seizing power there was a distinct lack of precision concerning most of the regime's social and economic goals. As Nasser himself admitted, 'it was necessary to improvise'.[75]

The manner – and context – of this improvisation requires highlighting. 'Disease, sickness and early death characterised the existence of almost all who inhabited the Nile valley,' observed Patrick O'Brien in his influential economic study of the Nasserite revolution; 'life expectancy for an Egyptian male at birth was only 36 years while an American could expect to live 69 years'.[76] If most of Egypt's immense problems were perhaps hazy in Nasser's mind, there was one thing about which he was always certain: that lasting political stability in Egypt would be impossible until all British troops had left. Consolidating power and expelling the British from the Canal Zone were thus part and parcel of the same process. In the meantime, the regime's embryonic social and economic programmes remained largely confined to lofty talk of 'ending feudalism'.

As a consequence, a mixture of heady nationalism and pragmatic responses to immediate concerns (usually to do with ensuring the survival of the regime) characterised meetings of Nasser and his co-conspirators. Thus, while Maher was outwardly serving as prime minister by day, backed by the genial presence of Neguib, the real power-brokers, the military high committee, met surreptitiously at night, often at Farouk's old yacht house on an island in the Nile, to plot their next moves. Sticky nights, smoky rooms and heated debates ended by majority vote – such was the executive of the new regime. The incongruence of Neguib's role was only addressed in mid-August by his being invited into the junta's inner circle, so bringing the total to fourteen officers.[77]

The junta's response to Kafr el Dawwar was thus all about political survival, but it placed enormous strains on relations with communists inside the Blessed Movement. Like the Muslim Brotherhood, the Democratic Movement for National Liberation (Egypt's largest communist faction) regarded the coup as very much a collaborative effort. While the support tasks allotted to both organisations before the uprising had actually proved largely superfluous, this did not stop either of them from expecting a prominent role in the regime.[78] Kafr el Dawwar came as a rude wake-up call to Egypt's communists, although a split did not as yet occur. A key reason for this was the regime's new focus on land reform.

'DOWN WITH THE PASHAS, AND UP WITH THE FELLAHEEN!'

In the fortnight after Kafr el Dawwar, British policymakers came to realise their mistake in not developing contacts with the Officers. 'These people are tasting power and popularity together and there is evidence that they like it', minuted one official a month after the coup.[79] Maher's real position was increasingly revealed by the junta's desire to push ahead with land reform, the main purpose of which was to undercut the political influence of the pashas. The slogans of the time may have called Egypt's agricultural structure 'feudal', but in truth it was more akin to land-capitalism. A feudal lord lives on the land and exploits it directly, governing and possessing both the land and the people on it. This was not the case in Egypt. Instead, the landowners typically lived in the cities off the income generated by their land.[80] Wealthy absentee landowners were the mainstay of Egypt's political elite, primarily because the *fellaheen* voted for who they were told to vote for. (It was the Wafd's organisational reach throughout the Nile Valley – it alone filed candidates for all constituencies – that guaranteed it electoral victories.) Meanwhile, the lifeblood of deputies and senators was patronage. To gain power within the political process, it was necessary to enlist as a supporter of a leading personality and when eventually in office to reward, in turn, one's own followers.[81] In seeking to break these old political networks, the junta's land reform proposals also constituted the first efforts at establishing a direct connection between the regime and the masses. Consolidation of power and 'revolution' went hand in hand.

The architects of the junta's reforms (which entailed limiting land holdings to 200 *feddans*, or roughly 200 acres, with an additional 100 *feddans* permissible if the family had two or more children) were el-Barawy, author of the first inside account of the coup, and military high committee member Ahmad Fuad. The Americans also attempted to get on board since land reform was one of their favoured methods for tackling the roots of communism globally. An expert from the US Technical Cooperation Administration was quickly dispatched to Egypt in the weeks after the coup, but his efforts were roundly rebuffed. The new regime saw land reform as a defining policy and did not want American fingerprints on the project.[82] For the first time in weeks, British officials could allow themselves a little smugness. Assessing el-Barawy's supposed Marxist views (he had been educated at the University of London where he was influenced by LSE professor and radical socialist Harold Laski), Roger Allen minuted, 'Senator McCarthy would have no doubts about him!'[83]

Like the Americans, Britain was pleased to see the new regime trying to tackle Egypt's rural problems, although the marginalisation of Maher remained a major worry.[84] A large landowner himself, Maher had been pressing for an upper ceiling of 500 *feddans*. His argument was that smaller holdings would result in a sharp decline of productivity and economic chaos. But even Winston Churchill was enthused by talk of breaking up the large holdings. In a letter to Foreign Secretary Anthony Eden, dated 26 August, he wrote: 'It is most important that we should not appear to be defending the landlords and pashas against long overdue reforms for the fellaheen.' He concluded: 'There might well be a policy, in which the US would join, of making a success of Neguib.'[85] But the Americans were far ahead of Churchill in this respect and they were not about to slow down to invite the British on board. Indeed, Caffery around this time was suspected by British diplomats of advising the coup leaders to keep them at arm's length, an allegation he reported back to Washington, probably to cover himself in case formal British complaints were made.[86]

By the start of September, Caffery was keen that his embassy's close relations with the military high committee be reflected officially back in Washington. Consequently, on 3 September, Dean Acheson issued a statement which praised recent developments in Egypt. British officials were incensed for not being consulted beforehand. They also feared that the junta would interpret the gesture as a blank cheque to adopt radical policies.[87] Sure enough, on the night of 5 September, sixty leading politicians and palace favourites were arrested. This was followed the next day by the dismissal of Maher as prime minister. 'Down with the Pashas, and up with the Fellaheen!', minuted Churchill, forgetting perhaps that British influence was entangled with the former.[88] Most of the politicians with whom Britain's embassy had dealt since 23 July were now under arrest. The agricultural reform law was promulgated on 7 September and Neguib became prime minister on the 8th.

When President Truman voiced concerns that Egypt was proceeding down the road to dictatorship, Acheson responded by asserting that recent events 'were a healthy sign of a desire of the military group to get on with land and other reforms'.[89] He did not trouble his chief with details of how the junta's first choice for prime minister, State Council president Abd al-Razzaq al-Sanhuri, had effectively been vetoed by Caffery (al-Sanhuri's involvement with the international peace movement made him suspect), nor of Caffery's similar blackballing of el-Barawy ('a commie') for a cabinet appointment.[90] The United States had indeed replaced Britain as the backstairs power in Egyptian political life.

Maher's dismissal prompted a heated debate among British and American policymakers over the relative merits of their post-coup policies. The US method for discouraging extremism and promoting stability had focused on establishing close and friendly relations with the junta; Britain, on the other hand, had followed a more reserved line, centring on support for Maher while never completely abandoning the threat of intervention as a deterrent.[91] In London's opinion, the contradictory character of these policies was brought to the fore by Acheson's statement on 3 September. By effectively removing the junta's fear of military intervention, it snapped the main prop of Britain's approach (which Caffery had condemned as 'medieval').[92] The Foreign Office looked for a scapegoat and found one: 'Caffery could not be worse', fumed Eden on 9 September.[93]

But the roots of Britain's problems went far deeper than these personality and policy clashes. The new character of Anglo-Egyptian relations was shaped by the particular mindset of the military regime, which had been forged by decades of accumulated nationalist grievances. Sadat especially was known for his uncompromising views. 'I have spent a total of seven years of my adult life in British concentration camps,' he told an American official over lunch, 'much of the time just because I was suspected of engaging in activities against the British. Under these circumstances I think you must admit that it is not surprising that I am not fond of your British cousins.'[94] Britain's overt policy of assisting the civilian elements of the post-coup government served only to heighten distrust.[95] While Caffery and his staff seemingly did nothing to discourage these views (and most probably manipulated them to their own advantage), a basic truth, which Stevenson aptly encapsulated, could not be escaped: to the young officers, British forces in the Canal Zone were 'as much an anachronism as the presence of a despotic king or parasitic pashas'.[96] No amount of diplomatic support from the Americans would have altered this belief.

SIX

• • • • • •

The Sudan Complication

In the autumn of 1952, the de facto ceasefire that had been in play since Black Saturday continued to shape Anglo-Egyptian relations over the future of the Canal Zone. Nevertheless, Egypt's new rulers wanted to rid their country of the British 'occupation'. Unlike in the past, however, this attitude was visceral and not merely linked to calculations of political survival. Equally committed, the Churchill-led Conservative government continued to see the British garrison astride the Suez Canal as absolutely vital to Britain's standing as a world military and imperial power. The prevailing attitude was that if Egypt was lost, other territories in Africa (the hub of the post-India empire) and the Middle East (the gateway to Africa and crucial in its own right because of oil) would quickly go the same way. In short, Egypt was regarded as a test case for Britain's continuing globalist ambitions.

With the stakes so high, it was little wonder that there was no desire on either side to resume the defence negotiations, which had been an intermittent and injurious feature of relations since 1946. Instead, Egypt's military junta stressed that internal politics remained their utmost priority, claims that had been underscored when Neguib ousted Ali Maher as prime minister in early September. But while British policymakers were similarly keen to avoid bilateral defence talks that autumn, they did have another pressing concern. This concern, moreover, had an unswerving habit of exacerbating the Canal Zone dispute. The issue in question was the future of the Sudan and, in particular, how it should be governed.

THE IMPERIAL AMBITIONS OF THE COLONISED

Egypt, Britain and, not least, the Sudanese themselves all wanted to determine this process. To the Egyptians, the Sudan was their vast southern neighbour which shared a preoccupation with the Nile waters. Indeed, Egypt's interest in *Bilad al-Sudan* (the land of black people) flowed from centuries of trade along the Nile artery, with merchants from the north settling as they went, taking with them the Arabic language and the Muslim religion. These cultural and ethnic affinities were bolstered by Ottoman subjugation under Muhammad Ali in 1820–1, which established a dynastic claim to the 'Unity of the Nile Valley' – the union of Egypt and the Sudan.

But the Sudan had broken free of Egypt following a religious-inspired revolt led by Mohamed Ahmed al-Mahdi (the 'rightly-guided one') in 1881. It was around this time that the British also began to take an interest in the Sudan, although not active enough for General Charles Gordon, who was famously killed by Mahdist forces in Khartoum in 1885. Towards the end of the nineteenth century, as rival European powers increasingly eyed the independent Mahdi state, Britain decided that a 'reconquest' was necessary, so termed because it was completed in 1898 under Egypt's name (thus reflecting the nature of Britain's 'veiled protectorate'). The upshot, however, was not the reinstitution of khedival control, but rather a mechanism of joint rule – the Sudan condominium (as established by an Anglo-Egyptian agreement signed in 1899).[1] A peculiar situation thus arose in which the colonising British worked with the colonised Egyptians to administer a third country.

In practice, however, joint rule was largely a fiction in that British officials routinely held all the key administrative posts, and the pretence was almost dropped altogether after Sir Lee Stack, Britain's most senior official in the Sudan, was murdered by Egyptian nationalists in 1924. By the early 1950s, the co-domini were partners in name only. The Sudan was effectively a British colonial possession; and here was the rub for the Sudanese who, like their counterparts elsewhere in the 'Third World', were increasingly motivated by the principle of self-determination.

Although there was a geographical logic to the Sudan in that it occupied a large part of the Nile basin, its political and cultural rationale was much less persuasive. The greatest divide, which occurred out of both accident and design, was a north–south split. It was an accident in that natural forces accounted for the White Nile merging with the Blue Nile at Khartoum to become the great Nile river. Proximity to these waterways brought trade and irrigation possibilities; distance from them usually brought hardship. The result across the Sudan was extremely uneven development.[2]

These accidents of nature were also exacerbated by Britain's policy of actively preventing political and economic integration. This approach ostensibly came out of a desire to 'protect' the impoverished Christian and pagan southerners from the more sophisticated, Arabicised and Muslim northerners. But there was also a self-serving motive in British policy. Looking after the underdeveloped southerners meant prolonging the imperial mission. These north–south divisions were the main arena for a long-standing Anglo-Egyptian struggle for supremacy in the Sudan which, after the Second World War, routinely exacerbated the Suez base dispute, and vice versa.

In the autumn of 1952, the Sudan–Suez connection, hitherto an aggravating sideshow in the Battle of the Canal Zone, shifted unceremoniously to centre-stage. The cause was an apparent U-turn in Egypt's traditional policy of 'Unity of the Nile Valley'. While Egypt's fledgling military regime would have preferred to concentrate on consolidating its power, it felt bound to maintain age-old interests in the Nile lifeline. In Britain, the Sudan became a highly contentious matter within the Conservative Party, during which the well-being of the Sudanese was only a small part of the picture. In fact, the main preoccupation was with what political developments in the Sudan revealed about the future direction of relations with Egypt. If hanging on to the Suez bastion was viewed by imperial diehards as the test case of empire, then maintaining the British position in the Sudan was, in turn, the test case of Britain's policy towards Egypt. Meanwhile, the quarrel over the Canal Zone, with America's role therein, provided the Sudanese with unique opportunities to play the condominium powers off against one another as they sought to free themselves from colonial rule.

A DIPLOMATIC REVOLUTION

On 24 September 1952, just over a fortnight since Egypt's military junta had dropped the pretence of civilian rule, Britain reintroduced the question of the Sudan's future into Anglo-Egyptian relations. It did so because of a timetable established during the previous winter's crisis – yet another legacy of the Canal Zone siege. The Wafd government's attempted nullification of the defence treaty of 1936 had been coupled with the abrogation of the Sudan condominium agreement of 1899. While the legislation had no direct impact on the essentially British administration, it did succeed in stirring up the

Sudanese political classes, and this was sufficient to prompt Britain, a month later, to declare that it would seek to implement constitutional reform in the Sudan by the end of the following year. It needs to be stressed, however, that Britain's idea of constitutional advancement still included a significant role for itself. Complete independence, which would have set a bad example for colonies elsewhere, was not the goal.

To this end, in May 1952 Governor-General Sir Robert Howe, who headed the British-run Sudan government, sent the co-domini a draft constitution for approval. Egypt's receipt of the draft was in line with London's policy of treating the abrogation action as unlawful owing to its unilateral nature. In an accompanying note, Howe stipulated that the constitution would be promulgated after six months if neither side expressed disapproval in the meantime.[3] Discussion of these measures was cut short, however, by al-Hilali's fall as prime minister in June 1952, and then further delayed by the Free Officers' coup. The military high committee subsequently insisted that their utmost priority was domestic reform, and the British accepted this as a necessity after the earlier procession of unstable palace-appointed governments.[4] Following Ali Maher's removal from office, however, Britain had less inclination to play along with the junta's political needs and, in any case, the Sudan was an issue that required immediate attention.

The timing was extremely awkward for the military regime. Its focus was squarely on the feverish activity of Egypt's political parties – the arrests and imprisonment of sixty leading politicians having taken place less than three weeks earlier. Even more importantly, the regime had also announced on 9 September a party reorganisation law compelling all parties to purify themselves by 7 October. Any party not complying with the new law (which stated that they must exclude any members who had corruption charges against them) would have their assets confiscated and donated to charity. In one of his secret tête-à-têtes, Nasser admitted to Lakeland that through these actions the junta was setting its sights on the opulent Wafd, and in particular its most powerful leader, Fuad Sirag al-Din, whom he described as 'a brilliant and dangerous politician'.[5] The former minister (one of the people arrested) was widely viewed as heir to the Wafd leadership should the septuagenarian al-Nahas resign. Once again, Nasser's tactical acumen was evident in his tackling the Wafd without a frontal assault and separating al-Nahas from his chief aide.

Thus, just as Britain was introducing the Sudan issue into proceedings, the coup leaders were preoccupied with taking on the greatest indigenous force in

Egyptian politics in the post-First World War era. Tackling the monarchy, the other pole of power, had proved easy: dissolute, reckless and fatalistic, Farouk was a pushover. Few grieved his deposition, let alone sought to prevent it. But the Wafd was different. For thirty years, it had presented itself as Egypt's only truly patriotic movement. Millions of Egyptians had listened and followed. Would the masses be ready to give up completely on the Wafd's leadership of the national struggle?

For Nasser, the aim was to focus power in a single group – his military regime. The British would consequently have no Egyptian elements to manipulate. The junta could then try to make the cost of Britain standing on its 1936 rights too high to sustain in terms of money, men and prestige. Moreover, Nasser well understood the dynamics of the struggle. Ending the occupation had become the key to political survival for any person, party or movement ambitious enough to hold power in Egypt. But by the same token, the British question was the main battleground for all rival political factions in their attempts either to acquire or regain power. This was the high-stakes Egyptian context for Sudanese constitutional reform.

The Americans were, of course, keen for the military regime to survive and prosper. In what was probably a State Department-inspired 'information' campaign, a spate of magazine articles appeared in the US during the autumn of 1952 which presented the July coup as Egypt's long-overdue 'bourgeois revolution'. Neguib was held up as 'a paragon of middle-class virtues' quite unlike the 'slothful, greedy and capricious' Farouk.[6] All this was well and good for Nasser, but there were also pitfalls. On the one hand, with 80,000 British troops stationed in the Canal Zone, he still needed Washington's help; on the other, the prevalence of rumours concerning US involvement in the coup was a serious problem – enough to prompt el-Barawy's first insider account, published that autumn, to dispute the stories head-on.[7] As for the Sudan complication, Washington had always pressed hard for a resolution of the Anglo-Egyptian rivalries so that their bigger concern of securing Egypt's allegiance in the Cold War could be achieved. In the context of late 1952, this entailed encouraging Egyptian involvement in the Sudanese constitutional reform process.

When Britain's ambassador met with Neguib on 24 September, there was, as always, a condition attached to Egypt's possible involvement in the new Sudanese constitution: Egypt must first acknowledge the Sudan's right to self-determination and self-government.[8] Because of popular sentiment surrounding the slogan 'Unity of the Nile Valley', this commitment had never before been given. It was consequently noted with much interest by the Americans (who were in close touch with both the British and the Egyptians on this issue) that during the meeting, Neguib made no mention of Egypt's long-standing dynastic links to the Sudan.[9] Might this stumbling block have finally disappeared along with Farouk? Neguib promised Stevenson a response in a week's time.[10] In fact, the junta's reply was not forthcoming until 2 November, a mere six days before the promulgation deadline of Howe's draft constitution.

During the intervening weeks, Egypt's military regime conducted offensives on two critical fronts. The first was domestic. In late September, Neguib undertook a three-day whistle-stop tour of the Nile Delta, the heartland of the Wafd. He was greeted by genuinely enthusiastic crowds along the way. 'The army is the nation and every Egyptian a soldier,' he repeated in his brief speeches.[11] Uncomplicated in his self-confidence and with a tendency to laugh heartily, this pipe-puffing, plain-speaking soldier possessed an obvious appeal. The timing of Neguib's tour made it something akin to a campaign trail ahead of the 7 October deadline for the submissions required under the party purification law.

Meanwhile, the Wafd had been wavering as to how best to respond to what was clearly designed to be a public humiliation. Although al-Nahas argued against appeasing the military regime while Sirag al-Din remained incarcerated, middle-ranking Wafdists, who had always resented the rapid rise of the former interior minister, were more willing to cooperate. When the junta stepped up the pressure by adding al-Nahas to their blacklist of politicians ineligible for party membership, his instinct, as a veteran of '1919', was for defiance. 'I remain in the hands of a faithful people, who alone are qualified to decide what has to be done with me,' he told the Wafdist daily El Misr, the circulation of which had been falling in recent weeks.[12] In the event, the Wafd's 'purification' submission attempted a compromise by showing al-Nahas to have resigned the party leadership, while being retained as 'honorary president'. The junta's response to all the submissions came in early November. Seven out of fifteen parties received certification (and thus remained legal), including a Wafdist bloc, but al-Nahas's new status was firmly rejected.[13] The al-Nahas–Sirag al-Din axis, the apex of power in the old parliamentary establishment, had thus been fractured.

The second offensive conducted by the junta entailed direct consultations in Cairo with representatives of the Sudanese political parties. Neguib was once again to the fore, the junta capitalising on his Sudanese mother, whom his father had married when posted as a soldier to Khartoum. A series of accords was signed in late October and early November by which Egypt finally accepted the principle of Sudanese self-determination, albeit only after a period of self-government during which the question of sovereignty would be deferred, the suggestion being that the Sudanese, when governing themselves, might eventually opt for union with Egypt. Other features included making the governor-general's powers subject to an international commission (thus emasculating this key administrative post, which had always been held by British officials), and 'Sudanisation' of all government posts to be completed within three years (which entailed removing all the other British administrators).[14]

With these agreements slotting into place, Neguib was finally able to respond to Britain's earlier démarche, only now it was from a position of strength. In contravention of all previous Egyptian policy, on 2 November the military regime accepted the basic tenets of Britain's position concerning the Sudan's fundamental rights to self-government and self-determination. The time-honoured policy of 'Unity of the Nile Valley' was thus abandoned, or so it seemed.[15] The 'revolution in the Egyptian attitude', as the head of the Sudan desk in the Foreign Office called Neguib's reply, meant that Egypt could henceforth assist the British in preparing the Sudanese for self-government.[16]

THE PAST AS PROLOGUE

The significance of Egypt's apparent U-turn is best gauged by comparison with the deadlock that ensued before it. Since the end of the Second World War, all previous attempts to negotiate a new Suez base agreement had been adversely affected or even blocked by what Ernest Bevin called the 'stone wall' of the Sudan.[17] The apparently intractable nature of the problem centred on widely differing British and Egyptian interpretations of Sudanese sovereignty.

It was possible to make three plausible legal arguments. Each started from the position that before the Mahdist revolt, the khedive of Egypt possessed the Sudan as part of the Ottoman sultan's jurisdiction. Case one held that Egyptian and Ottoman claims had been lost with the Mahdist revolt, and that because the Sudan was reconquered by both British and Egyptian forces,

'Jugular vein of empire.' The Suez Canal, early 1950s. *(Getty Images)*

Guarding the Canal. A British presence at Suez, 1951. *(Getty Images)*

Empire by treaty. British foreign secretary Anthony Eden (seated, right) watches as Egyptian prime minister Mustafa al-Nahas signs the defence treaty of 1936. *(Time Life Pictures/Getty Images)*

The Lampson legacy. Sir Miles Lampson (seated, right) oversees Egyptian affairs, *c.* 1938. A young Evelyn Shuckburgh (middle) looks to the future. *(Getty Images)*

A barbed-wire base. British installations on the outskirts of Ismailia. *(Time Life Pictures/Getty Images)*

Below, left: An Egyptian worker in the British engine shop at Tel el Kebir. *(Time Life Pictures/Getty Images) Right:* Friend or foe? Al-Nahas, c. 1938. In October 1951 his Wafd administration abrogated the Anglo-Egyptian defence treaty of 1936 and the Sudan condominium agreement of 1899. *(Getty Images)*

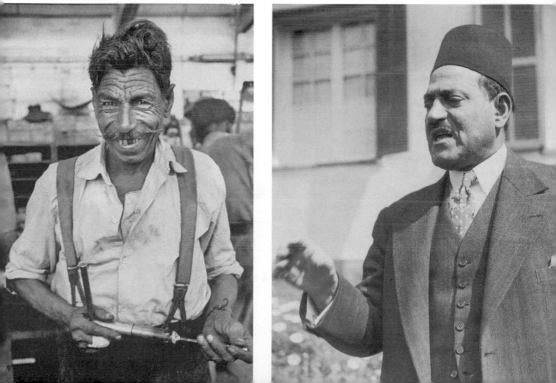

Above: living quarters for many British soldiers in the Canal Zone. *Below*: a place to have a pre-prandial drink for others – the terrace of the United Services Club, Fayid. *(Time Life Pictures/Getty Images)*

The sun sets on the Canal Zone. Tented accommodation may have been primitive, but it did at least afford greater security than the housing in Canal Zone towns. *(Time Life Pictures/Getty Images)*

An anti-British rally in Cairo, October 1951. The army Jeep suggests the involvement of the Egyptian government. *(Corbis)*

A sovereign country?
British soldiers search
an Egyptian train . . .
(IWM HV 71131)

set up road blocks . . . *(Getty Images)*

and stalk through villages, October and November
1951. *(Time Life Pictures/Getty Images)*

Above, left: Egyptians respond by decamping from Ismailia and ceasing to work for the British military. *(Time Life Pictures/Getty Images) Right:* An end to talking. Egyptian civilians plan an armed struggle. *(IWM HV 71084)*

A senior British officer contemplates the price Egyptian fedayeen have placed on his head. *(IWM HV 71081)*

Preparing to disarm Ismailia's auxiliary police. An outer cordon is established, January 1952. *(IWM HV 71076)*

'A sharp encounter.' Over five hours of battle ensued at Ismailia's Bureau Sanitaire, January 1952. *(IWM HV 71072)*

An honourable surrender. British perceptions of the fighting qualities of Egyptians are transformed by the 'Battle of Ismailia'. *(IWM HV 71105)*

The Egyptian wounded are carried out. *(IWM HV 71106)*

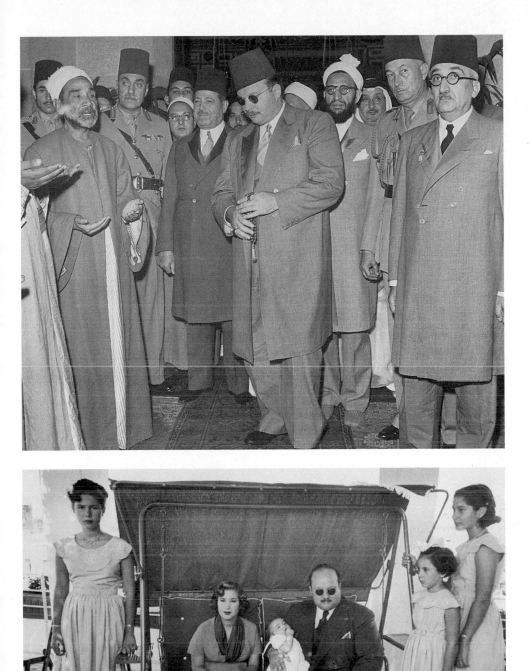

'The most effective baby-kissing politician in Egyptian history.' General Neguib smiles for the cameras; Colonel Nasser bides his time, 1953. *(Getty Images)*

Birth of a republic. Neguib takes the acclaim in celebrations to mark Egypt becoming a republic, June 1953. *(Getty Images)*

Above, left: British prime minister Winston Churchill and heir apparent Anthony Eden. Churchill regarded the Canal Zone negotiations as akin to 'Munich on the Nile'. *(Getty Images) Right:* All smiles. Eden and Churchill are greeted by President Eisenhower and the First Lady on the porch of the White House. John Foster Dulles waits at the side. *(Time Life Pictures/Getty Images)*

Below, left: An advocate of withdrawal. Sir Ralph Stevenson, Britain's ambassador to Egypt between 1950 and 1955. *(Getty Images) Right:* From Paris to Cairo. Jefferson Caffery, US ambassador to Egypt between 1949 and 1955, seen here on becoming the first career diplomat to head America's embassy in Paris, 1944. *(Time Life Pictures/Getty Images)*

At last a treaty which counts for Egypt. British minister of war Antony Head braces himself as Nasser signs the 'heads of agreement', July 1954. *(Corbis)*

Finishing the job. Anthony Nutting concludes the evacuation agreement, October 1954. The last British troops leave Egypt on 13 June, 1956. *(Getty Images)*

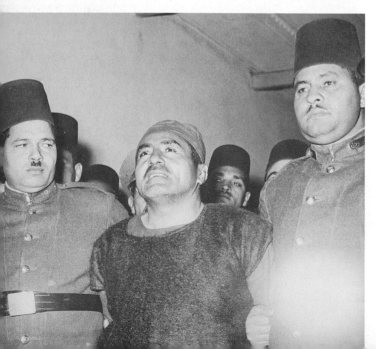

To the execution chamber. A member of the Muslim Brotherhood is led to his death in December 1954 for his alleged part in the assassination attempt on Nasser following the conclusion of the Canal Zone agreement. *(Corbis)*

With dignity. Egyptians at last defending the Canal. *(Corbis)*

Nasser returns to Cairo after announcing the nationalisation of the Suez Canal Company in Alexandria on 26 July 1956. *(Getty Images)*

Top: Back again. British troops at Port Said, November 1956. *(Getty Images)*

Centre: 'Separating the belligerents.' A British tank drives through Port Said as an Egyptian boy surveys the rubble. *(Corbis)*

Left: The General Service Medal, with Canal Zone Clasp, was finally instituted in 2003 by the British Government after many years of campaigning by veterans' groups. It is now available to all British servicemen who served in the Suez Canal Zone in the 1950s, subject to certain eligibility requirements. *(Jonathan Falconer)*

sovereignty was subsequently joint. Case two contended that the Ottoman–Egyptian title never lapsed and that the Sudan was reconquered on Egypt's behalf. Under this doctrine Egypt was the ultimate sovereign, though bound by the 1899 agreement to joint administration. Case three also assumed that Ottoman–Egyptian titular claims remained intact after the Mahdi's revolt, but argued that sovereignty over the Sudan passed from the Ottoman empire to the British empire when Britain declared a protectorate over Egypt in December 1914.[18] Successive British governments had always taken the first legal opinion as the correct one.

To Egyptian nationalists, however, the Sudanese were quite simply Egypt's flesh and blood, the Nile their common lifeline. True, water resources usually meant more than kinship to Cairo politicians: irrigation projects in the Sudan, where the population was relatively small, could not be allowed to affect Egypt's far greater need for the Nile's waters. But even these difficulties stemmed, it was felt, from the British divide and rule tactic of constantly portraying the Sudan as a separate entity.[19]

After the Second World War, the yardstick of all discussions was the ill-fated Bevin–Sidqi protocol of October 1946. This contentious document resulted from talks in London between Ismail Sidqi, Egypt's prime minister, and the British foreign secretary. As part of a general settlement that included military evacuation from Egypt by September 1949, Ernest Bevin formally recognised the Egyptian crown's claims to sovereignty over the Sudan. However, the protocol made clear, at least in British eyes, that this was to be a purely symbolic recognition. It would not affect the status quo or the eventual right of the Sudanese to self-determination. But when Sidqi returned to Egypt he ignored these qualifications. Bevin was therefore compelled to clarify publicly Britain's position, and the protocol soon collapsed amid great acrimony. Yet Britain had effectively admitted Egyptian titular claims over the Sudan and the ultimate failure of the negotiations could not cancel out this admission.

The British-staffed Political Service of the Sudan government was outraged by the protocol debacle. As an organisation, it had come to define its role as being to protect the interests of the Sudanese. By the late 1940s, this meant seeing itself as virtually autonomous of both co-domini. Underlying this attitude was the belief that Britain's priorities lay in Egypt and that London would 'sell out' the Sudanese to secure a settlement to the Canal Zone dispute. In this respect, it should be noted that Sudanese matters came under the responsibility of the Foreign Office, not the Colonial Office, for the simple reason that the Sudan condominium had always been connected to Britain's 'informal' imperial position in Egypt.

Among diplomats, it was a professional slur (the disease of 'localitis') to be accused of seeing events solely from the perspective of a particular posting; for colonial officials, on the other hand, often committed to one territory throughout their careers, it was a cause for pride. But the Sudan Political Service had taken this modus operandi to extremes. In the words of its most authoritative chronicler, Martin Daly, the officials suffered from 'an almost obsessive loyalty' to what they regarded as 'their' Sudan.[20] For them, the Bevin–Sidqi protocol was but more grist to the mill. In its wake, therefore, the Sudan government initiated their own 'Sudanisation' strategy as a weapon against Egyptian influence and London's double-dealing. A legislative assembly and an executive council were hastily established in 1948, the purpose being to train the Sudanese for self-government. Nevertheless, great care was taken to ensure that the imperial civilising mission was not rushed; very little legislation was ever produced by the two bodies.

Given the apprehensions of a surrender à la 1946, the Wafd's abrogation threat of November 1950 naturally caused great concern south of the border. The pro-independence factions, of which the largest was the Umma (Nation) party, responded by stepping up their demands for immediate self-government. Meanwhile, the most important of the pro-Egyptian unionist parties, the Ashigga (Brethren), maintained that the only way to real constitutional advancement (e.g. without Britain's continuing guiding hand) was to enlist the support of Cairo, the Egyptians being promised some form of confederation in recompense. Sectarian antipathies further fuelled these rivalries. Both main parties had sought greater popular support by obtaining the blessing of religious leaders. The Umma had the backing of Sayed Abdul Rahman, the posthumous son of the Mahdi and head of the Ansar (Mahdist) sect. The Ashigga had the patronage of Sayed Ali al-Mirghani, leader of the anti-Mahdist Khatmiyya sect. While Egypt suspected Rahman of wanting to be king of an independent Sudan (which they equated to his being a British stooge), Britain regarded al-Mirghani as a tool of Egyptian imperialism.

These entangling relationships, both real and perceived, gave weight to Egypt's contention that the Suez base and the Sudan issues were intrinsically linked, a contention that Britain persistently denied. This linkage became even more controversial in 1950–1 as a result of the onset of US involvement in Sudanese matters. Washington was drawn into the equation by the outbreak of war in Korea. With communism on the march in Asia, State Department officials urged London not to jeopardise strategic facilities in the Canal Zone because of outdated squabbles over the Sudan, a view Britain's embassy in Cairo tended to share. Thus, the geopolitics of the Cold War, not the desire to spread the principle of self-determination to the colonial world, motivated American actions.

Their ambassador in Cairo was particularly insistent that Britain conciliate Egyptian nationalism by withdrawing from the Sudan, an argument that earned him the lasting wrath of Sir James Robertson, head of the Sudan Political Service. In Robertson's memoirs, *Transition in Africa* (1974), Caffery is reported as saying that he could not understand Britain's concern for 'ten million bloody niggers'.[21] Although the authenticity of this quote has been questioned (Daly thinks 'niggers' rings true, but 'bloody' does not[22]), it nevertheless illustrates a common theme of the British 'official mind' in the 1950s, namely the hypocrisy of American anti-colonialism while segregation still prevailed in the United States.[23] The quote also offers a glimpse of the robust attitude for which Robertson was renowned (and he had a powerful physique to match).

Born in 1899 and educated at Oxford, where he gained a third class in classical honour moderations and a second in *literae humaniores*, Sir James was an archetype of officialdom in imperial Sudan. While Oxbridge graduates with first-class degrees tended to join the Indian Civil Service, the SPS had a strong preference for young men with sporting blues (Robertson's was for rugby) and a 'gentleman's third'.[24] Character, not intellect, was the key requirement, and this was more likely to be formed on the playing field than in the examination hall. Over the decades, a self-belief had developed among Britain's officials in the Sudan that was perhaps unmatched anywhere else in the empire. For these officials, obstinacy in 'defence' of the Sudanese was a matter of great principle, and in this respect Robertson was a worthy standard-bearer.

For many years, Britain had pursued a policy of separation for the black Africans in the south of the Sudan. Motivated by a desire to protect the primitive southern cultures from the more advanced northerners (including Arab slave traders), this approach had gone so far as to encourage closer links and even union with Uganda and other East African territories. But the reality was that none of these territories was willing to associate themselves with what they considered a vast and unproductive land. Moreover, when

economic penetration had occurred, it came, much to Britain's frustration
(and despite attempted restrictions), from the Muslim north. In the end, the
separatist approach was abandoned in favour of the aforementioned
legislative and executive structures developed in the wake of the Bevin–Sidqi
'sell out' crisis.

Apart from guiding both these processes (there was certainly to be no rapid
advancement towards full self-rule), Britain saw an even longer-term role for
itself via the provision of 'safeguards' for the southern Sudanese. This
approach aimed at creating a mechanism by which an informal imperial
presence in the Sudan could be maintained after formal imperial rule had
ended with the granting of independence, whenever that may be.[25] Thus,
Britain's insistence on safeguards for southern Sudan sounded very much like
an echo of the 'reserved points' in Egypt's independence charter of 1922.
It was not surprising that Egyptian governments were uniformly suspicious.

When it became clear in September 1951 that Egypt was going to abrogate
the 1899 and 1936 treaties come what may, Britain became preoccupied
with securing US support for the looming crisis. This resulted in a significant
shift in London's Sudan policy – a modification that was to be vitally
important a year later. The new approach was to promise the establishment of
an international commission to advise the co-domini on Sudanese
constitutional developments. Officials had at first been doubtful about their
political masters in the cabinet even conditionally accepting this move,
especially with a general election so close, but they need not have worried.[26]
By October (and certainly after the withdrawal from the Abadan oil complex
in Iran on the 3rd), the Labour government no longer regarded the Middle
East Command approach and any Sudan proposals tagged on as a basis for
negotiations (see Chapter 2). Instead, they were seen purely as a device to
strengthen Britain's international position in view of the imminent rupture
with Egypt. The cabinet therefore had little difficulty in accepting the
international commission 'concession' on 7 October.[27]

Egypt's abrogation of the 1899 condominium agreement on 15 October
1951 was coupled with the promulgation of a new constitution for the
Sudan, which was clearly a hypothetical exercise given Britain's complete
domination of the condominium's administrative structures. All the same, it
was a revealing document: Sudanese cabinets were to be appointed and
dismissed by the Egyptian king, who would also have the power to dissolve
and prorogue a house of representatives; and in matters relating to foreign

affairs, defence, the armed forces and currency, the pretence of collaboration was dropped altogether, since these were the exclusive preserve of the Egyptian monarch.[28]

With the exception of the pro-Egyptian Ashigga, all Sudanese political parties roundly condemned the arrogance of Cairo in seeking to impose a new constitution without first consulting them. Nevertheless, when Britain refused to recognise the legality of the Egyptian action and stated that it would continue to support the Sudan government in continuing to administer the territory in accordance with the condominium, the announcement was poorly received by Sudanese politicians. To them, the condominium framework had become a dead letter: quicker gains were to be had by openly playing Britain off against Egypt.[29]

It was to prevent the slow-is-best transitional process from being derailed that Anthony Eden, foreign secretary in the newly elected Conservative government, announced in the Commons on 15 November that 'a constitution for [Sudanese] self-government *may* be completed and in operation by the end of 1952 [author's italics]'.[30] This was the first time a specific date had ever been mentioned. Officials in the Sudan Political Service privately admitted that it was earlier (obviously) than they had envisioned.[31] Winston Churchill, the new occupant of 10 Downing Street, was also concerned about the pace: 'Surely we are not called upon to hurry this process in this way?', he enquired of Eden during the drafting of the statement.[32] The prime minister's preference had been to omit all references to timing, even though such vagueness was precisely the cause of discontent among the Sudanese. His doubts were eventually eased by the fact that the final draft specifically used the word 'may'. Cabinet approval was thus forthcoming.[33]

The next shot in the escalating battle for Sudanese opinion was fired by the Egyptian foreign minister at a meeting of the UN General Assembly on 16 November. 'As a challenge to the United Kingdom', Salah al-Din declared that Egypt would remove all its officials and armed forces from the Sudan if Britain did the same. (Egypt, of course, had few personnel of any sort in the Sudan, so it was not a big concession on his part.) This, he explained, would then 'allow the Sudanese freely to express their will through a plebiscite' arranged by the UN.[34] In making this offer, Salah al-Din's gaze was as much on Washington as the Sudan. His aim was to undermine Anglo-American solidarity on the Canal Zone by exposing British intransigence on the Sudan, which London was quick to pick up on. As expected, the State Department applied pressure for consideration of the offer, but Eden remained firmly opposed, asserting that any discussion would only 'be playing the Egyptian game'.[35]

By mid-December, following the publicity disaster of Kafr Abdu, the Americans were even more anxious for British concessions on the Sudan. The new line of thinking, outlined by the State Department on 14 December, was for a 'package deal' in which the four powers associated with the Middle East Command approach (Britain, the United States, France and Turkey) would all recognise Farouk as 'King of Sudan' on condition that Egypt agreed both to Sudanese self-determination and to the substance of the Command proposals.[36] But Eden was against any such horse-trading and firmly stuck to this line during his and Churchill's visit to Washington at the start of 1952.[37]

The shock of Cairo's Black Saturday riots prompted Britain to re-examine its objectives and responsibilities in respect of the Sudan. The moral dimension of the problem was identified in two often-repeated pledges: first, that there would be no change of status of the Sudan without consultation with the Sudanese people; and second, that the Sudanese would be free to decide their own future.[38] The practical side of the problem concerned the extent to which Britain wanted to keep the Egyptians out of Sudanese affairs. 'One must have every sympathy with people who do not wish to see the Sudan subjected to the unpleasant vagaries of Egyptian politics,' wrote Roger Allen on 16 February. 'At the same time, I think we are in danger of losing the true perspective. After all, the Sudan is, or was, the Anglo-Egyptian Sudan.' Britain, in other words, was not entitled to exclude Egypt from Sudanese affairs. 'If we are determined that self-determination for the Sudanese shall mean at all costs the exclusion of Egypt, then we are making a mockery of our pledges.'[39] The conclusion drawn by Sir James Bowker, the assistant under-secretary in charge of Middle Eastern affairs, was that while London could not impose Egyptian kingship on the Sudanese (as the Americans wanted), equally, British officials in Khartoum would have to refrain from attempts to dissuade the Sudanese from accepting it.[40]

This reassessment fed into Britain's policy of pushing ahead with Sudanese constitutional reform during 1952 (despite the earlier 'may' proviso), which in due course resulted in Egypt's apparent U-turn in attitude in November. In the meantime, the Free Officers' regime quickly came to realise that a continued insistence on 'Unity of the Nile Valley' would further diminish Egyptian influence in the Sudan.[41] With the imminent prospect of the draft constitution being promulgated, elections would be held and a representative body formed – major steps in the direction of self-government for the Sudanese. Moreover, while a continued administrative role in support of the new constitutional apparatus promised to sustain British influence, Egypt, if it persisted with its sovereignty claims, would be excluded completely from the process. Thus, the junta's break from the old 'Unity of the Nile Valley' mantra was actually a shrewd move to re-establish an Egyptian voice in Sudanese affairs.

THE UNRAVELLING OF BRITAIN'S POSITION

British policymakers were slow to see the real significance of the supposed revolution in Egypt's attitude. The agreements secured by Neguib with the Sudanese political parties should have sounded an alarm, but they did not; instead, complacency was the order of the day. Reports about the junta's new approach had been received in London (and Khartoum) in the first half of October. 'They had abandoned the slogan of unity of the Nile Valley and were working for genuine independence for the Sudan', telegraphed Stevenson on the 12th. 'That was a big change', he continued, 'and the officers expressed some nervousness of the reaction.' London's response was to worry about embarrassing poor Neguib over the 'surrender'.[42] More inexcusably, Howe's administration failed to see that the underlying purpose of the agreements was for Egypt to replace British influence in Sudanese affairs. With good reason, Neguib gloated in his memoirs that he had 'beat[en] the British at their own game simply by calling their bluff'.[43]

From this point on, Sudanese politicians looked more to Cairo, rather than to London or the (British) Sudan government, for guidance along the road to independence. This was of crucial importance because the route had yet to be properly delineated and signposts were still needed on two critical issues. The first was the question of whether safeguards were needed for southern Sudan. Britain wanted the governor-general to have special powers, whereas Egypt saw this as an attempt to maintain a British presence.[44] The second issue related to the relationship between the governor-general and the proposed international commission. London wanted to proceed with elections so as to let the final definition be settled by a Sudanese parliament, while Cairo insisted that all the governor-general's responsibilities be subject to the procedure of the international commission.[45]

Another complication was that the Sudan negotiations could not help but be affected by the domestic considerations of both disputants. On the Egyptian side, the party reorganisation law was causing great consternation. After the junta had refused to accept al-Nahas even as the 'honorary' leader of a purified party in early November, Wafdists of all complexions pulled together and challenged the legality of the legislation in the State Council, Egypt's highest court. In a preliminary hearing at the end of the month, Ibrahim Farag, who had previously been willing to appease the military regime, told the proceedings, 'the case before you is not of Mustafa al-Nahhas . . . but of parliamentary life in Egypt'.[46] The junta's popularity, meanwhile, was suffering as a consequence of economic problems caused by the year's cotton crop remaining unsold, which was in marked contrast to the previous two years when the early stages of the Korean War had stimulated cotton prices.

From early September there was also the question of the imprisoned politicians. Martial law permitted detention for three months unless charges were pressed, making 6 December the required release date. With insufficient evidence gathered, the military high committee reluctantly decided to free the detainees (including Sirag al-Din) in the days before the deadline. When al-Nahas met twice with Neguib shortly afterwards, British observers speculated that the general-cum-prime minister might be reinsuring himself against 'extremist elements' in the junta by assisting the Wafd. In a similar vein, rumours of a national unity government led by al-Nahas were reported in *Al-Ahram* on 7 and 8 December.[47]

This confused situation seemed to become clearer on 10 December when the regime announced the annulment of the Egyptian constitution as a prelude to a new one being written. The drafting was to be carried out by a committee of fifty experts drawn from all political affiliations, and the resulting document would be put to a popular referendum. But was this really a fresh start or was it the latest of Nasser's tactical gambits? Within a fortnight, the old-guard politicians were to discover that the scrapping of the constitution actually permitted the junta to do away with all the legal niceties that had previously hindered its prosecution of key opponents. On 22 December a special 'treason court' was established, followed by the issuing of a first set of indictments on 1 January 1953, with Sirag al-Din's topping the pile.[48] The regime's intentions for the new year were now clear to all.

Meanwhile, sentiment in Britain on the Sudan issue was being screwed up to a high pitch by a well-organised lobby, orchestrated through a series of networks between influential former members of the Sudan Political Service, the press, and the London-based Sudan agency (a quasi-embassy for the Sudan government). This campaign tapped into the prevailing mood within the Conservative Party. Although the one-year-old Churchill government had adapted with relative ease to the post-1945 domestic settlement of the welfare state and the mixed economy, it was struggling to accept the realities of the changed international order. The influence of the prime minister, a diehard imperialist, was clearly a critical factor in this respect, but there were also powerful currents of pro-empire opinion on the party's backbenches. With the memory of Munich still strong, it was easy for young MPs looking to make a name for themselves in Parliament, or alternatively old-timers wanting to salvage their reputations, to equate any talk of concessions with that dread word in British politics, appeasement.

In the winter of 1952/3, the Sudan issue brought together two such MPs. In the 'youthful ambition' category was Julian Amery. First elected in 1950, he had cut his teeth in the Commons by haranguing the Labour government for its handling of the Abadan crisis.[49] His background was Conservative through and through. The son of former cabinet minister Leo Amery, he had married the daughter of Harold Macmillan, minister for housing, and was well known for his exploits with Albanian partisans during the Second World War. Such advantages, coupled with a tendency to plot, could irritate colleagues, some of whom suspected him of using the Sudan and Canal Zone disputes as stepping stones for his political advancement[50] Captain Charles Waterhouse, on the other hand, was a Tory MP of the old school (the use of a military rank in peacetime was a giveaway), and, if anything, fitted into that second category of MPs who were perhaps looking for redemption. After entering Parliament in 1924, Waterhouse had distinguished himself as a whip for Neville Chamberlain at the time of Munich. His detractors, however, were less generous in their assessment of his motives. They pointed to his business interests in southern Africa as shaping his arch-imperialist attitudes, rather than any efforts at compensating for an earlier wrong.[51]

It was a chance meeting in January 1953 between Waterhouse and Amery in Cape Town (after Waterhouse had just visited Khartoum) that led them to form the 'Sudan Group'. In the words of Amery, their aim was to 'prevent a sell-out of the Sudan to Egypt'. With rumours also circulating that Eden was beginning to consider a withdrawal from the Suez base (under American pressure), a significant number of supporters were quickly gathered together. As Amery later recounted:

Among senior members these included Ralph Assheton, a privy councillor and former chairman of the Conservative party, Major John Morrison, deputy chairman of the 1922 Committee, Christopher Holland-Martin, the treasurer of the Conservative party. At the younger end were Fitzroy Maclean who had led the British mission to Tito during the war, Enoch Powell and later, Angus Maude. In the House of Lords we had the support of Lord Hankey who had been secretary to the War cabinet in World War I and a member of Neville Chamberlain's government, and Lord Killearn, former ambassador to Egypt.[52]

In total, there were about forty supporters in the Commons, twenty-eight of whom were hardcore (the government majority was seventeen), along with a wider circle who privately encouraged the group. These included no less a figure than Churchill himself. The importance of this faction – the Sudan Group soon morphed into the Suez Group – on Britain's descent to 1956 cannot be overstated.

One development that had little impact on the Sudan negotiations was the change in administration in America. Republican president-elect, Dwight D. Eisenhower, was fully expected to take the same line on Sudanese matters as his Democrat predecessors. Even so, the naming of John Foster Dulles as secretary of state-designate was not well received in the British Foreign Office because of his involvement in the McCarthyite allegations against the Truman administration for 'losing' China. According to Eden, 'Ike was almost apologetic' for the appointment.[53] Earlier in 1952, Eden had apparently confided to Eisenhower (during a NATO meeting in France) his hopes that Dulles would not be chosen to run the State Department if the Republicans won the presidential election. 'I do not think I would be able to work with him,' Eden reportedly stated.[54] The coolness of future interaction between Eden and Dulles suggests that the latter had learnt of this conversation.

The Dulles–Eden relationship started off muted and then got worse. Evelyn Shuckburgh, Eden's private secretary between 1951 and 1954, who made musical instruments in his leisure time, thought it because the tempo of their minds was always out of harmony: 'They were like two lute strings whose vibrations never coincide.'[55] 'Foster talks so slowly that Master does not wait to hear what he has to say,' Shuckburgh explained to a private office colleague in 1954, 'while our man talks in so roundabout and elusive a style that the other, being a lawyer, goes away having failed to make the right guesses.'[56] It might also be added that Eden's habit of addressing men as 'my dear' was not to the taste of many Americans, Dulles in particular. With his small wire-framed spectacles and grave countenance ('a great slab of a face', according to Churchill), Dulles looked like a stern preacher from the old Wild West. In fact, his grandfather had been secretary of state to President Benjamin Harrison, while his uncle, Robert Lansing, had served in the same capacity for Woodrow Wilson. Nevertheless, the Dulles–Eden discord went far beyond mere personality differences. Despite being moderate in comparison with some of his party colleagues, Eden remained a fitting representative of a Britain that was still anxious to cling on to its world role in a manner that failed to take fully into account America's recent ascendancy.

The thinking of the new Republican team on the Sudan was revealed to Churchill and Eden during a summit at Bermuda in early January 1953. As expected, it amounted to hardline reassertion of previous American policy. Dulles's brief for the discussion stated that the United States was 'deeply concerned lest failure of these negotiations should make impossible a resolution of the overall Egyptian question':

> We do not believe that vague fears for the future welfare of a relatively small number of . . . Sudanese should be allowed to stand in the way of a settlement deeply affecting, not only the security and interests of the Western powers, but also the security and welfare of many millions of Near Easterners. British rigidity on this issue could be disastrous.[57]

Here, indeed, was a clash of imperial missions.

The main outstanding problem in the Sudan negotiations continued to be the southern issue. The Egyptians saw the demand for safeguards as an excuse for Britain remaining in or even detaching the south, while northern Sudanese parties thought them yet another delaying tactic. To break this deadlock, junta member Major Salah Salem headed a delegation to Sudan in early January. Cairo Radio reported its aim as being to conduct direct talks with tribal leaders from the south, upon whose apprehensions British policymakers put such great store.[58] But Salem instead went straight to the northern political leaders, including those who were pro-independence, and persuaded them to sign a second set of agreements which specifically supported all Egypt's positions in the talks. Moreover, all future elections would be boycotted unless these points were accepted.[59] Announced on 11 January 1953, these agreements undercut the last remaining tenets of British policy. 'I doubt if we can recover much ground now with the Sudanese,' minuted Bowker a day later. 'I think our only course will be to get as best terms from the Egyptians as we can.'[60]

The Foreign Office was furious with the Sudan government. It felt that Egypt's past insistence on 'Unity of the Nile Valley' had made the British administrators blasé in their relations with the pro-independence parties. Little or nothing had been learnt from Neguib's triumph in the autumn when he had managed to lure usually dependable Sudanese parties to the Egyptian side. The damning assessment of the permanent under-secretary in the Foreign Office was that 'Sir R. Howe and his advisers' had 'sadly misjudged the situation and wasted much of our time and effort'.[61] Even the usually bullish James Robertson conceded that things had gone wrong. 'While I was playing cricket on Friday', he wrote in a private letter, '. . . our enemies were at work.'[62]

'MUNICH ON THE NILE'

Despite the bleak assessments of his officials, Eden refused to conclude that all was lost.[63] On 14 January he persuaded the cabinet to appoint a special subcommittee to deal with urgent questions arising from the Sudan situation. With himself in the chair, the committee included the lord president, the lord privy seal, the commonwealth secretary and the colonial secretary.[64] Apart from the newly cemented relationship between the Egyptian junta and the Sudanese political parties, the main danger identified was a possible rearguard action on the part of Conservative backbench critics (the nascent Sudan/Suez Group) who were making it known that they were opposed to the abandonment of Britain's role in the Sudan. The touchstone of their position was the attainment of 'special responsibilities' for the governor-general in the southern provinces. Eden clung to the hope that a solution could be found which would leave this matter to be decided by a Sudanese parliament.

Churchill's mind, on the other hand, was off in an altogether different direction. He regarded the junta's second diplomatic coup as a chance to relocate the Sudan negotiations back firmly in the context of the Canal Zone dispute with Egypt. 'Surely we should now confront Neguib resolutely and insist on execution of the (defence) Treaty till 1956 failing a satisfactory agreement,' he told Eden on 15 January, via a telegram from Jamaica (where he was on holiday following the Bermuda talks): 'I trust that no final decision need be taken before my return.'[65] Hitherto, the details of the Sudan, unlike those of the Suez base, had failed to interest the prime minister. This all changed when the alternatives became polarised between a clash with Egypt and a 'scuttle' in the Sudan.

Churchill's animation on this topic initially confounded officials in London. How was he getting the details in Jamaica? But it was not long before the Foreign Office identified Lord Beaverbrook, proprietor of the *Daily Express*, as responsible for influencing the prime minister while he was on holiday.[66] Meanwhile, Eden's sensitivity concerning the possibility that press barons might be turning against him was linked to a wider tension at the heart of the Conservative government as to who would succeed to the premiership. It had been widely assumed that Churchill would lead the country for a year or so after the election of 1951 before letting Eden, the 'heir apparent', take over. But the longer Churchill stayed on, the likelihood increased of another senior Conservative usurping Eden of his 'rightful' position. Rab Butler, the chancellor of the exchequer, was looking like the front runner in this regard.

Rumours in Whitehall were certainly rife. On 19 January 1953, for instance, Evelyn Shuckburgh visited Alan Lascelles, Queen Elizabeth II's private secretary, at Buckingham Palace, where he was surprised to be told that, 'If Winston were to die tomorrow there is no doubt at all the Queen would send for Anthony. But by the end of the year there will be doubt, if present trend continues. There might be at least 50 per cent opinion in the party and in the City by that time in favour of Butler.'[67] Eden, who was notoriously thin-skinned, was deeply troubled by such gossip and often seemed on the verge of a showdown with No. 10, only for his anger to subside as rapidly as it had risen. Churchill would also gear himself up for a major quarrel, before shying away from it at the last moment.

Shuckburgh again offers a fascinating glimpse of these tensions at the height of the Sudan dispute. His diary entry for 29 January reads:

Jock Colville [Churchill's private secretary] came round to see me in a great state of agitation. He said there was going to be a row. He had gone overnight to Southampton and travelled up with the PM [who had just returned from Jamaica]. The latter was in a rage again against A.E., speaking of 'appeasement' and saying that he never knew before that Munich was situated on the Nile. He described A.E. as having been a failure as Foreign Secretary and being 'tired, sick and bound up in detail'. Jock said that the Prime Minister would never give way over Egypt. He positively desired the talks on the Sudan to fail, just as he positively hoped we should not succeed in getting into conversations with the Egyptians on defence which might lead to our abandonment of the Canal Zone. Jock, who has hitherto sided strongly with the PM over this Egypt question, seemed seriously concerned. He said, 'The only hope is that Neguib will behave so badly that our two masters will see eye to eye.'[68]

Meanwhile, the military regime's successes on the Sudan front were all the more remarkable given the tumult of Egyptian domestic politics at this time. On 10 January 1953, the day before the second set of Sudan agreements was announced, there had been chaotic scenes in the State Council as the Wafdist case against the party reorganisation law had finally come before it. As in November, Ibrahim Farag led the defence, telling the court, 'The Wafd will never be dissolved. Only the people will dissolve the Wafd.'[69] The proceedings continued for three days after which they were adjourned with a verdict being promised in February.

But before a judgment could be delivered a counter-coup against Egypt's junta was apparently foiled, and in the days that followed both the court case and the constitutional deliberations fell by the wayside. On 17 January about twenty officers and half a dozen civilians were arrested on charges of plotting against the regime. The army element centred around Youssef Seddiq, the member of the military high committee who had figured so prominently on the first night of the coup. Sirag al-Din was arrested on charges of complicity soon afterwards. About ninety or so communist agitators were also interned. The junta, according to a report from Caffery, saw the plot as a coalition of Wafdists, communists and royalists, a combination that required an immediate draconian response. All political parties were immediately dissolved and their funds confiscated.[70]

On 23 January 1953, six months to the day after the coup, the Free Officers finally abandoned the fiction that their involvement in politics was going to be brief, and instead announced that Neguib, as 'Leader of the Revolution', would remain as prime minister for a further three-year period of transition. In line with this shift, the military high committee began to refer to itself as the Revolutionary Command Council (RCC). The purpose was twofold. As well as highlighting the radical intent of the army movement, it also gave greater prominence to the officers behind Neguib. A provisional constitutional charter legitimising the RCC was proclaimed on 10 February. To replace the factionalism of the political parties, a national movement called the Liberation Rally was formed, its purpose being to develop a mass popular base for the regime. Nasser was appointed its secretary-general. This new responsibility was to bring the real leader of the coup to public attention as never before.

Meanwhile, back in London, Churchill was eager for a showdown on the Sudan dispute. On 30 January he attended a meeting of Eden's special cabinet subcommittee. The minutes greyly record that he used the meeting to press the case for 'greater firmness' in the negotiations with Egypt, and that the present talks should be broken off if Neguib refused to accept Britain's position on the southern safeguards issue.[71] The chatter among Churchill and Eden's staff was, however, considerably more animated, and may be illustrative of how views were actually being aired among cabinet ministers. 'I spent a very uncomfortable half-hour with the Private Secretaries at No. 10', notes Shuckburgh in his diary, 'during which Colville, Pitblado and Montague Browne all attacked A.E. and the Foreign Office for their policy on Egypt':

They thought we should sit on the gippies and have a 'whiff of grapeshot'. If it meant letting the British communities in Alexandria and Cairo be massacred that could not be helped. Anyway, the soldiers were notoriously pessimistic and they thought it ridiculous that we should not be able to cope with the Egyptian Army with the eighty thousand men we have in the Zone. The Chiefs of Staff, they said (obviously quoting the Prime Minister), always say that the force available for any emergency is insufficient. You have to prove the contrary. If we go out of the Sudan and Egypt it will be another stage in the policy of scuttle which began in India and ended in Abadan. It will lead to the abandonment of our African colonies.[72]

The cabinet subcommittee reconvened the next day and it was decided that Howe in Khartoum should sound out the Sudanese political parties for one last time to see if they would reconsider Britain's stances on the outstanding issues. With rioting in the Sudan a distinct possibility if the talks looked like collapsing, the decision was also taken to place two Suez-based battalions on short notice to fly to Khartoum.[73]

Trouble was also in the air in the Canal Zone. The truce that had followed the Black Saturday riots had begun to falter by the end of 1952, encouraged by a spate of inflammatory statements by the Egyptian junta.[74] Instead of tapering off when the Sudan negotiations reached a delicate stage, the press campaign actually intensified, prompting Stevenson to make a formal complaint to Egypt's foreign minister in mid-January 1953.[75] Meanwhile, Britain's military authorities in Fayid and Ismailia regarded the prospect of moving some forces to Khartoum as likely to stir up further trouble in the Canal Zone, or worse still in Cairo and Alexandria. Field Marshal Sir John Harding, Slim's successor as chief of imperial general staff, fretted that such an eventuality might lead to the implementation of the dreaded Rodeo operations.[76]

On 3 February the full cabinet convened to discuss new instructions for Stevenson. It was at this meeting that Eden finally advised settling the southern issue in the manner desired by Egypt and the Sudanese political parties. With the Ministry of Defence backing the Foreign Office, the cabinet went along with Eden's recommendation.[77] Consequently, on 6 February Stevenson met representatives of the Egyptian junta. After five hours of clarification and discussion, all remaining differences were straightened out.[78] 'I believe that acceptance of this agreement is better than a deadlock and the ensuing difficulties and disturbances,' wrote a despondent Howe a day later, before adding that it was 'a blow to the prestige of HMG and the Sudan government, and a victory for Egypt in the Sudan'.[79]

The political will of Britain's Conservative government was now the only remaining obstacle to an agreement. With its small Commons majority, this final hurdle should not be underestimated, especially in view of Churchill's instinctive and emotional opposition to imperial retreat of any sort. Tuesday 11 February was to be the day of reckoning. At stake was not only the Sudan's orderly development towards self-government, but also the future of Anglo-Egyptian relations. It was widely expected that a collapse of the 6 February agreement would see an immediate return to widespread guerrilla warfare in the Canal Zone.

Undeterred by such worries, on the morning of the 11th Churchill's instinct was for fighting solutions. His latest scheme, which he outlined to the cabinet's defence committee, was to replace the Rodeo operations with a plan for rounding up and disarming that part of the Egyptian army located in the Sinai Peninsula. These forces could then serve as a bargaining chip in future negotiations.[80] One can only imagine the looks around the table as this suggestion was shot down. The prime minister's next gambit, at the first of two cabinet meetings held that day, was to raise the scarecrow of a backbench revolt if the Sudan agreement was carried through. But despite Churchill's best efforts, the balance of opinion in the cabinet rested on the side of an agreement. With realistic military considerations dictating compromise, not to mention the attitude of the Sudanese themselves, it was difficult to see what else could be done. Eden was therefore asked to explain the purpose of the settlement to a meeting of the Conservative Party's foreign affairs committee that evening, following which the cabinet would reconvene.[81]

Having spent so much of his career preoccupied with foreign affairs, Eden was never wholly at ease in the Commons. MPs found him distant and he found them (or rather the cut and thrust of parliamentary politics) a bother to the proper conduct of diplomacy. Still, he did as required on 11 February and went before Amery, Waterhouse and his other backbench critics. It was thus a great relief, albeit a temporary one, when the would-be rebels announced that they were going to hold their fire in preparation for what they considered the more serious battle of opposing the evacuation of the Canal Zone.[82] At 10.40 p.m. the cabinet sat again to hear Eden's report of what had transpired during the foreign affairs committee meeting. The minutes noted that the foreign secretary's explanation had 'removed many of the misunderstandings which had been current in the Party, and had gone a long way towards allaying the anxieties mentioned in the cabinet's discussions earlier in the day'. 'Although many of those present continued to be uneasy about the situation they now recognised that the course which the Government were proposing to follow was the most satisfactory of the alternatives now open to them.'[83] Eden was thus able to secure the cabinet's approval for a Sudan agreement. Had this not been achieved, he later claimed in his memoirs, he would have resigned.[84]

At 11 a.m. on 12 February 1953, Britain and Egypt signed the Sudan agreement, which formally established a three-year timetable for the end of the condominium. 'Dual administration' was terminated forthwith and replaced by three international commissions, with Sudanese participation. Elections were to be held as soon as they could be arranged.[85]

In September 1952, the British Foreign Office, because of a timetable established during the previous winter's abrogation crisis, had decided to make one last effort to include the Egyptians in the transitional process towards Sudanese self-government. Four months later, Britain's influence in the Sudan had been completely undermined by an Egyptian military regime that was unused to the intricacies of diplomacy, beset by internal difficulties and representative of a country that was widely – and rightly – suspected of imperial ambitions of its own in the Nile Valley. What had gone wrong? On one level, it would be easy to see Egypt's rise to a position of real influence (compared to the nominal role it had played before) as being the result of its diplomatic successes in the autumn of 1952 and January 1953, and the associated complacent performance of the British-run Sudan administration. Yet the underlying assumption in this is that Britain's own position in the Sudan had been impregnable, which it most certainly was not. Rather, the condominium was an outdated arrangement which had been at odds with Sudanese nationalism for many years. Moreover, the Sudan Political Service had become so obsessed with its own sense of imperial mission, and so inward-looking in its parochialism, that it had failed to grasp how earlier support for it had haemorrhaged long before the end of 1952.[86]

The timing and manner of the Sudan disengagement were shaped by the Battle of the Canal Zone, a struggle which had already helped produce a new ruling elite in Egypt, along with a new backstairs influence, America. To this list may be added an unstable state, riven by sectarianism – modern Sudan. The importance of the February 1953 agreement with regard to the Canal Zone dispute was that it set a precedent for withdrawal. Eden and Churchill, from their different perspectives, both appreciated this, as did imperialist-minded elements on the Conservative backbenches. Nasser, who had used the months since September 1952 to crack down on his political opponents, also knew this. Crucially, many of the key decisions taken by the British cabinet in January and February 1953 came at a time of increased guerrilla activity in the Canal Zone. This was not accidental. Egypt's military regime was now confident enough in its internal position to attempt to regulate fedayeen raids as a negotiating tool. The post-Black Saturday ceasefire was well and truly over: a new phase in the struggle had begun.

SEVEN

•••••••••••

Redefining Global Strategy

On 12 February 1953, the same day as the Sudan agreement was signed, British foreign secretary Anthony Eden instructed his officials to draft a cabinet paper setting out the reasons why a settlement of the Suez base dispute was also needed.[1] He was anxious to use the momentum of the Sudan negotiations to also press ahead on the defence issue. In previous talks since the Bevin–Sidqi protocol debacle of 1946, it had been an axiom of Britain's chiefs of staff that a peacetime presence in the Canal Zone was essential to their strategic planning requirements. However, in the last few months there had been major developments in military thinking, prompted by financial pressures, the testing of Britain's first atomic bomb, and, not least, the Canal Zone troubles. The upshot was that the Suez base was no longer seen as indispensable in peacetime. In purely military terms, therefore, an evacuation of the Canal Zone garrison was becoming a real possibility, albeit with the assumption that an agreement for wartime reactivation of the base could be secured.

To appreciate fully this shift in strategic thinking and its potential impact in the political sphere it is necessary to grasp the enormous influence of Britain's military planners in shaping the political requirements of informal empire in the Middle East following the onset of the Cold War in the second half of the 1940s. The Bevin-led Foreign Office had actually encouraged this greater emphasis on military considerations in order to shore up the wider imperial edifice (not least against Attlee's radicalism) at the time of Indian independence. However, during Eden's tenure there was mounting frustration with the continuing sway of the chiefs of staff over the general direction of Egyptian policy. The Canal Zone dispute was, after all, a major political problem for Britain. The fact that Egypt, in one form or another, was rarely off the cabinet agenda (at a time of twice-weekly meetings) was testimony to this. Thus, the prospect that the military planners might be more flexible in their Canal Zone requirements was a cause of guarded optimism in the Foreign Office. Nevertheless, there remained the formidable problem of Churchill, who, for more instinctive reasons connected with British prestige, continued to place a very high value on a working Suez base in peacetime.

Thus, when Eden wanted to press ahead with defence negotiations in the spring of 1953, the most important exchanges in the Battle of the Canal Zone were in the corridors of Whitehall rather than along the roads linking the base installations (which were prone to guerrilla attacks), or in the political and diplomatic struggle between London and Cairo. In the first instance, the bureaucratic military–civilian divide in Britain on the role of the Suez base still needed resolving: recent shifts in strategic thinking, if they were to mean anything, had to develop into new policies. Should this be achieved, Churchill and other imperial diehards in the Conservative ranks would then have to be convinced of the merits of trying to accommodate the demands of Egyptian nationalism. The initial hurdle, therefore, remained the huge influence of the service chiefs in determining the political requirements for a base in Egypt. In this respect, it is illuminating to quote the editor of the *British Documents on the End of Empire* (*BDEEP*) volume, which deals with Egypt and the defence of the Middle East between 1945 and 1956. 'The imperial role of military planners', observes John Kent, 'was to decide what needed to be done, often more for political than military reasons, and then to use an ostensible strategic rationale to promote a particular line of policy within the Whitehall bureaucracy.'[2]

NEW THINKING, OLD PLANNING

Eden's hopes of progress in the defence sphere after the conclusion of the Sudan negotiations were sparked by a chiefs of staff meeting on 21 October 1952, the result of which was the possibility of a whole new approach to the Suez base dispute. The Foreign Office had been represented at the meeting by Roger Allen. His appraisal for Stevenson in Cairo veered uncharacteristically towards the hopeful. 'The Chiefs of Staff', he remarked, 'were . . . not prepared to say, as they have hitherto said, that the existence of the Canal Zone base in peacetime was essential . . . I pointed out that this made a fundamental difference in our policy towards Egypt; it would be ridiculous to embark on negotiations designed to secure us a fully operative base in Egypt if it turned out that such a base was no longer militarily essential.' Allen's letter hinted at earlier frustrations: 'if we can get this confirmed in due course, our defence negotiations with Egypt might be on an entirely different footing and there might even be some prospect of a successful outcome'.[3] Earlier in the year, Allen had been deeply pessimistic about the chances of a settlement. The service chiefs, he stated in February 1952, had 'no intention of leaving the Canal Zone if they can possibly help it', adding rather undiplomatically, 'the British soldier seems willing to put up with a great deal of sniping and bomb-throwing for the sake of a few tennis-courts and amenities such as a place to have his pre-prandial drink'.[4]

Although the tensions between different agencies of Britain's government are revealing as to the nature of the Egyptian 'defence' question, in order to gauge the full significance of the October 1952 modification in strategic thinking it is necessary to take a much broader perspective – one which locates the dispute over the Suez base in the context of Britain's continuing expectations of remaining a global power following the Second World War. In systemic terms, the international environment that had allowed for European ascendancy in world affairs, and the empires that were part of that dominance, had effectively ceased in 1941 with the intervention of two continental-sized actors, the Soviet Union and the United States (prompted by Hitler's invasion and Pearl Harbor respectively). The upshot was a new bipolar international system in which the two 'superpowers' became ideological and geopolitical rivals.

With the Cold War a defining feature of this superpower rivalry, a crucial battleground related to the legacy of Europe's recent ascendancy, namely the vast parts of the planet still ruled or influenced by European powers, particularly Britain. In this respect, the contention often made in student textbooks that European decolonisation after 1945 can be explained by Moscow and Washington squeezing out the old guard needs to be qualified. Although this may be a contributory factor when encapsulating, say, a forty-year period, if the focus is narrowed to the first decade or two after 1945, another narrative reveals itself, and this is that the US regarded Britain's imperial presence around the world as, by and large, an asset in the Cold War. While it is important to look at the competitive elements in this alliance relationship (they were, after all, a key feature of the Battle of the Canal Zone), it was nevertheless a basic Anglo-American kinship, strained though it often was, that determined London's post-1945 approach to global strategic planning and the defence therein of the Middle East. Not surprisingly, therefore, British policymakers, when in discussions with Washington, would always stress the Cold War purposes of various interests in the region rather than their imperial raison d'être.

So what was the new Cold War role for Britain's long-standing imperial position in Egypt? There were two aspects to this, reflecting the dual nature of Cold War planning. The first saw the Canal Zone's significance in terms of concerted preparations for fighting a future hot war. When Labour prime minister Clement Attlee had pushed for a withdrawal from the Middle East c. 1945–7, the chiefs of staff, with Bevin in support, responded to this radicalism by arguing that the region, and the Suez base in particular, was vital not only for the survival of Britain as a world power, but also for the defence of Britain itself. Contingency plans were drawn up identifying the Canal Zone air base at Abu Sueir as an ideal location from which to bomb the industrial and oil-producing areas of southern Russia and the Caucasus, action which, in turn, would help weaken a Soviet offensive against Western Europe.[5] A primed Suez base in peacetime was thus a critical element of Britain's preparations for a global war, making any potential shift away from this basic planning assumption a matter of the utmost general strategic importance.

The second aspect of the Canal Zone's role in Cold War planning related to its political function, which was distinct from the efforts at deterring or fighting a war. The aim in this respect was to convince the Egyptian population of the Soviet military threat, so persuading them to see the British military presence as in their own defence interests, and thus a source of internal stability.[6] And yet, as the Canal Zone siege had recently shown, Britain's continuing 'occupation' had succeeded only in whipping up the nationalists (indigenous communists among them) and the increased instability had helped produce a *coup d'état*. It was, moreover, Britain's obvious shortcomings on the political side of the Cold War battle – it carried too much imperial baggage – that had impelled America's new-found interest in Egyptian internal affairs. Connected with these difficulties was the manner of the imperial withdrawal from Palestine in 1948: Arab nationalists blamed Britain for the creation of a Jewish state on Palestinian land. As a result, Israel and the British themselves were far more likely to be perceived as the real enemy in the eyes of the Arab world, rather than some distant Soviet threat.

The Palestine link also highlighted the interlocking nature of Britain's Middle East defence planning and the problems this produced. Concessions to Egyptian nationalist demands were very likely to prompt similar pressures elsewhere. The upshot would be an undermining of the entire Middle Eastern imperial position. Even after the loss of Palestine, Britain's regional interests remained extensive. Apart from the 'main base' by the Suez Canal, they included two air bases in Iraq, the command of Jordan's Arab Legion army, a naval base at Aden, numerous facilities in Cyprus, protectorates over the sheikhdoms of eastern Arabia (where new oil discoveries were being made), and, until 1951, extensive oil and refining interests in Iran. The methods of British influence were largely informal in that they tended to rely upon treaty relationships (the directly administered crown colonies of Aden and Cyprus being exceptions to this rule), but as with the Egyptian connection, these legal arrangements were generally unpopular with the local populations, and were consequently a source of growing instability. Given that Britain's primary Cold War political task in the Middle East was to prevent the spread of communism, it could be contended – and indeed increasingly was argued by the Americans – that London's rigid insistence on maintaining peacetime military bases was becoming more a handicap than an advantage.

In addition, Washington had never been impressed by Britain's anti-Soviet strategic planning in the Middle East. There was, it was felt, far too much concern with protecting the Suez base and not nearly enough emphasis given to defending the region as a whole. The first emergency plan (drafted when 'war by accident' seemed a distinct possibility following the onset of the Berlin blockade in 1948), entailed demolishing – not safeguarding – oil installations in Iraq and Iran, while trying 'to impose the maximum delay on the enemy as far from the Egypt base as administrative resources will allow'. Code-named Sandown, the plan went on to delineate a series of delaying and harassing operations by mobile forces in Jordan and what it was still calling 'Palestine'. The centrepiece of the plan was the construction of a defensive line from Jericho to Ramallah and on to Tel Aviv. 'The Allied land forces will not withdraw into it unless forced to: there they will fight it out and from this position there will be no withdrawal.'[7] Leaving aside the fact that Sandown offered the prospect of a great power war being waged on Israeli territory (a third of which, in any case, was to be unprotected), the idea that the new Jewish state, which owed Britain few favours, might welcome the construction of a defensive line through its territory, with an accompanying foreign garrison, was, to put it kindly, unrealistic.[8]

Little wonder that American planners were deeply unimpressed. Any amateur strategist could see that a genuine defence of the region could be achieved only from a more northerly position. When US officials therefore contended that Sandown was tantamount to the defence of Egypt alone and not the Middle East (and even in this it failed to provide adequate air cover), their British counterparts pointed out that they did not have the forces to defend a more forward position. Meanwhile, the bureaucratic function of the Tel Aviv–Ramallah holding operation within Whitehall was that it reaffirmed the need for the permanent stationing of British forces in the Canal Zone. There could be no more offers of peacetime evacuation of the base, as in 1946, nor even of reducing the troop levels to the 10,000 permitted by the 1936 treaty.[9]

Another crucial feature of the shift in strategic thinking in the autumn of 1952 was that Britain's military planners finally started to take into account years of American pressure to at least try and defend the Middle East as a whole, rather than merely the northerly approaches to the Suez bastion. The origins of this direct US interest in the region can be traced back to 1947, when it acquired a position of influence in Turkey. In February of that year, as Britain struggled against one of the coldest winters on record, London had informed Washington that it could no longer afford to provide economic assistance to Greece and Turkey. As anticipated, the United States stepped in and announced aid packages to help both countries resist communism, and in the process inaugurated the Truman Doctrine (entailing the global containment of communism). William Roger Louis has described this development as a triumph of British statecraft, arguing that, in taking on this burden in the eastern Mediterranean, the Truman administration was effectively underwriting Britain's empire in the Middle East (with the exception of Palestine).[10] Washington was thereafter anxious to link its interests in Turkey with those in Europe. Following the creation of NATO in 1949, efforts were consequently made to involve Turkey and Greece as associate members, which was achieved in late 1950.

Britain's military planners tried to deal with the obvious failings of the Tel Aviv–Ramallah Line, not least its patent unacceptability to the Israelis (so obvious as never to be tested in any bilateral defence talks). In an attempt to secure Israel's eventual cooperation, a new plan was proposed which entailed defending a more northerly line running through Lebanon and Jordan. But US planners, during talks in Washington in October 1950, were dismissive for familiar reasons: its primary purpose, they felt, was again the defence of Egypt and not the Middle East. America's preferred approach required the defence of an Outer Ring, a great arc from the Taurus mountains in central Turkey, running on to eastern Turkey (above Iraq), and south through the Zagros mountain range on the western border of Iran, before stretching another 400 miles or so to an inland position about 100 miles north of the Strait of Hormuz. (The Americans had long felt that the British ought to at least try to defend some of the oilfields in the Middle East.) However, in January 1951, Britain's chiefs of staff disregarded this US advice (again, because of lack of resources) and formally adopted the Lebanon–Jordan Line strategy.[11] But even with these more modest plans, an American military contribution was still needed. The Truman administration's reluctance to become involved stemmed from its existing massive commitments in the Far East and Western Europe, and it thus continued to see the Middle East as a British responsibility in the struggle against communism.

In a further attempt to secure US military input during 1951, Britain's military planners contemplated adjusting their Lebanon–Jordan approach so that a more northerly defence of the region could be attempted, albeit one much less ambitious than the Outer Ring strategy. The concept was named the Inner Ring. It followed a similar path to the Outer Ring at the Taurus mountains, before dropping down through the middle of Syria to Jordan (instead of going on past Iraq to the western borders of Iran).[12] These ongoing discussions about Middle Eastern strategy became enmeshed in a wider Anglo-American debate in 1951 about how Turkey should be involved in NATO's Mediterranean defence arrangements, and the extent to which these ought to be linked to contingency planning for the Middle East: London was for a strong connection; Washington and Ankara against.

The onset, in June, of discussions for the creation of a multilateral Middle East Command brought the talks full circle in the sense that Britain's primary motive was to 'cloak' a continued peacetime presence in the Canal Zone, and thereby convince the sceptical Americans of this requirement.[13] At the same time, Britain's military planners also wanted to ensure that the Mediterranean theatre of operations did not become a mere appendage – the southern flank – of NATO's European command.[14] The essential point, then, was to ensure a direct connection between the Mediterranean theatre and

Britain's Middle East defence responsibilities. A sense of urgency was added to these deliberations by the deteriorating relations with Egypt, and indeed by the end of the summer Britain's primary purpose in pursuing the Middle East Command approach had fundamentally shifted to being a mechanism by which American support could be secured prior to the anticipated onset of nationalist disturbances in the Canal Zone.[15]

The influence of the abrogation crisis (October 1951 to January 1952) on the shift in strategic thinking towards the end of 1952 was profound, even if there was still a tendency for Britain's military authorities in Egypt to dig in their heels. The most immediate and sensitive readings of the shock were registered by the embassy in Cairo. Even before the Ismailia incident and the ensuing Black Saturday riots, Stevenson had sent recommendations to London advocating a withdrawal of the Canal Zone garrison, but these had been categorically rejected by the British Defence Coordinating Committee for the Middle East. 'We do not agree that our base in the Canal Zone is rendered useless by Egyptian hostility,' the committee stated in a letter to the chiefs of staff on 16 December 1951. The committee went on to stress the symbolic significance of the base: Stevenson's proposals, they stated, would bring about 'a disastrous and world-wide loss of our prestige . . . The Arab states would lose all confidence in our leadership and our treaties with Iraq and Jordan would be placed in jeopardy.'[16]

After the bloody climax of the Canal Zone siege, Stevenson was even more convinced that Egypt's hostility would render the base useless in a future war. He was also deeply critical of the latest change in the plans for the defence of the Middle East. In December 1951, despite a continuing shortfall in forces, the chiefs of staff had abandoned the Lebanon–Jordan strategy in favour of the Inner Ring.[17] In Stevenson's opinion, the counter-offensive aspects of the new concept still seemed tailored to justifying a peacetime garrison in the Suez base, rather than to launching effective military operations. 'The communications north-eastwards from the Canal consist of the one line of railway from Kantara,' he wrote in an internal embassy minute on 22 February 1952:

> If reinforcements are going to be brought to fight in this part of the world surely they would be taken direct to Basra to support Iraq and to Alexandretta to bolster the Turkish right flank. It would be absurd, if we are going to fight as far forward as that, to bring all our reinforcements through the bottleneck of Suez. But the latter would of course be

invaluable later as a rearward base or in the case of having to fall back. All this is in favour of the Egyptian thesis of reactivating the base in the outbreak of war and not necessarily having it in existence in peacetime.[18]

This perceptive critique anticipated changes in military thinking made later in the year.[19]

While the chiefs of staff did not share Stevenson's view on the need to evacuate the Suez base, they did agree with him that a revised defence settlement with Egypt should at least be attempted. Their say had been vital to the cabinet decision in February 1952, which agreed the terms for the restart of negotiations. As Roger Allen noted, the service chiefs did not 'wish to see British troops placed once again in the position which we were at the beginning of this year'.[20] This attitude was underpinned, moreover, by a growing conviction that military planning based on the use of the Canal Zone base was, as the chiefs of staff themselves put it on 21 January, both 'academic and unrealistic'.[21] The renewed defence negotiations picked up from where the previous ones had left off – with the multilateral Middle East Command approach, albeit with Eden now also offering the 'withdrawal of British combatant forces from the Canal Zone'.[22]

In the meantime, the Labour government had been replaced by the Conservatives and new prime minister Winston Churchill made no bones about disliking his foreign secretary's policy, especially when Eden pressed to go even further in March by suggesting that Britain accept the principle of withdrawal in return for the Egyptians accepting the principle of a Middle East Command. 'What troubles me deeply', wrote the prime minister on 6 April, 'and what I really cannot understand is that we are giving everything into Egypt's power and have nothing in return, nor any means of securing the fulfilment of any understanding.'[23] On this occasion, Churchill's views prevailed. There could be no withdrawal from the Canal Zone until Middle East Command forces were already in place.[24] With significant concessions politically impossible, the British instead made a cosmetic alteration. In June 1952, the name of the proposed body was formally changed to the Middle East Defence Organisation, the word 'command' being belatedly perceived to have imperial connotations.[25]

Alongside the shock of the Canal Zone siege, three other developments helped bring about the major rethink in Britain's global strategic planning (and Egypt's role therein) during 1952. The first concerned financial difficulties. In late 1951, the incoming Conservative administration inherited a balance of payments problem which approached the disastrous proportions of the 1949 devaluation (when the worth of the pound had been slashed from US $4.03 to US $2.80). The new chancellor of the exchequer, Rab Butler, realised that immediate remedial measures were needed and he began by setting his sights on the £4,700 million defence programme established by the Attlee government during the early stages of the Korean War. This pressure for financial savings was felt in acute form by the service chiefs throughout 1952. The second push on military thinking related to technological advances in atomic warfare. Britain in October 1952 at last joined the exclusive nuclear club. At the same time, however, there was an awareness that the United States and, in all likelihood, Russia were on the verge of the next great leap forward – the hydrogen bomb. During Churchill and Eden's trip to Washington in January 1952, President Truman had briefed his guests on how America planned to utilise thermonuclear weapons in a future global war. Awed by the disclosures, British officials began to question the usefulness of massive conventional rearmament and instead saw a possible link between nuclear weapons and economic savings (what Americans would later speak of as 'more bang for the buck').[26] Until this point, Britain's own atomic bomb programme had been viewed primarily in terms of prestige, a notion Ernest Bevin had perfectly encapsulated in 1947 with his remark, 'We've got to have a bloody Union Jack fly on top of it.'[27] The third major influence on Britain's shift in strategic planning, especially as it affected Egypt, was Turkey's full admission into NATO in early 1952.

The confluence of these three developments took several months. Meanwhile, in a completely contradictory vein, Britain committed itself – via the Lisbon accords of February 1952 – to supplying ten divisions for NATO's use by 1954. The total size of the regular army, given its commitments in Germany, the Middle East, Malaya and Korea, was only eleven divisions.[28] While putting the 'O' into NATO may have seemed a good idea politically, it did not make much sense for Britain economically, nor for that matter strategically. Three months earlier, in November 1951, the chiefs of staff had agreed a revised planning estimate which held that the Soviet Union did not intend to start a total war and was instead far more likely to try to exploit Western weakness through 'Cold War methods and local aggression'.[29] The force levels set at Lisbon could, in this regard, easily become counter-productive in that economic weakness might result.

Having effectively taken a couple of steps back with the additional NATO commitments, Britain then proceeded to take a step forward by adopting a new overall deterrent posture. It was called the Long Haul, an oblique reference to the stretching of Labour's rearmament programme over a longer period. A one-off build-up of forces in the near future (the premise of the old posture) was no longer deemed necessary.[30] The most original aspect of the revised approach was its attempt to integrate the nuclear programme into the wider setting of Britain's conventional rearmament obligations and, most importantly, its economic predicament. Eden's private secretary, Evelyn Shuckburgh, in the privacy of his diary, scathingly cut to the essence of the policy: 'all it is really saying is we cannot spend more on defence, cannot reach our goals, better abandon them and make do with what we have. It is called the "New Look" and the "Long Haul" to make it sound impressive.'[31]

The economic imperative for defence savings dovetailed with reactions to the Canal Zone siege to make the base in Egypt a focus for potential cuts. In the upside-down manner of Whitehall military planning, all that remained to be done was the formulation of a new strategic rationale to justify a lessening of the Suez base's military importance. To this end, in the spring of 1952, Britain's chiefs of staff locked themselves away for a week at the Royal Navy's staff college in Greenwich and drew up a whole new basis for Britain's military planning. The 'Greenwich exercise' culminated in the 'global strategy paper' of 17 June 1952. Its main conclusion, which was a crystallisation of the Long Haul approach, stated that, 'provided the deterrents of atomic airpower and adequate forces on the ground in Europe were properly built up and maintained, the likelihood of war would be much diminished and we could in consequence ease our economic position by accepting a smaller and slower build up of forces, equipment and reserves for war'.[32]

The area where the service chiefs thought that cuts could be made was the Middle East. In the following weeks, it was decided that as soon as an agreement was reached with Egypt, Britain could reduce its Middle Eastern deployments to a level adequate for Cold War requirements alone. This so-called global strategy garrison was set at one division and 160 aircraft.[33] Reinforcements would be sent to the region in the event of an emergency. As the service chiefs admitted, this recommendation was made not because it was considered to be necessarily militarily sound, but because only in the Middle East could they see any way of significantly reducing overseas expenditure in the near future.[34] It was perhaps not merely fortuitous that, in the meantime, intelligence estimates had downgraded the Soviet threat to the Levant (and therefore Egypt) in the early stages of a war.[35] The logic of all this was that a peacetime base in Egypt was no longer a necessity: forces could be brought into position at the outset of a war.

THE LEVANT–IRAQ STRATEGY

This, then, was the fluid political, economic and military background to the chiefs of staff meeting on 21 October 1952, during which Britain's service chiefs admitted that the Suez base was no longer *necessarily* essential to Britain's strategic requirements in peacetime. On leaving the meeting Roger Allen dared to see an end to the Canal Zone dispute. As one of the leading advocates in British policymaking circles of a revised defence agreement with Egypt, Allen felt strongly that a settlement would only be possible if Britain's forces were first evacuated. The seventy-year imperial occupation had to be seen to end, and this meant all troops leaving the Canal Zone before any new Cold War defence arrangement could take its place.

During the winter of 1952/3, as the public focus of the Anglo-Egyptian struggle shifted to the Sudan, Britain's military planners did as Allen had hoped and mapped out a new strategic concept for the Middle East, which effectively downgraded the importance of the Suez base. As with the earlier developments, economic pressures within Britain continued to mesh with the ongoing responses to Egyptian nationalist demands. The revised approach (in accord with force-level targets established in the wake of June's landmark global strategy paper) entailed a much smaller covering force (approximately one division, plus Jordan's British-led Arab Legion) being permanently stationed in the Middle East. In the event of war, it was anticipated that rapid reinforcements would be sent by air and the Suez base fully reactivated.

The new battleplan was for a British, Iraqi and Arab Legion covering force to push up quickly into north-eastern Iraq and attempt to block the main entry points at the Ruwandiz, Penjwin and Panitak passes in the Zagros mountains. Air operations, raiding parties and extensive demolitions of the passes were envisaged. The plan also anticipated mobile Turkish forces, now viewed as much stronger after recent US military assistance, striking south of the flank of any Russian movement through Iraq. When making their recommendation to the chiefs of staff, the joint planners stated that an 'advantage of the Levant–Iraq strategy over the Inner Ring is that it allows for small forces, initially in the Middle East, to be deployed to the best advantage and it makes the enemy fight his way into, and perhaps through, Iraq':

> At worst it would retard the enemy's arrival on the Inner Ring. The grave risk in this strategy is that we may be forced back to an unprepared position on the Inner Ring before the reinforcing divisions from the United Kingdom are operational. We believe that this risk must be accepted . . . Were we to retain the use of the Egyptian base in peacetime we would still recommend this strategy.[36]

Formal approval for this Levant–Iraq strategy (or Forward Strategy as it was also known) was given on 14 November 1952.[37] There was a condition, however. Implementation of the new concept was made dependent on an Egyptian settlement – a sure indication that problems in the Canal Zone rather than possibilities in Turkey and Iraq were more influential in driving this shift. Nevertheless, the chances of an agreement had significantly improved now that a working base at Suez was no longer seen as a peacetime requirement. The relief of Britain's embassy in Cairo was almost palpable. An internal embassy minute dated 6 December described the recent changes as 'a very considerable advance in military thinking'.[38]

Major difficulties still remained, however, not least the problem of redeploying forces away from the Canal Zone. The military issues involved were, perhaps, the simplest to deal with. While the joint planners could pore over their maps and say what ought to be moved and why, their schemes had to bear at least a resemblance to economic and political realities. Financially, the continuing Treasury pressure for savings, which had been redoubled in the autumn with Rab Butler calling for a further 'Radical Review', was something of a two-edged sword as regards the possible shift away from an Egypt-based strategy. This was because the Levant–Iraq plan placed a greater emphasis on securing additional facilities in Jordan and Iraq, including the improvement of communications, and all this cost money at a time when significant cutbacks were being demanded. In addition, the need for increased logistical cooperation from other Arab states was a major political difficulty. If Britain reached an agreement on the Canal Zone based on apparent concessions, Egypt's neighbours who also held defence links would almost inevitably call for treaty revision themselves. In other words, Egypt's leadership status in the Arab world, reflected in the Arab League's headquarters being in Cairo and its secretary-general being an Egyptian, meant that its political importance remained constant even when its strategic worth was being whittled down.

Iraq's value to Britain would clearly increase the most once the new Forward Strategy was adopted. While geography was the main factor in this, a much greater contribution than before was also expected from its armed forces, once they were properly equipped and trained. It was thus a source of some concern for British officials that under the Anglo-Iraqi defence treaty of 1937, Iraq acquired the right to discuss treaty revision from October 1952. Despite good relations with the ruling Hashemite dynasty and its 'strong man' Nuri al-Said, Britain's ambassador in Baghdad fully expected a withdrawal from Egypt to evoke, because of nationalist pressures, an immediate demand for the evacuation of the RAF's Iraqi air bases at Habbaniya and Shaiba.[39]

Jordan similarly acquired an enhanced importance in the Levant–Iraq planning. In operational terms, the Arab Legion had been earmarked to assist in the defence of Turkey's right flank, as well as in the Iraqi mountain passes.[40] Britain's need to redeploy forces away from Egypt also contributed to Jordan's increased value: the reduced peacetime military presence in the Middle East would need to be situated somewhere. A top priority was finding an appropriate home for the armoured brigade presently stationed in the Canal Zone. Because of its proximity to Egypt (where the 'main base' would be reactivated in time of war), Jordan was the obvious choice. It would also be a visible sign of strength in the Arab world, another prerequisite for any withdrawal from Egypt.[41] But even in Jordan, which was long regarded as the most reliable of Britain's Arab allies, political difficulties were anticipated. The Foreign Office thought it highly unlikely that permission would be given for a large army base in Jordan, as required by a brigade group. Such a contingency was not covered by the Anglo-Jordan treaty of 1948 and, as elsewhere in the region, it would be at odds with the rising tide of nationalist opinion.[42]

In search of another option, Britain's military planners turned their attention to Libya, which had achieved statehood in December 1950 by virtue of a UN resolution that combined the former Italian colonies of Tripolitania and Cyrenaica. Britain's strategic interest was primarily in Cyrenaica, the more easterly of the two provinces. Its status in military planning had tended to rise and fall with the rhythms of the Egyptian problem. When Britain contemplated moving from the Canal Zone in 1946, Cyrenaica had been pencilled in as an alternative, but when it was decided to retain the Suez base irrespective of Egypt's attitude, Cyrenaica's strategic importance declined.[43] Naturally, it increased again in 1952–3: if additional base rights could not be acquired in Jordan, Libya was seen as offering a stop-gap for the armoured brigade group.[44] In the late 1940s, moreover, Cyrenaica had been seen as a location from which Britain could, if required, enter Egypt by force to secure base facilities in a future war.[45] A similar role was always possible should Egypt ever try and renege on the reactivation rights in a revised defence settlement.

In this jigsaw of military interests in the Arab world, Britain also hoped to find a place for Israel, whose geography, military potential and well-developed facilities made it impossible to ignore. In 1951, after the messy imperial disengagement from Palestine, a diplomatic rapprochement between London and Tel Aviv permitted Britain's military planners to consider more carefully, and realistically, the role Israel might play in a future war. The main obstacle was the ongoing Arab–Israeli dispute, which ruled out an Israeli contribution to a land battle against the USSR outside its own frontiers. Nevertheless, its forward position made it an ideal communications centre and listening post for early warning of attacks on the Canal Zone base.[46] After November 1952 and the adoption in principle of the Forward Strategy, Israel's military potential was extended to control and reporting functions for the air battle in the Iraqi passes.

Any eagerness to court the assistance of Israel had to be tempered, however, because of the danger that overt cooperation would arouse the strong opposition of the Arab world. Britain's service chiefs hoped that this problem could be circumvented if Israel confined its defence contribution to the air battle: it was believed that Arab permission for Israeli over-flying rights was more likely than permission for land movements. But Israel's military planners had different ideas, centring on their own defence concerns vis-à-vis the Arab states. A British exploratory military mission to Tel Aviv in October 1952 was informed that Israel intended to develop a balanced force structure able to meet land as well as air requirements. Britain regarded this as a waste of resources.[47] In any case, for so long as the Arab–Israeli dispute persisted, any coordinated Israeli contribution to regional defence was likely to be far less than Britain hoped.

The potential shift away from the Canal Zone, as allowed by the Levant–Iraq strategy, thus opened up all sorts of redeployment problems. Only with the crown colony of Cyprus, which did not have the same political delicacies as countries where Britain's 'informal' influence prevailed, was it possible to take a positive redeployment step without waiting on an Egyptian settlement. The impact of the Canal Zone siege was explicit in this decision. Following the previous winter's disturbances, it was accepted in military circles that the Middle East's joint headquarters for air and land forces needed to be relocated to a politically stable and secure area. There was no defiant talk of 'standing pat' in the Canal Zone, to use General Robertson's expression of March 1952.[48] And yet, in a clue to future developments with regard to the Egyptian problem, Conservative ministers were hesitant for their own political reasons to accept military advice. Moving the Middle East headquarters might be construed as the start of a policy of 'scuttle' in Egypt. In the end, the more northerly defence of the region contemplated from November onwards just succeeded in tipping the scales in favour of Cyprus. The relocation of the joint headquarters would take at least eighteen months. Preparatory building work was therefore necessary if this time factor was not to become an obstacle to an eventual defence agreement with Egypt. On 2 December the cabinet reluctantly allowed preliminary construction work to go ahead.[49]

THE RESTART OF DEFENCE NEGOTIATIONS

As the end of 1952 approached, British policymakers readied themselves for a new defence approach to Egypt with the aim of settling the Canal Zone dispute. But despite all the developments in strategic thinking, a crucial issue still needed resolving. While the proposed Levant–Iraq concept *allowed* for a peacetime evacuation of the Suez base, this had yet to be accepted as the way to proceed, either by the chiefs of staff or the Conservative government. The strategic rationale of having a well-established working base at Suez remained an extremely difficult proposition to abandon, even with the nationalist challenge from Egypt. Moreover, the chiefs of staff, as experienced Whitehall warriors, had been able to respond to the Treasury's pressure for cuts by emphasising the costs of redeployment away from the Canal Zone, thus keeping their options open. And as for the politics of the situation, the British garrison astride the Suez artery still served a massively important symbolic function in terms of prestige, which the revised strategic thinking did little to address.

In late November, Britain's joint planning staff outlined the military requirements for a revised defence treaty with Egypt. The document began by stating that, 'for military and financial reasons we would wish to retain a base in Egypt in peace, but in order to obtain Egyptian goodwill we may have to forego this facility'. It went on to emphasise the need for increased cooperation from other countries in the Middle East:

> Provided the necessary political agreements and expensive administrative arrangements can be made in peacetime, it is possible, without a base in Egypt, to maintain a forward strategy with small forces for a short period after the outbreak of war. After the first few months, however, when the Middle East forces are built up, the Canal Zone Base becomes essential.

The logic of this allowed the joint planners to identify three possible scenarios for an agreement with Egypt. 'Case A' entailed the transfer of the base area to Egyptian control but with the retention of some 7,500 British supervisors and technicians to run depots and installations. 'Case B' entailed holding war supplies in the Canal Zone and retaining heavy workshops, but with no British personnel present. Small inspection teams would visit from time to time. 'Case C' involved the complete evacuation of stores and personnel from the Canal Zone in peace, provided that a right of return was agreed in war or the imminent threat of war.[50]

When the report went before the chiefs of staff on 2 December 1952, the various cases were modified. Case A subsequently entailed the retention of 7,000 personnel, 5,000 of whom would be army and 2,000 RAF, the latter as part of a newly envisaged integrated Anglo-Egyptian air defence organisation. These air defence arrangements also featured as part of a new Case B, alongside the retention of between 500 and 1,000 British supervisory and technical personnel once the base had been passed to Egyptian control. Case C consequently became the same as the Joint Planning Staff's original Case B, while a new Case D was the former Case C.[51] After a further round of discussions with the Cairo embassy and the Foreign Office, the chiefs of staff came to the conclusion that, in military planning terms, something between cases B and C might be acceptable as a basis for the restart of defence negotiations with Egypt, a decision endorsed by the cabinet's defence committee on 11 December.[52] 'After all this time', observes the *BDEEP* editor, 'and after the adoption [in principle] of a new strategy, the COS were still hedging on complete evacuation in peacetime as only Cases C and D conceded this point.'[53]

The next step for Britain was to decide what precise role it wanted the United States to play in the new defence approach to Egypt. In general foreign policy terms, there was a desire to involve the Americans at every opportunity. Eden had articulated this view in a cabinet memorandum entitled 'British overseas obligations' in June 1952, written to complement the chiefs of staff's global strategy paper of that same month. As such, it may be viewed as the Foreign Office's response to the Treasury's government-wide demands for savings. Eden's underlying thesis was that reductions in Britain's responsibilities could only be made if damage to Britain's world position was not incurred. The way to do this was to avoid any immediate abandonment of interests, even minor ones. Instead, it was necessary to maintain all existing commitments so as to demonstrate to the US that Britain was making the maximum possible effort in the Cold War. The longer-term aim, however, was to transfer 'gradually and inconspicuously' Britain's 'real burdens . . . to American shoulders'. In reference to Egyptian policy, Eden had observed that it was 'beyond the resources of the United Kingdom to continue to assume the responsibility alone for the security of the Middle East . . . Our aim should be to make this area and in particular the Canal Zone an international responsibility. Hence every step should be taken to speed up the establishment of an Allied Middle East Defence Organisation.'[54]

The key question in early 1953, therefore, was not whether the Americans should be involved in the Anglo-Egyptian negotiations, but how to bring them on board. Given the emphasis on establishing a multilateral defence organisation, it was decided that the best way forward was through a joint approach to Egypt. The outgoing Truman administration agreed in principle to this, while leaving the details to be sorted out by the incoming Eisenhower presidency.

With the final phase of the Sudan negotiations preoccupying British policymakers for the first six weeks of 1953 (along with the changing of the White House guard in the US), it was not until a Sudan settlement had been achieved that further progress on the defence front could be made. As stated at the beginning of this chapter, Eden instructed his officials to prepare a cabinet paper setting out the reasons why a settlement of the Canal Zone dispute was needed. Roger Allen oversaw the drafting of the memorandum. He was especially keen to counter what he regarded as the military's tendency towards inertia. 'The truth of the matter', he minuted on 14 February, 'is that we are at present keeping 80,000 men in the Canal Zone for no purpose except to maintain themselves.'

It is their presence which creates the need for them to be there. This is at a time when it is vitally important that we should reduce our forces. We are no longer able to impose our will by force upon the countries of the Middle East, and therefore we should not fall between two stools as we are at present. It is useless to maintain our troops to be shot at.[55]

The finished memorandum, entitled 'Egypt: the alternatives', was circulated to ministers on 16 February. The imprint was clearly that of Allen, perhaps the most pro-settlement of the Foreign Office mandarins.

As a cabinet paper, it amounted to Eden's strongest statement to date of the need for an Anglo-Egyptian defence agreement, and it is therefore worth quoting at length (not least because it contained advice which he himself would have been wise to follow three and a half years later):

In the second half of the 20th century we cannot hope to maintain our position in the Middle East by the methods of the last century. However little we like it, we must face that fact.

. . . In most of the countries of the Middle East the social and economic aspirations of the common people are quickening and the tide of nationalism is rising fast. If we are to maintain our influence in this area, future policy must be designed to harness these movements rather than to struggle against them.

Our strategic purposes in the Middle East can no longer be served by arrangements which local nationalism will regard as military occupation by foreign troops. It is immaterial from what country those troops come. It would be a delusion to suppose that, in Egypt or elsewhere in the Middle East, local opinion would tolerate occupation by American or French forces any more readily than the Egyptians tolerate the British garrison on the Canal.

Our strategic interests in this area must in future be served by arrangements designed to enable its peoples to play a significant, if not a principal, part in its defence. They must at least appear to have a determining voice of the disposition of the defence forces for the area. But, if that principle is conceded, they may accept the assistance of ourselves, the Americans and the leading Powers of Western Europe in organising and equipping their own forces; and they may also be willing that the defence of the whole area shall be organised in association with those Powers.

The case for an agreement was as follows:

What other course could we follow? Could we stand on our rights under the 1936 Treaty? We may reproach Egypt for the unilateral renunciation of the Treaty. But let us not forget that we are ourselves in serious breach of it. It allows us to maintain not more than 10,000 troops in Egypt in time of peace: since 1936 we have rarely had so few there, and we now have nearer 80,000. Moreover, the Treaty expires at the end of 1956, and it will take at least 18 months to complete the withdrawal of our troops. Even if we decide to hang on until the Treaty expires, withdrawal will have to begin in two years' time. Thus, a policy of standing on the Treaty would be shaky in the present and barren for the future.

We could undoubtedly deal effectively with any immediate attempt by the Egyptians to eject us by force from the Canal Zone. But the situation which this would create would almost certainly compel us to re-occupy Egypt, with all the consequences which this would entail. We should be likely to have world opinion against us and would find it difficult to make a case if Egypt took us to the United Nations. It is hard to see what future there is for such a policy. We cannot afford to keep 80,000 men indefinitely in the Canal Zone . . .

With our limited resources, it is essential that we should concentrate on the points where our vital strategic needs or the necessities of our economic life are at stake and that we should utilise our strength in the most economical way. It is not possible for our present forces in the Canal Zone to support our peace-time interests elsewhere in the Middle East. If we leave them there in defiance of the Egyptians they will be wholly absorbed in coping with the situation which their very presence creates.[56]

Eden's memorandum succeeded in persuading the Conservative government of the need to restart the Canal Zone negotiations, and during the next month the details of a joint approach were agreed with the new US Republican administration.[57]

However, the policy that emerged failed to take advantage of the revised thinking among Britain's military planners from the previous autumn. Even the defence committee's earlier endorsement of a solution based somewhere between cases B and C was deemed impossible (B amounted to the establishment of an air defence organisation, plus 500–1,000 retained personnel, while C envisaged a withdrawal of all personnel, but with war supplies and heavy workshops being kept in place). Rather, the political requirement for the negotiations was set rigidly at Case A. Given that this entailed retaining 7,000 personnel in the Canal Zone (only 3,000 less than the number legally permitted under the hated 1936 defence treaty), the prospects for a settlement were, to say the least, slim.

Opinion within the Conservative Party accounted for this inflexibility, and constrained Eden in the process. As a consequence, the foreign secretary now effectively lagged behind the military planners, rather than the other way round. With a government majority of seventeen, Eden, no less than his cabinet colleagues, could not afford to ignore the newly formed Suez Group, which had at least twenty-five hardcore members. The upshot was that the value of the new defence approach was viewed less in terms of the concessions being made (Egypt had rejected similar terms already), than in the extras being added on, which were connected with the US's involvement as the co-sponsor. Thus, the Case A conditions were to be couched as part of a 'package deal' whereby a Canal Zone agreement would be linked to Egyptian participation in a Middle East Defence Organisation and an integrated air defence scheme, which in turn would result in America providing extensive military and economic assistance to the Egyptians. It was this overall package that Eden thought worth a renewed attempt at a settlement; Washington, for its part, hoped there would be some subsequent movement away from Case A.[58]

Great store was also placed on negotiating methods. London believed that a joint approach would make it impossible for the Egyptians to play the Americans off against the British, as they had in the past. The Foreign Office, moreover, hoped to have a say in what military and economic aid the US might confer on Egypt after an agreement.[59] A new mechanism for actually conducting the talks was also agreed. Rather than have Stevenson and Caffery lead the negotiations, it was decided to bring in two senior military officers to help.[60] Technical military talks, it could be argued, required specialist officials. In pushing for this, London was keen to have checks in place on both ambassadors in Cairo. Caffery, of course, was viewed as utterly unreliable by British officials: anything to circumvent his influence was a good thing. But there was also a question mark over Stevenson, resulting from his earlier criticisms of Britain's military authorities in Egypt.[61] Cabinet Secretary Sir Norman Brook, Britain's most senior civil servant, had asked Churchill if he wanted the ambassador replacing before the restart of the talks, but the suggestion was not taken up; nor was the idea of sending a minister over to Egypt, the feeling being in this instance that there would be too much pressure for a result.[62]

Instead, the decision was taken to have General Sir Brian Robertson, the commander-in-chief of Britain's Middle East Land Forces, serve as Stevenson's co-delegate. Robertson was immediately required to give up his command and move to a villa near the British embassy in Cairo.[63] On the American side, a more complicated situation arose. Appointing a co-delegate to work alongside Caffery would, it was felt, amount to a slight on the ambassador's work to date in Egypt. A 'special military adviser' was therefore judged more appropriate, a task which fell to General John E. Hull, the US army's vice chief of staff.[64]

But before it could even get off the ground, the Anglo-American joint approach collapsed amid a welter of acrimony between the supposed allies. On 15 March 1953 Egypt's military junta announced that it was not prepared to negotiate with the United States about the Canal Zone because any such talks would be interpreted in Egypt as discussions for a regional defence organisation, an issue the regime refused to contemplate until the evacuation issue had been resolved.[65] That same day, Caffery explained to the State Department that Neguib had told him that he could accomplish more in his 'behind-the-scenes role' than as 'an active negotiator'.[66]

While Eisenhower was content to condemn the whole affair as plain 'clumsy', British policymakers saw red and made a formal complaint about Caffery, the strong suspicion being that he had encouraged the Egyptians to reject the joint aspect so that he could continue to play his preferred role of mediator. According to Allen's general assessment, the US ambassador deliberately flattered and encouraged the military regime 'in order to build up his own position, and incidentally that of the US, at our expense', and that ultimately his aim was to present himself as the power behind the throne in

Egypt.[67] William Lakeland, the political counsellor at the US embassy in Cairo, also attracted criticism – Creswell describing him as 'notable for his youthful enthusiasm and idealistic, even sentimental, approach to the Egyptians untempered by realism and uncoloured by any feeling of solidarity with us'.[68] This disunity between the two allies did not go unnoticed by the Egyptian press. A cartoon in the Cairo daily *Al Akhbar* showed Caffery leaning over the ropes during a boxing match between Neguib and Churchill and whispering to the general, 'Do you want my help?' 'No thank you,' comes the reply, 'I can deal with him myself.'[69]

Although diplomacy was meant to be dominating the respective agendas of Egypt and Britain in April, it was clear to everyone involved that the new defence approach, which London decided to press ahead with on a bilateral basis, was doomed before it had ever truly started. Despite the bickering about Caffery and the public failure to get the United States jointly involved, the underlying cause was Britain's continuing unwillingness to evacuate the Suez base in peacetime. The shifts in strategic thinking in 1952, which were intimately entwined with the external push of Egyptian nationalism and the internal pull of Britain's financial infirmity, had looked like producing a compromise in the Canal Zone dispute, but in the end the old imperial inertia on a political level had stubbornly kicked in. Ironically, the dismantling of the Sudan 'stone wall' was pivotal in this respect. While one obstacle had been removed in the Egyptian context (Farouk's dynastic claims), a new obstruction had been created in British politics – the Suez Group.

The failure of the Conservative government to take advantage of the shift in military thinking concerning the peacetime necessity of the Suez base amounted to a major missed opportunity in relations with Egypt, and for Britain's position of influence in the Middle East generally. The Levant–Iraq concept was, above all else, a strategic planning justification for a peacetime withdrawal from the Suez base. For six years, Britain's service chiefs had effectively blocked a compromise solution in the Canal Zone dispute with their insistence that a working base in peacetime was essential to Britain's global strategic requirements. The result had been mounting Egyptian nationalist opposition, which eventually culminated in the Canal Zone siege and the Free Officers' *coup d'état*. The subsequent aggregation of power within Egypt into one centre (the military regime) meant that Britain's imperial tactic of manipulating the palace and political parties was no longer possible, at least not while the United States remained on friendly terms with the military rulers. It was these Egyptian developments that, in turn, pushed the British military planners into fundamentally reassessing the worth of the main regional base when surrounded by a hostile population.

It should also be emphasised that the Levant–Iraq concept served a second critical function. As a more forward strategy (which embraced the eastern half of Turkey), it was meant to entice Washington into assuming greater responsibility for the defence of the Middle East. The boldness of this new thinking was impressive. In one fell swoop, it attempted to resolve the two biggest difficulties in Britain's Cold War Middle East defence planning, lack of military resources and Egyptian nationalist opposition. But its appeal to the Churchill-led government, with its small Commons majority, was ultimately limited precisely because it only dealt with the Cold War problems. The Levant–Iraq strategy did not address the longer-standing imperial requirement for a British garrison to be seen astride the great Suez artery. Thus, it was no longer military inertia that prevented a solution to the Canal Zone dispute during the rest of 1953 – it was political inertia.

EIGHT

• • • • • • • • • • •

Inertia and its Discontents

Before the spring of 1953 there had been two fundamental stumbling blocks in the post-Second World War efforts at resolving the Anglo-Egyptian dispute over Britain's continuing occupation of the Suez base. One had been Farouk's dynastic claims to be king of the Sudan ('Unity of the Nile Valley'); the other, the insistence of Britain's military planners that a peacetime presence in the Canal Zone was essential to British global strategy in the Cold War. Time after time, these two concerns had caused negotiations to break down until finally, in October 1951, a major confrontation occurred. What started as a quarrel over possession of the Suez base (London maintained a legal right to be there by virtue of the 1936 defence treaty, whereas Cairo claimed to have abrogated that right) then developed into a triangular struggle for power and influence in Egypt. Internally, the long-standing rivalry between the Egyptian palace, the Wafd and the British was exacerbated to such an extent that there arose a crisis of governability, which paved the way for a *coup d'état* in July 1952. A new set of rivalries subsequently emerged as the junta, or the Revolutionary Command Council (RCC) as it called itself from early 1953, battled against its foes, mainly from the old landowning elite. Externally, meanwhile, there was a barely concealed struggle between Britain and the United States for influence in Egypt. This remained the situation following the latest formal break in the Suez negotiations on 6 May 1953. Only now the old excuses no longer held. The Sudan complication had been removed, along with Farouk; and although the Conservative government in Britain had yet to concede it, the Cold War military planning requirement for a peacetime presence in the Suez base had also effectively been abandoned. Stripped of these pretexts, the Canal Zone dispute finally presented itself in its primary colours – a clash between nationalism and imperialism.

While Eden felt that Britain's imperial interests were best served by attempting to accommodate the demands of the Egyptian nationalists, powerful forces within the Conservative Party, encouraged by Churchill, regarded any withdrawal from the mighty Suez garrison as a retreat too far. The postwar catalogue of disengagements – Palestine, India and Abadan under Labour, and now the Sudan under Eden's stewardship – had to stop. Meanwhile, for the coup leaders, securing the evacuation of British forces was their ticket to survival in Egyptian domestic politics; failure, or even delay, was likely to spell their demise. But a settlement of the dispute clearly required movement on both sides.

The core of Britain's latest offer had been the retention of 7,000 personnel in the Suez base. Compared with the 80,000 troops currently stationed there (the 1936 treaty permitted only 10,000), this seemed alarmingly generous in the eyes of imperial hardliners in Britain. To Egyptian nationalists, however, accepting such a number would be like tying Egypt to the terms of 1936 all over again, which would be suicidal for any administration. There were two routes to a compromise. The first, obviously, was for movement between 7,000 and zero. Indeed, this was necessary come what may. The second related to masking the continuation of a foreign military presence in Egypt, and this could undoubtedly have its uses for both disputants. Thus far, a couple of methods had been attempted, although one had been dropped almost immediately.

The more important by a considerable distance was Britain's desire to create a multilateral defence arrangement – the Middle East Command/Middle East Defence Organisation. Previously, in December 1950, Ernest Bevin had suggested another possible solution, namely, the maintenance of the Suez base by British technicians in civilian clothes, but this idea had been summarily scotched by the service chiefs.[1] The consequences of not reaching a compromise were already being felt. Following Egypt's refusal to contemplate formal US involvement in the negotiations in mid-March 1953, there had been a steady increase in the number of guerrilla incidents in the Canal Zone. Their aim, as earlier in the year during the Sudan negotiations, was to press Britain into making concessions. The effect instead was to strengthen the hand of the Suez Group in the Conservative Party.

While the immediate prospects for agreement were bleak, the future looked even worse. In April, Anthony Eden, the main British proponent of a compromise, underwent gall-bladder surgery, and after an initial operation had gone wrong was obliged to convalesce for six months. Churchill, who loathed the very idea of imperial disengagement, assumed control of the Foreign Office. Tellingly, he insisted that all telegrams on Egyptian matters be sent to his private office.[2] He also stopped the Foreign Office from making any more complaints to the RCC about inflammatory Egyptian statements: 'The more abusive and insulting they are,' he stated on 22 April, 'the easier it will be for us to take a calm line and also, if need be, a strong one.'[3] A day earlier he had requested to see the plans for the defence of Britain's embassy in Cairo in the event of a mob attack.[4] Under Churchill's supervision, negotiations were clearly not going to be prioritised.

THE DULLES VISIT TO CAIRO

The new Republican administration in the United States was extremely frustrated with the British and Egyptians for failing to capitalise on the momentum gained by the Sudan agreement in February. Rather than being a cornerstone of Western Cold War planning in the Middle East, Egypt was increasingly looking like its Achilles heel. Anxious to halt the current drift, John Foster Dulles decided that he should undertake a tour of the Middle East in order to clarify America's general policy towards the region, a task made more urgent after the 'joint approach' debacle in March. When informed of Dulles's intention to stop in Cairo on 11 May, the RCC upped the number of guerrilla attacks against the Suez garrison accordingly. The aim was to bring the dispute to a head in the hope that no less a person than the US secretary of state would step in and act as mediator.

The RCC's reliance on covertly sponsored fedayeen raids reflected its appreciation that a frontal attack by the Egyptian armed forces on British troops and installations in the Canal Zone was still out of the question. Colonel Nasser, the real leader of the junta despite the continued projection of General Neguib as prime minister, was nevertheless wary of the price that might have to be paid for these services. The fedayeen, after all, were mainly controlled by the Muslim Brotherhood. Although the Muslim Brotherhood remained regime 'insiders' (unlike earlier communist allies), the organisation's leadership had never been satisfied with their post-coup role and was divided over how to gain greater influence.[5]

Meanwhile, during the spring of 1953, Britain received reports that former Nazi officers had been hired by the RCC to teach the Egyptian army and its 'terrorist' auxiliaries techniques in sabotage and guerrilla warfare. It was estimated that 1,000 members of the Muslim Brotherhood were being trained to operate in armed bands of forty to fifty. In May Churchill issued an order that any suspicious Germans in or near the Canal Zone should be detained rather than expelled, as they had previously been.[6] There was certainly no doubting the increased number of incidents. A Foreign Office estimate put the total at seventy-seven (excluding cable thefts) in the period between the middle of March and the end of May, with a peak of intensity in the week of Dulles's visit.[7] British diplomats suspected that the intention was to incite the Suez forces into some heavy-handed action akin to the earlier Kafr Abdu and Ismailia incidents. 'While I cannot of course expect our military authorities not to take essential security precautions,' wrote Stevenson on 7 May, 'I think it would be much to our advantage to avoid being "provoked" until at any rate the [Dulles] party has left Cairo next week.'[8] The previous day, when the formal break in the negotiations occurred, the RCC had pronounced that Egyptian rights would have to be won by force.[9]

Events surrounding the Dulles visit to Cairo consequently came to resemble a war of nerves. According to British intelligence reports, in the weekend before he arrived some 4,000 Egyptian auxiliary police officers had left Cairo, a large proportion of whom were suspected of having moved to the Canal Zone.[10] There had also been significant troop movements by the Egyptian army in the preceding weeks. The main roads between Cairo and the Canal Zone were now all covered; the Egyptian garrison in Qantara East had been strengthened; extensive defences had been prepared on the east bank of the Suez Canal between Port Said and Ismailia; and a battalion group had been deployed at the El Firdan bridge. When briefed of these developments, Churchill was more worried by the police auxiliaries, the Wafd's weapon of choice in the winter of 1951/2, than the troop movements. He saw the latter as defensively arranged to counter the two Rodeo operations, the rescue missions for British nationals in Cairo and Alexandria. The Egyptian deployments, moreover, went a long way to confirming the suspicions from earlier in the year that the details of the Rodeo planning had been leaked to the Egyptians by an airman clerk.[11]

Meanwhile, Britain's escalatory measures tended to be psychological in nature, reflecting a greater appreciation of the need to be more subtle when trying to attract American support. Thus, on the day before Dulles was due to arrive in Cairo, Churchill wired Stevenson the text of warning to be delivered to the Egyptians in the event of a major clash. It read:

> An organised attack made on members of HM forces by Egyptians who are or have been members of the Egyptian armed forces, or by persons known to be trained or armed by the Egyptian forces would be regarded by HMG as tantamount to an act of war. British forces would therefore be obliged to use all necessary means in their own defence. Anyone found bearing arms and not in uniform would be liable to penalties in accordance with the customs of war.[12]

Such information was routinely shared with the US embassy. It was followed the next day (when Dulles was actually in Cairo) with the Foreign Office notifying Stevenson that the families of embassy staff could return to Britain at public expense. It also advised that a warning should be given to the British community to the effect that they should leave forthwith unless they had some pressing reason to stay.[13]

In the event, Dulles came away from the visit thoroughly disenchanted with the behaviour of both disputants. His meeting with Neguib was cordial – the Egyptian prime minister was presented with a pistol as a gift from Eisenhower: the British were aghast at the symbolism – but it left Dulles deeply disappointed with what he regarded as the military regime's parochial attitude. The crux of the problem was that Egypt would not allow even a small number of British soldiers to maintain the Suez base after a revised defence agreement. Unable to conceal his irritation, Dulles told Neguib that 'it seemed stupid to think that the great vision of a new Egypt can collapse on the point of who directs inventory-keepers'.[14] As for the British, he echoed earlier American concerns that they were in danger of leaving Egypt in an ignominious way. Publicly, however, he had made a statement, which Churchill regarded as 'excellent', backing the British need for the Suez base.[15]

The general disappointment felt by Dulles helped produce a major reorientation of US policy. On 1 June he informed the National Security Council that Egypt should no longer be the key to development of the West's strength in the Middle East, and that the efforts to form a Middle East Defence Organisation must be abandoned. From this point on, the United States began to focus instead on forming a defensive arrangement of 'Northern Tier' states, which Dulles identified as Turkey, Iraq, Syria and Pakistan.[16] Frustration with the ongoing Anglo-Egyptian quarrel lay at the heart of this decision.

The American abandonment of the Middle East Defence Organisation scheme was a major blow to Britain's Middle Eastern policies. This Egypt-based multilateral approach had been the main mechanism for attempting to secure US military involvement in the defence of the region since 1951. Of even greater significance, it was also the preferred method for cloaking a continued British presence in the Canal Zone. Moreover, since the final stages of the Sudan negotiations, when the Suez Group had emerged as a powerful force in British domestic politics, plans for a Middle East Defence Organisation had served a vital parliamentary function. Persuading the Conservative Party that a new Anglo-Egyptian treaty was the right way forward required some sort of guarantee above and beyond any paper agreement that might be signed, especially given Egypt's recent record of unilaterally abrogating treaties. A multilateral defence organisation served this purpose. In March 1953 Roger Allen had gone so far as to observe that the usefulness of a MEDO was 'not primarily in the Middle East, but in the House of Commons'.[17] The jettisoning of the approach thus made a Suez base withdrawal even more difficult politically in Britain.

The heightened tensions prompted by Dulles's visit to Cairo persisted after his departure. While US officials were busy formulating their new Northern Tier approach, Churchill continued to take an uncompromising stance towards Egypt's military junta. This entailed stepping up the preparations for maintaining Britain's position in the Canal Zone in the event of another siege-like crisis. To this end, on 19 May Stevenson met leaders of the British community in Cairo and Alexandria, and strongly advised that all British subjects leave the country.[18] Meanwhile, behind closed doors, attention was given to the possibility that Britain might have to assume responsibility for the administration of the whole Canal Zone, including the 160,000 Egyptian civilians, out of a total of 400,000, who were expected to stay put. Stockpiling of foodstuffs was initiated and, most sensitively, authorisation was given for the recruitment of senior-level civil affairs officers. In other words, active arrangements were afoot for the imposition of British military government in part of Egypt. It was indicative of Churchill's resolve that a commando brigade from Malta – 'teeth' fighting troops – was redeployed to further strengthen the Suez garrison.[19]

The Foreign Office and Cairo embassy became involved in these preparations in a time-honoured way, by re-examining the options for establishing an alternative government in Egypt. In London, the Egyptian politician who immediately came to mind was Ali Maher. Even moderates like Allen (which is to say pro-settlement officials) thought that bringing him to power 'would be preferable to a long drawn-out struggle with the present regime in Egypt'.[20] Old hands in Cairo agreed. The general view in the embassy, observed Michael Creswell on 22 May, was that there should be 'a fair chance' of finding a new administration if British troops had cause to enter Cairo: 'The present regime has made many enemies and few friends.'[21]

But as during the Canal Zone siege, the ambassador himself was markedly more cautious about interventionist solutions. In a telegram addressed to Churchill dated 27 May, Stevenson warned that although there was a sizeable group of Egyptians who were fearful of the present inflammatory atmosphere, they were nevertheless outnumbered by 'half-baked' elements, which was to say 'those with some pretensions to education but with no great claim to intelligence'. As well as being 'probably the most fervent supporters of the new regime', they amounted to 'an appreciable fraction of the politically conscious . . . In the event of disturbances they, together with the riffraff forming the bulk of the city mobs, would be the dangerous fanatical element.'[22] Stevenson added that within this assemblage the Muslim Brotherhood figured prominently, albeit also as a potential rival to the military junta:

At the moment the Moslem Brotherhood is the only reasonably well disciplined body in the country, apart from the army itself, and it is nearer to exercising real power than ever was the case in the past. It has no wish either to be pushed aside by the complete success of the Army Movement or to be destroyed with the movement if it goes down fighting. Nevertheless, there is little or no doubt that, if the struggle turns from cold to hot war, the Brotherhood and its Kataibs (or paramilitary formations) will be at the disposal of the military authorities.[23]

Given the rising temperatures during May on both sides of the Anglo-Egyptian dispute, Stevenson's concerns regarding the pitfalls of meddling in Egypt's internal affairs were, once again, a vital coolant in Britain's governmental machine.

It was a measure that Stevenson was doing an excellent job as ambassador that, at one time or another, he had managed to annoy most of the other centres of British policymaking towards Egypt and yet still be regarded as the right person for the appointment. True, there had been pressures to replace him, most notably by Britain's military authorities in Egypt during the dark days of December 1951. Moreover, his fitness to lead the defence negotiations on the British side had been found wanting earlier in 1953, hence the drafting in of General Sir Brian Robertson as co-delegate. But it was precisely his willingness to assert doggedly the case for further concessions or warn against clumsy military counter-measures that made him such a vital element in the decision-making process. In short, he was willing to go against the flow. If friction was the upshot, even with embassy colleagues, so be it. His relationship with Creswell, who as minister was the mission's 'number two', was the most awkward in this latter respect.

As chargé during the previous year's coup (when Stevenson had been on leave), Creswell had strongly advocated an interventionist approach. Tellingly, Stevenson was immediately called back to his post. Professional pressures spilled over into personal relations, and vice versa. One difficulty was a rift between their respective wives. Creswell's Dutch wife had previously been married to an ambassador and was therefore accustomed to entertaining other ambassadors. Lady Stevenson, who had married late and was perhaps a little too protective of her official consort capacity, took offence when Mrs Creswell invited heads of missions to the Creswell home, rather than number twos or below as etiquette demanded. The row had resulted in the Creswells moving outside Cairo and refusing to do any entertaining.[24] This could be left unmentioned were it not for Stevenson increasingly feeling the strains of his job. From 10 June 1953 he was obliged to take several months' sick leave. Creswell was passed over for the chargé role. The extent to which this was on account of his advice in July 1952 or the rift with Stevenson it is impossible to say. (Creswell ended his career as ambassador to Helsinki, hardly the most sought-after embassy.) In any case, the temporary replacement for Stevenson caused a great stir in Egyptian politics.

CHURCHILL'S 'PATIENT, SULKY PIG'

The person in question was Robin Hankey, an experienced Foreign Office diplomat handpicked by Churchill because of his right-wing views.[25] As the son of Lord (Maurice) Hankey, the former secretary to the Committee of Imperial Defence who sat on the board of the Suez Canal Company, it was assumed by Egyptian commentators that he would have the same views as his father. Alongside Lord Killearn (who was obviously very well known in Egypt), Hankey senior was the leading critic of the Canal Zone negotiations in the House of Lords. Before leaving for Cairo, Robin Hankey had received a personal briefing from Churchill over dinner. The minutes of the conversation were viewed by the Foreign Office as the fullest expression to date of the prime minister's thinking on Egypt. His basic line was that Britain did not need an agreement nearly as much as Neguib did. 'If H.M. Embassy did nothing for 6 months except avoid giving things away, he would be very content. We should be very polite and courteous and leave the Egyptians to make the running.' At one point, Churchill told Hankey that he should be a 'patient, sulky pig'. Churchill's attitude to 'physical trouble' was as follows:

Although we should not of course say so, he would in some ways welcome it. It would do the Egyptians no sort of good. We should certainly not take the initiative in precipitating trouble, but we should know how to deal with it and our position in no way would suffer . . .

There might be a nasty situation in Cairo. Obviously if the Egyptian army tried to occupy our Embassy, we should not resist. If the crowd attacked our Embassy, we should show all patience and not fire unless we must; but in the last resort we must defend it against the mob, conscious that Neguib and the Army would be obliged to restore order. If relations were broken, the Embassy should go to Fayid, and not leave Egypt if it could be avoided. The Egyptians would merely put themselves in the wrong if they did any of this.

As regards the last break in the defence negotiations, Churchill told Hankey that 'Case A [the retention of 7,000 personnel in the Suez base] already represented a sorry whittling down of our real needs, undertaken to secure American support.' He was therefore not prepared to accept anything much less than this, and in the meantime wanted to avoid the 'undignified' spectacle of 'always running to the Americans for help'.[26]

When Hankey arrived in Cairo in mid-June, the RCC was convinced that Britain had sent in a 'hard man' in order to engineer a complete rupture in relations, hence his every move was carefully monitored by a media circus.[27] His initial impressions of the Egyptian scene were revealing. He felt that Nasser was trying to be reasonable, but that he had a deep dislike of the British. As for the US embassy, Hankey reported that it included 'several uncoordinated and inexperienced enthusiasts' who were 'quite unpredictable'. The main problem, he felt, was Lakeland, 'the American Oriental Secretary' who was 'more Egyptian than the Egyptians'. In addition, Hankey interpreted Caffery's constant use of the first person singular when discussing Egyptian politics as a vanity 'over which he has little or no control'.[28]

Within days of the new chargé's arrival, a major development occurred in Egyptian politics. It was prompted by the RCC's growing appreciation that its tactics to get Dulles to play the role of mediator during his recent visit had seriously backfired: not only had the US's Republican administration failed to help Egypt, but Britain's Conservative government was now taking a much tougher stance. Moreover, an attempt from the end of May to bolster the junta's flagging domestic appeal through the holding of trials of old-regime politicians had rebounded in that the 'treason courts' had effectively created a public forum for Wafdist lawyers and other opposition elements.[29] When beset by earlier difficulties, the junta had developed a habit of undertaking bold new moves, last witnessed in January after a build-up of economic, political and legal pressures, and which saw all Egypt's political parties being summarily banned. This occasion was no different. On 18 June the RCC declared Egypt a republic. A note passed to the British embassy spoke of the 'abrogation of the monarchical regime and the end of the Mohamed Ali dynasty'. Neguib assumed the post of president (in addition to his existing position as prime minister), while Nasser for the first time assumed two government posts, the offices of deputy prime minister and interior minister.[30]

This was the strongest affirmation yet that Nasser was the power behind the regime, but it also gave further indication of a power struggle brewing inside the junta. As with earlier critical developments, rumours of sharp internal arguments reached the Americans.[31] According to Khalid Mohi El Din's first-hand account, Neguib had been strongly against proclaiming a republic because, under Nasser's plan, it entailed his resigning as head of the armed forces. The subsequent appointment of Abdul al-Hakim Amer as commander-in-chief was thus widely seen as a manoeuvre to strengthen Nasser's position within the RCC.[32] (Neguib's memoirs from 1955 are silent on this subject, apart from a general discussion of why Egyptian society was against authoritarian leaders in the Ataturk mould.[33]) Yet the birth of the republic failed to elicit much of a popular response in Egypt. The move had long been expected and, in any case, the monarchy, via the regency council, had meant little after Farouk's departure. With the anniversary of the coup little more than a month away (and with it the opportunity for proper celebrations), the rushed manner of the declaration, and its relatively flat reception, was indicative of growing problems for the regime.

On 23 June, less than a week after Egypt had become a republic, Churchill suffered a massive stroke. The circumstances of how the illness was covered up offer an insight into the Eden–Churchill relationship, which had been increasingly frayed over the direction of Britain's Egyptian policy. The stroke happened at the end of a dinner for the visiting Italian prime minister. Churchill had just given a rather slurred speech about the Roman conquest of Britain and was attempting to lead his guests from the drawing room when, after a few steps, he slumped down into a chair. It looked as though he had had too much to drink. The next morning he declared himself well enough to attend cabinet, despite having limited use of his left arm; his mouth was also drooping badly. At the meeting, no mention whatsoever was made of his ailment. Ministerial colleagues came away thinking he was a bit quieter than usual, and perhaps a little white, but nothing untoward beyond this.

However, over the next few days the symptoms worsened, prompting Churchill to give strict orders to his private secretary 'not to let it be known that he was temporarily incapacitated and to ensure that the administration continued to function as if he were in full control'. His aim was to avoid a constitutional crisis during which the Queen might be obliged to appoint Rab Butler as prime minister since Eden, long the 'heir apparent', was also on his sick bed. Hiding the stroke was thus an act of loyalty to Eden, despite the foreign secretary's attitude to the Canal Zone dispute. The cabinet was only informed of the stroke on 29 June and an arrangement was reached whereby Lord Salisbury, lord president of the council, assumed control of foreign policy, while Butler looked after domestic issues.[34] So it came to be that the Egyptian issue acquired a new ministerial head in Britain.

THE SALISBURY PERIOD

To senior officials accustomed to Eden, who was known for his quick temper, and Churchill, who regarded diplomats as appeasers at heart, the 'calm and aristocratic atmosphere' of the Foreign Office under Lord Salisbury was something of a welcome relief.[35] He also offered an element of continuity in that he had long been regarded as an Edenite, having served under Eden in the 'national' governments of the 1930s, and indeed having resigned with him in 1938 in protest against the appeasement of Mussolini. At the same time, however, Salisbury's reputation in post-1945 politics was as an arch-imperialist. The prospects for the Egyptian negotiations, therefore, did not look good. One of his first responsibilities as acting foreign secretary was to visit Washington in mid-July.

Not coincidentally, just before Salisbury arrived, Neguib wrote to President Eisenhower to remind him that the RCC was 'greatly relying upon' his 'frequently expressed sentiments of friendship and support for Egypt's right to be a fully free and independent state'. The letter went on to give Egypt's latest proposals on the base issue.[36] This missive topped the agenda at the first meeting between Salisbury and Dulles on 14 July. Salisbury suggested that if no response had been sent a non-committal reply on the substance of Egypt's proposals should be given. The key point was to indicate that the United States would not be playing the role of mediator in future negotiations. The meeting then proceeded to a frank exchange about what had gone wrong in Anglo-Egyptian relations. Dulles pointed out that some Americans had the impression that the British attitude towards countries such as Egypt was that 'the right way to deal with such people was to be completely stern and firm and to deliver a well placed kick when they made difficulties'. Salisbury, in turn, explained why Britain found it necessary to exceed the 10,000 troops legally permitted in Egypt, albeit without mentioning the actual garrison size. 'British troops were there', he stated, 'by reason of a Treaty freely negotiated, and they were the minimum necessary to secure our rights under that Treaty.'[37] Although Dulles had a lecturing tone at times, Salisbury's composed rejoinders resulted in the discussion ending in a fruitful way, at least as far as the British were concerned. Thus, Eisenhower's response to Neguib's letter was to be kept vague, while the 'general blessing' of the US government was given to Britain's stance in the Canal Zone negotiations.[38]

The frankness of Dulles's discussion with Salisbury on 14 July was probably linked to the latest incident in the Canal Zone, which happened the day before. In response to reports that a serviceman had been abducted in Ismailia, General Festing, Erskine's successor as officer in charge of British troops in Egypt, ordered the implementation of a military operation (code-named Diameter), which aimed at securing all routes into and out of the Canal Zone by the extensive use of road blocks. A statement was also issued to the Egyptian sub-governor of Ismailia, which, because of its imprecision, gave the impression that Britain was about to take full control of Ismailia, as well as cut off oil supplies from the Agrud pumping station (a tactic last used during the early stages of the abrogation crisis).

The RCC was convinced that the Canal Zone was about to be fully taken over and responded with a series of violent speeches against the British, which generally had the effect of encouraging fedayeen attacks. The thinking of the regime seems to have been that Hankey, who had visited the Suez base on 11 July, was out to scupper the proposals contained in Neguib's letter to Eisenhower and thus fulfil Churchill's supposed mission of destroying any prospect of an agreement.[39] In fact, British policymakers were astounded by Festing's resort to Diameter. For one thing, the scale of the operation was such that he was expected at least to consult Britain's civilian authorities in Egypt and, if time permitted, London also. Even Churchill, who never hid his robust attitude on Egyptian matters, described Diameter as 'a case of using a steam hammer to crack a nut'.[40] A second statement was therefore quickly issued correcting the impression made by the first, and was followed by the easing of the road blocks.

Nevertheless, the furore persisted because of its proximity to the first anniversary of the July coup. Junta-inspired press attacks on the British were a welcome distraction from domestic concerns. 'We want Mr Hankey because he represents true imperialism,' stated Major Gamal Salem, the minister of national guidance, in one such instance: 'The only victory we seek is the ousting of the occupant, not of Hankey. Let him stay in Cairo as a monument to remind us of the bitterness of occupation.'[41] The British chargé's complaints to the Egyptian foreign ministry about the personal nature of the attacks had little effect, so instead he bided his time until he had a chance to confront Salem in person. His account of the meeting, which occurred during a function at the Pakistan mission, suggested vindication for Dulles's earlier lecturing to Salisbury. 'When [Salem] takes off his dark glasses, which he usually wears,' wrote Hankey to a colleague in London on 3 August, 'he has lustrous and appealing brown eyes like a dog that knows it is about to be bashed! He went as near as apologising as could be reasonably expected.'[42]

The balance sheet for the first year of military rule in Egypt was as follows: in one column, a cabal of largely thirty-something officers with disparate aims had seized political power, forced Farouk's abdication, pushed through land reform measures, banned political parties, secured an agreement (to Egypt's advantage) on the long-standing Sudan dispute, and most recently made Egypt a republic, while all the time keeping the British, and their interventionist tendencies, at bay. In the other column, the British military occupation persisted. As Nasser well understood, no matter how impressive the various feats, only a complete evacuation of foreign troops would bring about the long-term survival of the regime, not to mention his position within it. In the meantime, Egypt's continuing economic problems and the prospect of further internal crises (so far they had been occurring at roughly two-monthly intervals) served as encouragement to the regime's unbowed domestic opponents, as well as to its supposed friends. In this latter respect, question marks especially hung over the ambitions of Neguib and the Muslim Brotherhood.

On 28 July, with the anniversary celebrations over (and thus the need for a mini crisis), Nasser initiated contacts with the British embassy with a view to restarting the negotiations concerning the future of the Canal Zone base. By mid-August, four meetings had been held, which both sides preferred to keep secret. Three issues dominated the discussions. The first concerned the number of technicians allowed to maintain the base. Britain was still insisting on a Case A-type figure of 7,000, but was willing to reduce the number to 3,000 after four and a half years. Meanwhile, the air defence organisation idea had been dropped altogether because of a shortage of British warplanes. The second issue related to the duration of an agreement. Egypt wanted three years (e.g. up until the 1936 defence treaty was due to expire), the British much longer. The third matter was the reactivation clause. Britain was pressing not only for automatic availability in the event of an attack on an Arab state, Turkey or Iran, but also for consultation rights when such attacks were threatened.[43]

While Lord Salisbury was satisfied with Britain's firm approach, the Robertson–Hankey negotiating team in Egypt was showing signs of wanting greater flexibility. After the previous break in the negotiations, General Robertson had sent Churchill a personal report on the situation, dated 12 May, which stated that Case A was out of the question for Egypt and that the RCC would only accept, at the very best, the presence of British technicians for a short term only.[44] Like Stevenson before him, Robertson had become convinced that a settlement of the dispute was urgently needed. The continuing financial pressures to reduce Britain's overseas military commitments and the conviction that the Suez base was useless without Egyptian cooperation shaped his new-found moderation. His shift in thinking was such that the Foreign Office asked him to address MPs on the Canal Zone issue, but a meeting proved impossible to arrange during the weeks he was in London before the negotiations restarted.[45] Hankey was similarly inclined to press for additional concessions. In particular, he saw little point in bickering over the duration clause. The chances of the RCC lasting ten years, he wrote on 14 September, were 'slender even to the most optimistic of us'.[46]

One compromise that was forthcoming concerned the latest instalment in a Cairo–Tehran linkage which had punctuated Anglo-Egyptian relations in the early 1950s. In May 1951 Iran's parliament had passed legislation nationalising the petroleum industry, including the holdings of the Anglo-Iranian Oil Company (AIOC). When the last British workers were forced to leave on 3 October 1951, a powerful signal had been sent to Egyptian nationalists that they could achieve a similar result as regards the Suez garrison. Less than a fortnight later, Egypt's Wafd government had abrogated the defence treaty of 1936 and the Sudan agreement of 1899. In the preceding months, meanwhile, Britain's Attlee administration had been seriously considering a military solution to the AIOC issue. However, the seizure of the Abadan area using forces from the Suez base (Operation Buccaneer) had been put on hold following US pressure for restraint. President Truman believed that such an invasion would stir up nationalist opinion throughout the region, and possibly draw the Soviet Union into the northern part of Iran. Losing Abadan had consequently become a formative moment in the birth of the Suez Group.

For nearly two years thereafter, Churchill's Conservative government had been contemplating action of one sort or another against the errant Iranian prime minister, Muhammad Mossedeq. Finally, on 19 August 1953, a joint Anglo-American covert operation helped remove Mossedeq from power and installed a pro-Western government in Iran. The timing of America's participation was in no small part shaped by Dulles's abandonment of the Egypt-centred Middle East Defence Organisation project following his recent visit to Cairo and his subsequent focus on a Northern Tier arrangement, which Iran could slot into.[47] Within a few days of this success, British officials informed Nasser that they were now willing to drop Iran from the reactivation clause in the Suez base negotiations. It was further stressed, however, that the greatest importance was still attached to Turkey's inclusion. But Nasser could not accept the trade-off. As well as the emotional issue of Turkey's recent past as the Ottoman rulers of Egypt, there was also the major problem of its current membership of NATO.[48]

Nevertheless, there were two signs of progress around this time. The first related back to the incident of the missing serviceman in July, which had prompted the implementation of Operation Diameter. Following the uproar surrounding the sealing of the Canal Zone, it became a matter of some political delicacy to have the serviceman returned to Britain's military authorities. Egypt's security forces detained him, but refused to admit that they had him. Meanwhile, British officials were reluctant to recede from their position that the Egyptians knew where he was, a situation that made negotiating his release problematic to say the least. To complicate matters further, the soldier's plight had exacerbated hardline opinion within the House of Commons. Thus, it was a measure of both Britain and Egypt's desire to make progress in the Canal Zone negotiations that the affair was resolved by the serviceman being secretly transported to Paris by the Egyptian government.[49] The second indication of an improvement in relations related to British claims for compensation arising from the Black Saturday riots. In early September, the RCC presented Britain's embassy in Cairo with a cheque for £95,000.[50]

Hankey's assessment in early September was that it would be 'difficult to foresee better circumstances for concluding an agreement at any time before 1956'. 'The present [RCC] government', he stated on the 5th, 'cannot solve its economic problems or survive unless it settles the Canal Zone dispute and that in a manner that can be shown to satisfy Egyptian aspiration for liberation', before adding, 'no better government is in sight whatever happens'. In the event of another break in the negotiations, the chargé predicted trouble in the Canal Zone, spreading eventually to Cairo and Alexandria.[51] His co-delegate, Robertson, who made a special visit to London, underlined to the cabinet on 8 September the areas where an agreement was likely. It was felt that Egypt might accept a seven-year agreement, provided that combatant troops were withdrawn in the first eighteen months. This would leave 4,000 technicians for a further three years, after which the total could be reduced again for the final two and a half years. With respect to 'reactivation', the RCC would only accept automatic rights in the event of an attack on an Arab League state. Recent efforts at including a reference in the proposed settlement to freedom of navigation in the Suez Canal had proved unacceptable.

The cabinet's response was to insist that a reference to the principle of freedom of transit through the Canal should at the very least appear in the preamble to an agreement. This was seen as essential for squaring parliamentary opposition to an agreement in that it would give Britain a legal peg in the event of an Egyptian violation. As regards the availability issue, the latest idea was to seek additional reactivation rights via 'UN action to resist aggression'.[52] On 16 September the cabinet met again and Churchill, who had recovered from his stroke with remarkable speed, reluctantly accepted the seven-year duration figure, but added that the government must be prepared to face a breakdown of the negotiations on this issue. Instructions based on the cabinet's conclusions were issued to the British delegation two days later.[53]

With Egyptian expectations raised by Robertson's visit to London, two highly productive negotiating sessions were held on 21 and 22 September, before a third meeting on the 23rd ended acrimoniously when Nasser stormed out. The issue, and indeed the eventual breaking point of the negotiations, was over what clothing the British technicians would wear. For the British, the right of their servicemen to wear the Queen's uniform when carrying out their duties was fundamental. It was also a matter of prestige. Nasser, on the other hand, was adamant that civilian attire for the technicians was an absolute necessity. The military occupation had to be seen to end.[54] Egyptian efforts to breathe life back into the negotiations at the start of October received short shrift from Churchill.[55]

EDEN'S RETURN

Thin and frail but in good spirits, Eden returned to the Foreign Office on 5 October. During his lengthy convalescence, he had been kept informed about Egyptian developments, albeit not with the detail he preferred. The caretaker foreign secretary, Lord Salisbury, had moved the Canal Zone dispute close to the point of resolution, but, like Churchill, was in no mood for further concessions and was reportedly feeling 'very bellicose about the Egyptians'.[56]

After a similar period of intimate involvement in the Anglo-Egyptian negotiations (as well as first-hand experience of the counter-insurgency side of the dispute), General Robertson had ended up being positively dovish in comparison. Having initially regarded the RCC as 'miserable fellows', over the last six months he had developed a considerable respect for the new rulers of Egypt, which he wanted to put on record for Roger Allen, the newly appointed assistant under-secretary in charge of Middle Eastern affairs. 'They are ruthless young men and they have done many things which we condemn as bad or foolish,' wrote Robertson in October; yet they had also 'shown a determination and capacity to exact obedience; they live austerely and are not enriching themselves; they work hard and they put the interests of Egypt before their individual interests'. 'They can make this agreement work if they wish to,' he concluded.[57]

In mid-October the two co-delegates in Cairo made another push for a settlement, which in the first instance meant persuading the Conservative government to revise its stance that further concessions were impossible. The differences remaining were adjudged 'relatively small in substance'.[58] Eden was certainly keen and managed to take the cabinet at least partially with him. On the uniform issue, however, it was Churchill who set the terms. These centred on an official definition to be included in any agreement, coupled with an informal statement of how it would work in practice. The recommended treaty text was as follows: 'Within the Base installations and in transit between them British personnel will be entitled to wear the uniform of the Service to which they belong and to carry a weapon for their personal protection. Outside the area of the Base they will wear plain clothes.' When presenting this, Robertson and Hankey would be authorised 'to inform the Egyptians orally that the British technicians when at work would normally wear overalls or shorts and shirts with rank distinctions'.[59]

Despite having his way on this matter, Churchill remained deeply worried about Conservative backbench opinion. At the party's conference in Margate earlier in the month, the delegates had given rapturous applause to combative speeches by Suez Group members. Of particular note was Julian Amery's warning to the government that the British had already endured 'the scuttle from Palestine and the shame of Abadan', but would not tolerate the evacuation of 'the hinge of our imperial strength'.[60] The cabinet's decision to make another bid for an agreement with Egypt was consequently coupled with further efforts at winning over the Conservative critics.

To this end, Eden persuaded Lord Alexander, the minister of defence, to present the military reasons for an agreement to a Foreign Affairs Committee meeting on 21 October. This was a parliamentary body for those holding the Conservative whip. Alexander bluntly told those present that the Suez base was costing £50 million a year and that it was a 'dead corpse' without Egyptian cooperation. In a move that was meant to signal the prime minister's support for the withdrawal policy, Eden also persuaded Churchill to attend the meeting. The plan backfired, however, in that he sat glum-faced throughout the talk.[61] The next day twenty-six Conservative MPs, the core of the Suez Group, wrote to the prime minister opposing an evacuation from the Canal Zone.[62]

But their fears that an agreement was about to be signed were misplaced. On the same day as the Foreign Affairs Committee meeting, the British and Egyptian negotiating teams effectively broke off the talks. Egypt's final word on the uniform issue failed to meet Britain's requirements. It read: 'Outside the base area and when off duty within it, British personnel will wear civilian clothes. When on duty within the installations, and in transit between them, they will wear a unified civilian dress to be agreed upon. They may carry a pistol for their personal protection.' There was also disagreement concerning the availability clause: the Egyptian delegation refused to accept UN action as a cause for reactivating the base.[63]

The break in negotiations produced a by now predictable flourish of bickering between the British and Americans. Caffery was furious at the uniform issue in particular, which he dismissed as mere 'haberdashery'.[64] His indiscreet comments to an Australian diplomat that 'the British had bungled these negotiations from the start' were reported back to Britain's Cairo embassy and prompted a further spate of Foreign Office complaints to the State Department. Eden wanted Caffery replaced as ambassador, but all that Dulles was willing to do was to recall him for consultations, and only then if Britain specifically requested it. 'The President spoke to me alone but most emphatically even vehemently of his dislike of Caffery,' Eden minuted: 'It is a commentary on his lack of grip that Caffery is still there.'[65]

In November General Robertson left Egypt to become chairman of the British Transport Commission. During his last evening in the country, he called upon Nasser for a candid farewell talk. Talking as one officer to another, Robertson observed that, 'it would be most irresponsible, when no difference of substance existed, not to carry matters to a successful conclusion . . . he appreciated a soldier's impatience at the delay (he himself felt such impatience and even irritation after the last meeting of the delegations) but having assumed political responsibility Colonel Nasser and his colleagues had to go through with it'. When Nasser expressed worries about Egyptian reactions to an agreement, Robertson reassured him that once it was signed his regime would be able to claim credit for securing an end to the British occupation.[66] Just before boarding his plane for London the next day, Sir Brian was given a parcel from Nasser. Assuming it was some sweets, he did not open it until he arrived home, at which point he discovered that it was an antique silver salver.[67]

The break in the negotiations resulted in an upsurge of guerrilla incidents against the British garrison. As head of Egypt's Directorate of Military Intelligence (under the Interior Ministry), Nasser was responsible for regulating the frequency and scale of the attacks, as far as this was possible. The chain of command between the RCC and the Muslim Brotherhood's irregular warfare units was anything but clear. Moreover, this dependency, as Nasser was well aware, also carried risks in terms of having to increase the political rewards for the Muslim Brotherhood's leadership, which in the longer run could threaten the secular character of the regime.

Britain's response to the increased number of incidents was to revert back to the abrogation crisis tactic of detaining known troublemakers without trial. Handing them over to the Egyptian police force, which also came under the control of Nasser's Interior Ministry, was seen to be pointless. By mid-November, eighteen Egyptians were being detained and of those ten were believed to be capable of seriously prejudicing the security of British forces.[68] The Foreign Office backed this approach provided that the numbers held were kept low. 'If our military authorities were to retain all of the hundreds of malefactors that pass through their hands in the Canal Zone, it would be difficult to justify their action,' noted an official on 8 December. 'The fact that they have detained only 18 makes it relatively easy.'[69] Other measures taken by the Suez garrison included the imposition of curfews, the setting up of mobile road blocks, and the searching of villages thought to harbour fedayeen.[70] This latter tactic was regarded as 'sheer dynamite' by the Cairo embassy, but as was the case during the winter of 1951/2, the head of the British Middle East Office tended to side with the Canal Zone military authorities.[71] Meanwhile, Eden, determined not to give his backbench critics additional ammunition, did his best to keep the often murderous incidents out of the news.[72]

In November and early December 1953, the first national elections in the Sudan, organised in accordance with the Anglo-Egyptian agreement of February that year, further heightened tensions in the Canal Zone. The Suez Group and, independently, Churchill kept a close eye on developments, hopeful that an excuse might be found for compelling the Foreign Office to abandon its policy of 'scuttle' in Egypt. From the British perspective, the

Sudanese election results were a disappointment. The pro-Egyptian National Unionist Party emerged as the largest party, taking fifty-one out of ninety-seven seats in the House of Representatives, and twenty-two out of thirty elective seats in the Senate. The pro-independence Umma Party, London's choice, took twenty-two and three seats respectively.[73] Eden's first reaction to this news, on 3 December, was to stress that it was more important 'to keep our friends in the Sudan in good heart' than 'not to upset critics in the House of Commons'.[74] The pressure to do otherwise, however, was great, especially if sectarian violence broke out in Khartoum. Most dramatically, on 11 December, Churchill outlined to Eden a plan for turning the Sudan setback into, as he put it, an 'opportunity':

> The exit from all your troubles about Egypt, the Suez Canal, the Sudan, the Southern Sudan and later on in the Middle East will be found in deeds not words, in action not treaties . . . Let me tell you the action, which, although apparently local, I believe would be comprehensive and decisive. Find some reason to send 2 Battalions of infantry and 3 or 4 squadrons RAF by air to Khartoum. The Governor could perhaps claim that public order required it . . . Once this sign of strength and action of policy and design had been shown all the Conservative troubles here would be quenched. The negotiations with Egypt would of course be broken off or lapse, but the evacuation would be declared and would begin none the less, and the redeployment of our troops to the extent of the armoured Division or 4 Brigades in the Middle East and Cyprus could begin and proceed as fast as convenient.[75]

Eden had yet to acquire the stomach for engineering a short colonial war and so instructed his officials to kill the idea.[76]

As 1953 drew to a close, the pressures on Nasser and Eden's respective domestic positions, as a consequence of the continuing inertia in the Canal Zone dispute, were intense. Nasser needed the British 'occupation' to be seen to end. The stability of the military junta and his leadership within it depended on such an outcome. During the recent negotiations, the minutiae of this issue had boiled down to bickering over the colour of clothes the small number of British technicians would wear once the vast majority of the garrison had departed. It seemed a trivial issue (Caffery certainly thought so), but at its heart was a fundamental question of national pride and, more particularly, the perception of sovereignty. If the technicians wore khaki shirts with rank epaulettes, this would constitute a military uniform, which in turn would amount to the continuation of the occupation, no matter how small the numbers involved. The politically vital boast of securing a complete evacuation of all foreign troops could not be made. The centrality of perception in this dispute may be seen in the fact that the issue of carrying side-arms was not contentious. Epaulettes mattered more than guns.

By the same token, Britain's Conservative government had to be seen to leave a small troop presence in the Canal Zone for reasons of prestige, even though the soldiers concerned were essentially store-keepers. Sovereignty also lay at the heart of the 'availability' issue. Aggression against an Arab League state could be presented as aggression against Egyptian interests. Egypt, after all, had founded the inter-governmental organisation in 1945 as a means of promoting its own interests in the region, and indeed led the body from headquarters in Cairo. But Britain, by insisting on a clause relating to reactivation of the Suez base in the event of UN action, was looking to bypass Egypt's sovereign rights as an independent nation-state. Both these outstanding issues cut to the quick of Britain's pretensions to remaining a world power. Even a few hundred soldiers astride the Suez Canal had an important symbolic value. An attack on military personnel (rather than technicians clad in civilian clothes) would constitute an attack on Britain's state interests, which could trigger an appropriate response. Availability rights, moreover, signalled future intentions.

In mid-December US embassy officials in London were briefed by Roger Allen to the effect that Churchill might, at any time, reverse government policy and take a line advocated by the Tory rebels.[77] This mounting concern stemmed from the frustrations of the failed negotiations, the increased number of violent incidents in the Canal Zone and the spoiling efforts of the Suez Group prior to a major foreign affairs debate in the Commons scheduled for 17 December.

Eden in the meantime was still doing his best to placate the critics of his Suez policy. One such effort entailed inviting the leading dissidents to a dinner with General Robertson so that he could give them a confidential briefing on the military facts underlying the 'withdrawal' policy.[78] In addition, several ministers – Butler, Lloyd, Alexander and minister of war Antony Head (but not Eden himself, who had a UN commitment in Paris) – addressed the Conservative Party's Foreign Affairs Committee on 16 December in order to reiterate the financial, military and political reasons behind the government's position.[79] But the rebels remained undeterred and went into the debate the next day with a motion urging the government 'to suspend the negotiations and to retain in the Canal Zone sufficient troops to discharge British responsibilities for the defence of the Canal'.[80] Eden's speech, which was drafted by his private secretary, was given a 'once over' by Churchill. 'He liked it', stated Shuckburgh, 'but he is longing for a break.' 'It has been my constant fear', the prime minister was reported as saying, 'that the Egyptians might accept . . . If they attack us, that would be war, and you can do a lot of things then.'[81]

Eden's attempts to secure a settlement of the Canal Zone dispute amounted to a policy of trying to preserve, so far as possible, Britain's interests in Egypt, the Middle East, and indeed across the world. His approach entailed modifying the various methods of exerting British power and influence, a process initiated by the Labour administrations between 1945 and 1951. It was not a policy of scuttle, as his critics alleged, the prime minister among them. In this respect, Eden was the realist and progressive, Churchill the romantic and reactionary. Yet the problem for Eden was that within broader Conservative Party politics his policy was being increasingly branded as weak. As heir apparent to the premiership, the foreign secretary thus displayed strength of character in sticking to his Egyptian policy, despite the accusations of appeasement. Others in a similar position, especially considering the government's small majority, may well have been tempted to tap into jingoistic sentiments. But for how long could this last?

Christmas Day 1953 found Britain's foreign secretary in a reflective mood: 'I am weary of the fickle friendship of the Arabs,' he gloomily minuted.[82] According to Shuckburgh, Eden was seriously considering whether he should 'throw over the Arabs altogether' and instead rely on Turkey and Israel as pillars of Western defence in the Middle East.[83] Churchill, a Zionist by conviction, had long advocated such a line when being bloody-minded or mischievous.[84] If Eden switched to the prime minister's uncompromising approach to the Egyptian question, there could be little doubt that a major showdown in the Canal Zone would ensue, possibly leading to the reoccupation of Cairo with all the mayhem that this would entail.

NINE

· · · · · · · ·

The Politics of Disengagement

As Anthony Eden's closest adviser, Evelyn Shuckburgh was perfectly placed to describe the pressures acting on the Conservative minister as he sought to resolve the Canal Zone dispute. The role of private secretary, observes Shuckburgh, was the 'point of contact between the political and professional forces which contribute to the formulation of policy'. 'One came to see what an enormous proportion of the Foreign Secretary's emotional and mental energy is burned up by parliamentary anxieties and by the strains of the House of Commons, so that the immense task of coping with the conduct of Britain's foreign relations is only a part – and perhaps the lesser part – of his burden.'[1] Not surprisingly, at the start of 1954, pro-settlement officials within Whitehall were worried that months of time and effort spent either in negotiations or working out alternative defence arrangements might be wasted if Eden, whose medical problems had not fully cleared (he was prone to fevers), reacted to these enormous stresses and switched to the diehard approach advocated by the Suez Group.

Meanwhile, Nasser had mounting worries of his own. The failure of the Canal Zone negotiations, which he personally conducted on the Egyptian side, had resulted in the military junta relying increasingly on guerrilla warfare. The upshot was a greater dependency on the Muslim Brotherhood. Moreover, the disappointments of the base talks starkly contrasted with the regime's successes in shaping the direction of the Sudan's development, first with the agreement signed in February 1953 and then with the Sudanese election results in December. A native of Khartoum, Neguib considered these achievements a personal victory. As both president of the Egyptian republic and prime minister, he had always been acutely conscious that there was a considerable gap between his official appointments and the limited powers he wielded in actuality. Towards the end of 1953, he was feeling confident enough to push his case for closing this gap, which he did in the first instance by competing with his RCC colleagues in terms of patriotic public statements. It was a familiar card to play in Egyptian politics, but no less dangerous to Nasser's own leadership position for that. In short, 1954 was shaping up to be a make or break year for both the leading personalities in the Canal Zone dispute.

DOMESTIC POLITICS – THE BRITISH CONTEXT

The new year began in London with Foreign Office officials working hard to dispel Eden's downcast talk about throwing over the Arabs and relying instead on Turkey and Israel. A pessimistic end to 1953 was thus replaced with a sense of renewed determination for an agreement with Egypt. In a cabinet paper dated 7 January 1954, Eden strongly argued the case for a settlement: 'If we do not succeed, we are in a bad position. We must either remain in the Canal Zone indefinitely by force, a policy which, among other things would not enable us to meet the Chancellor of the Exchequer's demands [for cost-cutting], or we must leave Egypt of our own volition. However we do this it will look more or less like we are running away.'[2] Meanwhile, the chiefs of staff went to task on Churchill's latest idea, made in the final cabinet of 1953, for issuing Egypt with an ultimatum, following which Britain would carry out a 'vigorous and effective redeployment' in its own time.[3] Apart from the physical difficulties of liquidating the base when it was surrounded by a hostile population, such a plan, the service chiefs stated, would rule out the possibility of acquiring stockpiling facilities in Egypt. Even more importantly, it would also undermine Britain's relations with Iraq and Jordan where facilities were crucial to the more northerly defence of the region envisaged under the Levant–Iraq strategy.[4]

With Eden again eager for progress in the Canal Zone negotiations, Churchill resurrected a ploy he had last used in September 1953, when there had been similar pressures for a settlement. He raised the issue of unrestricted access through the Suez Canal. Egypt's recent extension of the blockade on Israeli-bound shipping to include foodstuffs and anything else that could be interpreted as contributing to war potential gave the prime minister the necessary pretext.[5] His previous tactic had been to press for a reference to freedom of transit through the Canal in any final settlement, but a special

cabinet committee had watered down this proposal by concluding that a
formula in the preamble of an agreement would suffice.[6] Now he argued that
Britain should make a formal protest at the United Nations against the
Egyptian blockade. Such a course, he stated on 21 January 1954, would win
the support of MPs of all parties and transfer the differences with Egypt from
the Suez base to the Canal.[7] Eden responded by pointing out that the issue
was one which all maritime powers should tackle, not just Britain. The
cabinet agreed and asked the foreign secretary to enlist the support of other
powers for a protest in the Security Council.[8] As Eden no doubt expected,
Washington poured cold water on the proposal. The last formal complaint on
this matter had been in September 1951, with little effect and only after
much hesitation on the part of the United States.[9]

Two other interrelated dangers faced Eden's Egyptian policy in early 1954.
The first was due to his absence from London for close to a month between
22 January and 19 February to attend a conference in Berlin on the future of
Germany. The day before he left, Churchill warned him that it would not be
possible to take decisions on Egypt by telephoning Berlin all the time. 'The
power of prompt action if needed by events must rest here,' he said.[10] Eden's
permanent under-secretary, Sir Ivone Kirkpatrick, was sufficiently worried by
the message to contact the prime minister and remind him in no uncertain
terms 'that the Secretary of State was in charge of the Office' and that he, as
his senior adviser, would decide when it was necessary to communicate with
him.[11]

The second danger to Eden's Canal Zone policy concerned the sympathies
of Selwyn Lloyd, minister of state in the Foreign Office, towards a proposal
made by the Suez Group in December 1953. The so-called 'Waterhouse plan'
was for Britain to reduce the number of troops in Egypt to the 10,000 legally
permitted under the 1936 treaty and then put the Canal Zone dispute to
international arbitration. The aim was to extend the 1936 terms beyond
1956, as provided for in the original agreement. (A catch in the withdrawal
conditions stated that Egypt's armed forces must be able to ensure security of
navigation in the Canal before a British evacuation could take place.) Roger
Allen considered the plan 'hopeless'. 'We maintain ourselves in Egypt because
the Egyptians are afraid of us. They are afraid of us because we have
overwhelming power. If they ceased to be afraid of us (and still hated us),
they would soon harry the life out of us.' In parentheses, he added,
'I shouldn't like to be among the last 10,000.'[12] But despite these strong

departmental views, as well as Eden's own attitude, Lloyd proceeded to champion the Waterhouse plan (known in cabinet memoranda as 'Course C') during the foreign secretary's absence.

Lloyd's first opportunity came within days of Eden leaving for Berlin, thanks to Churchill's mischievous request for a full review of Egyptian policy at a cabinet meeting scheduled for 28 January.[13] Not unnaturally, Eden was anxious that his own views on the Waterhouse plan, as well as those of the chiefs of staff, be forcefully reiterated at the session. Consequently, on the day of the meeting, Eden sent Lloyd a sharp telegram telling him, 'We must on no account let the Cabinet have too optimistic a view of course (C). This is worse than a treaty and I have always said so.' Shuckburgh summed up his master's mood in Berlin: 'More talk of resignation when he gets back, unless the Old Man will go.'[14]

But against Eden's express instructions, Lloyd circulated a paper describing the scheme in approving terms. It was, he stated, the policy most defensible with 'British opinion' (meaning the government's backbench critics); troops could be kept in Egypt 'for several critical years'; and when the British did eventually leave the Canal Zone, it would be because of a ruling of an international tribunal, rather than Egyptian clamour.[15] For ministers who were tired of party disunity, this option increasingly looked like an attractive proposition. Even the minister of defence was beguiled. The meeting concluded by recommending further detailed consideration of the proposal.[16] After this episode, Eden's confidence in Lloyd naturally plummeted.[17] It was telling, moreover, that when the foreign secretary returned to London on 19 February, his minister of state shrewdly made himself absent from the Foreign Office.[18]

The upshot of Lloyd's attitude was that no progress occurred in the Canal Zone negotiations during Eden's spell in Berlin. Ironically, however, the scope for movement was perhaps greater than it had been for a long time. On 25 January Nasser had intimated that he was willing to extend the availability formula to include Turkey.[19] This was a major concession because Turkey was a member of NATO and an indirect link would thereby be established between the defence concerns of the Middle East and those of Western Europe. In making this offer, Nasser was well aware that his domestic opponents would accuse him of tying Egypt to a Western defence organisation. His willingness to take this risk was predicated by his anxiety to get the Canal Zone talks going again, lest the mounting pressure on the Conservative government result in the abandonment of the negotiations altogether.

Yet no one in London was prepared to undertake a detailed consideration of the Turkey concession. Eden tried his best to hurry things along from Berlin, but with little effect. A telegram to Lloyd on 9 February, two weeks after Nasser's original soundings, asked if he and the department were concerned over the delay in reopening the discussions with Cairo 'now that the Egyptians seemed to be moving towards us?'[20] Lloyd, however, remained unruffled: as the main advocate of remaining in Egypt and awaiting arbitration, Turkey's inclusion in the availability clause was neither here nor there. His reply some five days later merely stressed the Conservative Party's difficulty in making a quid pro quo, as Nasser expected, over the uniform dispute.[21]

DOMESTIC POLITICS – THE EGYPTIAN CONTEXT

This delay played into the hands of Nasser's opponents. The most powerful of these were no longer political parties or palace cronies, they were rivals within the junta. It was probably not unconnected, therefore, that before Nasser felt able to signal the concession over Turkey, he first moved against one of his ostensible allies, the Muslim Brotherhood. As a broad-based movement within the armed forces, the Free Officers had always maintained links with the Brotherhood. Nevertheless, the underlying danger for Nasser was that this politically orientated Islamic pressure group could swamp the military regime.

It was consequently to his advantage that the Brotherhood had been plagued by internal divisions since the assassination of its founding supreme guide, Hasan al-Banna, in 1949. Hudaybi, al-Banna's successor, had always struggled to control the secret military apparatus of the society. Indeed, according to British intelligence sources, Nasser covertly exacerbated these divisions throughout 1953, as he meanwhile tried to build up his own mass organisation, the Liberation Rally.[22] Yet these divide-and-rule tactics were effectively taken away from him in late 1953 when Hudaybi finally succeeded in asserting his authority over the whole of the Muslim Brotherhood. The timing for Nasser, given his anxiety to push through a Canal Zone settlement, could not have been worse. Adding to his worries were reports that Neguib was busy trying to develop personal contacts with the newly potent Hudaybi.[23]

Difficult times called for drastic measures. On 15 January 1954 the RCC announced that the Muslim Brotherhood would henceforth count as a political party and was therefore subject to the decree dissolving all such bodies. The statement was preceded by the arrest of about 500 members, including most of the leadership, plus individuals in the army and police. A clash between rival student factions in Cairo on 12 January was the immediate cause of the action, although the clash may have been provoked by the government. In any case, it certainly convinced Nasser of the need to move. For a month or so before this incident, there had been discussions within the RCC concerning the possibility of banning the Muslim Brotherhood.[24]

No one doubted that attempting to emasculate the main Islamic organisation in Egyptian society would be the riskiest action to date for the military regime. Unlike the discredited politicians, the Brotherhood was responsible for concerted welfare provision throughout the land via schools, hospitals and clinics. It had also played the lead role in the patriotic battle against the Canal Zone garrison. Nasser's strategy against the organisation entailed trying to discredit its leadership – secret contacts with the British were repeatedly mentioned – rather than the Islamic revivalist idea per se.[25] The Brotherhood responded by mounting a wave of attacks against British personnel in the Suez base, in an effort to prove that it could still flex its muscles. On 20 January or thereabouts, three servicemen were killed in the space of two days. In the opinion of Ralph Stevenson, who had returned to Cairo as ambassador at the end of 1953 after a long period of sick leave, the situation was as bad as that around the Dulles visit to Cairo the previous May.[26]

The British government interpreted the banning of the Muslim Brotherhood as evidence of the RCC's weakening internal position.[27] Neguib was also perceived to be under threat because of his private contacts with the Brotherhood in late 1953.[28] In light of this deteriorating situation, Britain began to consider reviving its old practice of making and breaking Egyptian governments. On 27 January (two days after Nasser's Turkey concession), Eden issued a directive to his officials enquiring if there was a Wafdist or other political leader with whom Britain could get in touch, and also whether it was possible 'to start any subversive activities in Egypt'. The Foreign Office's African department was duly instructed to consider whom Britain could back if Neguib was murdered or deposed and anarchy threatened. Likely scenarios included a new coup by a different military clique (possibly backed by the Wafd), or an extended period of mob rule followed by a seizure of power by either the Muslim Brotherhood or the Wafd.[29]

On that same day (the 27th), Sirag al-Din's trial for culpability in the Black Saturday riots came to a conclusion in Cairo. The former interior minister was sentenced to fifteen years' imprisonment.[30] The prosecution had successfully argued that the Wafd government abrogated the 1936 defence treaty solely as a means of keeping themselves in office, and that the absence of preparations for the subsequent breakdown in Anglo-Egyptian relations amounted to 'high treason'.[31]

As was customary, Britain's embassy in Cairo was asked by the African department for its assessment of the stability of the existing Egyptian government, along with its views on the possible alternatives. Equally routine was Stevenson's reply that there was no viable alternative to the RCC. Instead, the prospects for the regime's survival were assessed as being 'very good', provided that key members were not assassinated and there was no grave deterioration in the economic situation. 'The main sources of support', he pointed out, 'are the Armed Forces, the National Guard and the Liberation Rally. Peasantry and urban proletariats are generally in sympathy.' Meanwhile, opposition came 'mainly from the old political parties, [the] upper classes, some dissatisfied elements of the Army, police and civil service, some business and labour organisations, and [the] communists'.[32] Officials in the Foreign Office agreed. Even if Nasser or Neguib were assassinated, it was felt that the RCC would close its ranks and ruthlessly suppress the culprits.[33]

Nasser waited for more than a fortnight for a British response to his Turkey offer before asking the Americans to try to move things along. His influence in the RCC, he confided, was being jeopardised by the delays.[34] These were not empty words. In the third week of February, while Britain's Conservative government was still equivocating, the RCC underwent its severest test to date when the long-simmering rivalry between Nasser and Neguib boiled over into a major internal crisis.

The origins of this showdown can be traced back to when Neguib took much of the credit for the Sudan settlement a year earlier. The friction seemed to stem from conflicting personalities, but underlying this was a problem of dependency. Easy-going, instantly likeable and, above all, popular with the Egyptian people, Neguib gave the junta much-needed mass support. Nasser, meanwhile, was nothing if not intense and remained somewhat stilted and shifty in public forums. The loyalty he commanded among soldiers and co-conspirators did not easily translate into popular appeal; in any case, how could it when he was usually obliged to stand behind the genial, pipe-smoking general? An American journalist writing in 1959 captured the source of Nasser's frustration when he described Neguib as 'the most effective baby-kissing politician in Egyptian history'.[35] There was also a generational element to the divide. Born in 1901, Neguib was practically old enough to have been the father of any of the other RCC members. In the early days of the regime, this age issue had presented itself more as a matter of style than content. Although Neguib lacked the younger officers' enthusiasm for rapid reform, he generally shared their views on the measures needed. By 1954, however, he had come to perceive an increasing zealotry in the behaviour of his colleagues, and with Nasser especially.

The internal crisis began with Neguib tendering his resignation as president and prime minister on 22 February. RCC colleagues immediately suspected that it was a pressure tactic.[36] American embassy dispatches suggested that he was influenced by his wife and presidential legal adviser, both of whom wanted him to secure extra powers. His own explanation, in his 1955 memoirs, emphasised the problems with the regime's 'committee government'. What was needed, he argued, was a clear chain of command with himself at the top.[37] The timing of his move, which he did not admit to, was determined by the delicate state of the Canal Zone talks and the impending inauguration of the Sudanese parliament, scheduled for 1 March.

Nasser and his RCC colleagues spent three days trying to persuade Neguib to change his mind before finally accepting the decision on Thursday 25 February.[38] News of the resignation was broken with an explanatory communiqué from the regime. After detailing the history and aims of the revolutionary movement, the document stated that Neguib had suffered a 'psychological crisis' as a result of the RCC presenting him as their leader when he was no more than the president of a committee of equals. Within six months of the revolution, it continued, he had begun demanding powers exceeding those of an ordinary member.[39]

In accepting Neguib's resignation, the younger officers woefully misjudged both the mood of the country and the attitude inside the army. 'Cairo was thoroughly crestfallen on the morning of the 26th of February,' write the Lacoutures: 'Neguib's portraits were still smiling in the shop windows, but the newspaper-sellers and their customers were not in a mood for joking.'[40] That night, encouraged by the widespread public dismay, a counter-coup was attempted within the army. It was led by Khaled Mohi el-Din, a Marxist member of the RCC whom Nasser counted as a personal friend. As the commander of the motorised cavalry, Mohi el-Din carried with him a powerful section of the army. His self-ascribed motive was a desire to see the resumption of parliamentary life in Egypt.[41] His colleague Anwar Sadat offered a more cynical explanation: 'By using the strength of his Cavalry Corps, Khaled thought he could impose a dictatorship of the left (under the pretence of wanting to restore democracy and the party system).'[42]

At first, the attempted counter-coup had the air of a collegiate quarrel. Cavalry officers led by Mohi el-Din met Nasser at the Abbassia barracks on the outskirts of Cairo to protest against Neguib's removal. Fearing that the army might be splitting, Nasser acceded to the calls for Neguib's reinstatement as president and also accepted Mohi el-Din's appointment as prime minister, along with a programme for restoring constitutional government. However, as soon as the meeting was over, Nasser ordered loyal units to surround the Abbassia barracks, and Mohi el-Din and forty-one cavalry officers were arrested. Neguib was also apprehended and held prisoner.[43]

But on Saturday 27 February, it was the turn of the population to show their loyalty to Neguib and the crisis took on a much broader significance. Seeing the former president as their best chance for returning to legality, the Muslim Brotherhood organised pro-Neguib demonstrations, which resulted in a genuine groundswell of support. Having underestimated Neguib's popularity, the RCC completed a humiliating U-turn and restored him as president on 28 February. Mohi el-Din fared less well. Because the cavalry revolt had not spread to other sections of the armed forces, his claims to be prime minister were resisted and he was instead exiled to Europe as a trade delegate. Nasser subsequently became the new prime minister (so dropping the 'deputy' pretence), in addition to his role as interior minister.[44]

The next month was the making of Nasser: not only was he able to reverse the climbdown of Neguib's reappointment, but he also became, in Britain's hitherto sceptical eyes, a leader capable of both concluding a Canal Zone agreement and, even more importantly, carrying the Egyptian people with him. Furthermore, the Sudan issue, for once, worked against Neguib.

On 1 March the reinstated president arrived in Khartoum to represent Egypt at the opening of the Sudan's first parliament, elected the previous December. Selwyn Lloyd represented Britain, the other former co-dominium partner. Prior to the planned inauguration ceremony, both dignitaries headed for the governor-general's palace, which had been built on the site of the one destroyed in 1885 – the place where General Gordon had been speared to death. Lloyd arrived first and managed to get a few hours' sleep before being awoken by the sounds of a carefully orchestrated pro-Neguib demonstration outside the palace gates. He went downstairs and found Neguib having coffee. Lloyd asked about the situation in Cairo: 'Young men like Nasser', replied Neguib in words that echoed Ali Maher's after the July coup, 'thought they knew everything, but he had them exactly where he wanted them.'[45]

Later that morning, Lloyd joined the British governor-general on the veranda and watched with concern as the mood of the crowd changed. The pro-Neguib demonstration had melted away, but had been replaced by irate Mahdists – the dervishes of imperial notoriety. Lloyd takes up the story:

I returned to my room, and just as I got there I heard what sounded like shots. I went up on the flat roof, from which I had a good view of Kitchener Square. There was a huge mob there. Sporadic fighting was taking place. The police were shooting and using tear gas. Dead and wounded were being carried through the west gate, and some bodies were being fished out of the Nile.[46]

The anger of the crowd, which numbered in the tens of thousands, stemmed from the fact that they felt cheated out of being able to make a peaceful protest against the Egyptian president as he was driven from the airfield to the palace, Neguib having taken a circuitous route to avoid them. In the subsequent clashes, the British police commander was brutally killed by the mob. Seven fellow officers also died, along with at least twenty civilians and many more injured. Meanwhile, inside the palace, Lloyd worried that history was about to repeat itself.

I went down to see the Governor-General. On the landing I met Neguib. The main staircase splits into two half-way up. I said to Neguib how thoughtful I felt the architect had been when the palace was rebuilt after its destruction by the Mahdi. Gordon had been stabbed to death at the top of a single staircase. We were there representing the two condomini [sic] – there was a place for both of us, one at the head of each staircase. He did not seem very amused.[47]

In the event, a British official, William Luce, managed to barge his way through the throng (a brave act indeed) and ordered Sayed Abdul Rahman to restrain his followers. It was a subdued and shaken Neguib at dinner that evening, no doubt realising that his stock back in Egypt would be badly damaged by the fact that British lives had been lost trying to protect him.[48]

Nasser was certainly given a much-needed boost in his struggle with Neguib. Since yielding to the public clamour for the general's return on 28 February, Nasser had been deliberating on how to avoid the associated commitment of returning Egypt to parliamentary politics. Encouraged by the latest Sudan episode, his strategy was to mount a psychological campaign that made widespread unrest appear inevitable in Egypt. In pursuance of this approach, all censorship was lifted on 5 March. Over the next three weeks, press reports, radio broadcasts, pamphlets and word of mouth all worked together to fashion a mood in which considerable disorder was seen as more than a possibility. It became widely accepted that the RCC was doomed and that Neguib was being used by the Wafd to facilitate their return to power.[49]

In the meantime, Nasser tightened his control over the armed forces, especially the cavalry. Measures were also taken to neutralise the Muslim Brotherhood. Emissaries visited its imprisoned leader, Hudaybi, in mid-March and a deal was struck whereby Nasser promised to restore the movement's legal status, while Hudaybi committed himself to an ambivalent stance on the legalisation of political parties.[50] On 21 March Lakeland and the head of the State Department's Near Eastern Affairs section, Parker Hart, visited Nasser at his home. A two-hour long meeting ensued in which the Egyptian prime minister explained his audacious plan: he was letting the situation deteriorate 'in order to demonstrate to the people what would be in store for the country if party elections were carried out now'.[51]

Four days later the junta announced that political parties were again legal and elections would soon be held, adding that the RCC would not itself form a political party. The 'revolution' was to be formally declared over on 24 July. Hundreds of Muslim Brothers, including Hudaybi, were released from prison.[52] Also on Friday 25 March, Nasser initiated the activist element to his strategy. Railway, tram and bus workers in Cairo and other major cities took part in government-organised 'spontaneous' strikes. The strikers' key demand was that there should be no legalisation of political parties or electoral campaigning until the evacuation of British forces had been achieved.[53] Mass demonstrations were also staged by the old political parties calling for an immediate return to parliamentary life.

On the Saturday evening representatives from the Egyptian armed forces presented a resolution to the RCC declaring their opposition to the reconstitution of the political parties, thus completing the circle that began a month earlier with the cavalry protest.[54] Nasser continued to keep the US embassy well briefed. In the 'forthcoming political melee', Caffery informed the State Department on the 26th, the RCC would stand aloof while Neguib and the other party groups sullied themselves. The upshot would be a 'resurgence [of] public sympathy for the "clean" revolution leaders', so allowing the RCC to reverse the trend towards parliamentary democracy.[55] Sure enough, the next day the junta used the demonstrations to justify a reassertion of its control over the country. At 7 p.m. a statement was issued cancelling the elections, banning political parties, and reinstating censorship. Instead, a national advisory council was to be established which would represent organisations and districts. Nasser resisted the hardline members of the junta who wanted Neguib arrested: keeping him as president, emasculated in the confines of the RCC, was the preferred solution.[56]

With the crisis over, Stevenson observed that Nasser had proved himself to be 'an astute, if unscrupulous politician'. Caffery, while not approving all his methods, nevertheless felt that Nasser was the 'only man in Egypt with strength enough and guts enough to put over an agreement with Britain'.[57]

TOWARDS A CANAL ZONE AGREEMENT

On 11 March a meeting was held in the British Foreign Office for all those dealing with the Egyptian question. Everyone present – Eden, Kirkpatrick, Allen, Shuckburgh, Lloyd and parliamentary under-secretary for foreign affairs, Anthony Nutting – realised that the Neguib–Nasser split in Cairo, together with the recent rioting in Khartoum, made an immediate restart of the negotiations if not impossible then at least undesirable. Eden was close to going one step further and breaking off the negotiations until the Egyptians 'behaved better'. Churchill had already used the reports of the rioting to repeat his case for a minor war and a guns-blazing retreat.[58]

To forestall this, Shuckburgh suggested turning Eden's attitude into the basis of a positive new approach. His plan was to inform the RCC that Britain would produce a solution to the uniform issue provided that 'conditions of confidence' were created in the Sudan and the Canal Zone. The concession in mind was to have civilian technicians maintain the base, an idea first proposed by Bevin in December 1950. Eden agreed and a memorandum was drafted ready for the cabinet's consideration on 15 March.[59] The key passage in the paper related to the unsatisfactory nature of the existing policy on the uniform question. Leaving '4,000 soldiers in the Canal Zone, scattered on technical duties, whether in uniform or not' was, it stated, 'offering hostages to fortune'.[60] A second memorandum was also circulated highlighting Washington's view that no further time should be lost in resuming the negotiations on the basis of Nasser's Turkey offer, made some six weeks earlier.[61]

The cabinet met on the evening of 15 March. Already that day the chiefs of staff committee had concluded that there would be no insuperable difficulty with civilian technicians provided that reputable contractors could be found to undertake the work.[62] Before the cabinet meeting, Shuckburgh anxiously gauged the various ministerial positions towards his scheme. Eden was indecisive, despite the fact that it was officially his paper about to be discussed. Salisbury apparently liked the plan, but thought it might be more difficult to sell to the party. On the other side, Butler was deemed to be dubious, thinking all the stores would be stolen by the Egyptian army. The silence from No. 10 was taken to mean that Churchill did not approve.[63] It was a perceptive assessment.

As the cabinet minutes record, Butler and Churchill were indeed the main critics of the proposals. Summing up the prime minister's contribution to the discussion, Shuckburgh noted that he 'wanted all the usual things – a brigade to Khartoum, 10,000 men on the Canal, etc. and a break in the negotiations'.[64] A more general opinion was that the civilian contractors scheme would be less justifiable to the government's own backbenchers. The evacuation of all troops, it was noted, 'could easily be presented as a complete surrender to the more extreme demands of the Egyptian Government'. However, rather than reject the idea outright, the cabinet decided to sound out the Americans as to whether they would join in the project. The political value of having US personnel involved was that it could be presented to the Commons as a powerful guarantee that the technicians would not be harassed.[65] Against Caffery's advice, the State Department responded positively to the suggestion five days later.[66] The proponents of an evacuation agreement were thus left with a glimmer of hope in the dark days of March 1954.

Churchill, in the meantime, was worried. The civilian contractors scheme did indeed look like circumventing the last remaining hurdle in the base negotiations, provided that the Egyptian political scene became stable enough to push through a new agreement. The day after the cabinet meeting, the prime minister consequently spent ninety minutes grilling the chief of the imperial general staff on the pros and cons of Course C. Britain's most senior soldier apparently crumbled under the pressure. Harding 'has turned his coat on Egypt', grumbled Shuckburgh in his diary on 17 March.[67]

The specifics of Course C had been worked out in February and entailed a withdrawal from Tel el Kebir, followed by a progressive rounding up from the south until, at the end of two years, the final garrison was concentrated in an area in and between Ismailia and Abu Sueir.[68] Ever the cautious soldier, Harding's only modification to this plan following his discussion with Churchill was to argue that 15,000 troops must be kept in the base.[69] But given the arbitration aspect of Course C (which first entailed reducing the garrison size to the legally permitted maximum of 10,000 troops), this insistence on an extra 5,000 personnel defeated the purpose of the exercise. This may have been Harding's point. In any case, buoyed by the CIGS's seeming defection, Churchill wrote to Eden on 18 March stressing the need 'for deeds, not words, with the Egyptians'.[70] In reply, Eden pointed out that Harding had taken 'a different view' from all the previous ones by the chiefs of staff. Furthermore, he felt that leaving 15,000 men in the Canal Zone could easily lead Britain into 'open conflict with Egypt'.[71] The heads of the Royal Navy and the Royal Air Force must have thought likewise because they reaffirmed their support for a negotiated Canal Zone settlement on 22 March.[72]

It was around this time that the RCC descended into the second phase of its internal crisis, with strikes and demonstrations. The Conservative government closely monitored events in case it became necessary to reoccupy the Nile Delta to protect British lives in Cairo and Alexandria. The tense situation was exacerbated by widespread doubts about the efficacy of the Rodeo plans. While these concerns had been around since the winter of 1951/2, it was not until the Canal Zone negotiations stalled in October 1953 that a long-overdue re-examination of the operations was sanctioned.[73]

By March 1954 the military view had crystallised enough for Harding to recommend the complete abandonment of the Rodeo plans. Two main factors influenced his decision. First, future troop withdrawals, whether through an Eden-type settlement or via the politically popular Course C, would make the Rodeo plans impossible to implement. Secondly, Britain's military authorities now accorded increased respect to Egyptian resistance capabilities after the Ismailia police barracks incident of January 1952. 'We must always be prepared to carry out a rescue dash on Cairo by a strong mobile column,' Harding explained, 'but we cannot continue to contemplate a major military adventure such as Rodeo which would have no hope of achieving its primary object of preventing a wholesale massacre of British subjects, and which would inevitably lead us into the military occupation of the whole Delta.'[74] Harding's brusquely expressed solution was to 'cut down the size of the target'. This meant encouraging all British subjects to leave Egypt as soon as trouble threatened. The rescue mission could then be limited to picking up officials compelled to remain in Cairo on government business. The chiefs of staff gave their backing to Harding's proposals at their committee meeting on 18 March.[75]

The Foreign Office was deeply unimpressed with the recommendations of the chiefs of staff. It was 'surely impossible', noted one official on 27 March (the day Egypt's internal crisis reached its climax), 'morally and politically, to limit the object of Rodeo to the protection of British officials, as opposed to British subjects in general'.[76] Moreover, in addition to the 4,000 to 5,000 Britons who may or may not have left Cairo at the first sign of trouble, there were also 12,000 Maltese and Cypriots, plus an unspecified number of Americans, French, Italians and Greeks, many of whom might need protecting.[77]

On 31 March (when Cairo was once again calm), the service chiefs sought a compromise with the Foreign Office. While ready to concede that all British subjects ought to be rescued, they added two provisos. The first was that the evacuees should be instructed to make their own way to a prearranged rendezvous point. The second stated that the operation should not go beyond the scope of a rescue mission. In other words, the wider plans to restore order and maintain control of the Delta should be dropped.[78] The subtext was that Britain's military authorities no longer wanted to play the Foreign Office's old game of interfering in Egypt's internal affairs, whether to prop up a sympathetic government or to topple an unsympathetic one.

The cabinet discussed the revised plans on 15 April. Eden began by speaking out against limiting the Rodeo operations to rescue missions: 'If a situation arose which called for intervention by us', he stated, 'we might have an opportunity to set up an alternative government and we should be ill-advised to miss such an opportunity . . . The Egyptians already knew that we had plans for occupying the Delta and this knowledge was a powerful guarantee of their good behaviour. If we restricted our plans in the way proposed by the Chiefs of Staff, we should be abandoning this useful negotiating card.'[79]

Harding responded in a way which implied that Eden could not have his cake and eat it: 'The object of the modified plan was to enable a start to be made with the redeployment of the fighting troops in the Canal Zone.' He continued, 'So long as we accepted a firm commitment to occupy the Delta in an emergency, no reduction could be made in the garrison of the Canal Zone. Moreover, if we had to restore order in Cairo and Alexandria and support an alternative government, it was likely that reinforcements would be needed from the United Kingdom.'[80]

This argument left the foreign secretary seemingly guilty of inconsistency. It was possible, however, that Eden was trying to impress upon his colleagues the dangers of open-ended Egyptian hostility, as could be expected with Course C. A minute by the cabinet secretary to the prime minister, dated 15 April, gives credence to this supposition. According to Brook, the foreign secretary wanted to show that substantial reinforcements would be needed for a reoccupation of the Nile Delta, but because this could not be afforded, he felt that Britain 'must avoid the risk of it by concluding a defence agreement with Egypt'.[81] Over the following weeks, the serious question marks over the feasibility of the two Rodeo plans helped steer many cabinet members away from Course C and back towards the policy of seeking a Canal Zone settlement.

For the second time in 1954, an International conference – this time held in Geneva to discuss Indo-China (where the French empire was collapsing) – militated against speedy progress in the Canal Zone negotiations. With Eden again often absent from the Foreign Office between 22 April and 21 July, the requisite high-level political guidance on Egyptian matters was lacking. Meanwhile, to Britain's Suez 'rebels', Eden's advocacy of a partition solution for Vietnam was privately viewed as 'selling out' French interests, not unlike his willingness to scuttle Britain's position in the Canal Zone.[82] Nevertheless, Eden's role in producing a settlement and thus helping avert a wider war gave him great personal prestige elsewhere in the Conservative Party and in the country at large. As for Egyptian opinion, an understandably more self-centred lesson was learnt from events in Indo-China. The fall of the large French garrison at Dien Bien Phu in May was interpreted as a victory for all nationalists against Western imperialism.[83]

Another setback for progress in the Suez base talks came when Dulles, en route to Geneva, called at London and backtracked on American participation in the civilian contractors scheme. While confirming that President Eisenhower approved the plan in principle, Dulles alluded to a distinct lack of enthusiasm in other quarters.[84] No names were mentioned, but Caffery's influence was plain to see. As if to prove the point, Dulles also stated that the US would not participate in the negotiations on this matter unless the Egyptians invited them to do so. The imprint was unmistakably that of Caffery and his aversion to 'ganging up'.[85] Eden angrily minuted that this attitude was 'absurd'. 'This scheme has no appeal unless Americans really come into it. If they want to slide out on one pretext or another – for fear of agreeing with their allies – we had better call the whole thing off, and just stay in the Canal for the time being anyway. The whole point is to be "ganging up" – and to be seen to be "ganging up".'[86]

In line with Britain's conditions for tabling a new offer, Nasser brought about a period of relative calm in the Canal Zone from 18 April. But when Britain had not responded in any way by the end of May, Nasser reverted to pressure tactics and lifted his controls on fedayeen raids. A British serviceman was murdered by a mob in Ismailia on the 30th and another soldier was found shot the next day.[87] Over the next month or so, the Foreign Office struggled to keep the temperature down in Parliament, with MPs asking awkward questions about how many British servicemen had been killed in Egypt. The official line, as always, was not to give full details because they would 'produce a rather poor impression'.[88]

By the end of May, Harding was back to fully supporting an evacuation agreement, not least because, as he himself put it, the implications of Rodeo were 'so great that it must on all accounts be avoided'.[89] Positive news was also at hand concerning the War Office's recent discussions with British industrialists. A number of high-profile firms, including Shell Oil, ICI and Austin Motors, were prepared to join the civilian labour scheme. No one doubted that it was an expensive and inefficient way to run the base, but the political advantages outweighed these concerns.[90] The momentum in the direction of an agreement was thus becoming irresistible. Significantly, it was under Selwyn Lloyd's name – hitherto Lloyd was the main ministerial proponent of Course C – that the first detailed discussion paper on the technicians scheme was circulated to the cabinet on 3 June. The 'essential thing', Lloyd stated, was that Britain left Egypt with an agreement that permitted the right to return in war. It also suggested that the extra expense of civilian labour could be overcome by having 'a minimum form of nucleus base'.[91]

The key breakthrough in respect of Churchill's attitude came at a cabinet meeting on 22 June. With Eden briefly back from Geneva, the Foreign Office had prepared a draft heads of agreement for discussion. The plan was to reduce substantially the size of the Suez base and have it maintained by civilian technicians; in return, Eden wanted to press for an agreement of longer duration. Although Britain and Egypt had previously agreed on seven years, he was now looking for ten to twenty years. Churchill responded by conceding that he had finally accepted the military case for redeployment (presumably because of the implications for the Rodeo operations of a much-reduced garrison size), but continued to be worried by the political disadvantages of abandoning the position. It was this political dimension that also worried the Suez Group. In the discussion that followed, the cabinet isolated the problem to one of presentation. Following this diagnosis, a prescription was soon recommended. The thinking was to link the evacuation of Egypt with the advent of the hydrogen bomb.[92]

There had been widespread nervous excitement in March 1954 when news of the h-bomb had broken to an unsuspecting public (the first tests actually occurred in November 1952). But while a mood of impending doom had characterised the British press at the time, the impact on the Canal Zone negotiations had been nil and indeed remained so until the Conservative government came up with the idea of presenting the withdrawal from Egypt as a result of a reassessment of strategic needs in the thermonuclear age. The target for this blatant example of spin was Britain's domestic political scene and, above all, the Suez Group rebels.

One other matter still needing resolution concerned America's role in the new package. Learning from previous experience, Eden decided not to seek US participation in a joint approach. Instead, he sought a strong affirmation of the basis of the settlement, a tacit link between the signing of an agreement and American financial aid, and a public endorsement of freedom of transit through the Suez Canal. Eisenhower and Dulles readily agreed to these points, relieved no doubt not to be asked to 'gang up' on the Egyptians.[93] The cabinet's formal approval for the reopening of negotiations came on 7 July.[94] Two days later, in accordance with the sterling releases agreement of 1951, Britain unblocked £10 million from Egypt's sterling accounts, which the RCC had been asking for since the start of the year.[95] This conciliatory gesture immediately set alarm bells ringing among the Suez Group MPs.

Once again, the Conservative government tried to win over the backbench critics. On 13 July Churchill told a meeting of the party's army committee that an agreement was essential for strategic, economic and political reasons. 'Well, I did your dirty work for you,' he commented afterwards to one Foreign Office official.[96] Although clearly not reconciled to the policy of withdrawal, Churchill was nevertheless no longer opposing an agreement. The Suez Group had lost their most powerful (tacit) ally. Not to be deterred, the rebels issued a statement later that day informing the government 'that they would vote against any treaty made with Egypt which involves the removal of all fighting troops from the Suez Canal area'.[97] This was followed twenty-four hours later by Major Harry Legge-Bourke, an aide-de-camp to Sir Miles Lampson at the time of the Abdin palace incident in 1942, giving up the Conservative whip in protest. Waterhouse kept the Suez Group's activities in the newspapers a few days later by resigning as chairman of the parliamentary Conservative Party's Defence Committee.[98]

RESOLUTION

Meanwhile, informal discussions between Stevenson and Nasser began on 10 July. The talks centred on the British-drafted heads of agreement. Nasser immediately liked what he saw regarding the uniform problem, but took exception to Britain's attempts to extend the duration. 'I agreed to seven years,' he commented. 'Why change?'[99] Another meeting took place on 19 July, but there was no give on either side.[100] Nasser's predictable response meant that some British backtracking was necessary. In London, Shuckburgh wrote a minute to Lloyd considering the probability that an agreement would be either lost or gained on the duration issue. 'Can we contemplate losing it?' he asked rhetorically.

> Personally I think not. There is a lot to be said for the view that in dealing with unreliable and improvident people like the Egyptians you do well to have short arrangements which, if they work, can be extended, and if they do not work do not become a symbol of 'mainmorte', as the 1936 Treaty has . . . We have waited over two years for a concatenation of circumstances here and in Egypt which would make an agreement possible. If we

let the talks break down now I doubt very much if another opportunity will occur. There have been very few occasions since 1882 when we could 'start afresh' with Egypt. 1936 was one. Today is another and we should seize it. There is to my mind everything to be lost and nothing to be gained by extending the argument beyond the coming week.[101]

The government had assured the rebels that the signing of the heads of agreement would be debated in the Commons before a final treaty was concluded. Parliament was set for summer recess at the start of August. This left two weeks to sign the initial settlement.

Shuckburgh had been living and breathing the Canal Zone issue since August 1951, first as Herbert Morrison's private secretary and then in the same capacity for Eden. He also had a better sense of Egyptian grievances than most, having been private secretary to Lampson between 1937 and 1939. In May 1954 Shuckburgh moved from Eden's private office to become assistant under-secretary of state in charge of Middle Eastern affairs, replacing Roger Allen, the other main Foreign Office proponent of an Egyptian agreement. Like Allen, Shuckburgh was utterly convinced that Britain must evacuate its garrison from the Canal Zone or face serious consequences. He had, of course, been the official responsible for keeping Eden on track in late 1953/early 1954 and for resurrecting Bevin's hitherto forgotten civilian contractors idea.

Not surprisingly, then, Shuckburgh was adamant that the new approach on 'duration' had to be modified. Part of this issue concerned the time that would be permitted for the garrison to be withdrawn. Egypt insisted on a fifteen-month maximum, whereas Britain's military authorities wanted up to two years. Indeed, the chiefs of staff actually considered it more important to secure a longer withdrawal period than to extend the duration terms. Extra stores could be saved that way. From the political angle, however, the priority was the other way round. Nevertheless, at their meeting on 21 July the service chiefs were so desirous of an agreement that they were prepared to accept, if necessary, both a fifteen-month withdrawal period and a seven-year duration.[102] The prospect of an agreement was clearly too precious to miss.

Churchill, for his part, was now ready to get 'this melancholy business' over with as quickly as possible.[103] Decisions on the duration issue and withdrawal period were due to be taken at the cabinet meeting on 23 July – the two-year anniversary of Egypt's *coup d'état*. Like the service chiefs, the

Foreign Office was willing to accept the existing timetables if the alternative was to lose the agreement.[104] According to the cabinet minutes, Churchill made no comments and the case for greater flexibility on the outstanding issues was agreed.[105]

On 24 July, Britain's secretary of state for war, Antony Head, flew to Cairo with Shuckburgh to tie up the final points of an agreement. The choice of Head rather than Eden was important for domestic political purposes in that it underlined the military reasons for a withdrawal. During the flight, tactics for the negotiations were decided. To explain away Britain's previous insistence on anything up to twenty years as a duration period, Head suggested reusing the line about hydrogen bombs and strategic reassessments. (The Conservative Party, after all, was being similarly misinformed.) The outcome of this 'review' was that Britain had decided 'that a short duration with good evacuation time and a friendly Egypt was of more importance than a long one bargained out of them'. It was further reasoned that Egypt might accept a twenty-month evacuation period because it could be fulfilled within a month of the lapse of the 1936 treaty. Cabinet approval for this approach was granted on 26 July.[106]

The two negotiating teams met on the evening of the 26th at what had been a royal residence adjacent to the Giza pyramids. Proceedings began with a good dinner, during which the atmosphere was kept friendly despite the obvious tensions. The parties then moved to another room and got down to business. Shuckburgh takes up the story: Head, he writes, stated the British proposition 'in a brief, soldierly and effective statement'.

> The Egyptians did not bat an eyelid when he announced our concessions, but when he had finished and suggested we might adjourn till tomorrow, they at once said they would prefer to retire for half an hour and give their answer tonight and a settlement was quickly reached. We had expected this and agreed, though we were anxious not to get into a detailed argument about any except the main points. While they were out I walked up and down outside the rest-house under the Pyramid with Head. Dark night, sky full of stars and the lights of Cairo away down on the plain. We thought they would accept.

The Egyptian delegation came back looking cheerful. It was, as Shuckburgh himself expressed it, 'in the bag'.[107]

Drafting details were tied up the next morning. With the initialling ceremony scheduled for later that day, Shuckburgh spent part of the afternoon sailing on the Nile with John Hamilton, his old Lampson-era colleague from the 1930s (and an embassy fixture ever since): 'He is entirely with us over this agreement and bitter about the attitude of Killearn and [Maurice] Hankey.'[108]

The initialling ceremony was a crowded affair and rather uncomfortable given the heat, but it did not stop the Egyptians present from embracing one another with great joy. As soon as the final agreement could be signed, the twenty-month evacuation period would begin. The British occupation would finally end. Thereafter, the base was set to be maintained by up to 800 British civilian technicians for a further five years and four months, making the total duration period seven years. During that time, Britain could remilitarise the base if there was a direct attack on a member state of the Arab League or Turkey. In an emergency or a threatened attack, Egypt's sole obligation was to consult with Britain. In the preamble of the agreement, Egypt pledged its adherence to free transit through the Canal, in line with the 1888 Convention of Constantinople.[109]

The agreement contained no references to control boards, joint air defence systems, or automatic rights of re-entry whenever Britain thought it justifiable. There was to be no British-led Middle East Command or Defence Organisation. The terms severely curtailed Britain's ability to reactivate the base effectively in a future war. The availability clause meant that reoccupation would probably have to take place in wartime conditions. In addition, the base would be a lot smaller, with far fewer facilities. While the settlement allowed Britain over-flying, landing and servicing rights, permission nevertheless had to be sought first and this could be refused. As a sop, Britain was granted most-favoured-nation status, which meant that full diplomatic procedure would not be necessary to clear each flight or landing.[110]

A footnote to the signing of the Canal Zone agreement (but a major debacle in the annals of Israel's early statehood) was an attempt by a Jewish espionage ring in Egypt to derail the final stages of the negotiations. At the bidding of hardline activists in Israeli military intelligence (though not necessarily with the prior knowledge of defence minister Pinhas Lavon, after whom the affair is named), a sleeper cell was activated in early July with instructions to fake anti-British and anti-American incidents aimed at showing the Nasser regime to be too weak to protect Western interests or make a defence agreement work. The fear motivating the action was that if Britain withdrew its garrison from the Canal Zone, Egypt would stop worrying about the enemy in its own backyard and instead concentrate on a 'second round' against Israel.

But the execution of the operation was inept to say the least. Incendiary devices were placed in mailboxes in Alexandria on 2 July, and against American libraries and information offices in Cairo and Alexandria on 14 July, all with minor effect. On the anniversary of the coup, the attacks were stepped up to include a number of cinemas showing British and American films – but disaster struck. One of the crude bombs went off in the pocket of an agent (the timing mechanism entailed acid burning through a contraceptive 'rubber'), causing him to run out of the cinema with his trouser leg on fire. His subsequent capture led to the rest of the ring being rounded up.[111]

SELLING THE AGREEMENT

The House of Commons was officially informed of the heads of agreement on 29 July and debated it that same day. Political considerations within the Conservative Party had done much to delay the settlement of the dispute. The domestic test of this policy was now at hand. The debate started with a review by Antony Head of the terms of the settlement and why they were needed. Clement Attlee then opened for the opposition, making it plain how much he had resented the Conservative taunts of 'scuttle' during his 1945–51 administrations. The Labour Party nevertheless agreed in principle with the settlement. As long expected, the real opposition came from the Conservative backbench Suez Group. Waterhouse, for one, was not fooled by all the references to thermonuclear weapons. 'If the hydrogen bomb is making our position in the Suez Canal completely untenable,' he asked not unreasonably, 'why have we been fiercely arguing for six, eight or ten months about the power of re-entry?'[112] Amery added – and this had always been the key point for the rebels – that there were political interests to uphold, apart from any military rationales for withdrawal. Britain, he argued, must also 'consider what will happen if there is no war'.[113]

Ministerial contributions all emphasised the need for an agreement. 'What was the alternative?' asked Macmillan in his memoirs: 'To sit indefinitely on the Canal with 80,000 troops and at huge expense.' Lloyd in turn referred to Turkey's entry into NATO, along with the Suez base being 'unpopular and bad for recruiting'. Eden concluded by speaking of the need for 'smaller bases, redeployment and dispersal'.[114] But the high point of the debate came when a Labour MP, Major R. Paget, accused Churchill of conspiring with 'a back-bench cabal' against the policy favoured by Eden and Head. Churchill immediately rose to his feet and made a miniature speech in the form of an intervention:

I behaved with perfect correctness in my relations with my colleagues and members of the House. I have not in the slightest degree concealed in public speech how much I regretted the course of events in Egypt. But I had not held my mind closed to the tremendous changes that have taken place in the whole strategic position in the world which makes the thoughts which were well formed and well knit together a year ago utterly obsolete and which have changed the opinions of every competent soldier that I have been able to meet.[115]

In the division lobby, twenty-six Conservative MPs voted against the agreement. Two others acted as tellers. The Labour Party abstained, allowing the government to win a comfortable majority of 259 to 28.[116]

Although the agreement was a great personal achievement for Nasser (succeeding where all his predecessors had failed), he was ever the realist and so allowed just one full day of public celebrations, on 28 July, before demonstrations were again banned. Wafdists, communists and the Muslim Brotherhood all predictably opposed the agreement.[117] Hudaybi, in an article published in a Beirut newspaper on 31 July, articulated what became the standard opposition view. It held that the 1936 treaty would have expired within less than two years, whereupon Britain would have been required to evacuate the base. (This was not the case, hence the serious consideration given to the Course C arbitration option.) In addition, the reactivation clause, because of Turkey's inclusion, was said to have bound the Arab states to the Western powers. And, finally, it was held that the maintenance contractors would be military personnel in civilian attire. The RCC responded by conducting a propaganda campaign against the Brotherhood which emphasised secret contacts between the supreme guide and the British from earlier in the year, as well as his 'relations with the former ruling classes'.

Fearful of arrest or assassination attempts, Hudaybi went into hiding towards the end of August.[118]

These continuing domestic pressures on Nasser made him reluctant to accept the long-held promise of US aid. The irony in this was that for the previous two years Washington and London had bickered about when the best time would be to offer assistance to the RCC. American policymakers tended to think the earlier the better, and offered such explanations as it would help stabilise the regime, counter tendencies towards neutralism, and encourage a spirit of compromise in the Canal Zone negotiations. British officials, on the other hand, believed that aid, particularly if it included military equipment, would make the junta more intractable, and it might, moreover, be used against British forces in the Canal Zone.[119] This dispute was waged at the very highest levels of government. Churchill and Eisenhower even corresponded on the matter. In December 1953 Churchill went so far as to warn the US president that economic aid to Egypt at that time would have a 'grave effect' on Anglo-American relations. Feeling for Washington's weak point, the British prime minister even suggested that the Labour opposition might press for 'Red' China's inclusion in the UN, which the Conservative government, with its slender majority and 'disturbed and increasingly angered section', might find hard to resist.[120] In short, the basic British line was that US aid must follow a Canal Zone agreement, not come before.

Exceptions to this rule tended to be so trivial as to excite ridicule. For instance, shipments of American-variety chickens (with excellent egg-producing records) in 1953–4, though sufficiently unthreatening as not to ruffle any British feathers, signally failed to capture Egyptian hearts and minds. Indeed, in September 1954 Nasser thought it judicious to publicly mock the past efforts, while at the same time privately telling Caffery that the time was not right to accept increased assistance. 'Everyone jokes about it,' Egypt's prime minister told *US News and World Report*: 'They all laugh about American "chicken aid". The saying is that, after all the talk about American aid, all we got were a lot of chickens.' The US embassy's public affairs officer conceded that 'favourable publicity' for the programme had been 'overshadowed by the wisecracks'.[121]

Over the next two years, Nasser gradually tilted Egyptian foreign policy in a new direction – towards the Soviet bloc. The need to distance himself from NATO (and so counteract Turkey's inclusion in the reactivation clause of the

Canal Zone agreement) may be seen to have prompted this process. His regime's close relations with the US embassy in Cairo, moreover, had served their purpose: the British occupation was coming to an end. Nasser, we might reasonably assume, never saw himself as the Egyptian leader who would replace the waning imperialism of Britain with the waxing influence of the United States. A 1950s equivalent of Khedive Tawfiq was not in the offing.

Negotiations for the definitive Canal Zone agreement went on until 19 October 1954. Issues that needed settling included the precise number of civilian contractors and their accommodation sites, what military equipment would remain in place, and the method for ratifying the treaty. The delay allowed an unrepentant Israel to try again to destabilise the Anglo-Egyptian rapprochement, this time by attempting to send the *Bat Galim*, a small Israeli-flagged vessel, through the Suez Canal to Haifa. Sure enough, the ship was stopped at the southern entrance to the Canal and its crew imprisoned. Needless to say, the British and American governments did not appreciate Israel's spoiling tactics and were consequently disinclined to put pressure on Egypt to back down. 'All it did', observes Avi Shlaim, 'was demonstrate to the Egyptians that for the time being the blockade could be continued with impunity.'[122]

Nasser, meanwhile, was showing himself to be a leader of moderate views. September saw the publication of his book *The Philosophy of the Revolution*. Ghosted over the previous year by his journalist friend and confidante Mohamed Heikal, this slender tome had a breadth of vision that surprised British officials. Stevenson saw in it a 'humanity and idealism which one might be excused for not expecting from a man of his [Nasser's] background'.[123] 'For a dictator', agreed Shuckburgh, 'Nasser has a rather attractive lack of subtlety and at least does not try and hold himself up as a prophet.'[124] There was also candour in the way Nasser expressed his disappointment at the reaction of the Egyptian people to the July coup. 'The masses did come,' he writes. 'But they came struggling in scattered groups . . . It was then that I realised, with an embittered heart, that the vanguard's mission had not ended at that hour but had just begun.'[125] Despite these positive initial British reactions, Eden two years later had no qualms about branding *The Philosophy of the Revolution* as Nasser's *Mein Kampf*.[126]

The final signing ceremony for the Anglo-Egyptian agreement (so termed to distinguish it from the hated 1936 treaty) took place in the Pharaonic Hall of the Egyptian parliament. Anthony Nutting signed for Britain and Nasser completed the process for Egypt.[127] Without a parliament to submit the agreement to, the RCC instead used other methods for gaining the approval of the people. The rector of al-Azhar, the great mosque and Islamic university, presented himself at the hall immediately after the initialling to congratulate the Egyptian delegation. Mass meetings were then held by professional organisations, trade unions and other institutions so that support for the regime could be pledged. Meanwhile, the only former prime minister to immediately congratulate Nasser was Hussein Sirri. Ali Maher, perhaps understandably, was less prompt and less enthusiastic.[128] The 20th and 21st were given over to public holidays in Egypt and well-organised demonstrations were staged in the main cities, but they lacked the enthusiasm of the July events. Caffery put this down to the drawn-out negotiations. Neguib was conspicuously absent from the celebrations.[129]

Nasser's struggle to consolidate his power by ending the British occupation was not, however, over. While addressing a mass meeting in Alexandria on 26 October, about eight revolver shots were fired at him in an apparent attempt to end his life. All missed, though shattered glass slightly injured some bystanders. Four members of the Muslim Brotherhood were immediately arrested. Tense but in control, Nasser exhorted the crowd to stay in place and he went on to complete the speech, which was being recorded, by making political capital out of the incident: 'Remember that, if anything should happen to me, the Revolution will go on, for each of you is a Gamal Abdel Nasser.'[130] The speech was repeatedly broadcast to excellent effect. The next day demonstrators burnt down the headquarters of the Muslim Brotherhood in Cairo. Because the assassination attempt was such a boon to Nasser's popularity, rumours quickly spread that it had been staged. Caffery rejected this theory, but acknowledged that the Egyptian revolution at last had its 'hero'.[131]

Nasser used his new-found popularity to remove Neguib from office and crack down, once and for all, on the Muslim Brotherhood. The trial of the alleged would-be assassins served as the means to this end. During the court hearings, Neguib was frequently mentioned by witnesses as being in collusion with the Muslim Brotherhood. Although in Caffery's view no conclusive evidence was provided, Nasser nevertheless ousted Neguib on 14 November, with a public announcement being made on the 19th.[132] The British were also unconvinced by the evidence and felt that Neguib was mentioned in the trials as an excuse for 'getting him out the way'.[133] (He was to remain under house arrest for eighteen years, until released by Nasser's successor, President Anwar Sadat in 1972.) Meanwhile, the process of imprisoning thousands of Muslim Brothers began, leaving Nasser without serious internal rivals. On 9 December 1954, six members of the society were hanged, after guilty verdicts had been delivered five days earlier. Pleas for clemency from around the Arab world were ignored. Egypt was stunned. Demonstrations of protest occurred in several Muslim countries.[134] It took Britain's reinvasion of Egypt in the autumn of 1956, alongside France and Israel, to transform Nasser into the Arab hero we remember.

CONCLUSION

The ultimate reason for Britain's withdrawal from the Canal Zone bastion resulted from the Churchill government's realisation that to stay in the base would be to run the risk of having to reoccupy the whole of Egypt. Yet after the Ismailia incident of January 1952, the military plans to seize control of Cairo and Alexandria, let alone any subsequent efforts to administer the vast regions to the south, were regarded as dangerously flawed. Hardliners within the Conservative cabinet only came to appreciate this when serious consideration was given, following Treasury demands for savings, to remaining in the Canal Zone in accord with the actual terms of the 1936 treaty. If the Rodeo operations were seen as too risky with 80,000 troops, what were their prospects with one-eighth of that number? Meanwhile, American influence with Nasser's military regime meant that British policymakers were prevented from manipulating Egypt's internal politics, as they had in the past. The fallout from Ismailia was again a turning point in this respect.

In the terminology of imperial historians, 'metropolitan' financial infirmity meshed with the 'peripheral' challenge of a more focused indigenous nationalist movement, which was abetted by the self-interest and Cold War preoccupations of the US government, to produce a withdrawal agreement that all but ended Britain's informal imperial position in Egypt. Churchill's talk of thermonuclear weapons served as an unconvincing fig leaf for this retreat.[135] Imperial diehards like the prime minister had always maintained that the base's ultimate worth stemmed from its peacetime uses, particularly in sustaining British prestige, rather than from any past or future wartime roles.

The single-mindedness and incorruptibility of Egypt's new military rulers succeeded where all their predecessors since 1882 had failed. They secured an end to the misnamed 'temporary occupation' and gained for their country real independence. No longer would there be a foreign garrison which had the power to make and break Egyptian governments. But this freedom from outside interference came at a high price. In order to secure the evacuation of British forces (and concomitantly his own position at the head of the RCC), Nasser repressed, with steadily increasing ruthlessness, the vibrant pluralism of Egypt's parliamentary system, and thereby inaugurated a period of authoritarian rule which persists to this day.

In the final analysis, the Anglo-Egyptian defence agreement of 1954 was part of a wider process that had preoccupied British policymakers since the end of the Second World War. This process entailed replacing the old symbols of domination – the 1936 defence treaty in this instance – with arrangements based on the principle of equality. Anthony Eden's hard-fought achievement had been Ernest Bevin's earlier goal. The crucial feature of this new Anglo-Egyptian 'partnership' was the agreement's reactivation clause. If Turkey or an Arab League state were attacked, Egypt would be required to make the Suez base available to British forces. Britain, in other words, was not *completely* surrendering its interests in Egypt. What, then, was Eden's purpose in accepting such a liberal settlement, rather than making an imperious guns-blazing retreat as Churchill often craved? The answer to this question lies in the fact that disengagement from the Canal Zone was not simply about retreat. It was also about redeploying the massive Suez garrison to the best effect in the rapidly changing circumstances of the postwar world. This meant preserving good relations across the rest of the Middle East, particularly with Iraq and Jordan – whose enhanced roles in Britain's Levant–Iraq military planning finally came into play with the Egyptian agreement. The road to the Suez War of 1956 hereafter went via Baghdad and Amman.

Epilogue

IN SEARCH OF DIGNITY

'It is the determination of the Egyptian Government', wrote Nasser to Eden a few days after the signing of the 1954 settlement, 'to carry out in letter and in spirit the new Agreement and make it really inaugurate a new and happier chapter in the relations between our two countries.'[1] But this was not to be. After a brief honeymoon period, an increasingly bitter separation ensued. Psychologically, the notion of 'partnership' proved impossible to foster in a relationship hitherto defined by its inequality. As Sir Humphrey Trevelyan, Stevenson's successor as Britain's ambassador to Egypt, admitted, '1955 was the first year of real Egyptian independence'.[2] Having been patronised and bullied over the previous seven decades, Egypt now sought the restoration of 'dignity'. 'The concept of dignity was rather vague,' writes Ali Hillal Dessouki, a former professor at Cairo University (and a student there in 1956), 'but the vagueness itself corresponded to the *mélange* of amorphous feelings of resentment towards major powers, a yearning for past glories, and aspirations towards a brighter future.'[3] In practical terms, Nasser's pursuit of dignity became closely tied to the search for Arab unity, which sought the abandonment of the artificial boundaries imposed on the Middle East after the First World War.

The main challenge to Nasser's ambitions in this regard came from the Baghdad Pact, a defence organisation with a mixed and troubled Anglo-American parentage. Its membership, by the end of 1955, included, in order of accession, Iraq and Turkey (both in February), Britain (April), Pakistan (September) and Iran (October), but, significantly, no formal US association. The creation and development of the pact undermined the already fragile relations between the Arab states. Pan-Arabism, it should be noted, had always been a competitive idea in the various regional capitals, and there was certainly no consensus as to whether it meant unity around, for example, a Greater Syria or the Hashemite kingdoms of Iraq and Jordan. Connected with this, the pact also threatened to establish Iraq as a rival centre of leadership to Egypt, which in turn tended to dominate the Arab League. As all the books on 'Suez 1956' attest, the formation of the Baghdad Pact constituted a critical milestone on the road to war. It is worth emphasising, therefore, how the tributaries of the Suez crisis flowed from the Battle of the Canal Zone.

Firstly, Britain's move to an Iraq-centred Middle East defence approach was clearly prompted by the siege-like conditions in the Suez base during the winter of 1951/2. Although the embassy in Cairo was the first to identify the need for this shift (because of the push of Egyptian nationalism), it took the additional pull of Treasury demands for savings to persuade the military planners that a more northerly defence of the region might be desirable. The upshot was the Levant–Iraq concept, agreed in principle by Britain's chiefs of staff in late 1952. With the conclusion of the Anglo-Egyptian base negotiations in October 1954, this so-called Forward Strategy finally came into play, and in the process made Iraq the new focus of Britain's regional military planning.

A second tributary may be seen in Washington's abandonment of the British-led efforts to establish a Middle East Defence Organisation and its subsequent adoption of a Northern Tier approach. This pivotal development came about after Dulles's highly disappointing visit to Cairo in May 1953, at a time of one of the most violent periods of the Canal Zone struggle. The significance of this, moreover, was that the United States had effectively stopped deferring to the British across the Middle East, and not just in Egypt (as had been happening since the coup). The Turco-Pakistani pact of April 1954, followed closely by military assistance to Iraq, was the first major sign of this.[4] Egypt's hostile reaction was a clear portent of things to come. Even at this early stage, Nasser was convinced that the Western powers were seeking to detach Egypt from the other Arab states (what Caffery called an 'isolation complex') and set up a regional defence arrangement.[5] In truth, Britain was also worried by the American actions, the feeling being that allies like Jordan and Iraq might start looking to Washington instead of London.[6]

When Eden and Nasser met for the only time on 20 February 1955 (at a British embassy-hosted dinner in Cairo), the recent conclusion of the

Turkey–Iraq agreement figured prominently in discussion. The Egyptian leader wanted Britain to oppose the final signature of the pact, in the spirit of their own recent agreement, but Eden had by this stage come round to seeing the American-inspired initiative as a means by which Britain could secure its own increased defence needs in Iraq (hence Britain's accession to the pact in April). Despite this particular disagreement, the meeting went reasonably well. 'I was impressed by Nasser,' wrote Eden to Churchill; he 'seemed forthright and friendly although not open to conviction on the Turkish-Iraqi business. No doubt jealousy plays a part in this and a frustrated desire to lead the Arab world.'[7]

Only later, after relations were irredeemably poisoned, was another gloss put on the encounter. In 1986, Nasser's confidante Mohamed Heikal wrote of Eden showing off to his young wife, Clarissa, by dropping Arabic proverbs into pre-dinner small talk about ancient Islamic civilisation. But the key point in this, surely, was that no one had bothered to tell Nasser that Eden spoke Arabic (having gained a first in oriental languages at Oxford), an indictment, if anything, of Egypt's administrative machinery under the new military rulers. Nasser also supposedly felt slighted by Sir Anthony and Lady Eden's attire. According to Heikal, the Egyptian leader's first reaction on being driven away at the end of the evening was to comment on the sartorial contrasts: 'He and his party had been in uniform or lounge suits, their hosts in dinner-jackets or, in the case of the ladies, in long gowns and jewels. "What elegance!" he exclaimed. "It was made to look as if we were beggars and they were princes!".'[8] Yet this makes little sense (unless joking) in that such dress was par for the course in diplomatic circles, something Nasser would have been familiar with by this stage given his regime's close contacts with the Caffery embassy.

The Anglo-Egyptian split over the Baghdad Pact reached its nadir in December 1955 as a result of the Templer mission to Amman. General Sir Gerald Templer, Britain's new chief of imperial staff (and feted veteran of the Malayan emergency) was instructed to try to persuade the Jordanian monarch, King Hussein, of the benefits of accession to the burgeoning defence organisation. Jordan, of course, was another crucial element in Britain's new Levant–Iraq strategic planning. But Nasser perceived Amman's potential inclusion in the pact as breaking an informal agreement made in April, which specified that the Arab membership of the organisation would be frozen with Iraq (all the other members being Muslim but not Arab countries).[9] With Anwar Sadat orchestrating opinion via Egypt's Amman embassy, senior Jordanian ministers persuaded Hussein that Jordan's best interests lay outside the grouping. 'Tiger Templer' was consequently rebuffed, and in the following weeks Egyptian propaganda succeeded in fomenting disorder in Amman to the point where the fragile Hashemite kingdom seemed close to collapse.[10]

Jordan, hitherto Britain's most loyal ally in the Middle East, played another important part in the deterioration in Anglo-Egyptian relations during 1955, this time in relation to the Arab–Israeli dispute over Palestine. Following the conclusion of the Suez base negotiations in October 1954, British and American policymakers immediately set about trying to heal this running sore by conducting highly secret mediation efforts between Israel and Egypt (Project Alpha), the assumption being that if Nasser could arrive at a settlement, other Arab leaders would follow closely behind. Yet these efforts were repeatedly disrupted by clashes along the Jordan–Israel border. The mounting sense of insecurity on both sides was directly linked to Britain's withdrawal from the Suez base. London's commitment to come to Jordan's defence (under a treaty signed in 1948) had seemed far more plausible when 80,000 troops were conveniently stationed in the Canal Zone.

Israel, for its part, had already expressed its fears over the evacuation agreement by means of the bombing campaign in Cairo and Alexandria in July 1954 and the *Bat Galim* incident the following September. The Gaza raid of 28 February 1955, the most serious clash between Israel and Egypt since the end of the Palestine War, was an indirect legacy of these interventions. Conducted with ruthless expertise by Israeli forces led by future prime minister Ariel Sharon (thirty-seven Egyptian soldiers were killed), the underlying purpose of the operation was to take Nasser down a peg or two. The immediate reason for the raid had been the execution of two members of the Jewish spy ring apprehended in Egypt the previous July and convicted in late January 1955. Having overseen the trial and execution of several members of the Muslim Brotherhood for the assassination attempt on his life, Nasser could not be seen to be more lenient to the Jewish terrorists. A chain of events that began with the rather pathetic prophylactic incendiary bombings had thus led to the Gaza raid, which in turn initiated an inexorable drift to a 'second round' in the Arab–Israeli conflict.

From this point on, Nasser was consumed by the threat from Israel. According to Avi Shlaim, the raid exposed 'the military impotence of Nasser's regime just at the time when he needed to demonstrate its strength in order to ward off the threat to his leadership posed by the emergent Baghdad Pact'.[11] The upshot was Egypt turning to Moscow and an arms deal of September 1955 (worth $100 million), which John Foster Dulles described as the 'most dangerous development since Korea'.[12] Again, it is not difficult to see the origins of this move in Britain's persistent efforts to stop the United States supplying arms to Egypt in advance of a base settlement, lest they be used against the Canal Zone garrison. Once an evacuation timetable had been agreed upon, however, Nasser was less inclined to accept Washington's assistance, and indeed needed to distance himself from the Western powers because of Turkey's inclusion, as a NATO member, in the agreement's reactivation clause. There was also, of course, America's connection with Israel to consider. News of the arms purchase was greeted joyously by the Arab masses as a 'slap in the face for the West' and a commitment to the dispossessed Palestinians.[13]

Within a year of the 1954 agreement, Britain began to contemplate, once again, the removal of Nasser, their supposed partner in a new era of relations. Like David Ben-Gurion, Israel's founding statesman, Eden was developing a deep-seated aversion to the Egyptian leader. But whereas Ben-Gurion feared an Ataturk-type figure who would modernise his country and thereby threaten Israel's very existence, Eden, who had finally succeeded Churchill as prime minister in April 1955, feared something a little more prosaic – political humiliation. Even so, the stakes were high. As the minister responsible for pushing through the Suez withdrawal against considerable opposition from within his own party, Eden now saw his belated premiership as being tarnished by Nasser's behaviour, both in Egypt (with his acceptance of Soviet arms) and across the Middle East (with his propaganda attacks on the Baghdad Pact). The last straw came with the dismissal of General Sir John Glubb as commander of Jordan's Arab Legion on 1 March 1956, which Eden wrongly attributed to Egyptian influence.

A few days later, Anthony Nutting was having dinner at the Savoy when he was called to the telephone. As he subsequently recounted:

> 'It's me,' said a voice which I recognised as the Prime Minister's. If his esoteric self-introduction was meant to conceal his identity from the Savoy Hotel switchboard, our subsequent conversation could hardly have done more to defeat his purpose.

'What's all this poppycock you've sent me?' he shouted. 'I don't agree with a single word of it.'

Nutting replied that it was an attempt to rationalise Britain's position in the Middle East so as to avoid future blows to prestige, as just experienced with the Glubb dismissal. Eden's alleged response is among the most quoted statements in the Suez story:

> But what's all this nonsense about isolating Nasser or 'neutralising' him, as you call it? I want him destroyed, can't you understand? I want him removed, and if you and the Foreign Office don't agree, then you'd better come to the Cabinet and explain why.[14]

A BBC documentary transmitted in 1986 stated that Nutting actually sanitised Eden's words by inserting 'destroyed' for 'murdered'.[15]

Having assisted Nasser in his efforts to consolidate power and promoted his ascendancy as Egypt's long awaited 'bourgeois revolution', the US was naturally slower to lose faith in the regime he led. Indeed, it was a testament to the bonds formed between the CIA and the RCC while scheming against the latter's domestic opponents that even the Soviet arms deal did not immediately derail the relationship. 'Tell him the arms are coming from Czechoslovakia,' was CIA operative Kim Roosevelt's advice to Nasser on 23 September, as Humphrey Trevelyan's Bentley drove the short distance from the British embassy to the RCC headquarters (after he had urgently requested an appointment to discuss the matter).[16] By calling it the 'Czech arms deal', the Americans hoped to lessen the impact of the transaction so that Nasser could be enticed back into the fold.

It took a British intelligence source code-named Lucky Break, which apparently began providing information in November 1955, finally to convince the Americans that Nasser was getting ever closer to the Russians, and was also planning to attack Israel. Two theories have thus far been put forward as to who or what Lucky Break was. The first suggests that it was a British embassy contact within the government; the second hypothesis, influenced by the work of Scott Lucas, sees the whole thing as a figment of the imagination of MI6 hawks.[17] Yet neither of these seem wholly persuasive given that Britain had the difficult task of convincing the Americans that Nasser (their 'boy' since July 1952) had incontrovertibly shifted to the communist side. A third possibility, albeit based on anecdotal evidence, should therefore be considered, namely that Lucky Break actually referred to a signals communication source.[18] This type of intelligence would obviously have been the most persuasive with Washington. A related tale is that Britain actually stumbled across the source (hence its code name) while physically clearing out of the Canal Zone base.

Lucky Break helped produce a major shift in US policy. From March 1956 onwards, the British and American intelligence and foreign policy establishments cooperated in an operation (code-named Omega) which aimed at isolating Nasser both domestically and internationally. Working over a period of many months, there was to be a gradual squeeze on the Egyptian economy in order to stir up popular dissatisfaction against the military leaders. In the meantime, black propaganda radio broadcasts would emphasise the republican nature of the regime and the threat it posed to monarchies across the region, Egypt's main ally Saudi Arabia included.[19] (Heikal has since written that the disinformation campaign focused on Nasser's 'ambitions' to topple the old feudal regimes in Arabia so as to centralise oil production for Egyptian, and by extension Soviet, ends.[20]) The ultimate aim of Omega was either to remove Nasser from power or, as some US officials still hoped, to make him behave better.

America's intimate relations with Egypt since the July coup had thus yielded highly disappointing results. With one foot in the Soviet camp, Nasser was demonstrating that Egypt could use its new-found real independence to play the field between East and West. The US connection had worked extremely well for him, but had served its purpose with the Canal Zone evacuation agreement, and was becoming a liability after the Gaza raid, thanks to Jewish influence in Washington. Still, there was *something* to show for the relationship in Cairo, albeit not as Kim Roosevelt's CIA team would have desired. In late 1953, fellow operative Miles Copeland had arranged for '$3,000,000 of unvouchered funds' to be given discreetly to Nasser via the head of his bodyguard. Half annoyed and half amused by the clumsiness of the attempted bribe, Nasser ordered the construction of 'something unidentifiable, but very large, very conspicuous, very enduring and very expensive – costing, oh, say something in the neighbourhood of three million dollars'. The 'Tower of Cairo' on the Gezira side of the Nile was the result. Nasser's aides had a lewd nickname for the monument – 'Roosevelt's erection'. It was, they jibed, a 'non-functional' structure.[21]

While Anglo-Egyptian relations deteriorated rapidly during 1955, London was at least satisfied with how the Sudan's three-year transition period (which began with the February 1953 agreement) concluded. British officials had been quick to see Neguib's removal as Egyptian president in November 1954 (linked, of course, to the signing of the Canal Zone agreement) as marking a new era for the Sudan. Without Neguib's great popularity to call upon among the Sudanese, the RCC was not expected to maintain its existing levels of influence.[22] Nasser himself was fairly uninterested in the Sudan issue, as signalled, to Eden's surprise, by his acceptance of a British official to succeed Robert Howe as governor-general in early 1955.[23] At the same time, however, he was concerned that his regime should not lose face as Sudanese opinion shifted away from wanting a constitutional link with Egypt to favouring independence.[24] The solution was to advance slightly the end of the condominium to 1 January 1956, so that all the interested parties could claim the credit. Nevertheless, a bleak future was in store for Egypt's southern neighbour. Parliamentary politics in the new sovereign state of Sudan lasted until November 1958. Civil war, at best smouldering, has been a feature ever since. Looking back at the Battle of the Canal Zone and its critical influence on the Sudan agreement of 1953, one might be forgiven for arguing that the Sudanese gained their independence too soon.

On 13 June 1956, the last British troops vacated the Canal Zone base and boarded a waiting ship at Port Said. The seventy-four-year 'occupation' was well and truly over. The occasion, which went unmarked by any special ceremony, was six days early.[25] It was not quite a moonlight flit, but that was the intention. Meanwhile, Nasser had arranged for Wednesday 20 June to be celebrated as 'Independence Day'. A military parade was planned for Cairo, and British dignitaries were invited to attend. Eden, however, was not keen for there to be any official British representatives (apart from the usual embassy staff), but after pressure from Trevelyan, it was decided that Brian Robertson should attend on a strictly personal basis. Upon arriving in Cairo, Sir Brian found Nasser much surer of himself since the last time they had met in late 1953, though not in a good way: 'a bit pompous and apt to talk down to people' was Robertson's assessment. During the four-day visit, a lunch was held for British officials and civilian base contractors at the Fayid officers' club. The Egyptians made sure that a MiG fighter was visible on a nearby airfield. On the big day, a long (and in the opinion of the British observers, tiresome) military procession took place.[26] Despite the professed tedium, this event symbolised what Albert Hourani has called the greatest change in the Middle East's balance of power since the settlements at the end of the First World War – Britain's withdrawal from Egypt.[27]

SWANSONG

Roughly 1,000 hours after the final British troops left Egyptian soil, Nasser gave a momentous speech in Alexandria to mark the fourth anniversary of the 'July Revolution'. The date was Thursday 26 July 1956. A week earlier, Britain and the United States had withdrawn an offer made in 1955 to help finance the construction of a high dam at Aswan. Such a project, they stated in deliberately insulting terms, was beyond Egypt's economic capabilities. Nasser's response, before 250,000 people in Alexandria's Menishiyeh Square, was that Egypt would pay for the flagship project itself from money raised by the nationalisation of the Suez Canal Company, which was to have immediate effect. A ten-minute ovation greeted the announcement. Egypt's last symbol of foreign occupation had been removed.

Eden responded to this latest humiliation by abandoning the Omega planning (it was too long-term), and instead began to prepare for a much swifter reinvasion of Egypt with the express aim of toppling Nasser from power. Having shown great principle and tremendous strength of character to push through the Suez evacuation agreement, Eden was hereafter intent on overturning all his good work, although, of course, he did not see it this way. This reversal meant disregarding compelling arguments that he himself had advanced, not least that in the second half of the twentieth century Britain could not hope to maintain its position in the Middle East by the methods of the previous century.

Eden's mental state in 1956 has since been the subject of much speculation among historians. Anthony Nutting's first-hand account *No End of a Lesson*, published in 1967, helped set the ball rolling. The passage in question reads:

In 1953, when undergoing an operation to remove his gall-bladder, he had suffered grave damage to his bile-duct, the 'exhaust-pipe' of the human system. A famous American surgeon had patched him up, but the patchwork was liable to wear under extreme nervous pressure. And from now on [Eden had just become prime minister in Nutting's narrative] the nervous pressures and tensions were to grow greater almost week by week . . .[28]

This pseudo-scientific explanation has led to debates about whether recurrent bouts of fever or a diet of painkillers and other prescription drugs clouded Eden's judgement during the Suez crisis. Yet such speculation ignores the fact that he had been living with his health problems for the previous three years, during which time he willingly risked his ascent to the prime minister's job by sticking firmly to his convictions on the Suez withdrawal policy. Moreover, fevers might produce a temporary delirium lasting hours, but Britain's invasion planning in 1956 lasted many weeks, and involved the collective action of senior ministers, all of whom were well versed in the arguments that had justified the 1954 agreement. On appraising Nutting's book in 1967, Lord Avon (as Eden had become in 1961) made copious typed notes. The passage cited above received the following brief dismissal: 'References to my illness erroneous. The bile duct wound was entirely physical and not generally affected by nervous pressures.'[29]

Rather than focusing on the supposed effects of one man's ailments, the Eden government's actions in the autumn of 1956 are best understood in relation to the legacy of Churchill's leadership of the Conservative Party, whether in facing the dictators during the Second World War or their alleged tin-pot successors in the 1950s. After being harangued for three years for not standing up to Nasser or 'Negwib' (as Churchill pronounced Neguib), Eden finally relented after 26 July. Senior ministerial colleagues, and most notably the chancellor, Harold Macmillan, fully supported and encouraged such a fighting solution. We can only ponder what might have been if Churchill had retired earlier in his peacetime administration, as had been expected, and given Eden a longer run as prime minister.

The linkage between the Canal Zone struggle of 1951 to 1954 and the Suez crisis of 1956 was especially strong in relation to military planning. According to Frank Brenchley, who represented the Foreign Office at numerous chiefs of staff meetings during which invasion planning was discussed, far too much emphasis was placed on the resistance capabilities of Egyptian forces. This stemmed from a misreading of the Ismailia incident in January 1952. The unheeded lesson was not that the Egyptians had suddenly become good fighters; it was that they should not be backed into a corner without an escape route. As a result, in 1956 far too long was taken assembling an unnecessarily large invasion force.[30] Any suggestion of using lighter forces in a swifter operation was opposed in the strongest terms. When, at 11 p.m. on 26 July, Eden summoned a meeting of senior ministers, the military chiefs, the French ambassador (France being the other main shareholder in the Suez Canal Company) and the American chargé, the chiefs of staff threatened to resign if immediate operations were pursued. Military action, they insisted the next day, must have 'overwhelming force from the outset'.[31] In the event, Lieutenant-General Sir Hugh Stockwell, the commander of the joint land action at Suez, had about 80,000 personnel under his command – tellingly, the same size as the Canal Zone garrison for much of the period between 1951 and 1954.[32]

Another military connection between the two Suez crises related to expected casualty figures. Britain's earlier Rodeo planning was deemed to be fundamentally flawed because of the likely number of civilian deaths on both sides. With guerrilla warfare seen as a bigger threat than the Egyptian army, it was anticipated that British forces would have to fight themselves into Egypt's two main cities against fedayeen. Extensive urban destruction and large numbers of casualties would be the result. An appreciation of likely domestic and international reactions had consequently been enough to keep the British garrison firmly ensconced in the Canal Zone. Britain's initial planning in 1956 (which was code-named Musketeer in a nod to having a French ally) entailed invading Egypt through Alexandria, before moving down to Cairo. But while a heavy bombardment of Alexandria may have been acceptable in 1882, there was a growing appreciation that it would not be in 1956. In early September the plan was therefore altered (hence its amended name Musketeer Revise) so that the allied landings took place at Port Said. It also placed a much greater emphasis on psychological warfare methods to bring down the Nasser regime. A common view among senior officers thereafter was that the Suez operation had 'ceased to be strategically sound'.[33] Apart from the uncertainties of the 'psy-war' aspect, Port Said was a poor choice for landings because the town effectively sat on an island and was connected to the mainland by some 30 miles of easily blockable narrow causeway. 'Port Said', remarked Stockwell, 'was like a cork in a bottle with a very long neck.'[34]

After spending the previous seventy-or-so years manipulating Egyptian politics, Britain went into the Suez War believing that it would have few problems finding an alternative government to Nasser's. Yet a key lesson of the 1951–4 crisis, at least as far as Britain's embassy in Cairo was concerned, was that a stable successor administration would be hard, if not impossible, to come by. Trevelyan later summarised the content of his embassy's reporting during the 1956 crisis:

> We commented that . . . the Egyptians would organise guerrilla warfare and it would be difficult for us to disengage without long and widespread operations against guerrillas organised by Nasser or, if he had fallen, by his proclaimed successor. No government set up by the occupying Forces would last. Only a government untainted by collaboration with the British could hold its position.

Another preoccupation of the Trevelyan embassy was the safety of British and foreign nationals in Egypt in the event of an invasion: 'Whatever was done, we should not endanger the lives of the large non-Egyptian population in Cairo, Alexandria and on the Canal. A breakdown of internal security in the cities might have the most serious consequences for Egyptians and others, for which we should bear a heavy responsibility.'[35] As the architect of the 1954 withdrawal agreement, Eden was well versed in this logic. He now simply chose to ignore it. 'Tell him to cheer up!', he minuted on one of Trevelyan's telegrams warning of prolonged guerrilla warfare.[36]

Despite Trevelyan's misgivings about military action, his embassy was still obliged to advise London on the Egyptian personalities who might be encouraged to form a successor administration. The organising principle of the guidance was to include as many of the parliamentary parties as possible. In practice, this meant trying to co-opt prominent personalities (since party machines had been dismantled in January 1953) into a 'national' government.[37] It was also accepted that elements of the Egyptian armed forces would have to be brought on board, so that the maintenance of internal security after Nasser's fall could be delegated (a lesson the Americans and British failed to observe during their invasion of Iraq in 2003 to topple Saddam Hussein). Given that General Neguib was a key element in Britain's planning, the influence of Egypt's internal crisis of March 1954 was seemingly strong. Moreover, some four and a half years after Black Saturday, British officials were also willing to forgive and forget past Wafd misdemeanours in the interests of ousting Nasser. As the Cairo embassy well understood, the viability of a successor government would hinge on popular support and a democratic veneer, and this meant including senior Wafdists. Former foreign secretary Dr Muhammad Salah al-Din, the main proponent of the popularist anti-British policy which led to the Battle of the Canal Zone, was seen as having the perfect credentials in this respect. MI6 contacts in August indicated that he was game. Ali Maher, a leading 'independent' politician of Egypt's parliamentary order, was also reckoned to be interested. If all this seemed like trying to turn back the clock, it should at least be recalled that Nasser's consolidation of power between 1952 and 1954 had entailed making many powerful internal enemies.[38]

Incidentally, a key figure from the old days whom the British did not bother trying to contact was Farouk. In this respect, the clock was instead being re-set to 1914. Although London could not bring back Khedive Abbas Hilmi II, whom they deposed for 'pro-Turkish' sympathies following the outbreak of the First World War (he died in 1944), they did apparently look to include his 57-year-old son, Prince Muhammad Abdel Moneim, in a successor regime.[39] Whether this would have meant the return of the palace as a centre of power in Egyptian politics, it is not possible to say.

The Anglo-American split over Suez is, of course, one of the most discussed aspects of the 1956 crisis. The roots of this falling-out were planted and nourished in the acrimony engendered by the US's role in the Canal Zone negotiations: London wanted an ally, Washington preferred to mediate. The same was equally true after 26 July. Underlying this friction (which had also been evident elsewhere in the Middle East)[40] was Britain's reluctance to admit that its days of acting independently of the United States in the region were numbered. Plenty of signs were discernible beforehand, but Suez demonstrated this beyond any shadow of a doubt. Iran was a case in point. In 1951 the Attlee government accepted that its military plans to seize control of the Abadan oil complex (following Mossedeq's nationalisation of the Anglo-Iranian concession) could not be implemented without American support, which was patently lacking. Instead, Mossedeq was eventually overthrown by covert methods in 1953, but on collaborative terms which left Britain a junior partner to the United States. The problem of Nasser in 1956 presented a similar predicament: should the Eden government stick with the US partnership and all its constraints (e.g. the long-term nature of Omega's covert methods) or should it strike out for a quick prestige-enhancing result without its Atlantic partner (Musketeer Revise)? Eden chose the latter, by means of an unholy triple alliance with old imperial rival, France, and upstart, Israel.

At first sight, the story of the infamous war plot at Sèvres can seem so far-fetched that its well-documented occurrence may be dismissed as an aberration. Between 22 and 24 October, in a private villa on the outskirts of Paris, representatives of the British, French and Israeli governments hatched a plan whereby Israel would attack the Egyptian army near the Suez Canal on 29 October, which would then serve as a pretext for Britain and France invading Egypt in order to separate the belligerents and protect the international waterway.[41] (In the event, Israeli forces were again led by Ariel Sharon.) On the final day of the plotting a document was drafted in French, and signed by each of the three parties, detailing the precise terms of the collusion. This document later became known as the Protocol of Sèvres. It is hard to imagine another 'smoking gun' being so neatly and concisely crafted. Eden, who had not dignified the highly secret meetings with his own presence, was dismayed that the plot had been committed to paper, and instructed that the British copy, and any translations made, be destroyed. He then insisted that two officials fly back to Paris and ask that the same be done to any other copies of the agreement. Suspicious that Britain might be trying to worm out of the deal, Israel and France refused the request.

Aberrations, however, come out of nowhere – this compact did not. During the earlier Canal Zone troubles, Churchill had repeatedly berated Eden on the need to keep open the option of Israel being a military ally. In December 1951, for instance, he had growled, 'Tell them [the Egyptians] that if we have any more of their cheek we will set the Jews on them and drive them back into the gutter, from which they should never have emerged.'[42] On another occasion, when the chiefs of staff were considering an Israeli contribution to Britain's Levant–Iraq strategic concept in early 1953, Churchill had railed against the Foreign Office's line that nothing should be done to upset Arab opinion: 'The idea of selling Israel down the drain in order to persuade Egypt to kick us out of the Canal Zone more gently is not one which attracts me.'[43] Eden, it will be recalled, subsequently dallied with the Israeli option at the end of 1953, before his officials pulled him back from the brink. In late October 1956, he decided to keep most of the civil service, and indeed many ministers, out of the loop. Having been in Churchill's shadow for so long, Eden finally succumbed to the pressure to stage a short colonial war – with Israel as a secret ally.

On 31 October, as per the Sèvres terms, Britain launched the bombing campaign that preceded the reinvasion of Suez. It was a mere four and a half months since the last British troops had left the Canal Zone. In the days that followed, Eden knew that the pretence of separating the belligerents could be unequivocally exposed at some future date. Suspicions were rampant from the start. The Anglo-French landings at Port Said followed six days later (a period of domestic uproar and political polarisation in Britain), only for the efforts to be halted at midnight British time that same day (2 a.m., 7 November, Egyptian time). With Macmillan telling the cabinet that £100 million of Britain's currency reserves had been lost during the previous week's run on sterling, the pressure of imminent bankruptcy (or so it seemed) caused a shattering loss of nerve. Only later did it transpire that the real figure for the sterling losses was nearer £32 million, and that at no time on 5–6 November had Treasury officials advised the chancellor in such black terms.[44] (Macmillan, the hawk turned dove, succeeded Eden as prime minister in January 1957.) Meanwhile, in Egypt, Britain's forces were obliged to stop about 4 miles north of Qantara, less than halfway down the Suez Canal. Ismailia was an impossible prize in the distance.

Shortly before he died in 1965, Churchill was asked by his former private secretary Jock Colville if he would have gambled on launching the Suez expedition. 'I would never have dared,' he replied, 'and if I had dared, I would never have dared stop.'[45]

38002014274148

Notes

INTRODUCTION

1. George Orwell, *The Lion and the Unicorn*, reprinted in Peter Davison (ed.), *Orwell's Politics* (London, 2001), pp. 256, 258.
2. On this theme, see the introduction in John Kent (ed.), 'Egypt and the Defence of the Middle East', *British Documents on the End of Empire*, Series B, vol. 4 (London, 1998) (hereafter cited as *BDEEP*).
3. Wm Roger Louis, The Leonard Stein Lectures, June 2005, St Antony's College, Oxford.
4. The National Archives (TNA): Public Record Office (PRO) FO 371/102761 JE1052/16G, Churchill to Eden, 15 January 1953.
5. M.A. Fitzsimons, *Empire by Treaty: Britain and the Middle East in the Twentieth Century* (Notre Dame, 1964).
6. On Bevin's 'grand strategy', see Wm Roger Louis, *The British Empire in the Middle East, 1945–1951: Arab Nationalism, the United States, and Post-War Imperialism* (Oxford, 1984), p. 1; see also *idem*, 'The Tragedy of the Anglo-Egyptian Settlement of 1954', in Wm Roger Louis and Roger Owen (eds), *Suez 1956: The Crisis and its Consequences* (Oxford, 1991), p. 43.
7. John Darwin, 'Decolonization and the End of Empire', in Robin Winks (ed.), *The Oxford History of the British Empire* (Oxford, 1999), 'Historiography', vol. 5, p. 551.
8. This description is a paraphrasing of that given in: Cm. 5999, Cabinet Office, *The Naval General Service Medal and General Service Medal (Army and Royal Air Force): Service in the Suez Canal Zone between 16 October 1951 and 19 October 1954* (SO, 2003), p. 4.
9. J.C. Hurewitz, 'The Historical Context', in Louis and Owen (eds), *Suez 1956*, p. 24.
10. Albert Hourani, 'The Middle East and the Crisis of 1956', in St Antony's Papers, No. 4, (London, 1958), 24. One of the fascinating aspects of writing this book has been to compare the insights given in Hourani's scrupulously balanced essays on the Egyptian dispute written in the 1950s and '60s with the version of events given in British and American government papers. See also *idem*, 'The Anglo-Egyptian Agreement: Some Causes and Implications', *Middle East Journal*,

9/3 (1955); and 'Independence and the Imperial Legacy', *Middle East Forum*, 42/3 (1966). His 'Conclusion', in Louis and Owen (eds), *Suez 1956*, allows him to take stock magisterially of the archive-based research some thirty odd years after the events.

CHAPTER ONE

1. Quoted in D.A. Farnie, *East and West of Suez: The Suez Canal in History, 1854–1956* (London, 1969), p. 126.
2. On this period, see especially Roger Owen, *Lord Cromer: Victorian Imperialist, Edwardian Proconsul* (Oxford, 2004).
3. Quoted in M.E. Yapp (ed.), *Politics and Diplomacy in Egypt: The Diaries of Sir Miles Lampson, 1935–1937* (Oxford, 1997), p. 984. Yapp includes the complete text of the treaty as an appendix.
4. Laila Morsey, 'The Military Clauses of the Anglo-Egyptian Treaty of Friendship and Alliance, 1936', *International Journal of Middle Eastern Studies*, 16 (1984), p. 88.
5. Trefor Evans (ed.), *The Killearn Diaries, 1934–1946* (London, 1972). This volume of Lampson's diaries focuses on the war years. The full manuscript of the diaries is deposited at St Antony's College, Oxford: the Middle East Centre Archive.
6. TNA: PRO FO 371/90110, Stevenson to Bevin, 28 February 1951.
7. Elizabeth Monroe, 'British Interests in the Middle East', *Middle East Journal*, 2/2 (1948), p. 143.
8. Anthony Nutting, *Nasser* (London, 1972), p. 35.
9. *BDEEP*, ed. Kent, part 1, lii–liii.
10. See Richard Aldrich and John Zametica, 'The Rise and Decline of a Strategic Concept: The Middle East 1945 51', in Richard Aldrich (ed.), *British Intelligence, Strategy and the Cold War, 1945–51* (London, 1992); and Michael J. Cohen, *Fighting World War Three from the Middle East: Allied Contingency Plans, 1945–1954* (London, 1997).
11. TNA: PRO FO 800/476 ME/47, Bevin to Attlee, 9 January 1947.
12. See Avi Shlaim, 'The Debate About 1948', *International Journal of Middle Eastern Studies*, 27/3 (August 1995).
13. This is one of the main themes of Michael Doran in his *Pan Arabism before Nasser: Egyptian Power Politics and the Palestine Question* (New York, 1999). See also Michael T. Thornhill, 'Britain and the Politics of the Arab League, 1943–50', in Michael J. Cohen and Martin Kolinsky (eds), *Demise of the British Empire in the Middle East: Britain's Reponses to Nationalist Movements, 1943–55* (London, 1998).
14. Fawaz A. Gerges, 'Egypt and the 1948 War: Internal Conflict and Regional Ambition', in Eugene L. Rogan and Avi Shlaim (eds), *The War for Palestine* (Cambridge, 2001), pp. 160–1.
15. Gamal Abdel Nasser, 'The Egyptian Revolution', *Foreign Affairs*, 33/2 (January 1955), p. 20.
16. Joel Gordon, *Nasser's Blessed Movement: Egypt's Free Officers and the July Revolution* (New York, 1992), p. 47.

17. TNA: PRO FO 371/73464 J5644, minute by Wright, 28 June 1949.
18. Robert Vitalis, *When Capitalists Collide: Business Conflict and the End of Empire in Egypt* (Berkeley and Los Angeles, 1995), p. 173.

CHAPTER TWO

1. See especially Joel Gordon, 'The False Hopes of 1950: The Wafd's Last Hurrah and the Demise of Egypt's Old Order', *International Journal of Middle Eastern Studies*, 21 (1989).
2. Hoda Gamal Abdel Nasser, *Britain and the Egyptian Nationalist Movement 1936–1952* (Reading, 1994), p. 205.
3. Shaden Shehab, 'The Last Pasha', *Al-Ahram Weekly*, Issue no. 495, 17–23 August 2000.
4. Alaa al-Din al-Hadidy, 'Mustafa al-Nahas', in Charles Tripp (ed.), *Contemporary Egypt: Through Egyptian Eyes* (London, 1993), p. 85.
5. For a balanced view, see Jacques Berque, *Egypt: Imperialism and Revolution* (London, 1972), p. 521.
6. Al-Hadidy, 'Mustafa al-Nahas', in Tripp (ed.), *Contemporary Egypt*, pp. 77–8.
7. Jean and Simonne Lacouture, *Egypt in Transition* (London, 1958), p. 373.
8. Vitalis, *When Capitalists Collide*, p. 178.
9. Gordon, 'The False Hopes of 1950', pp. 199–202.
10. David R. Devereux, *The Formulation of British Defence Policy towards the Middle East, 1948–56* (London, 1990), p. 28.
11. Bevin's secret undertakings are detailed in TNA: PRO FO 371/90176 JE1194/14G, minute by Allen, 7 February 1951. They are not included in the published record of these meetings which came out later in 1951. See Cmd. 8419: *Anglo-Egyptian Conversations on the Defence of the Suez Canal and the Sudan, December 1950–November 1951*, Egypt No. 2 (HMSO, 1951).
12. TNA: PRO FO 371/90177 JE1194/30G, minute by Allen, 16 March 1951.
13. TNA: PRO CAB 131/10 D (51) 6, 19 March 1951; see also TNA: PRO FO 371/90176 JE1194/29G, minute by Allen, 10 March 1951; and TNA: PRO FO 371/90176 JE1194/24G, Bevin to Attlee, 18 February 1951.
14. *BDEEP*, ed. Kent, part 1, xxxvii.
15. TNA: PRO FO 371/90174 JE1192/21, minute by Morrison, 31 March 1951.
16. TNA: PRO T 236/4096 91–92, Waight to Flett, 12 March 1951.
17. Hansard, 5th Series, 1951, c. 2333–56; see also TNA: PRO T 236/4097 8–9, Waight to Flett, 28 March 1951.
18. TNA: PRO CAB 129/45 CP (51) 95, 30 March 1951.
19. *Foreign Relations of the United States*, 1951, vol. 5, *The Near and Middle East*, pp. 361–3, Caffery to State Department, 14 April 1951 (hereafter cited as FRUS).
20. TNA: PRO CAB 129/45 CP (51) 140, 28 May 1951.
21. TNA: PRO FO 371/91185 E1024/24G, record of US–UK politico-military talks, 17 May 1951; TNA: PRO FO 371/90133 JE1051/115G, State Department aide-mémoire, 21 May 1951.
22. *FRUS*, 1951, pp. 344–7, Caffery to State Department, 13 February 1951; see also George McGhee, *Envoy to the Middle World: Adventures in Diplomacy* (New York, 1983), p. 380.

23. TNA: PRO FO 371/91185 E1024/30G, record of Foreign Office meeting on 29 May by Dudgeon, 30 May 1951.

24. TNA: PRO FO 371/91185 JE1051/131G, minute by Allen, 4 July 1951.

25. TNA: PRO FO 371/901185 E1024/34G, Steel to Foreign Office, 25 June 1951; TNA: PRO FO 371/91185 E1024/36G, record of meeting on Allied Command in the Middle East, 29 June 1951; and TNA: PRO FO 141/1442 1077/25/51G, Strang to Stevenson, 30 July 1951.

26. As a consequence of these domestic pressures, on 1 September Britain managed to persuade the United States into supporting a Security Council resolution which called upon Egypt to end all restrictions on commercial shipping passing through the Suez Canal. As expected, Egypt ignored the resolution and no attempt was made to enforce it. See Peter L. Hahn, *The United States, Great Britain and Egypt, 1945–1956: Strategy and Diplomacy in the Early Cold War* (Chapel Hill, 1991), pp. 117–22.

27. TNA: PRO FO 141/1442 1077/25/51G, Stevenson to Foreign Office, 28 July 1951.

28. TNA: PRO FO 371/90135 JE1051/167G, Foreign Office to Franks, 15 August 1951.

29. TNA: PRO FO 371/90137 JE1051/196G, minute by Bendall, 30 August 1951; TNA: PRO FO 371/90136 JE1051/179G, Stevenson to Bowker, 14 August 1951.

30. TNA: PRO FO 141/1442 1077/25/51G, Strang to Stevenson, 30 July 1951.

31. TNA: PRO CAB 128/20 CM (51) 58, 4 September 1951.

32. TNA: PRO FO 141/1452 11914/179/51G, minute by Creswell, 3 October 1951; TNA: PRO FO 141/1452 11914/213/51G, minute by Wall, 10 October 1951.

33. Quoted in L.M. Fabunmi, *The Sudan in Anglo-Egyptian Relations: A Case Study in Power Politics, 1800–1956* (London, 1960), p. 289; the cabinet's special committee meeting is discussed in Devereux, *Formulation of British Defence Policy*, pp. 59 60.

34. Previous accounts of the diplomacy leading up to the presentation of the MEC proposals have argued that Britain was wrong to proceed with the approach as it was bound to fail. But, as has just been shown, such interpretations judge the policy by a different set of criteria from those considered by officials at the time. See Peter L. Hahn, 'Containment and Egyptian Nationalism: The Unsuccessful Effort to Establish the Middle East Command, 1950–1953', *Diplomatic History*, 11/1 (1987); Louis, *British Empire in the Middle East*, p. 713; and Devereux, *Formulation of British Defence Policy*, pp. 58–63.

35. TNA: PRO FO 800/649 ME/51/15, Morrison to Attlee, 12 October 1951.

36. See *FRUS*, 1951, pp. 397–8, editorial note; the US statement is contained in *The State Department Bulletin*, 25/643 (22 October 1951), pp. 647–8.

37. TNA: PRO FO 141/1452 11914/243/51G, Allen to Stevenson, 11 October 1951.

38. A story in the *News Chronicle* on 11 October had reported that the Cairo embassy was opposed to the presentation of the new proposals. As a consequence, Stevenson became worried that the Foreign Office might think that he was 'secretly sabotaging the proposals out of spite!' TNA: PRO FO 141/1452 11914/243/51G, minute by Stevenson, 12 October 1951 on the FO to Alexandria telegram, dated 11 October 1951.

CHAPTER THREE

1. Quoted in Ahmed Abdalla, *The Student Movement and National Politics in Egypt* (London, 1985), p. 78.
2. This account of the Ismailia riots on 16 October is largely taken from the newsletter of the Lancashire Fusiliers, *Gallipoli Gazette* (April 1952), a copy of which is held in the Museum of the Lancashire Fusiliers. It is reprinted on the website http://www.britains-smallwars.com/Canal/ISMAILIA-RIOTS.htm, 'The Suppressed Story: The Canal Zone, 1951 to 1954'. See also Farnie, *East and West of Suez*, p. 698.
3. TNA: PRO FO 371/90146 JE1051/412G, minute by Dixon of meeting in Morrison's office, 12 October 1951.
4. TNA: PRO FO 371/90141 JE1051/298G, Morrison to Acheson, 12 October 1951; *FRUS* 1951, pp. 404–5, Acheson to Morrison, 17 October 1951; and TNA: PRO FO 371/90142 JE1051/319G, minute by Allen, 20 October 1951.
5. TNA: PRO FO 371/90146 JE1051/428, minute by Bowker, 27 October 1951; TNA: PRO PREM 11/92 111–12, Foreign Office to Stevenson, 2 November 1951.
6. TNA: PRO FO 800/769 EG/52/72, Foreign Office to Stevenson, 4 November 1951; N[ational] A[rchives, Washington DC]: RG59 773/521/1–1952, Caffery to State Department, 19 January 1952.
7. TNA: PRO FO 371/45920 J1238, Killearn to Foreign Office, 6 April 1945; TNA: PRO FO 371/45920 J1275, Killearn to Foreign Office, 13 April 1945.
8. TNA: PRO PREM 11/92 111–12, Foreign Office to Stevenson, 2 November 1951.
9. TNA: PRO CAB 131/11 DO (51) 108, 4 October 1951.
10. NA: RG59 641.74/10-2351, Caffery to State Department, 23 October 1951.
11. TNA: PRO FO 141/1440 1041/2/128/51G, Robertson to COS, 27 October 1951; see TNA: PRO FO 371/90145 JE1051/383G for the chiefs of staff minutes on 29 October.
12. Quoted in Charles Richardson, 'Robertson, Brian Hubert', in Robert Blake and C.S. Nicholls (eds), *Dictionary of National Biography 1971–1980* (Oxford, 1986), pp. 728–9.
13. TNA: PRO FO 141/1439 1041/2/83/51G, Stevenson to Foreign Office, 25 October 1951.
14. TNA: PRO FO 371/90200 JE1261/311, Churchill to Eden, 28 October 1951.
15. TNA: PRO FO 141/1440 1041/2/201/51G, COS to Robertson, 2 November 1951; TNA: PRO FO 371/90200 JE1261/311, Foreign Office to Stevenson, 2 November 1951.
16. *FRUS*, 1951, p. 410, Caffery to State Department, 25 October 1951; TNA: PRO FO 371/90145 JE1051/381G, Franks to Foreign Office, 1 November 1951; TNA: PRO FO 371/90145 JE1051/385, Franks to Foreign Office, 3 November 1951.
17. TNA: PRO WO 216/796 20A, Robertson to Brownjohn, 2 November 1951; also, same date, 21A.
18. Rapp writes in his memoirs that the BMEO had 'a strange medley of functions'. 'It was set up in 1945 by Mr Bevin to fill in a partial way the gap left by the dismantling of our wartime organisation in the Middle East', and 'it was [also] thought advantageous to retain an office at the official level to study problems

that affected the region as a whole.' St Antony's College, Oxford: Middle East Centre Archive: Rapp Papers, 'Memoirs' [unpublished], pp. 370, 373.

19. Rapp Papers, 'Memoirs', pp. 403–4; TNA: PRO FO 371/90145 JE1051/391G, Rapp to Strang, 2 November 1951.

20. TNA: PRO WO 216/796 20A, Robertson to Brownjohn, 2 November 1951.

21. TNA: PRO FO 371/90146 JE1051/418G, COS to Strang, 8 November 1951.

22. TNA: PRO FO 371/90146 JE1051/418G, Minute by Eden, 15 November 1951, on COS to Strang, 8 November 1951.

23. TNA: PRO FO 371/90146 JE1051/418G, Strang to chiefs of staff, 12 November 1951.

24. TNA: PRO FO 141/1440 1041/2/311/51G, minute by Burroughs, 12 November 1951; see also, TNA: PRO FO 371/90115 JE10110/29, Stevenson to Bowker, 5 October 1951.

25. TNA: PRO FO 141/1440 1041/2/253/51G, minute by Creswell, 6 November 1951; TNA: PRO FO 141/1451 10121/22/51G, minute by Creswell, 20 November 1951.

26. BDEEP, ed. Kent, part 1, p. lxv.

27. According to British intelligence reports, Sirag al-Din was paying large amounts of money to the socialist party while Salah al-Din was trying to curry favour with the Muslim Brotherhood. TNA: PRO FO 371/90119 JE10110/106, minute by Morris, 7 November 1951.

28. Amira Ibrahim, 'For national dignity', Al-Ahram Weekly, Issue no. 570, 24–30 January 2002.

29. Charles Tripp, 'Egypt 1945–52: The Uses of Disorder', in Cohen and Kolinsky (eds), Demise of the British Empire in the Middle East, p. 132.

30. Sir Thomas Russell (Russell Pasha), the Cairo police chief between 1913 and 1946, had regarded the auxiliary police (in contrast to his own men) as 'riff raff'. See Rapp Papers, 'Memoirs', p. 408.

31. This account is based on that given in Douglas J. Findlay, White Knees Brown Knees: Suez Canal Zone 1951–1954 – The Forgotten Years (Edinburgh, 2003), pp. 19–20. See also Farnie, East and West of Suez, p. 699.

32. TNA: PRO PREM 11/92 73–4, BDCC (ME) to COS, 12 November 1951; TNA: PRO PREM 11/92 141–2, BDCC (ME) to COS, 22 December 1951; and TNA: PRO PREM 11/632 136–8, McClean to Minister of Defence, 11 January 1952.

33. TNA: PRO FO 371/90120 JE10110/145G, 'Suez Canal Zone: Implications of Military Government': Foreign Office comments on COS paper, 22 November 1951; TNA: PRO FO 371/96918 JE1051/22G, minute by Allen, 28 December 1951.

34. TNA: PRO CAB 128/23 CM (51) 15, 7 December 1951; also, TNA: PRO FO 371/90150 JE1051/484G, minutes of COS meeting on 4 December 1951.

35. Vitalis, When Capitalists Collide, p. 186.

36. Amira Ibrahim, 'For national dignity', Al-Ahram Weekly, Issue no. 570, 24–30 January 2002; see also Farnie, East and West of Suez, p. 699.

37. TNA: PRO WO 216/800 5A, Brownjohn to Robertson, 1 December 1951.

38. TNA: PRO WO 236/11, EGYFOR (Ismailia) to 17 Infantry Brigade, 5 December 1951.

39. TNA: PRO FO 371/90121 JE10110/165, Stevenson to Foreign Office, 7 December 1951.

40. St Antony's College, Oxford: Middle East Centre Archive: Monroe Papers, interview with John Hamilton by Elizabeth Monroe, September 1959.

41. TNA: PRO FO 141/1440 1041/2/386/51G, Allen to Creswell, 15 December 1951.

42. The figures are reported in TNA: PRO FO 371/90123 JE10110/233, Stevenson to Foreign Office, 13 December 1951.

43. Gregory Blaxland, *Objective Egypt* (London, 1966), p. 166.

44. NA: RG59 974.61/12-2051, Caffery to State Department, 20 December 1951; TNA: PRO FO 371/90121 JE10110/182, Stevenson to Foreign Office, 11 December 1951; *FRUS*, 1951, p. 434 (footnote), Caffery to State Department, 14 December 1951.

45. *FRUS*, 1951, pp. 424–5, Caffery to State Department, 24 November 1951; TNA: PRO FO 141/1440 1041/2/386/51G, Allen to Creswell, 15 December 1951.

46. TNA: PRO FO 371/90151 JE1051/528G, Stevenson to Foreign Office, 22 December 1951; TNA: PRO FO 371/90151 JE1051/532, Stevenson to Foreign Office, 24 December 1951.

47. TNA: PRO WO 216/798, Robertson to Brownjohn, 7 December 1951. According to Robertson's biographer, Sir Brian felt that Stevenson lived 'in the stratosphere' and was out of contact with Egyptian opinion; instead the ambassador relied too much on the advice of local British businessmen 'whose main desire was simply to return to the luxurious life they led before the troubles started'. See David Williamson, *A Most Diplomatic General: The Life of General Lord Robertson of Oakridge* (London, 1996), p. 164.

48. *FRUS*, 1951, pp. 438–40, Acheson to Gifford, 14 December 1951; for the joint US–UK Cairo embassy appreciation, see TNA: PRO FO 371/90148 JE1051/467, Stevenson to Foreign Office, 1 December 1951.

49. TNA: PRO FO 371/90151 JE1051/528G, Bowker to Stevenson, 5 January 1952.

50. On the publicity point, see TNA: PRO FO 953/1319 PG11637/8, minute by Nicholls, 9 January 1952.

51. TNA: PRO FO 371/90169 JE1112/101, Stevenson to Foreign Office, 23 December 1951.

52. TNA: PRO FO 371/90151 JE1051/524, minute by Allen, 21 December 1951; *FRUS*, 1951, p. 44, Gifford to State Department, 17 December 1951.

53. *FRUS*, 1951, p. 443, Caffery to State Department, 18 December 1951.

54. This account is taken from 'The Suppressed Story: The Canal Zone, 1951–54' – An Anti-Terrorist Patrol, http://www.britains-smallwars.com/Canal/ISMAILIA-RIOTS.htm; see also, Farnie, *East and West of Suez*, p. 700.

55. TNA: PRO FO 371/96918 JE1052/22G, brief for Eden's visit to Washington (drafted by Allen), 28 December 1951.

56. Churchill's ill-advised initiative also undermined the Foreign Office's low-key efforts from the end of 1951 to attract American, French, Dutch and Norwegian technicians to the Canal Zone in order to operate tugs and carry out other essential harbour work previously completed by Egyptian labour. State Department officials drew little distinction between these moves and Churchill's

request, since both sought to entangle the US in the 'Egyptian mess'. TNA: PRO PREM 11/632 140, Brook to Churchill, 8 January 1952; NA: RG59 974.5301/1-2352, memo by Raynor to Perkins, 21 January 1952; NA: RG59 974.5301/1-2352, Deputy Secretary of Defence to Acheson, 23 January 1952; and Martin Gilbert, *Never Despair: Winston S. Churchill*, vol. 8 (London, 1988), pp. 676–80.

57. The speech is reprinted in: *State Department Bulletin*, 26/657 (28 January 1952), p. 118.
58. TNA: PRO FO 371/90110 210, Stevenson to Foreign Office, 20 December 1951.
59. TNA: PRO PREM 11/632 130–2, COS meeting, 24 January 1952; *FRUS*, 1952–4, p. 1753, Holmes to State Department, 24 January 1952; TNA: PRO PREM 11/91 244, Eden to Churchill, 25 January 1952; and TNA: PRO CAB 128/24 CM (52) 7, 25 January 1952.
60. Minute by Dixon, 23 January 1952, in *BDEEP*, ed. Kent, part 2, pp. 320–1. Dixon was a deputy under-secretary of state.
61. TNA: PRO WO 236/13, Brigadier R.K. Exham, 'Report on Operation Eagle', 25 January 1952.
62. TNA: PRO WO 216/801 1A, Robertson to Slim, 25 January 1952.
63. Rapp Papers, 'Memoirs', pp. 413–14.

CHAPTER FOUR

1. Anwar el-Sadat, *Revolt on the Nile* (London, 1957), p. 99.
2. William Stadiem, *Too Rich: The High Life and Tragic Death of King Farouk* (New York, 1991), pp. 315–16.
3. The following sources are used for this description of events: TNA: PRO FO 371/96873 JE1018/86, Stevenson to Eden, 'Ambassador's Investigation Committee Report on the Egyptian Rioting of 26th January 1952'; Berque, *Egypt*; Lacouture, *Egypt in Transition*; Blaxland, *Objective Egypt*; Rapp Papers, 'Memoirs'; 'Endgame' special supplement [on Black Saturday] in *Al-Ahram Weekly*, Issue no. 570, 24–30 January 2002.
4. See in particular 'Ambassador's Investigation Committee Report on the Egyptian Rioting of 26th January 1952', cited above.
5. Maurice Guindi, 'Arson and Upheaval', *Al-Ahram Weekly*, Issue no. 570, 24–30 January 2002.
6. It is indicative of the organised character of the arson attacks that the Gezira Sporting Club, a 150-acre site about ten minutes' carriage ride from the scene of the riots, was left unharmed. Established in the early years of the British occupation, the club – called the Khedivial Sporting Club until Britain deposed Khedive Abbas Hilmi in 1914 – was the alternate social centre of the higher British community when they were not at the Turf Club. Although Egyptian membership (drawn from the elite) had increased during the previous forty or so years, Egyptians had never been made to feel especially welcome. The tennis and squash courts, hockey and cricket grounds, croquet lawns, golf and race courses and four polo pitches were all primarily for the relaxation of the foreign elites. The presidency of the club had been held by Britain's agent and consul-general and his successors. However, all this was already changing around the time of

the Black Saturday riots, hence its survival on the day when similar sites were being violently set upon. Once again the hand of Sirag al-Din was evident. Following the British bulldozing incident at Kafr Abdu in December 1951, the interior minister had announced that the Gezira Sporting Club was to be taken over for public utility purposes. This Egyptianisation process was formalised by the club's governorate on 24 January 1952, and signalled by the resignation of the British ambassador from the presidency, along with the rest of the general committee. See Samir Raafat, 'Gezira Sporting Club Milestones', *Egyptian Mail*, 10–17 February, 1996.

7. Erskine letter (in retirement), cited in Blaxland, *Objective Egypt*, p. 169.

8. TNA: PRO PREM 11/632 130–2, COS meeting, 24 January 1952; see also Anthony Eden, *Full Circle* (London, 1960), pp. 231–3; Blaxland, *Objective Egypt*, p. 169.

9. Blaxland, *Objective Egypt*, p. 170. For Stevenson's worries about the inception of military government, see Chapter 3.

10. Lacouture, *Egypt in Transition*, p. 112.

11. TNA: PRO FO 141/1453 1011/15/52G, minute by Hamilton, 13 February 1952; see also Brian Lapping, *End of Empire* (London, 1985), p. 252.

12. TNA: PRO FO 371/96846 JE10113/5, Stevenson to Foreign Office, 14 February 1952.

13. St Antony's College, Oxford: Middle East Centre Archive: Hamilton Papers, lecture by John Hamilton at the Imperial Defence College, 4 May 1960, p. 15.

14. TNA: PRO FO 371/96872 JE1018/78, Chancery to African department, 18 February 1952. See also 'Ambassador's Investigation Committee Report on the Egyptian Rioting of 26th January 1952'; Berque, *Egypt*, p. 671; and Tripp, 'Egypt 1945–52: The Uses of Disorder', in Cohen and Kolinsky (eds), *Demise of the British Empire in the Middle East*, p. 135.

15. 'The beginning of the end', Anne-Claire Kerboeuf, *Cairo Times*, vol. 6, Issue no. 20, 18–24 July 2002.

16. Berque, *Egypt*, p. 460.

17. TNA: PRO FO 141/1456 1041/29/52G, Stevenson to Foreign Office, 28 January 1952.

18. TNA: PRO PREM 11/91 187–8, Eden to Stevenson, 28 January 1952.

19. TNA: PRO FO 800/768 Eg/52/15, Churchill to Eden, 30 January 1952.

20. TNA: PRO FO 371/96921 JE1052/83, Franks to Foreign Office, 29 January 1952; TNA: PRO FO 141/1453 1011/17/52G, meeting with Cecil Campbell, 14 February 1952.

21. See Chapter 6.

22. See Evans (ed.), *The Killearn Diaries*, 19; Yapp (ed.), *Politics and Diplomacy in Egypt*, pp. 693 and 759.

23. TNA: PRO FO 141/1456 1041/48/52G, minute by Hamilton, 13 February 1952; TNA: PRO FO 141/1453 1011/17/52G, minute by Creswell, 14 February 1952. Smart still lived in Cairo with his Egyptian wife who was the daughter of Dr Faris Nimr Pasha, an Egyptian senator and newspaper proprietor. Nimr's other daughter had married the political activist and author George Antonius, whose book *The Arab Awakening* (1938) was widely viewed as a landmark in the development of Arab nationalist thought.

24. TNA: PRO FO 371/96923 JE1052/142G, Stevenson to Foreign Office, 25 February 1952.
25. TNA: PRO FO 371/96923 JE1052/142G, minute by Allen, 13 March 1952; also, TNA: PRO FO 371/96923 JE1052/142G, FO 141/1462 1043/1/52G, Foreign Office to Stevenson, 20 February 1952.
26. 'Happy birthday, Your Majesty' by Amina Elbendary, *Al-Ahram Weekly*, Issue no. 572, 7–13 February 2002.
27. TNA: PRO WO 216/754 2A, Robertson to Brownjohn, 12 February 1952.
28. TNA: PRO WO 216/754 2A, Brownjohn to Robertson, 25 February 1952.
29. 'Profile of Mustafa Rifaat: To the last bullet', *Al-Ahram Weekly*, Issue no. 570, 24–30 January 2002.
30. Hassan Youssef, 'Before the fall', *Al-Ahram Weekly*, Issue no. 576, 7–13 March 2002 [Hassan Youssef was a senior courtier in Farouk's palace. His memoirs, written in Arabic, are entitled *The Role Played by the Royal Cabinet in Egyptian Politics, 1922–1952*]. See also TNA: PRO FO 371/96874 JE1018/108, Stevenson to Foreign Office, 10 March 1952; and *FRUS*, 1952–4, pp. 1772–3, Berry to Acheson, 3 March 1952.
31. Tellingly, this telegram was not found in the normal run of Foreign Office documents (FO 371) which tends to be heavily weeded (e.g. 'retained in department of origin' under the Official Secrets Act) whenever documents discuss interventions in the internal affairs of another country. Rather, it was in a War Office file where the weeder was probably looking out for other types of sensitive topics. See TNA: PRO WO 236/12, Stevenson to Foreign Office, 1 March 1952.
32. Miles Copeland, *Game of Nations: The Amorality of Power Politics* (New York, 1970), pp. 51–2.
33. *FRUS*, 1952–4, pp. 1755–6, conversation between Franks and Acheson, 27 January 1952.
34. Quoted in Hahn, *The United States, Great Britain, and Egypt*, p. 140.
35. Ahmed Mortada Al-Maraghi, *Oddities from Farouk's Reign* (Beirut, 1976); and Hahn, *The United States, Great Britain, and Egypt*, pp. 140–1.
36. Unless otherwise cited, this section draws on first-hand accounts from Findlay's *White Knees Brown Knees* and veterans' websites.
37. Rapp Papers, 'Memoirs', pp. 403–4.
38. Doris Golder, 'A Woman's View', in Findlay, *White Knees Brown Knees*, pp. 212–15.
39. Niall Ferguson, *Empire: How Britain Made the Modern World* (London, 2003), p. 354.
40. Findlay, *White Knees Brown Knees*, p. 18.
41. TNA: PRO CAB 129/50 CP (52) 63, 5 March 1952; TNA: PRO FO 141/1451 10121/26/51G, minute by Creswell, 28 November 1951; *FRUS*, 1952–4, pp. 1772–3, Berry to Acheson, 3 March 1952.
42. TNA: PRO CAB 129/50 CP (52) 63, 5 March 1952.
43. TNA: PRO FO 371/96985 JE1202/1G, Churchill to Eden, 9 March 1952.
44. TNA: PRO FO 371/96985 JE1202/2, Eden to Churchill, 10 March 1952.
45. TNA: PRO FO 141/1457 1041/52G, minute by Wall, 3 April 1952; TNA: PRO FO 371/96875 JE1018/146, Creswell to Eden, 26 April 1952.

46. NA: RG59 774.00/3-3152, Ortiz to Stabler, 31 March 1952.
47. TNA: PRO FO 371/96927 JE1052/229, Foreign Office to Stevenson, 4 April 1952.
48. NA: RG59 774.00/4-1452, Stabler to Jones, 14 April 1952.
49. TNA: PRO CAB 128/24 CM (52) 35, 1 April 1952; also 36th meeting, 3 April 1952, 37th meeting, 4 April, 40th meeting on 9 April, and 43rd meeting on 16 April.
50. TNA: PRO CAB 128/24 CM (52) 47, 29 April 1952.
51. TNA: PRO FO 371/96930, JE1052/338, Stevenson to Bowker, 9 May 1952.
52. TNA: PRO FO 371/96930 JE1052/332, Stevenson to Foreign Office, 13 May 1952.
53. TNA: PRO FO 371/96874 JE1018/117, Stevenson to Foreign Office, 15 March 1952; see also Gordon, *Nasser's Blessed Movement*, pp. 29–30.
54. Abdalla, *The Student Movement and National Politics in Egypt*, p. 79; Richard P. Mitchell, *The Society of Muslim Brothers* (London, 1969), pp. 94–5.
55. TNA: PRO FO 141/1453 1011/53/52G, Creswell to Foreign Office, 2 July 1952.
56. TNA: PRO FO 371/96876 JE1018/174, minute by Allen, 2 July 1952; *FRUS*, 1952–4, pp. 1826–7, Bruce to Caffery, 2 July 1952.
57. TNA: PRO FO 141/1453 1011/66/52G, Eden to Alexandria, 13 July 1952.
58. TNA: PRO FO 371/96877 JE1018/222, Alexandria to Foreign Office, 17 July 1952.
59. *FRUS*, 1952–4, pp. 1826–7, Bruce to Caffery, 2 July 1952; TNA: PRO FO 371/96876 JE1018G, minute by Morris, 3 July 1952; TNA: PRO FO 371/96876 JE1018/183, minute by Allen, 30 June 1952.
60. TNA: PRO FO 141/1456 1041/60/52G, Allen to Creswell, 26 February 1952.
61. TNA: PRO FO 371/96930 JE1052/350G, Allen to Creswell, 23 May 1952.
62. TNA: PRO FO 141/1456 1041/60/52G, Creswell to Allen, 3 March 1952.
63. The latest British assessment along these lines was: TNA: PRO FO 371/96876 JE1018/192, Creswell to Foreign Office, 7 July 1952.
64. TNA: PRO FO 141/1462 1043/12/52G, memorandum by Creswell, Operation Jolt, enclosed in letter from Creswell to Allen, 12 May 1952.
65. TNA: PRO FO 371/96930 JE1052/350G, Allen to Creswell, 23 May 1952.
66. TNA: PRO FO 371/98244 E1026/1, memorandum by Fellowes (quoting Arnold Toynbee's *Study of History*), 2 March 1952.
67. TNA: PRO FO 371/96923 JE1052/129G, minute by Allen, 27 February 1952.
68. TNA: PRO FO 953/1320 PG11637/26, meeting of Middle East Discussion Group, RIIA, 14 March 1952.
69. As we have seen, this arms sales monopoly was only modified for the first time earlier that year after Britain reluctantly allowed the US to help the Egyptian authorities develop a *carabinieri*-like security force to replace the auxiliary police.
70. See, for instance, TNA: PRO FO 371/90120 JE10110/136, Rapp to Foreign Office, 16 November 1951.
71. TNA: PRO FO 953/1320 PG11637/26, meeting of Middle East Discussion Group, RIIA, 14 March 1952.
72. TNA: PRO FO 371/96929 JE1052/309G, minute by Stevenson, 30 April 1952.

73. TNA: PRO FO 371/96876 JE1018/192, Creswell to Foreign Office, 7 July 1952.
74. TNA: PRO FO 141/1453 1011/71/52G, Creswell to Robertson (repeated to Foreign Office), 20 July 1952; TNA: PRO FO 371/90877 JE1018/198G, minute by Bowker, 21 July 1952.
75. Sadat, *Revolt on the Nile*, p. 110.
76. Gordon, *Nasser's Blessed Movement*, p. 51.
77. *FRUS*, 1952–4, pp. 1837–8, Fowler to Stabler, 21 July 1952; TNA: PRO FO 371/96877, Creswell to Foreign Office, 22 July 1952.
78. Gordon, *Nasser's Blessed Movement*, p. 52.

CHAPTER FIVE

1. Sadat, *Revolt on the Nile*, p. 116.
2. Gordon, *Nasser's Blessed Movement*, p. 52.
3. Joachim Joesten, *Nasser: The Rise to Power* (London, 1960), p. 88. This was one of the first biographies of Nasser written in English and benefited from interviews with the subject and his family at a time when he refused to talk to French and British correspondents, and was wary of being misquoted by American journalists.
4. Khaled Mohi El Din, *Memories of a Revolution: Egypt 1952* (Cairo, 1992), p. 104.
5. This initial coup exchange between the Free Officers and the Americans is well documented in most sources. The evidence for Britain interpreting the move as a means of avoiding undue antagonism is: TNA: PRO FO 371/96880 JE1018/210G, minute by Morris, 28 July 1952.
6. NA: RG59 774.521/10-542, 'Biographical Data: Members of the Military High Committee', Caffery to State Department, 4 October 1952.
7. Wilbur Crane Eveland, *Ropes of Sand: America's Failure in the Middle East* (New York, 1980), pp. 97–8; see also Barry Rubin, 'America and the Egyptian Revolution, 1950–1957', *Political Science Quarterly*, 97/1 (1982), p. 76.
8. Hahn, *The United States, Great Britain, and Egypt*, p. 146.
9. *FRUS*, 1952–4, p. 213, editorial note; Eveland, *Ropes of Sand*, p. 60.
10. TNA: PRO FO 371/96931 JE1052/363, minute by Allen, 6 June 1952; TNA: PRO FO 371/96930 JE1052/329, Stevenson to Foreign Office, 10 May 1952.
11. *FRUS*, 1952–4, pp. 237–41, State Department minutes of State–joint chiefs of staff meeting, 18 June 1952.
12. *FRUS* 1952–4, pp. 1838–43, Byroade to Acheson, 21 July 1952.
13. Mohi El Din, *Memories of a Revolution*, pp. 78–9. Egyptian openness, however, is by no means uniform. Nasser's confidant, the leading Arab journalist Mohamed Heikal, wrote in *Cutting the Lion's Tale: Suez through Egyptian Eyes* (London, 1986) that while Roosevelt 'had been a familiar figure in Cairo before the revolution', his contacts were with 'many leading figures in King Farouk's circle' (p. 64).
14. *Revolt on the Nile* is a notable exception to this rule. In this early account (which was clearly sensitive to America's role), Sadat details a stirring but wholly fictitious story of Ali Sabri going directly to the British embassy and warning 'Councillor Sir Walter Stuart' (he meant Sir Walter Smart, despite the fact that

this official had retired several years earlier) 'that what had happened was a purely internal affair, and that the least sign of intervention would be regarded as an act of hostility' (p. 118). Ironically, Sadat's memory served him much better when he was writing his autobiography *In Search of Identity* (London, 1978). In this version of events, Sabri actually contacted his 'friend' at the American embassy, the US military attaché (pp. 133–4).

15. Sadat, *Revolt on the Nile*, pp. 117–18; also Khaled Dawoud, 'The Red Major', *Al-Ahram Weekly*, Issue no. 595, 18–24 July 2002.
16. Mohi El Din, *Memories of a Revolution*, pp. 78–9.
17. *Ibid.* During the Suez crisis of 1956, Britain, France and Israel all made assassination attempts on Nasser, so such methods in the 1950s Egyptian context were clearly not unpalatable. See Jeremy Bennett (director), 'The Suez Crisis', BBC1, transmission October 1996; and Heikal, *Cutting the Lion's Tail*, p. 231.
18. TNA: PRO FO 371/96877 JE1018/204, Creswell to Foreign Office, 23 July 1952.
19. Sadat, *Revolt on the Nile*, p. 119; see also Rashed el-Barawy, *The Military Coup: An Analytic Study* (Cairo, 1952), pp. 7–8.
20. 'Announcing the revolution', interview with Fahmi Omar by Omaya Abdel-Latif, *Al-Ahram Weekly*, Issue no. 595, 18–24 July 2002.
21. Lacouture, *Egypt in Transition*, p. 152.
22. Tom Little, *Egypt* (London, 1958), p. 191.
23. Robert Stephens, *Nasser* (London, 1971), p. 106.
24. Lacouture, *Egypt in Transition*, p. 152.
25. TNA: PRO FO 371/96877 JE1018/211 (B), Creswell to Foreign Office, 23 July 1952.
26. Gordon, *Nasser's Blessed Movement*, p. 60.
27. See David Tresilian interview with Eric Rouleau, 'A View from Paris', *Al-Ahram Weekly*, Issue no. 595, 18–24 July 2002.
28. Edward Luttwak, *Coup d'état* (New York, 1968), pp. 57–9.
29. TNA: PRO FO 371/96877 JE1018/211(B), minutes by Allen and Strang, 23 July 1952.
30. TNA: PRO FO 141/1453 1011/96/52G, Creswell to Foreign Office, 23 July 1952.
31. TNA: PRO FO 371/96877 JE1018/211(B), minute by Allen, 23 July 1952.
32. TNA: PRO FO 371/96877 JE1018/211(B), Creswell to Foreign Office, 23 July 1952.
33. TNA: PRO FO 371/96877, JE1018/210G, Minute by Allen, 23 July 1952.
34. TNA: PRO FO 371/96877 JE1018/217, Creswell to Foreign Office, 23 July 1952.
35. 'Announcing the revolution', interview with Fahmi Omar by Omaya Abdel-Latif, *Al-Ahram Weekly*, Issue no. 595, 18–24 July 2002.
36. TNA: PRO FO 141/1453 1011/88/152G, Creswell to Foreign Office, 24 July 1952.
37. For Hamilton's instructions for the meeting, see: TNA: PRO FO 371/96878, JE1018/229, Foreign Office to Creswell, 'Emergency/Secret', 24 July 1952.

38. Blaxland, *Objective Egypt*, p. 176. (This account erroneously gives the date of the meeting as 23 July.)
39. St Antony's College, Oxford: Middle East Centre Archive: John Hamilton Papers, lecture by John Hamilton at the Imperial Defence College, 4 May 1960.
40. For further background on this decision, see TNA: PRO FO 141/1453 1011/133/52G, Allen to Creswell, 25 July 1952.
41. Sadat, *Revolt on the Nile*, pp. 122–3. Nasser's aversion to bloodshed comes through in his booklet *The Philosophy of the Revolution*, published in 1954 (English edn, Buffalo, 1959), in which he describes being involved in a botched political assassination attempt, and feeling enormous relief at reports that the person survived, pp. 32–3. The full text of *Philosophy* is included in E.S. Farag (ed.), *Nasser Speaks: Basic Documents* (London, 1972).
42. See TNA: PRO FO 371/96878 JE1018/241, Creswell to Foreign Office, 25 July 1952; American reports are recounted in TNA: PRO FO 371/96878 JE1018/240, Franks to Foreign Office, 25 July 1952.
43. TNA: PRO FO 371/96879 JE1018/273, Goulburn to Creswell, 28 July 1952; also TNA: PRO FO 371/96879 JE1018/273, minute by Morris, 29 July 1952.
44. Sadat, *Revolt on the Nile*, p. 122.
45. Quoted in Lacouture, *Egypt in Transition*, p. 156.
46. St Antony's College, Oxford: Middle East Centre Archives: Slade-Baker Papers, 'Instructions 9 April' [handwritten notes].
47. St Antony's College, Oxford: Middle East Centre Archives: Slade-Baker Papers, 'Coup d' etat by Egyptian army', memorandum by Colonel Slade-Baker [undated but with a textual reference citing 25 July as the day it was written]. It should also be noted that Slade-Baker's subsequent standing with Egypt's military regime was such that during the Suez crisis of 1956 he was one of the few British journalists whom Nasser agreed to meet. See St Antony's College, Oxford: Middle East Centre Archives: Slade-Baker [unpublished] Diaries, 17 August 1956.
48. Mohi El Din, *Memories of a Revolution*, p. 110.
49. El-Barawy, *Military Coup*, pp. 13–14; slightly different translations appear in Little, *Egypt* (p. 198) and Lacouture, *Egypt in Transition* (p. 157).
50. El-Barawy, *Military Coup*, p. 14; Mohi El Din, *Memories of a Revolution*, p. 111.
51. For a report of Caffery's account, see TNA: PRO FO 371/96878 JE1018/263, Creswell to Foreign Office, 26 July 1952; see also *The Times*, 27 July 1952, a copy of which is with: TNA: PRO FO 371/96878 JE1018/263 (B), minute by Parsons, 28 July 1952.
52. El-Barawy, *Military Coup*, p. 18.
53. A photograph of this telegram is included in Evelyn Shuckburgh, *Descent to Suez: Diaries, 1951–1956* (London, 1986), p. 22.
54. TNA: PRO FO 141/1453 1011/144/52G, Creswell to Foreign Office, 28 July 1952.
55. NA: RG59 774.00/7-3152, Caffery to Acheson, 31 July 1952.
56. Gordon, *Nasser's Blessed Movement*, p. 61.
57. NA: RG59 774.00/7-3152, Caffery to State Department, 31 July 1951; NA: RG59 774.00/8-752, Caffery to State Department, 7 August 1952; NA: RG59,

774.00 (W)/8-852, Caffery to State Department, 8 August 1952; TNA: PRO FO 371/96932 JE1052/393G, minute by Bowker, 30 July 1952.

58. TNA: PRO FO 141/1453 1011/96/52G, Foreign Office to Creswell, 24 July 1952; TNA: PRO FO 141/1453 1011/138/52G, Foreign Office to Alexandria, 28 July 1952; also TNA: PRO CAB 128/25 CM (52) 75, 31 July 1952.

59. TNA: PRO FO 371/96879 JE1018/301 Stevenson to Eden, 2 August 1952; also TNA: PRO FO 141/1454 1011/156/52G, minute by Evans, 8 August 1952.

60. TNA: PRO FO 141/1454 1011/156/52G, Stevenson to Bowker, 16 August 1952.

61. Robert D. Schulzinger, 'Caffery, Jefferson (1886–1974)', in John A. Garraty and Mark C. Carnes (general eds), *American National Biography* (New York, 1998); see also Philip F. Dur, 'Caffery of Louisiana: Highlights of his Career', *Louisiana History*, 15/1 (winter 1974).

62. In *Ropes of Sand*, Eveland describes a protocol-ridden dinner with the Cafferys: 'black tie was the uniform, red roses for the ambassador's wife were to arrive precisely one hour before us, and there was to be no talk of business until Jefferson Caffery took us to the smoking room for brandy, coffee, and exactly one whiskey nightcap' (p. 104).

63. Robert D. Kaplan, *The Arabists: The Romance of an American Elite* (New York, 1995), p. 128.

64. Jon B. Alterman, *Egypt and American Foreign Assistance, 1952–1956: Hopes Dashed* (New York, 2002), p. 3; see also the recent biography of Nasser by Saïd K. Aburish for a perceptive assessment of Lakeland's role: *Nasser: The Last Arab* (London, 2004).

65. NA: RG59 774.00/3-3154, Hart to Byroade, 31 March 1954.

66. Copeland, *Game of Nations*, p. 53; W. Scott Lucas's *Divided We Stand: Britain, the US and the Suez Crisis* (London, 1991) also accords Lakeland a significant role, based on the Copeland memoirs.

67. See pp. 153 and 164.

68. Selma Botman, 'Egyptian Communists and the Free Officers: 1950–54', in *Middle East Studies*, 22/3 (July 1986), pp. 355–8; Joel Beinin and Zachary Lockman, *Workers on the Nile: Nationalism, Communism, Islam and the Egyptian Working Class, 1882–1954* (Princeton, 1987), pp. 421–6.

69. See 'All the Revolution's Men', *Al-Ahram Weekly*, Issue no. 595, 18–24 July 2002.

70. NA: RG59 774.521/10-4524, Caffery to State Department, 'Biographic Data – Members of the Military High Committee', 4 October 1951. For an American account of the dinner mentioned in the last sentence, see *FRUS*, 1952–4, pp. 1851–2, Caffery to State Department, 20 August 1952. An Egyptian perspective can be found in Mohi El Din's *Memories of a Revolution*, pp. 127–8.

71. Following Caffery's first dinner engagement with members of the military high committee, he went on record as saying that the rumours concerning Neguib being a figurehead were 'untrue': 'he is not brilliant but he has good common sense and some qualities of leadership'. As for the younger officers, 'they are all well intentioned, patriotic and filled with desire to do something for Egypt. On [the] other hand they are woefully ignorant of matters economic, financial,

political and international'. *FRUS*, 1952–4, pp. 1851–2, Caffery to State Department, 20 August 1952.

72. NA: RG59 774.521/10-4524, Caffery to State Department, 'Biographic Data – Members of the Military High Committee', 4 October 1952. See also NA: RG59 774.521/1-1053, Caffery to State Department, 'Confidential Biographic Data – Lt. Colonel Gamal Abd Al Nasir', 10 January 1953.

73. Lacouture, *Egypt in Transition*, p. 164.

74. Selma Botman interview with Khaled Mohi El Din, April 1980, quoted in Botman's 'Egyptian Communists and the Free Officers', p. 352.

75. Quoted in Stephens, *Nasser*, p. 112.

76. Patrick O'Brien, *The Revolution in Egypt's Economic System* (London, 1966), p. 3.

77. Mohi El Din, *Memories of a Revolution*, p. 118; Lacouture, *Egypt in Transition*, p. 163; and Stephens, *Nasser*, p. 111.

78. The Muslim Brotherhood had been given five 'support' tasks. These were: 1) the protection of foreign nationals, along with their businesses and embassies; 2) the provision of popular support for the uprising should it be lacking for the military; 3) the maintenance of order generally if the police failed to cooperate with the army; 4) to help the Free Officers escape if the uprising failed; and 5) to commit acts of sabotage against Canal Zone forces in the event of British intervention. Similarly, Ahmed Hamroush, leader of the DMNL's military branch, had been personally briefed by Nasser on 22 July to mobilise loyal army units in Alexandria, and on the day of the uprising was joined in Alexandria by Nasser's two brothers. Unlike in Cairo, however, the units in Alexandria were not asked to move until reinforcements arrived on the 25th. See Mitchell, *Society of Muslim Brothers*, pp. 103–4; Botman, 'Egyptian Communists and the Free Officers', p. 351; and Gamal Nkrumah, 'Ahmed Hamroush: For Corps and Country', *Al-Ahram Weekly*, Issue no. 544, 26 July–1 August 2001.

79. TNA: PRO FO 371/96880 JE1018/328, minute by Ledward, 23 August 1952.

80. Lacouture, *Egypt in Transition*, p. 323.

81. Yapp, *Politics and Diplomacy in Egypt*, p. 14.

82. Alterman, *Egypt and American Foreign Assistance*, pp. 42–4.

83. TNA: PRO FO 371/96881 JE1018/369, minute by Allen, 11 September 1952; TNA: PRO FO 371/96881 JE1018/369, Cairo to Foreign Office, 6 September 1952.

84. TNA: PRO FO 371/96880 JE1018/347, minute by Allen, 1 September 1952.

85. TNA: PRO FO 800/769 ME/52/64, Churchill to Eden, 26 August 1952.

86. NA: RG59 774.00/8-2852, Caffery to State Department, 28 August 1952.

87. The British embassy in Washington complained to the State Department over the lack of consultation. An apology of sorts was received but not on the substance of the matter. TNA: PRO FO 371/96896 JE10345/19, Franks to Foreign Office, 3 September 1952; *FRUS*, 1952–4, pp. 1857–8, Acheson to Caffery, 8 September 1952; TNA: PRO FO 371/96896 JE10345/10, Steel to Foreign Office, 9 September 1952.

88. TNA: PRO PREM 11/392 210–11, minute Churchill, 7 September 1952, on Stevenson to Foreign Office, 6 September 1952.

89. NA: RG59 774.00/9-852, memorandum of conversation between Truman and Acheson, 8 September.

90. Gordon, *Nasser's Blessed Movement*, p. 167.
91. NA: RG59 774.00/9-952, Caffery to State Department, 9 September 1952; NA: RG59 774.00/9-852, Gifford to State Department, 8 September 1952; TNA: PRO FO 371/96896 JE10345/15, minute by Morris, 8 September 1952.
92. TNA: PRO FO 141/1454 1011/166/52G, Bowker to Stevenson, 11 September 1952; NA: RG59 774.00/9-952, Caffery to State Department, 9 September 1952; and NA: RG59 774.00/9-852, Gifford to State Department, 8 September 1952.
93. See Eden's comments on TNA: PRO FO 371/96896 JE10345/18, Steel to Foreign Office, 9 September 1952.
94. NA: RG59 774.521/10-4524, Caffery to State Department 'Biographic Data – Members of the Military High Committee', 4 October 1951.
95. Maher's fall, observed Caffery on 8 October, has left Britain 'out in [the] cold here in Egypt'. The junta 'will not only have nothing whatever to do with them but are convinced that the British are attempting to sabotage their movement'. *FRUS*, 1952–4, p. 1856, Caffery to State Department, 8 September 1952.
96. TNA: PRO FO 371/96883 JE1018/450, Stevenson to Foreign Office, 2 December 1952.

CHAPTER SIX

1. The agreement is included as appendix 1 in Douglas H. Johnson (ed.), 'Sudan', *British Documents on End of Empire Project*, Series B, vol. 5 (London, 1996).
2. Heather J. Sharkey, *Living with Colonialism: Nationalism and Culture in the Anglo-Egyptian Sudan* (Berkeley and Los Angeles, 2003), pp. 5–6.
3. TNA: PRO CAB 129/55 CP (52) 308, 25 September 1952.
4. TNA: PRO FO 371/96933 JE1052/407, minute by Bowker, 7 August 1952. This priority also meant leaving Israeli peace-feelers unexplored in August 1952. See Michael B. Oren, *Origins of the Second Arab–Israeli War: Egypt, Israel and the Great Powers* (London, 1992), pp. 13–14.
5. NA: RG59 774.34/11-1052, Caffery to State Department, 10 November 1952.
6. See Alterman, *Egypt and American Foreign Assistance*, p. 9.
7. El-Barawy, *The Military Coup in Egypt*, pp. 30–42.
8. TNA: PRO CAB 129/55 CP (52) 308, 25 September 1952.
9. *FRUS*, 1952–4, pp. 1861–2, Caffery to State Department, 24 September 1952.
10. TNA: PRO CAB 129/55 CP (52) 308, 25 September 1952.
11. Quoted in Gordon, *Nasser's Blessed Movement*, p. 74.
12. Lacouture, *Egypt in Transition*, p. 169; and Gordon, *Nasser's Blessed Movement*, p. 73.
13. Gordon, *Nasser's Blessed Movement*, pp. 73–4.
14. Martin W. Daly, *Imperial Sudan: The Anglo-Egyptian Condominium, 1934–56* (Cambridge, 1991), p. 296.
15. TNA: PRO FO 371/96911 JE1051/346, Stevenson to Foreign Office, 2 November 1952; also TNA: PRO FO 371/96913 JE1051/406, Strang to Churchill, 19 November 1952.
16. TNA: PRO FO 371/96913 JE1051/411, minute by Morris, 20 November 1952; and TNA: PRO FO 371/96913 JE1051/411, minute by Allen, 20 November 1952.

17. W. Travis Hanes III, 'Sir Hubert Huddleston and the Independence of the Sudan', in *Journal of Imperial and Commonwealth History*, 20/2 (1992), p. 249.

18. These legal arguments are outlined in: TNA: PRO FO 371/96902 JE1051/11G, minute by Allen, 16 January 1952.

19. See Yunan Labib Rizk, 'Out of Sudan', *Al-Ahram Weekly*, Issue no. 437, 8–14 July 1999.

20. Daly, *Imperial Sudan*, p. 399.

21. James Robertson, *Transition in Africa: From Direct Rule to Independence* (New York, 1974), p. 150. (The entry was in 1951.)

22. Daly, *Imperial Sudan*, p. 435.

23. Wm Roger Louis, 'American Anti-Colonialism and the Dissolution of the British Empire', *International Affairs*, 61/3 (1985), p. 411.

24. See A.H.M. Kirk-Greene, 'Robertson, Sir James Wilson', in Brian Harrison and H.C.G. Matthew (eds), *Oxford Dictionary of National Biography* (Oxford, 2004); and *idem*, *On Crown Service: A History of HM Colonial and Overseas Civil Services, 1837–1997* (London, 1999).

25. In the jargon of imperial historians, the 'formal' and 'informal' terms do not quite fit Britain's experience in the Sudan. On the one hand, Britain directly administered the Sudan, which suggests it was part of the 'formal' empire; on the other, this rule operated under the umbrella of a legal instrument with Egypt, which in turn was part of Britain's 'informal' empire; and as already mentioned, the British-led Sudan government was overseen by the Foreign Office and not the Colonial Office. More curiously still, members of the Sudan Political Service were only invited to British imperial conferences as observers.

26. TNA: PRO FO 141/1452 11914/147/51G, Bowker to Stevenson, 2 October 1951.

27. Reported in *FRUS*, 1951, p. 390, Acheson to Caffery, 8 October 1951. The Sudan proposals which accompanied the Middle East Command approach can be found in Cmd 8419.

28. Graham Thomas, *Sudan 1950–1985: Death of a Dream* (London, 1990), p. 38.

29. TNA: PRO FO 371/90154 JE1052/55, Howe to Eden, 17 October 1951.

30. Eden, *Full Circle*, p. 229.

31. Daly, *Imperial Sudan*, p. 285.

32. TNA: PRO FO 371/90113 JE1017/48, Churchill to Eden, 11 November 1951.

33. *Ibid.*; TNA: PRO FO 371/90113 JE1017/48, Strang to Churchill, 12 November 1951; TNA: PRO CAB 128/23 CM (51) 7, 15 November 1951.

34. *FRUS*, 1951, p. 425, footnote 2.

35. TNA: PRO FO 800/826 Sud/51/4, Foreign Office to Franks, 5 December 1951; also *FRUS*, 1951, pp. 425–6, Gifford to State Department, 24 November 1951.

36. *FRUS*, 1951, pp. 438–40, Acheson to Gifford, 14 December 1951.

37. *FRUS*, 1951, p. 440, Gifford to State Department, 17 December 1951; Hahn, *The United States, Great Britain, and Egypt*, pp. 137–8.

38. TNA: PRO FO 371/96905 JE1051/107G, minute by Mackworth-Young, 22 April 1952.

39. TNA: PRO FO 371/96903 JE1051/50G, minute by Allen, 16 February 1952.

40. TNA: PRO FO 371/96903 JE1051/50G, minute by Bowker, 19 February 1952.

41. Husain Zulfakar Sabri, *Sovereignty for Sudan* (London, 1982), pp. 55–60.
42. Quoted in Daly, *Imperial Sudan*, p. 295.
43. Mohammed Neguib, *Egypt's Destiny* (London, 1955), pp. 241–2.
44. TNA: PRO CAB 128/25 CM (52) 102, 4 December 1952.
45. TNA: PRO FO 371/96912 JE1051/373, minute by Strang, 6 November 1952; *FRUS*, 1952–4, pp. 1882–3, Gifford to State Department, 15 November 1952.
46. Quoted in Gordon, *Nasser's Blessed Movement*, p. 75.
47. TNA: PRO FO 371/96883 JE1018/465, minute by Allen, 5 January 1953; Gordon, *Nasser's Blessed Movement*, p. 76.
48. Gordon, *Nasser's Blessed Movement*, p. 76.
49. See Sue Onslow, 'Battle lines for Suez: The Conservatives and the Abadan Crisis 1950–51', *Contemporary British History*, 17/2 (2003).
50. Sue Onslow, *Backbench Debate within the Conservative Party and its Influence on British Foreign Policy, 1948–57* (Basingstoke, 1997), pp. 110–11; Patrick Cosgrave, Amery, [Harold] Julian (1919–96), Harrison and Matthew (eds), *Oxford Dictionary of National Biography*.
51. Onslow, *Backbench Debate within the Conservative Party*, pp. 109–10; and Philip Murphy, *Party Politics and Decolonization: The Conservative Party and British Colonial Policy in Tropical Africa, 1951–1964* (Oxford, 1995), p. 95; see also, Andrew Roberts, *Eminent Churchillians* (London, 1994).
52. Julian Amery, 'The Suez Group: A Retrospective on Suez', in Selwyn Ilan Troen and Moshe Shemesh (eds), *The Suez–Sinai Crisis of 1956: Retrospective and Reappraisal* (London, 1990), p. 111.
53. TNA: PRO PREM 11/323 9, Eden to Churchill, 21 November 1952.
54. Herman Finer, *Dulles over Suez* (London, 1964), p. 85.
55. Shuckburgh, *Descent to Suez*, p. 23.
56. This is quoted in *ibid.*, p. 23.
57. *FRUS*, 1952–4, pp. 1928–31, Perkins to Dulles, 31 December 1952.
58. TNA: PRO FO 371/102736 JE1051/5, minute by Allen, 1 January 1953.
59. Daly, *Imperial Sudan*, p. 299.
60. TNA: PRO FO 371/102738 JE1051/52, minute by Bowker, 12 January 1953.
61. TNA: PRO FO 371/102738 JE1051/52, minute by Strang, 12 January 1953.
62. Quoted in Daly, *Imperial Sudan*, p. 299.
63. 'This is too defeatist', wrote the foreign secretary on the margin of Bowker's 12 January minute. See TNA: PRO FO 371/102738 JE1051/52, minute by Bowker, 12 January 1953.
64. TNA: PRO CAB 128/26 CM (53) 2, 14 January 1953.
65. TNA: PRO FO 371/102761 JE1052/16G, Churchill to Eden, 15 January 1953.
66. Shuckburgh, *Descent to Suez*, pp. 74–5.
67. *Ibid.*, p. 74.
68. *Ibid.*, p. 75.
69. Quoted in Gordon, *Nasser's Blessed Movement*, p. 77.
70. NA: RG59 774.00 (W)/11-653 NR 813, Caffery to State Department, 17 January 1953. A few weeks later, the oriental counsellor at the British embassy in Cairo corroborated Caffery's account: 'The High Military Command admit that there was no fully worked out plot. There seems no doubt, however,

that real trouble was brewing, that the High Military Command was seriously worried (even from the point of view of their own personal safety) and that the "conspiracy" was not merely a convenient excuse for liquidating the parties.' See TNA: PRO FO 371/102704 JE1015/43, Evans to Crossman, 5 February 1953.

71. TNA: PRO CAB 130/83 Gen 421 2, 30 January 1953.
72. Shuckburgh, *Descent to Suez*, pp. 75–6.
73. TNA: PRO CAB 130/83 Gen 421 3, 31 January 1953; TNA: PRO FO 371/102742 JE1051/171G, Minister of Defence to GHQ, MELF (Fayid), 31 January 1953.
74. NA: RG59 774.00 (W)/1-353 NR 806, Caffery to State Department, 3 January 1953.
75. TNA: PRO FO 371/102738 JE1051/63, Stevenson to Foreign Office, 17 January 1953.
76. TNA: PRO DEFE 4/59 COS (53) 4, 13 January 1953. See also TNA: PRO FO 371/102740 JE1051/136, minute by Allen, 2 February 1953.
77. TNA: PRO CAB 128/26 CM (53) 6, 3 February 1953.
78. Reported in *FRUS*, 1952 4, p. 1983, Caffery to State Department, 7 February 1953.
79. TNA: PRO FO 371/102743 JE1051/188, Howe to Foreign Office, 8 February 1953.
80. TNA: PRO CAB 131/13 D (53) 2, 11 February 1953 (11.30 a.m.).
81. TNA: PRO CAB 128/26 CM (53) 9, 11 February 1953 (6.30 p.m.).
82. Andrew Roth, *Enoch Powell* (London, 1970), p. 100.
83. TNA: PRO CAB 128/26 CM (53) 10, 11 February 1953 (10.40 p.m.).
84. Eden, *Full Circle*, p. 247.
85. Glen Balfour-Paul, *The End of Empire in the Middle East: Britain's Relinquishment of Power in her Last Three Arab Dependencies* (Cambridge, 1991), p. 38; TNA: PRO FO 371/102744 JE1051/210, Stevenson to Foreign Office, 12 February 1953.
86. See TNA: PRO FO 371/102752, JE1051/426, report by Morris, 17 March 1953.

CHAPTER SEVEN

1. TNA: PRO FO 371/102798 JE1192/54G, minute by Shuckburgh, 12 February 1953.
2. *BDEEP*, ed. Kent, xlii. This three-part volume of British government documents is particularly central to the concerns of the present chapter and as such many of the official papers cited are also reprinted in this source. These instances will hereafter be denoted by the *BDEEP* abbreviation, followed by a document number e.g. [*BDEEP* no. 330].
3. TNA: PRO FO 141/1402 1043/35/52G, Allen to Stevenson, 23 October 1952 [*BDEEP* no. 330]; see also TNA: PRO DEFE 4/57 COS (52) 147, 21 October 1952 [*BDEEP* no. 329].
4. TNA: PRO FO 141/1456 1041/60/52G, Allen to Creswell, 26 February 1952 [*BDEEP* no. 278].
5. See pp. 18–19.
6. *BDEEP*, ed. Kent, p. xxxvi.
7. TNA: PRO DEFE 4/16, COS (48) 145, annexes, 11 October 1948 [*BDEEP* no. 125].

8. See also Michael J. Cohen, *Fighting World War Three from the Middle East: Allied Contingency Plans, 1945–1954* (London, 1997), p. 169.

9. John Kent, 'The Egyptian Base and the Defence of the Middle East, 1945–54', *Journal of Imperial and Commonwealth History*, 21/3 (1993), p. 48.

10. Louis, *The British Empire in the Middle East, 1945–51*, p. 100.

11. *BDEEP*, ed. Kent, p. lix; and Devereux, *Formulation of British Defence Policy towards the Middle East*, pp. 40–1.

12. *BDEEP*, ed. Kent, p. lxii.

13. See p. 33.

14. TNA: PRO CAB 131/10 DO (51) 15, 7 June 1951.

15. See p. 36.

16. TNA: PRO FO 141/1438 1041/66/51G, BDCC (ME) to COS, 16 December 1951 [*BDEEP* no. 254].

17. TNA: PRO DEFE 5/35, COS (51) 755, annex 'Defence of the Middle East Dec 1951–Dec 1954': COS Committee memorandum [*BDEEP* no. 257]; and TNA: PRO DEFE 5/35, COS (51) 759, annex 'Middle East strategy: Brief by the COS Committee for Mr Churchill on the Importance of the Middle East [*BDEEP* no. 258].

18. TNA: PRO FO 141/1456 1041/48/52G, minute by Stevenson, 22 February 1952.

19. In the aforementioned chiefs of staff meeting on 21 October 1952, chief of air staff, Sir John Slessor, commented that, with the battle likely to be fought in more forward positions, 'Alexandretta and Basra might provide alternative bases, and, as the war in the Middle East developed, we could move back and resuscitate the Egyptian base.' TNA: PRO DEFE 4/57 COS (52) 147, 21 October 1952.

20. TNA: PRO FO 371/96929 JE1052/289, minute by Allen, 8 March 1952.

21. TNA: PRO DEFE 4/51 COS (52) 10, 21 January 1952.

22. The quote is from TNA: PRO FO 800/807 ME/52/21, Eden to Churchill, 30 August 1952; for the actual cabinet meeting, see TNA: PRO CAB 128/24 (CM) 18, 18 February 1952 [*BDEEP* no. 274].

23. TNA: PRO FO 800/768 Eg/52/34, Churchill to Eden, 6 April 1952; Kent, 'The Egyptian Base and the Defence of the Middle East, 1945–54', p. 52.

24. TNA: PRO CAB 128/ 24 CC (52) 35, 1 April 1952 [*BDEEP* no. 293]; and TNA: PRO CAB 128/ 24 CM (52) 37, 4 April 1952 [*BDEEP* no. 294].

25. TNA: PRO DEFE 4/54 COS (52) 71, 23 May 1952; *FRUS*, 1952–4, pp. 247–9, Acheson to Aldrich, 21 June 1952.

26. Eric Grove, *Vanguard to Trident: British Naval Policy since World War Two* (Annapolis, 1987), pp. 77 and 81; Devereux, *Formulation of British Defence Policy towards the Middle East*, pp. 113–14.

27. Brian Cathcart, *Test of Greatness: Britain's Struggle for the Atomic Bomb* (London, 1994), p. 21.

28. Michael Dockrill, *British Defence since 1945* (Oxford, 1988), p. 50; the size of the army is cited in TNA: PRO CAB 129/54 CP (52) 253, 22 July 1952.

29. Grove, *Vanguard to Trident*, p. 81.

30. *Ibid.*, pp. 81–2.

31. Shuckburgh, *Descent to Suez*, p. 119.
32. This summarised conclusion is taken from: TNA: PRO DEFE 5/41 COS (52) 514, 2 October 1952. The full global strategy paper of 17 June, minus a few deletions under section 5.1 of the Public Records Act, is printed in *BDEEP*, ed. Kent, no. 308.
33. TNA: PRO DEFE 4/55 COS (52) 98, 7 July 1952: see annex JP (52) 69 (Final).
34. TNA: PRO DEFE 5/41 COS (52) 54 514, 2 October 1952.
35. *BDEEP*, ed. Kent, p. lxix.
36. TNA: PRO DEFE 6/22 JP (52) 129 (Final), 12 November 1952.
37. TNA: PRO DEFE 4/57 COS (52) 157, 14 November 1952 [*BDEEP* no. 337].
38. TNA: PRO FO 141/1462 1043/62/52G, minute by Creswell, 6 December 1952.
39. TNA: PRO DEFE 4/59 COS (53) 3, 8 January 1953 – see annex, JP (52) 149 (Final), 22 December 1952; see also TNA: PRO FO 141/1464 1043/79/52G, Rapp to Bowker, 22 December 1952 [*BDEEP* no. 350].
40. TNA: PRO FO 141/1464 1043/81/52G, COS to Elliot (British Joint Staffs Mission, Washington), 19 December 1952.
41. TNA: PRO DEFE 4/60 COS (53) 19, 6 February 1953; TNA: PRO CAB 131/13 D (53) 10, 23 February 1953.
42. See Foreign Office comments at TNA: PRO DEFE 4/60 COS (53) 8, 19 January 1953.
43. Devereux, *Formulation of British Defence Policy towards the Middle East*, pp. 17–18.
44. TNA: PRO PREM 11/487 28–9, Head to Churchill, 8 September 1953.
45. Richard Aldrich and John Zametica, 'The Rise and Decline of a Strategic Concept', in Richard Aldrich (ed.), *British Intelligence, Strategy and the Cold War, 1945–1951* (London, 1992), p. 256.
46. TNA: PRO DEFE 4/52 COS (52) 44, 27 March 1952.
47. TNA: PRO CAB 131/13 D (53) 21, memorandum by chiefs of staff: 'Israel and Middle East Defence: Discussions with the Americans', 26 March 1953.
48. TNA: PRO WO 216/518 1A, Robertson to Brownjohn, 27 March 1952.
49. TNA: PRO CAB 128/25 CM (52) 101, 2 December 1952; and TNA: PRO FO 371/104234 E1195/1, minute by Allen, 15 January 1953.
50. TNA: PRO DEFE 4/58, COS 164 (52) 1 – see annex, 'Military basis of defence negotiations with Egypt': report by the JPS to the COS on the requirements in Egypt of the forward strategy, 28 November 1952 (JP (52) 141) [*BDEEP* no. 339].
51. TNA: PRO DEFE 4/58, COS 164 (52) 1, 2 December 1952 [*BDEEP* no. 340].
52. TNA: PRO CAB 131/12, COS 12 (52) 4, 11 December 1952.
53. *BDEEP*, ed. Kent, p. lxxiii.
54. TNA: PRO CAB 129/53 CP (52) 202, 18 June 1952.
55. TNA: PRO FO 371/102796 JE1192/18G, minute by Allen, 14 February 1953 [*BDEEP* no. 359].
56. TNA: PRO CAB 129/59 CP (53) 65, 16 February 1953 [*BDEEP* no. 361].
57. TNA: PRO CAB 128/26 CC (53) 12, 17 February 1953 [*BDEEP* no. 364].
58. TNA: PRO CAB 128/26 CC (53) 17, 9 March 1953 [*BDEEP* no. 374]; Steven Z. Freiberger, *Dawn over Suez: The Rise of American Power in the Middle East, 1953–1957* (Chicago, 1992), p. 63.

59. TNA: PRO FO 371/102798 JE1192/53G, minute by Allen, 9 March 1953.

60. TNA: PRO FO 371/102802 JE1192/130G (O), Jebb to Foreign Office, 10 March 1953; also TNA: PRO FO 371/102802 JE1192/130W, Makins to Foreign Office, 11 March 1953.

61. During the Canal Zone siege, rumours had circulated that he might be recalled (see p. 52).

62. TNA: PRO PREM 11/486, Brook to Churchill, 14 February 1953.

63. The former chief of imperial general staff, Field Marshal Sir William Slim, was initially chosen to act in this capacity, but he was subsequently offered the governor-generalship of Australia and he did not want to delay his appointment. See TNA: PRO PREM 11/704 185–6, Swinton to Churchill, 17 February 1953; and Williamson, *A Most Diplomatic General*, pp. 169–70.

64. *FRUS*, 1952–4, pp. 2016–17, Dulles to Caffery, 11 March 1953.

65. TNA: PRO FO 371/102802 JE1192/130 (W), Stevenson to Foreign Office, 15 March 1953.

66. *FRUS*, 1952–4, pp. 2019–20, Caffery to State Department, 15 March 1953.

67. TNA: PRO PREM 11/431 44, Eisenhower to Eden, 16 March 1953; also TNA: PRO FO 371/102803 JE1192/155G, minutes by Allen (23rd), Strang (24th), Eden (27th) and Strang 30 March [*BDEEP* no. 383].

68. TNA: PRO FO 371/102803 JE1192/155G, Creswell to Allen, 19 March 1953 [*BDEEP* no. 378].

69. NA: RG59 774.5/3-2353, Aldrich to State Department, 23 March 1953.

CHAPTER EIGHT

1. See p. 28.

2. TNA: PRO FO 800/772 Eg/53/96, Churchill to Strang, 20 March 1953; TNA: PRO FO 800/772 Eg/53/96A, Strang to Churchill, 21 April 1953.

3. TNA: PRO PREM 11/392 119, Churchill to Creswell, 22 April 1953.

4. TNA: PRO CAB 131/13 D (53) 25, 21 April 1953.

5. Mitchell, *Society of Muslim Brothers*, pp. 119–21.

6. TNA: PRO CAB 131/13 D (53) 9, 13 May 1953; and TNA: PRO PREM 11/392, Lloyd to Churchill, 21 April 1953.

7. TNA: PRO FO 371/102848 JE11914/47, minute by Allen, 31 May 1953.

8. TNA: PRO PREM 11/392, Stevenson to Foreign Office, 7 May 1953; see also TNA: PRO FO 371/102847 JE11914/1, Festing to Creswell, 23 April 1953.

9. TNA: PRO FO 371/102807 JE1192/259, minute by Parsons, 7 May 1953.

10. TNA: PRO CAB 131/13 D (53) 9, 13 May 1953.

11. *Ibid.*; and TNA: PRO PREM 11/632 61, BDCC (ME) to COS, 12 January 1953.

12. TNA: PRO FO 371/102847 JE11914 /22, Churchill to Stevenson, 10 May 1953.

13. TNA: PRO FO 800/773 Eg/53/120, Foreign Office to Stevenson, 11 May 1953.

14. *FRUS*, 1952–4, pp. 5–9, Caffery [on behalf of Dulles] to State Department, 12 May 1952.

15. Ritchie Ovendale, 'Egypt and the Suez Base Agreement', in John W. Young (ed.), *The Foreign Policy of Churchill's Peacetime Administration, 1951–1955* (Leicester, 1988), p. 145.

16. *FRUS*, 1952–4, pp. 379–86, memo of discussion of 147th meeting of the NSC, 1 June 1953; for a British overview of US policy after the Dulles tour, see TNA: PRO FO 371/104258 E10345G, Makins to Foreign Office, 6 November 1953.

17. TNA: PRO FO 371/102798 JE1192/64, minute by Allen, 23 March 1953; see also TNA: PRO FO 371/102780 JE1027/3G, Bowker to Stevenson, 30 March 1953.

18. Reported in NA: RG59 774.00 (W) /5-2153, Caffery to State Department, 22 May 1953.

19. TNA: PRO CAB 131/13 D (53) 9, 13 May 1953; TNA: PRO FO 371/102765 JE1052/117G, minute by Allen, 13 May 1953.

20. TNA: PRO FO 371/102765 JE1052/117G, minute by Allen, 13 May 1953.

21. TNA: PRO FO 371/102766 JE1052/130G, Creswell to Allen, 22 May 1953.

22. TNA: PRO PREM 11/392, Stevenson to Churchill, 27 May 1953.

23. *Ibid.*

24. Private information.

25. Wm Roger Louis, 'Churchill and Egypt 1946–1956', in Robert Blake and Wm Roger Louis (eds), *Churchill* (Oxford, 1993), p. 479.

26. TNA: PRO FO 371/102765 JE1052/121G, minute by Hankey, 22 May 1953.

27. TNA: PRO PREM 11/629 92–3, Hankey to Foreign Office, 19 June 1953.

28. TNA: PRO FO 371/102766 JE1052/133, Hankey to Bowker, 17 June 1953; TNA: PRO FO 371/102811 JE1192/374G, Hankey to Strang, 23 June 1953; TNA: PRO FO 371/102766, JE1052/143, Hankey to Allen, 3 August 1953.

29. Gordon, *Nasser's Blessed Movement*, pp. 83–6.

30. See TNA: PRO FO 371/102845 JE11913/8, minute by Bowker, 20 June 1953; TNA: PRO FO 371/102723 JE1025/4, Hankey to Foreign Office, 22 June 1953.

31. See NA: RG59 774.00/6-2353, Dulles to Caffery, 24 June 1953; and NA: RG59 774.00/6-2353, Caffery to Dulles, 24 June 1953.

32. Mohi El Din, *Memories of a Revolution*, pp. 156–7; see also, Sadat, *In Search of Identity*, pp. 154–5.

33. Neguib, *Egypt's Destiny*, pp. 188–90.

34. Gilbert, *Never Despair*, pp. 846–57.

35. Shuckburgh, *Descent to Suez*, p. 89.

36. *FRUS*, 1952–4, pp. 2115–17, Neguib to Eisenhower, 11 July 1953.

37. TNA: PRO FO 371/102732 JE10345/28G, 'UK record of Anglo-American conversations held in the State Department, Washington, July 14 1953 at 10.30 a.m.'.

38. TNA: PRO FO 371/102732 JE10345/28G, Salisbury to Foreign Office, 14 July 1953.

39. TNA: PRO FO 371/102851 JE11914/121, Duke to Allen, 23 July 1953.

40. TNA: PRO FO 371/102850 JE119414/87, Churchill to Lloyd, 15 July 1953.

41. Reported in TNA: PRO FO 371/102924 JE1897/3, Hankey to Foreign Office, 18 July 1953.

42. TNA: PRO FO 371/102766 JE1152/143, Hankey to Allen, 3 August 1953; TNA: PRO FO 371/102924 JE1897/4, Hankey to Foreign Office, 18 July 1953.

43. TNA: PRO CAB 128/62 C (53) 232, 15 August 1953.

44. Williamson, *A Most Diplomatic General*, pp. 170–1.

45. *Ibid.*, pp. 171–2.

46. TNA: PRO FO 371/102816 JE1192/482G, Hankey to Bowker, 14 September 1953.

47. See generally, Henry W. Brands, 'The Cairo–Tehran Connection in Anglo-American Rivalry in the Middle East, 1951–1953', *International History Review*, 11/3 (1989).

48. TNA: PRO FO 371/102859 JE11915/55G, Hankey to Foreign Office, 24 August 1953.

49. TNA: PRO FO 371/102924 JE1897/1, Hankey to Foreign Office, 17 July 1953; TNA: PRO FO 371/102851 JE11914/121, Duke to Allen, 23 July 1953; TNA: PRO FO 371/102853 JE11914/150G, Hankey to Foreign Office, 26 August 1953; TNA: PRO FO 371/102853 JE11914/158G, minute by Morris, 30 August 1953; TNA: PRO FO 371/102853 JE11914/158G, Hankey to Foreign Office, 30 August 1953 (and accompanying minute); and TNA: PRO FO 371/102854 JE11914/165, Hankey to Foreign Office, 10 September 1953.

50. NA: RG59 774.00/9-1653, Caffery to State Department, 3 September 1953.

51. TNA: PRO FO 371/102860 JE11915/65, Hankey to Foreign Office, 5 September 1953.

52. TNA: PRO CAB 128/26 CM (53) 51, 8 September 1953; TNA: PRO CAB 130/95 Gen 442/3, 12 September 1953; TNA: PRO CAB 128/26 CM (53) 53, 16 September 1953.

53. *Ibid.*

54. TNA: PRO FO 371/102816 JE1192/486, minute by Allen, 24 September 1953; NA: RG59 774.00 (W)/9-2553, Caffery to State Department, 25 September 1953.

55. TNA: PRO CAB 128/26 CM (53) 54, 2 October 1953.

56. Shuckburgh, *Descent to Suez*, pp. 105–6.

57. TNA: PRO FO 371/102861 JE11915/100G, Robertson to Allen, 17 October 1953.

58. Letter from Robertson and Hankey to Eden, 12 October 1953; circulated to the cabinet as TNA: PRO CAB 129/63 CP (53) 281, 14 October 1953.

59. TNA: PRO CAB 128/26 CM 58 (53) 4, 15 October 1953.

60. Farnie, *East and West of Suez*, p. 706; see also Onslow, *Backbench Debate within the Conservative Party*, p. 176.

61. Bodleian Library, Oxford: Conservative Party Archives, CRD 2/34/1, Foreign Affairs Committee Minutes 1946–55, meeting on 21 October 1953. For a reference to Churchill's demeanour, see Bodleian Library, Oxford: Conservative Party Archives, CRD 2/34/1, Foreign Affairs Committee Minutes 1946–55, meeting on 16 December 1953.

62. TNA: PRO FO 371/102821, Waterhouse *et al.* to Churchill, 22 October 1953.

63. TNA: PRO PREM 11/484, Hankey to Foreign Office, 21 October 1953.

64. *FRUS*, 1952–4, p. 2151, Caffery to State Department, 22 October 1953.

65. TNA: PRO FO 371/102820 JE1192/595G, Creswell to Allen, 28 October 1953; TNA: PRO FO 371/102820 JE1192/590, minute by Eden, 29 October 1953; TNA: PRO FO 371/102818 JE1192/560G, Hankey to Foreign Office, 23 October 1953; TNA: PRO FO 371/102818 JE1192/560G, minute by Allen,

23 October 1953; TNA: PRO FO 371/102818 JE1192/569G, Makins to Foreign Office, 26 October 1953; and TNA: PRO FO 371/102820 JE1192/590, minute by Allen, 29 October 1953.

66. TNA: PRO FO 371/12808, Cairo to Foreign Office, 19 November 1953.
67. Williamson, *A Most Diplomatic General*, p. 176.
68. TNA: PRO FO 371/102856 JE11914/205, Duke to Boothby, 18 November 1953.
69. TNA: PRO FO 371/102857, minute by Ledward, 8 December 1953.
70. TNA: PRO CAB 131/13 D (53) 58, 'Egypt – Review of the situation in the Canal Zone', memo by the COS, 30 November 1953.
71. TNA: PRO FO 371 /102857 JE11914/222G, Sterndale-Bennett to Allen, 7 December 1953.
72. TNA: PRO FO 371/102855, JE11914/190G, marginal comments by Eden on Creswell to Foreign Office, 18 November 1953.
73. Daly, *Imperial Sudan*, p. 360.
74. TNA: PRO FO 800/827 Sud/53/52, Eden to Lloyd, 3 December 1953.
75. TNA: PRO FO 371/102823 JE1192/656G, Churchill to Eden, 11 December 1953.
76. Shuckburgh, *Descent to Suez*, 12 December 1953, p. 118.
77. *FRUS*, 1952–4, pp. 2173–4, Butterworth to State Department, 14 December 1953.
78. TNA: PRO CAB 128/26 CM (53) 78, 14 December 1953; TNA: PRO CAB 128/26 CM (53) 79, 15 December 1953.
79. Bodleian Library, Oxford: Conservative Party Archives: Foreign Affairs Committee Minutes, CRD 2/34/1, meeting on 16 December 1953.
80. *The Times*, 16 December 1953, p. 6.
81. Shuckburgh, *Descent to Suez*, p. 121.
82. Quoted in Y.J. Tenembaum, 'British Policy towards Israel and the Arab–Israeli Dispute, 1951–54' (unpublished Oxford D.Phil., 1991), p. 298.
83. Shuckburgh, *Descent to Suez*, p. 125.
84. In the spring of 1953, for instance, when the issue of an Israeli contribution to Middle East defence planning was being discussed, Churchill had stated, 'We have probably got to have a showdown with Neguib, and Israel will be an important factor both Parliamentary and military. We must not throw away any important card we have in our hand. TNA: PRO PREM 11/463 10–11, Churchill to Strang, 23 April 1953.

Chapter Nine

1. Shuckburgh, *Descent to Suez*, p. 10.
2. TNA: PRO CAB 129/65 CP (54) 6, 7 January 1954.
3. TNA: PRO CAB 128/26 CC (53) 81, 29 December 1953.
4. TNA: PRO CAB 129/65 CP (54) 9, 9 January 1954; see also TNA: PRO DEFE 4/67 COS (53) 146, 31 December 1953.
5. TNA: PRO FO 3871/108503 JE1261/9, minute by Boothby, 22 January 1954.
6. TNA: PRO CAB 130/95 Gen 442/3, 12 September 1953; see pp. 170–1.
7. TNA: PRO CAB 128/27 CC (54) 4, 21 January 1954.

8. *Ibid.*
9. See p. 34.
10. TNA: PRO PREM 11/701 262–3, Churchill to Eden, 21 January 1954 (not sent but the purport of it telephoned).
11. TNA: PRO FO 371/108463 JE11912/9G, Kirkpatrick to Shuckburgh, 22 January 1952.
12. TNA: PRO FO 371/102823 JE1192/678, minute by Allen, 16 December 1953; see pp. 12–13 for conditions relating to the revision of the 1936 treaty.
13. TNA: PRO CAB 128/27 CC (54) 5, 26 January 1954.
14. TNA: PRO FO 371/800/775 Eg/54/10, Eden to Lloyd, 28 January 1954; and Shuckburgh, *Descent to Suez*, p. 129; TNA: PRO CAB 129/65 CP (54) 6, 7 January 1954.
15. TNA: PRO CAB 129/65 CP (54) 29, 27 January 1954.
16. TNA: PRO CAB 128/27 CC (54) 6, 28 January 1954.
17. Shuckburgh, *Descent to Suez*, p. 131.
18. Perhaps rather defensively on this matter, Lloyd's biographer notes that his subject had a long-standing engagement in his Wirral constituency on 19 February. See D.R. Thorpe, *Selwyn Lloyd* (London, 1989), p. 176.
19. *FRUS*, 1952–4, pp. 2208–9, Caffery to State Department, 26 January 1954.
20. TNA: PRO FO 800/775 Eg/54/24, Eden to Lloyd, 9 February 1954.
21. TNA: PRO FO 800/775 Eg/54/26, Lloyd to Eden, 14 February 1954; TNA: PRO FO 371/108464 JE119112/21, minute by Allen, 15 February 1954.
22. TNA: PRO FO 371/108319 JE1016/1, Chancery (Cairo embassy) to African department (Foreign Office), 30 December 1953.
23. Mitchell, *Society of Muslim Brothers*, pp. 120–4; and Gordon, *Nasser's Blessed Movement*, pp. 104–5.
24. NA: RG59 774.00 (W)/1-2254, Caffery to State Department, 22 January 1954; Mitchell, *Society of Muslim Brothers*, p. 126, footnote 59; and Gordon, *Nasser's Blessed Movement*, p. 105.
25. See Mohi El Din, *Memories of Revolution*, p. 174; NA: RG59 774.00 (W)/1-2254, Caffery to State Department, 22 January 1954.
26. TNA: PRO FO 371/108446 JE1193/13, minute by Boothby, 21 January 1954; TNA: PRO FO 371/108447 JE1193/14, Stevenson to Foreign Office, 22 January 1954.
27. TNA: PRO CAB 128/27 CC (54) 3, 18 January 1954.
28. TNA: PRO FO 371/108319 JE1016/4, minute by Morris, 18 January 1954; see also NA: RG59 774.00 (W) 1-2254, Caffery to State Department, 22 January 1954.
29. TNA: PRO FO 371/108375 JE1056/2G, Shuckburgh to Kirkpatrick, 27 January 1954.
30. NA: RG59 774.00 (W) 2-554, Caffery to State Department, 27 January 1954. Sirag al-Din was released after three years in gaol but was imprisoned again in 1981 after reviving the Wafd in 1978. See Shaden Shehab, 'The Last Pasha' [obituary], *Al-Ahram Weekly*, Issue no. 495, 17–23 August 2000.
31. Quoted in NA: RG59 774.11/1-1854, Caffery to State Department, 18 January 1954.

32. TNA: PRO FO 371/108315 JE1015/2, Stevenson to Foreign Office, 4 February 1954.
33. TNA: PRO FO 371/108375 JE1056/3G, minute by Boothby, 20 February 1954.
34. *FRUS*, 1952–4, pp. 2215–16, Caffery to State Department, 12 February 1954.
35. Wilton Wynn, *Nasser of Egypt: The Search for Dignity* (Cambridge MA, 1959), p. 95.
36. Mohi El Din, *Memories of a Revolution*, p. 179.
37. Neguib, *Egypt's Destiny*, pp. 213–14; *FRUS*, 1952–4, pp. 2221–2, Caffery to State Department, 25 February 1954.
38. *FRUS*, 1952–4, pp. 2221–2, Caffery to State Department, 25 February 1954.
39. TNA: PRO FO 371/108327 JE1018/3, Stevenson to Foreign Office, 25 February 1954; *FRUS*, 1952–4, pp. 2221–2, Caffery to State Department, 25 February 1954; see also Neguib, *Egypt's Destiny*, pp. 222–3.
40. Lacouture, *Egypt in Transition*, p. 179.
41. Mohi El Din, *Memories of a Revolution*, p. 177.
42. Sadat, *In Search of Identity*, pp. 163–4.
43. *FRUS*, 1952–4, pp. 2223–4, Caffery to State Department, 27 February 1954.
44. *FRUS*, 1952–4, pp. 2224–5, Caffery to State Department, 28 February 1954; Little, *Egypt*, pp. 232–3.
45. Lloyd, *Suez 1956*, p. 17.
46. *Ibid.*, pp. 18–19.
47. *Ibid.*
48. *Ibid.*; see also Daly, *Imperial Sudan*, pp. 368–89.
49. NA: RG59 774.00 3-2554, Payne to Caffery, 25 March 1954.
50. Gordon, *Nasser's Blessed Movement*, p. 135.
51. *FRUS*, 1952–4, pp. 2242–4, Caffery to State Department, 23 March 1954.
52. *FRUS*, 1952–4, p. 2252, Caffery to State Department, 30 March 1954; NA: RG59 774.00 (W)/4-254, Caffery to State Department, 3 April 1954.
53. *Ibid.*; and *FRUS*, 1952–4, pp. 2247–9, Caffery to State Department, 28 March 1954.
54. TNA: PRO FO 371/108316 JE1015/18A, minute by Bromley, 29 March 1954.
55. *FRUS*, 1952–4, p. 2246, Caffery to State Department, 26 March 1954.
56. *FRUS*, 1952–4, pp. 2250–1, Caffery to State Department, 29 March 1954; *FRUS*, 1952–4, p. 2253, Caffery to State Department, 30 March 1954; TNA: PRO FO 371/108316 JE1015/29, Stevenson to Eden, 15 April 1954.
57. TNA: PRO FO 371/108316 JE1015/29, Stevenson to Eden, 15 April 1954; and NA: RG59 774.00/3-3154, Caffery to Dulles, 31 March 1954.
58. TNA: PRO CAB 128/27 CC (54) 13, 1 March 1954.
59. Shuckburgh, *Descent to Suez*, pp. 126, 155; TNA: PRO CAB 129/66 CP (54) 99, 13 March 1954.
60. TNA: PRO CAB 129/66 CP (54) 99, 13 March 1954.
61. TNA: PRO CAB 129/67 CP (54) 102, 15 March 1954.
62. TNA: PRO DEFE 4/69 COS (54) 28, 15 March 1954.
63. Shuckburgh, *Descent to Suez*, p. 148.
64. *Ibid.*; and TNA: PRO CAB 128/27 CC (54) 18, 15 March 1954.
65. TNA: PRO CAB 128/27 CC (54) 18, 15 March 1954.
66. *FRUS*, 1952–4, pp. 2240–1, Caffery to State Department, 20 March 1954; and *FRUS*, 1952–4, p. 2239, Dulles to Aldrich, 20 March 1954.

67. Shuckburgh, *Descent to Suez*, p. 149.
68. TNA: PRO CAB 129/65 CP (54) 74, 25 February 1954.
69. TNA: PRO PREM 11/701 49–50, Harding to Churchill, 17 March 1954.
70. TNA: PRO PREM 11/701 M 55/54 47, Churchill to Eden, 18 March 1954.
71. TNA: PRO FO 800/775 Eg/54/36, Eden to Churchill, 18 March 1954.
72. TNA: PRO DEFE 4/69 COS (54) 32, 22 March 1954.
73. TNA: PRO FO 371/108545 JE1536/2G, minute by Millard, 27 March 1954.
74. TNA: PRO PREM 11/701 49–50, Harding to Churchill, 17 March 1954.
75. *Ibid.*; and TNA: PRO DEFE 4/69 COS (54) 29, 18 March 1954.
76. TNA: PRO FO 371/108545 JE1536/2G, minute by Millard, 27 March 1954.
77. Figures cited in TNA: PRO PREM 11/632 5, Brook to Churchill, 15 April 1954.
78. TNA: PRO DEFE 4/69 COS (54) 36, 31 March 1954.
79. TNA: PRO CAB 128/27 CC (54) 29, 15 April 1954.
80. *Ibid.*
81. TNA: PRO PREM 11/632 5, Brook to Churchill, 15 April 1954.
82. Roth, *Enoch Powell*, p. 112.
83. NA: RG59 774.00 (W)/5-1354, Caffery to State Department, 14 May 1954.
84. *FRUS*, 1952–4, pp. 2261–2, Dulles to State Department, 13 April 1954.
85. TNA: PRO FO 371/108479 JE11929/33G, minute by Bromley, 14 April 1954.
86. TNA: PRO FO 371/108479 JE11929/33G, minute by Eden, 14 April 1954.
87. TNA: PRO FO 371/108454 JE1195/30, minute by Street, 1 June 1954.
88. TNA: PRO FO 371/108450 JE1193/111, minute by Bromley, 14 June 1954.
89. TNA: PRO WO 216/867 8, note of meeting between Harding and Keightley, 27 May 1954.
90. TNA: PRO FO 371/108479 JE11929/42G, Head to Eden, 29 April 1954.
91. TNA: PRO CAB 129/68 CP (54) 187, 3 June 1954.
92. TNA: PRO CAB 128 CC (54) 43, 22 June 1954.
93. TNA: PRO CAB 129/69 CP (54) 220, 6 July 1954; also TNA: PRO FO 371/108419 JE1192/134G, minute by Bromley, 30 June 1954.
94. TNA: PRO CAB 128/27 CC (54) 47, 7 July 1954.
95. *The Times*, 19 July 1954, p. 6.
96. The comment was made to Frank Roberts and is reported in Shuckburgh, *Descent to Suez*, p. 224.
97. *The Times*, 19 July 1954, p. 6.
98. *The Times*, 15 July 1954, p. 8; and *The Times*, 22 July 1954, p. 6.
99. *FRUS*, 1952–4, pp. 2279–80, Caffery to State Department, 11 July 1954.
100. TNA: PRO FO 371/108424 JE1192/209G, Stevenson to Foreign Office, 20 July 1954.
101. TNA: PRO FO 371/108424 JE1192/215G, Shuckburgh to Lloyd, 17 July 1954.
102. TNA: PRO DEFE 4/71 COS (54) 84, 21 July 1954; see also TNA: PRO FO 371/108424 JE1192/229G, minute by Shuckburgh, 21 July 1954.
103. TNA: PRO AIR 8/1863 420/8, Churchill to Alexander and chiefs of staff, 21 July 1954.
104. Eden circulated two cabinet papers, one arguing the case for an agreement, the other detailing the final terms for the negotiations. TNA: PRO CAB 129/69 CP (54) 248, 23 July 1954; TNA: PRO CAB 129 CP (54) 251, 23 July 1954.

105. TNA: PRO CAB 128/27 CC (54) 52, 23 July 1954.
106. Shuckburgh, *Descent to Suez*, p. 230; TNA: PRO CAB 128/27 CC (54), 26 July 1954.
107. *Ibid.*, pp. 231–2.
108. *Ibid.*, pp. 233–4.
109. TNA: PRO FO 371/108425 JE1192/258, the signed 'heads of agreement' can be found at Stevenson to Foreign Office, 29 July 1954.
110. For the relevant passage of the agreement on air matters and British comments upon it, see TNA: PRO AIR 8/1863 420/8, 29 July 1954.
111. Avi Shlaim, *The Iron Wall: Israel and the Arab World* (London, 2001), pp. 110–12; see also Aburish, *Nasser*, pp. 67–71.
112. Hansard, 5th Series, House of Commons Debates, vol. 531, col. 743, 29 July 1954.
113. *Ibid.*, col. 772, 29 July 1954.
114. See Harold Macmillan, *Tides of Fortune, 1945–55* (London, 1969), p. 502; Selywn Lloyd, *Suez 1956* (London, 1978), p. 21; and Eden, *Full Circle*, p. 261.
115. Hansard, 5th Series, House of Commons Debates, vol. 531, col. 750, 29 July 1954.
116. *The Times*, 30 July 1954.
117. NA: RG59 774.00 (W) NR 1-158, Caffery to State Department, 31 July 1954.
118. Mitchell, *The Society of Muslim Brothers*, pp. 136–9.
119. Hahn, *The United States, Great Britain, and Egypt*, pp. 165–7.
120. Churchill to Eisenhower, 19 December 1953, in Peter G. Boyle (ed.), *The Churchill–Eisenhower Correspondence, 1953–1955* (Chapel Hill, 1990), pp. 114–15.
121. Alterman, *Egypt and American Foreign Assistance*, p. 54; *FRUS*, 1952–4, pp. 2297–8, Caffery to State Department, 29 August 1954.
122. Shlaim, *The Iron Wall*, p. 113.
123. TNA: PRO FO 371/108317 JE1015/54, Stevenson to Foreign Office, 14 September 1954.
124. TNA: PRO FO 371/108317 JE1015/54, minute by Shuckburgh, 4 October 1954.
125. Gamal Abdel Nasser, *The Philosophy of the Revolution*, reprinted in Farag (ed.), *Nasser Speaks*, p. 23.
126. Kyle, *Suez*, p. 54.
127. The terms were published as a white paper: *Agreement regarding the Suez Canal Base, Egypt* No. 2 Cmd 9298 (HMSO, 1954); on the final negotiations, see TNA: PRO CAB 129/70 CP (54) 299, 28 September 1954, and TNA: PRO PREM 11/702 6, Murray to Eden, 3 November 1954.
128. TNA: PRO PREM 11/702 6, Murray to Eden, 3 November 1954.
129. NA: RG59 774.00 (W) NR 1-205, Caffery to State Department, 23 October 1954.
130. Stephens, *Nasser*, p. 136.
131. NA: RG59 774.00 (W)/10-2954 NR 1209, Caffery to State Department, 29 October 1954; see also TNA: PRO PREM 11/702 6, Murray to Eden, 3 November 1954.
132. NA: RG59 774.00 (W)/11-1254 NR 1218, Caffery to State Department, 19 November 1954.

133. TNA: PRO FO 371/108319 JE1016/24, minute by Street, 12 December 1954.

134. Mitchell, *Society of Muslim Brothers*, pp. 160–1.

135. For an assessment of the 1954 agreement which places a much greater emphasis on the importance of the hydrogen bomb, see Louis, 'The Tragedy of the Anglo-Egyptian Settlement of 1954', in Louis and Owen (eds), *Suez 1956*, pp. 66–8.

EPILOGUE

1. TNA: PRO FO 371/108426 JE1192/285, Nasser to Eden, 6 August 1954; this correspondence was initiated by a letter from Eden to Nasser on 31 July, see TNA: PRO FO 371/108426 JE1192/271.

2. TNA: PRO FO 371/118830 JE1011/1, Trevelyan to Lloyd, 31 January 1956.

3. Ali E. Hillal Dessouki, 'Nasser and the Struggle for Independence', in Louis and Owen (eds), *Suez 1956*, p. 32.

4. Ayesha Jalal, 'Towards the Baghdad Pact: South Asia and Middle East Defence in the Cold War, 1947–1955', *International History Review*, 11/3 (August 1989), p. 431.

5. NA: RG59 774.00 (W)/5-2854 NR 1123, Caffery to State Department, 28 May 1954.

6. TNA: PRO CAB 129 CP (54) 181, 31 May 1954.

7. TNA: PRO FO 371/115492 V1073/289, Cairo to Foreign Office, 21 February 1955.

8. Heikal, *Cutting the Lion's Tale*, p. 78.

9. Churchill College, Cambridge: Selwyn Lloyd Papers: Selo 6/202, Eden to Lloyd, 14 June 1966 (discussing questions from Kennett Love, author of *Suez: The Twice-Fought War* (New York, 1969)).

10. Kyle, *Suez*, pp. 90–1.

11. Shlaim, *The Iron Wall*, p. 126.

12. Geoffrey Aronson, *From Sideshow to Center Stage: US Policy towards Egypt, 1946-1956* (Boulder, 1986), p. 200.

13. Aburish, *Nasser*, p. 84.

14. Anthony Nutting, *No End of a Lesson: The Story of Suez* (London, 1967), pp. 34–5.

15. Kyle, *Suez*, p. 99.

16. Copeland, *Game of Nations*, pp. 134–5. Scott Lucas points out that Roosevelt's suggestion was probably superfluous in that the Soviet ambassador to Egypt had already suggested such a course. See Lucas, *Divided We Stand*, p. 340.

17. Robert McNamara, *Britain, Nasser and the Balance of Power in the Middle East, 1952–1967* (London, 2003), p. 45.

18. This was suggested to me by a relative of Sir Ralph Murray, minister at the Cairo embassy between 1954 and 1956. See also Murray's entry in *Oxford Dictionary of National Biography*.

19. Lucas, *Divided We Stand*, pp. 111–12.

20. Heikal, *Cutting the Lion's Tale*, p. 118.

21. As related by Copeland himself in *Game of Nations*, pp. 149–50.

22. Reported in NA: RG59 774.11/11-1954, Aldrich to State Department, 19 November 1954.

23. TNA: PRO FO 800/828 Sud/54/28, Eden to Churchill, 9 December 1954; and Daly, *Imperial Sudan*, p. 379.

24. TNA: PRO FO 371/118830 JE1011/1, Trevelyan to Lloyd, 31 January 1956.

25. TNA: PRO PREM 11/1470 35, Head to Eden, 15 November 1955. This gives the official withdrawal date as 19 June 1956.

26. Williamson, *A Most Diplomatic General*, pp. 177–8.

27. Hourani, 'The Anglo-Egyptian Agreement', p. 239.

28. Nutting, *No End of a Lesson*, p. 26.

29. Birmingham University: Avon Papers: AP20/49/19A, comments on Nutting's *No End of a Lesson*.

30. Author's interview with Frank Brenchley, Oxford, 27 April 1999.

31. Lucas, *Divided We Stand*, p. 143.

32. 'Suez: Success or Disaster?', interview with General Sir Hugh Stockwell by Frank Gillard, *The Listener*, 4 November 1976, p. 563.

33. Churchill College, Cambridge: Cowley Papers: CWLY 1/3, note by Sir John Cowley, vice chief of imperial general staff (undated but said to be written shortly after the events).

34. Kyle, *Suez*, p. 173.

35. Humphrey Trevelyan, *Middle East in Revolution* (London, 1970), pp. 105–6.

36. See TNA: PRO PREM 11/1099, Trevelyan to Foreign Office, 15 August 1956.

37. Adam Watson to author, 15 March 1997. Watson was head of the Foreign Office's African department in 1956.

38. Michael T. Thornhill, 'Alternatives to Nasser: Humphrey Trevelyan, Ambassador to Egypt', *Contemporary British History*, 13/2 (1999), 17–22.

39. According to Kennett Love's sources for *Twice-Fought War*, Prince Abdel Moneim was to head the successor regime. See Churchill College, Cambridge: Selwyn Lloyd Papers: SELO 6/202, Love to Lloyd, 29 January 1966.

40. Britain's position as the paramount power in the sheikhdoms of eastern Arabia – from Kuwait running down to Trucial Oman – was, for instance, being increasingly challenged by the rise of the US's interests in Saudi Arabia. A particular source of friction was the Saudi–Abu Dhabi dispute over ownership of the Buraimi oasis, which soured Anglo-American relations between 1952 and 1956.

41. See especially Avi Shlaim, 'The Protocol of Sèvres, 1956: Anatomy of a War Plot', *International Affairs*, 73/3 (1997).

42. Shuckburgh, *Descent to Suez*, p. 29.

43. TNA: PRO PREM 11/463 10–11, Churchill to Strang, 23 April 1953.

44. Kyle, *Suez*, p. 464.

45. Gilbert, *Never Despair*, p. 1222.

Bibliography

(1) OFFICIAL SOURCES

The National Archives of the United Kingdom (TNA): Public Record Office (PRO), London:

AIR 8	Chief of Air Staff Papers
CAB 128	Cabinet Minutes
CAB 129	Cabinet Papers
CAB 130	Cabinet Committee (ad hoc) Files
CAB 131	Defence Committee Minutes
DEFE 4	Chiefs of Staff Committee Minutes
DEFE 5	Chiefs of Staff Memoranda
DEFE 6	Joint Planning Staff Memoranda
FO 141	Embassy and Consular Archives, Cairo
FO 371	Foreign Office, General Political Correspondence
FO 800	Records of the Foreign Secretary's Office
FO 953	Foreign Office, Information Department
PREM 11	Records of the Prime Minister's Office
T 236	Treasury Overseas Finance Division Files
WO 216	Chief of Imperial General Staff Papers

National Archives of the United States of America, Washington DC:

RG59	General Records of the Department of State
Class 6	International Political Relations
Class 7	Internal Political and National Defence Affairs
Class 8	Internal Economic, Industrial and Social Affairs
Class 9	Communications/Public Press

(2) PRIVATE COLLECTIONS

Birmingham University Library:
 Avon Papers

Bodleian Library, Oxford:
 Clement Attlee Papers
 William Clark Papers

Churchill College, Cambridge:
  Selwyn Lloyd Papers
  John Cowley Papers

St Antony's College, Oxford, Middle East Centre Archive:
  John Glubb Papers
  John Hamilton Papers
  Elizabeth Monroe Papers
  Thomas Rapp Papers
  John Slade-Baker Papers

(3) POLITICAL PARTY RECORDS
Bodleian Library, Oxford, Conservative Party Archive:
  CRD 2/34/1   Parliamentary Foreign Affairs Committee Minutes
  CRD 2/34/6   Parliamentary Foreign Affairs Committee Briefs

(4) PUBLISHED OFFICIAL SOURCES
Cmd. 8336, *Sterling Releases Agreement*, Treaty Series No. 67 (HMSO, 1951)
Cmd. 8419, *Anglo-Egyptian Conversations on the Defence of the Suez Canal and the Sudan, December 1950–November 1951*, Egypt No. 2 (HMSO, 1951)
Cmd. 8767, *Documents concerning Constitutional Development in the Sudan and the Agreement between the Government of Great Britain and Northern Ireland and the Egyptian Government concerning Self-Determination for the Sudan* (HMSO, 1953)
Cmd. 9230, *Heads of Agreement: Anglo-Egyptian Defence Negotiations regarding the Suez Canal Base*, Egypt No. 1 (HMSO, 1954)
Cmd. 9290, *Agreement regarding the Suez Canal Base*, Egypt No. 2 (HMSO, 1954)
Foreign Office List and Consular Year Book (London, 1951 to 1961 inclusive)
Foreign Relations of the United States, 1951, vol. 5 (US Government Printing Office, 1982)
Foreign Relations of the United States, 1952–4, vol. 9 (US Government Printing Office, 1982)
Cm. 5999, *The Naval General Service Medal and the General Service Medal (Army and Royal Air Force): Service in the Suez Canal Zone between 16 October 1951 and 19 October 1954* (SO, 2003)

(5) PARLIAMENTARY PROCEEDINGS
Hansard, House of Commons Debates

(6) NEWSPAPERS
Al-Ahram Weekly (Cairo)
Cairo Times (Cairo)
Egyptian Mail (Cairo)
The Times (London)

(7) EDITED COLLECTIONS OF OFFICIAL PAPERS
British Documents on the End of Empire, Series B, vol. 4, 'Egypt and the Defence of the Middle East', parts 1, 2 and 3, ed. John Kent (London, 1998)

British Documents on the End of Empire, Series B, vol. 5, 'Sudan', ed. Douglas H. Johnson (London, 1996)

(8) SECONDARY SOURCES

Abadi, Jacob, *Britain's Withdrawal from the Middle East: The Economic and Strategic Imperatives* (Princeton, 1982)

Abdalla, Ahmed, *The Student Movement and National Politics in Egypt* (London, 1985)

Aburish, Saïd K., *Nasser: The Last Arab* (London, 2004)

Acheson, Dean, *Present at the Creation* (London, 1969)

Aldrich, Richard J., *British Intelligence, Strategy and the Cold War, 1945–51* (London, 1992)

—— and Hopkins, Michael F. (eds), *Intelligence, Defence and Diplomacy: British Policy in the Post-War World* (London, 1994)

Alterman, Jon B., *Egypt and American Foreign Assistance, 1952–1956: Hopes Dashed* (New York, 2002)

Aronson, Geoffrey, *From Sideshow to Center Stage: US Policy towards Egypt, 1945–1956* (Boulder, 1986)

Ashton, Nigel John, *Eisenhower, Macmillan and the Problem of Nasser: American Relations and Arab Nationalism, 1955–59* (Basingstoke, 1996)

Balfour-Paul, Glen, *The End of Empire in the Middle East: Britain's Relinquishment of Power in her Last Three Arab Dependencies* (Cambridge, 1991)

Barawy, Rashid el, *The Military Coup: An Analytic Study* (Cairo, 1952)

Beinin, Joel and Lockman, Zachary, *Workers on the Nile: Nationalism, Communism, Islam and the Egyptian Working Class, 1882–1954* (Princeton, 1987)

Berque, Jacques, *Egypt: Imperialism and Revolution* (London, 1972)

Beshir, Mohamed Omer, *The Southern Sudan: Background to Conflict* (London, 1968)

Bill, James, and Louis, Wm Roger (eds), *Mussadiq, Iranian Nationalism and Oil* (London, 1988)

Blake, Robert and Louis, Wm Roger (eds), *Churchill* (Oxford, 1993)

Blake, Robert and Nicholls, Christine (eds), *Dictionary of National Biography, 1971–1980* (Oxford, 1986)

Blaxland, Gregory, *Objective Egypt* (London, 1966)

Botman, Selma, 'Egyptian Communists and the Free Officers: 1950–1954', *Middle East Studies*, 222/3 (July 1986)

Boyd-Orr, Lord, *As I Recall* (London, 1967)

Boyle, Peter G. (ed.), *The Churchill–Eisenhower Correspondence, 1953–1955* (Chapel Hill, 1990)

Brands, Henry W., 'The Cairo–Tehran Connection in Anglo-American Rivalry in the Middle East, 1951–1953', *International History Review*, 11/3 (1989)

Bullock, Alan, *Ernest Bevin: Foreign Secretary, 1945–1951* (London, 1983)

Butler, David, *The General Election of 1951* (London, 1952)

Cable, James, *The Geneva Conference of 1954 on Indochina* (London, 1986)

——, *Intervention at Abadan* (London, 1991)

Campbell, John C., *Defense of the Middle East: Problems of American Policy* (New York, 1958)

Carlton, David, *Anthony Eden* (London, 1981)

Cathcart, Brian, *Test of Greatness: Britain's Struggle for the Atomic Bomb* (London, 1994)

Charmley, John, *Churchill's Grand Alliance: The Anglo-American Relationship, 1940–1957* (London, 1995)

Childers, Erskine, *The Road to Suez: A Study in Western–Arab Relations* (London, 1962)

Cohen, Michael J., *Fighting World War Three from the Middle East: Allied Contingency Plans, 1945–1954* (London, 1997)

—— and Kolinsky, Martin (eds), *Demise of the British Empire in the Middle East: Britain's Responses to Nationalist Movements, 1943–55* (London, 1998)

Colville, Jock, *The Fringes of Power: 10 Downing Street Diaries, 1939–1955* (New York, 1985)

Copeland, Miles, *Game of Nations: The Amorality of Power Politics* (New York, 1970)

Daly, Martin W., *Imperial Sudan: The Anglo-Egyptian Condominium, 1934–1956* (Cambridge, 1991)

—— (ed.), *The Cambridge History of Egypt*, vol. 2 (Cambridge, 1998)

Danchev, Alex, *Oliver Franks: Founding Father* (Oxford, 1983)

Darby, Phillip, *British Defence Policy East of Suez, 1947–1968* (London, 1973)

Darwin, John, *Britain, Egypt and the Middle East: Imperial Policy in the Aftermath of War, 1918–1922* (London, 1981)

Devereux, David R., *The Formulation of British Defence Policy towards the Middle East, 1948–1956* (London, 1990)

Davison, Peter (ed.), *Orwell's Politics* (London, 2001)

Dockrill, Michael, *British Defence Policy since 1945* (Oxford, 1988)

Doran, Michael, *Pan-Arabism Before Nasser: Egyptian Power Politics and the Palestine Question* (New York, 1999)

Dur, Philip F., 'Jefferson Caffery of Louisiana: Highlights of His Career', *Louisiana History*, 15/1 (winter 1974)

Eden, Anthony, *Full Circle* (London, 1960)

Evans, Trefor (ed.), *The Killearn Diaries 1934–1946* (London, 1972)

Eveland, Wilbur Crane, *Ropes of Sand: America's Failure in the Middle East* (New York, 1980)

Fabunmi, L.M., *The Sudan in Anglo-Egyptian Relations: A Case Study in Power Politics, 1800–1956* (London, 1960)

Farag, E.S. (ed.), *Nasser Speaks: Basic Documents* (London, 1972)

Farnie, D.A., *East and West of Suez: The Suez Canal in History, 1854–1956* (London, 1969)

Fawzi, Mahmud, *Suez 1956: An Egyptian Perspective* (London, 1987)

Ferguson, Niall, *Empire: How Britain Made the Modern World* (London, 2003)

Findlay, Douglas J., *White Knees Brown Knees: Suez Canal Zone 1951–1954 – the Forgotten Years* (Edinburgh, 2003)

Finer, Herman, *Dulles Over Suez* (London, 1964)

Fitzsimons, M.A., *Empire by Treaty: Britain and the Middle East in the Twentieth Century* (Notre Dame, 1964)

Freiburger, Steven Z., *Dawn over Suez: The Rise of American Power in the Middle East, 1953–1957* (Chicago, 1992)

Garraty, John A. and Carnes, Mark C. (eds), *American National Biography* (New York, 1998)

Ghali, Waguih, *Beer in the Snooker Club* (London, 1964)

Gershoni, Israel and Jankowski, James P., *Redefining the Egyptian Nation, 1930–1945* (Cambridge, 1995)

Gilbert, Martin, *Never Despair: Winston S. Churchill*, vol. 8 (London, 1988)

Goldschmidt, Arthur, *Biographical Dictionary of Modern Egypt* (Boulder, 2000)

Goodhart, P., *The 1922: The Story of the 1922 Committee* (London, 1973)

Gordon, Joel, 'The False Hopes of 1950: The Wafd's Last Hurrah and the Demise of Egypt's Old Order', *International Journal of Middle Eastern Studies*, 21 (1989)

——, *Nasser's Blessed Movement: Egypt's Free Officers and the July Revolution* (New York, 1992)

Grove, Eric, *Vanguard to Trident: British Naval Policy since World War II* (Annapolis, 1987)

Hahn, Peter L., 'Containment and Egyptian Nationalism: The Unsuccessful Effort to Establish the Middle East Command, 1950–1953', *Diplomatic History*, 11/1 (1987)

——, *The United States, Great Britain, and Egypt, 1945–1956: Strategy and Diplomacy in the Early Cold War* (Chapel Hill, 1991)

Hanes III, Travis W., 'Sir Hubert Huddleston and the Independence of the Sudan', *Journal of Imperial and Commonwealth History*, 20/2 (1992)

——, *Imperial Diplomacy in the Era of Decolonization: The Sudan and Anglo-Egyptian Relations, 1945–1956* (Westport, 1995)

Harris, Kenneth, *Attlee* (London, 1982)

Harrison, Brian and Matthew, H.C.G. (eds), *Oxford Dictionary of National Biography* (Oxford, 2004)

Heikal, Mohamed, *Cutting the Lion's Tale: Suez through Egyptian Eyes* (London, 1986)

Holt, P.M., *A Modern History of the Sudan* (London, 1961)

Hopwood, Derek, *Egypt: Politics and Society, 1945–1990* (London, 1991)

Horne, Alistair, *Macmillan, 1894–1956* (London, 1986)

Hourani, Albert, 'The Anglo-Egyptian Agreement: Some Causes and Implications', *Middle East Journal*, 9/3 (1955)

——, 'The Middle East and the Crisis of 1956', *St Antony's Papers*, No. 4 (London, 1958)

——, 'Independence and the Imperial Legacy', *Middle East Forum*, 42/3 (1966)

Ibrahim, H.A., *The 1936 Anglo-Egyptian Treaty* (Khartoum, 1976)

Idris, Yusif, *City of Love and Ashes* (Cairo, 1999)

James, Robert Rhodes, *Anthony Eden* (London, 1986)

Jalal, Ayesha, 'Towards the Baghdad Pact: South Asia and Middle East Defence in the Cold War, 1947–1955', *International History Review*, 11/3 (1989)

Jenkins, Roy, *Churchill: A Biography* (London, 2002)

Joesten, Joachim, *Nasser: The Rise to Power* (London, 1960)

Kaplan, Robert D., *The Arabists: The Romance of an American Elite* (New York, 1995)

Kent, John, 'The Egyptian Base and the Defence of the Middle East, 1945–1954', *Journal of Imperial and Commonwealth History*, 21/3 (1993)

Kirk-Greene, A.H.M., *On Crown Service: A History of H.M. Colonial and Overseas Services, 1837–1997* (London, 1999)

Kolinsky, Martin, *Britain's War in the Middle East: Strategy and Diplomacy, 1936–42* (Basingstoke, 1999)

Kyle, Keith, *Suez* (London, 1991)

Lacouture, Jean and Simonne, *Egypt in Transition* (London, 1958)

Lapping, Brian, *End of Empire* (London, 1985)

Little, Tom, *Egypt* (London, 1958)

Lloyd, Selwyn, *Suez 1956* (London, 1978)

Louis, Wm Roger, *The British Empire in the Middle East, 1945–1951: Arab Nationalism, the United States, and Post-War Imperialism* (Oxford, 1984)

——, 'American Anti-Colonialism and the Dissolution of the British Empire', *International Affairs*, 61/3 (1985)

—— and Robinson, Ronald, 'The Imperialism of Decolonization', *Journal of Imperial and Commonwealth History*, 22/3 (1994)

—— and Owen, Roger (eds), *Suez 1956: The Crisis and its Consequences* (Oxford, 1991)

Love, Kennett, *Suez: The Twice-Fought War* (New York, 1969)

Lucas, W. Scott, *Divided We Stand: Britain, the US and the Suez Crisis* (London, 1991)

Luttwak, Edward, *Coup d'état* (New York, 1968)

Macmillan, Harold, *Tides of Fortune, 1945–55* (London, 1969)

——, *The Macmillan Diaries: Cabinet Years 1951–1957*, ed. Peter Catterall (London, 2004)

Mason, Michael, 'The Decisive Volley: The Battle of Ismailia and the Decline of British Influence in Egypt, January–July 1952', *Journal of Imperial and Commonwealth History*, 19/1 (1991)

——, 'Inside Knowledge: The Antinomies of British Intelligence in Egypt, 1945–1952' (unpublished article, *c.* 1992)

Mansfield, Peter, *The British in Egypt* (London, 1971)

——, *Nasser* (Gateshead, 1969)

Marlowe, John, *A History of Modern Egypt and Anglo-Egyptian Relations* (London, 1965)

McBride, Barrie St Clair, *Farouk of Egypt* (London, 1967)

McGhee, George, *Envoy to the Middle of the World: Adventures in Diplomacy* (New York, 1983)

McNamara, Robert, *Britain, Nasser and the Balance of Power in the Middle East, 1952–1967* (London, 2003)

Mitchell, Richard P., *The Society of Muslim Brothers* (London, 1969)

Mohi El Din, Khaled, *Memories of a Revolution: Egypt 1952* (Cairo, 1992)

Monroe, Elizabeth, 'British Interests in the Middle East', *Middle East Journal*, 2/2 (1948)

——, *Britain's Moment in the Middle East, 1914–1956* (London, 1963)

Moran, Lord, *Winston Churchill: The Struggle for Survival, 1940–1965* (London, 1968)

Morris, Benny, *Israel's Border Wars, 1949–1956* (Oxford, 1993)

Morsey, Laila, 'The Military Clauses of the Anglo-Egyptian Treaty of Friendship and Alliance, 1936', *International Journal of Middle Eastern Studies*, 16 (1984)

Mortada, Ahmed Al-Maraghi, *Oddities from Farouk's Reign* (Beirut, 1976)

Mostyn, Trevor, *Egypt's Belle Epoque: Cairo 1869–1952* (London, 1989)

Murphy, Philip, *Party Politics and Decolonization: The Conservative Party and British Colonial Policy in Tropical Africa, 1951–1964* (Oxford, 1995)

Nasser, Gamal Abdel, 'The Egyptian Revolution', *Foreign Affairs*, 33/2 (January 1955)

——, *The Philosophy of the Revolution* (Engl. lang. edn: Buffalo, 1959)

Nasser, Hoda Gamal Abdel, *Britain and the Egyptian Nationalist Movement, 1936–1952* (Reading, 1992)

Neguib, Mohammed, *Egypt's Destiny* (London, 1955)

Nutting, Anthony, *No End of a Lesson: The Story of Suez* (London, 1967)

——, *Nasser* (London, 1972)

O'Brien, Patrick, *The Revolution in Egypt's Economic System* (London, 1966)

Onslow, Sue, *Backbench Debate within the Conservative Party and its Influence on British Foreign Policy 1948–57* (Basingstoke, 1997)

——, 'Battle Lines for Suez: The Conservatives and the Abadan Crisis 1950–51', *Contemporary British History*, 17/2 (2003)

Oren, Michael B., *Origins of the Second Arab–Israeli War: Egypt, Israel and the Great Powers, 1952–1956* (London, 1992)

Owen, Roger, *State, Power and Politics in the Making of the Modern Middle East* (London, 1992)

——, *Lord Cromer: Victorian Imperialist, Edwardian Proconsul* (Oxford, 2004)

Rahman, H., *A British Defence Problem in the Middle East: The Failure of the 1946 Negotiations* (Reading, 1994)

Roberts, Andrew, *Eminent Churchillians* (London, 1994)

Robertson, James, *Transition in Africa: From Direct Rule to Independence* (New York, 1974)

Rogan, Eugene L. and Shlaim, Avi (eds), *The War for Palestine* (Cambridge, 2001)

Roth, Andrew, *Enoch Powell* (London, 1970)

Rubin, Barry, 'America and the Egyptian Revolution, 1950–1957', *Political Science Quarterly*, 97/1 (1982)

Sabit, Adel M., *A King Betrayed: The Ill-Fated Reign of Farouk of Egypt* (London, 1989)

Sabri, Husain Zulfakar, *Sovereignty for Sudan* (London, 1982)

Sadat, Anwar el, *Revolt on the Nile* (London, 1957)

——, *In Search of Identity* (London, 1978)

Safran, Nadav, *Egypt in Search of Political Community* (Cambridge, 1961)

Sayed-Ahmed, Muhammad Abd el-Wahab, *Nasser and American Foreign Policy, 1952–1956* (London, 1989)

Shamir, Shimon (ed.), *Egypt from Monarchy to Republic: A Reassessment of Revolution and Change* (Boulder, 1995)

Sharkey, Heather J., *Living With Colonialism: Nationalism and Culture in the Anglo-Egyptian Sudan* (Berkeley and Los Angeles, 2003)

Shlaim, Avi, 'The Debate About 1948', *International Journal of Middle Eastern Studies*, 27/3 (August 1995)

——, 'The Protocol of Sèvres, 1956: Anatomy of a War Plot', *International Affairs*, 73/3 (1997)

——, *The Iron Wall: Israel and the Arab World* (London, 2001)

Shuckburgh, Evelyn, *Descent to Suez: Diaries, 1951–1956* (London, 1986)

Slonin, Shlomo, 'Origins of the 1950 Tripartite Declaration on the Middle East', *Middle East Studies*, 23/2 (1987)

Stadiem, William, *Too Rich: The High Life and Tragic Death of King Farouk* (New York, 1991)

Stephens, Robert, *Nasser* (London, 1971)

Taykeh, Ray, *Origins of the Eisenhower Doctrine: The United States, Britain and Nasser's Egypt, 1953–1957* (Basingstoke, 2001)

Tenenbaum, Y.J., 'British Policy towards Israel and the Arab–Israeli Dispute, 1951–54' (unpublished Oxford D.Phil. thesis, 1991)

Terry, Janice, *The Wafd 1919–1952* (London, 1982)

Thomas, Graham, *Sudan 1950–1985: Death of a Dream* (London, 1990)

Thornhill, Michael T., 'Alternatives to Nasser: Humphrey Trevelyan, Ambassador to Egypt', *Contemporary British History*, 13/3 (1999)

——, 'Britain and the Collapse of Egypt's Constitutional Order, 1950–1952', *Diplomacy and Statecraft*, 13/1 (2002)

——, 'Britain, the United States and the Rise of an Egyptian Leader: The Politics and Diplomacy of Nasser's Consolidation of Power, 1952–1954', *English Historical Review*, 119/483 (2004)

Thomas, Hugh, *The Suez Affair* (London, 1967)

Thorpe, D.R., *Selwyn Lloyd* (London, 1989)

——, *Eden: The Life and Times of Anthony Eden, First Earl of Avon, 1897–1977* (London, 2004)

Trevelyan, Humphrey, *The Middle East in Revolution* (London, 1970)

——, *Public and Private* (London, 1980)

Tripp, Charles (ed.), *Contemporary Egypt: Through Egyptian Eyes* (London, 1993)

Troen, Selwyn Illan and Shemesh, Moshe (eds), *The Suez–Sinai Crisis of 1956: Retrospective and Reappraisal* (London, 1990)

Vatikiotis, P.J., *The Egyptian Army in Politics* (Bloomington, 1961)

——, *Nasser and his Generation* (London, 1978)

——, *Modern History of Egypt* (London, 1991)

Vitalis, Robert, *When Capitalists Collide: Business Conflict and the End of Empire in Egypt* (Berkeley and Los Angeles, 1995)

Warburg, Gabriel R., *Egypt and the Sudan* (London, 1985)

Williamson, David, *A Most Diplomatic General: The Life of General Lord Robertson of Oakridge* (London, 1996)

Wilson, Keith M. (ed.), *Imperialism and Nationalism in the Middle East: The Anglo-Egyptian Experience 1882–1982* (London, 1983)

Winks, Robin (ed.), *The Oxford History of the British Empire*, 'Historiography', vol. 5 (Oxford, 1999)

Wynn, Wilton, *Nasser of Egypt: The Search for Dignity* (Cambridge, 1959)

Yapp, M.E. (ed.), *Politics and Diplomacy in Egypt: The Diaries of Sir Miles Lampson, 1935–1937* (Oxford, 1997)

Young, John W. (ed.), *The Foreign Policy of Churchill's Peacetime Administration, 1951–1955* (Leicester, 1988)

(9) WEBSITES

http://britains-smallwars.com/Canal/index.html

http://www.suezveteransassociation.co.uk/

http: //www.nasser.org

Index